Edited by Katherine Arnup

$\mathscr{L}$ESBIAN PARENTING

Living with Pride & Prejudice

gynergy
books

10 9 8 7 6 5 4 3 2 1

Printed and bound in Canada by: Best Book Manufacturers

*gynergy books acknowledges the generous support
of the Canada Council.*

Published by:
gynergy books
P.O. Box 2023
Charlottetown, P.E.I.
Canada, C1A 7N7

Acknowledgements
Thanks to Spinster's Ink for kind permission to reprint
"Another View of Choosing Children," by Angela Bowen, from *Lesbians
at Midlife: The Creative Transition*, B. Sang, J. Warshow and A. Smith (eds.),
(Minneapolis: Spinster's Ink, 1991). Available from Spinster's Ink,
P.O. Box 300170, Minneapolis, MN 55403.

Thanks to *Hot Wire: The Journal of Women's Music and Culture* for kind
permission to reprint, "A Mother-Daughter Conversation: Alix Dobkin and
Adrian Hood," as told to Toni Armstrong Jr., (May 1989).

"Another Kind of Baby Story," by Yvette Perreault, was first published in
The Lesbian Health Guide, Regan McClure and Anne Vespry (eds.),
(Toronto: Queer Press, 1994).

Canadian Cataloguing in Publication Data
Main entry under title:

Lesbian parenting

Includes bibliographical references.
ISBN 0-921881-33-9

1. Lesbian mothers.   I. Arnup, Katherine, 1949-

HQ75.53.L47 1995   306.874'3'086643   C95-950025-1

Contents

～❧～

Introduction

Mothers in our society may be odd or strange, but never "queer" — or so most people believe. Lesbians obviously can't have children. Theirs is a "sterile" relationship that is nonprocreative. "Poor things, they will go through life without ever being fulfilled as women — never knowing the joys and heartaches of motherhood," or so the story goes.

Well, the news is that many lesbians are mothers, and they are raising their children well, or raising them poorly or raising them indifferently, just as their heterosexual counterparts do.[1]

WHEN DEL MARTIN AND PHYLLIS LYON, FOUNDERS OF THE DAUGHTERS OF Bilitis, made that observation in their 1972 book, *Lesbian/Woman*, few people outside of the "homosexual" community knew of the existence of lesbian mothers. Indeed, "lesbian mother" was considered a contradiction in terms — a physical and social impossibility. In just over two decades, that situation has changed dramatically. Widely cited figures suggest that ten percent of women are lesbians and that between twenty and thirty percent of lesbians are mothers.[2] A recent study estimated that there are "between 3 and 8 million gay and lesbian parents in the United States, raising between 6 and 14 million children."[3] While no figures are available for Canada, we can assume that, proportionately, the number of lesbian mothers is equally high.

Lesbian mothers first came to public attention as they began to fight for custody of their children conceived within heterosexual relationships. In the past dozen years, increasing numbers of lesbians have chosen to conceive and give birth to children within the context of lesbian relationships. Today, lesbians come to parenthood in many ways. From the woman fighting for custody of her children conceived within a hetero-sexual marriage, to the lesbian co-parent coaching her partner through labour, eagerly anticipating the birth of their first child; from the lesbian foster mother quietly applying to adopt her child, to the lesbian couple travelling to Latin America to adopt a baby — lesbian mothers are as diverse as any group of women in society. We are found in all classes, races, communities, and countries. The articles in this collection speak eloquently about the diversity of lesbian motherhood. In this book, you will find the stories of dozens of lesbian parents from across Canada and the United States. You will hear of the ways in which issues of disability, race, generation, and class have affected our lives with our children. You will find accounts of courageous women dealing with the profoundly homophobic institutions of the state — from adoption agencies to child welfare services, from schools to day care centres, from hospitals to courtrooms. Lesbian mothers and our children are literally everywhere, finding support and love in unexpected places. We are grand-mothers, aunts, co-mothers, mothers without custody, and mommy wanna-be's.

Several years ago I wrote an article about lesbian mothers, which I entitled "Mothers Just Like Others." I chose that title not because I was sure we *were* in fact "mothers just like others," but to invoke a slogan from women's demonstrations, a slogan that demanded custody rights for lesbian mothers. Now, as I edit the first Canadian collection of articles on lesbian motherhood, I find myself asking the same questions: are we just like others? or do we mother in ways that are profoundly different from heterosexual mothers? The answer, I think, is both yes and no. There are women in this collection who are very different from me, in many ways; by the same token, there are heterosexual mothers on my street who are very much like my partner and I. Whether we are different or the same, how-ever, we deserve the same rights as other mothers, and it is for those rights that we are fighting.

Nearly three years have passed since I first agreed to take on the task of editing this collection. As I worked three jobs, and prepared to move houses and cities, the prospect of editing a book on lesbian motherhood seemed like a welcome relief from the academic "rat race" in which I was embroiled. Little did I realize just how much time and energy this book would require — how many calls for papers, letters, telephone calls, and faxes would cross the country in the seemingly never-ending search for contributors. Interest in the book has been tremendous — virtually every woman I spoke with talked about the need for such a book. But interest, I learned, does not always translate into an article.

Working on this book reminded me, if I ever needed reminding, of how full our lives as mothers are. Raising children, holding down jobs, juggling political and personal lives, overcoming barriers placed in our way because of our race, class or ability, lesbian parents find it nearly impossible to steal the hours necessary to pause long enough to reflect upon, process, and eventually produce an article about their lives. I've long since lost track of how many crises have prevented authors from meeting deadlines, or have forced would-be authors to abandon their efforts altogether. For women who are already vulnerable, whether because of poverty or race or disability — for whatever reason — the dangers of coming out are magnified. It is not surprising, then, that despite concerted efforts to reach out to diverse communities and constituencies, the women represented in this collection are, for the most part, white, middle class, and able-bodied.

Writing about our lives as lesbian parents presents a number of risks. For many women, the prospect of losing custody of their children is never far from view. For all of us, the threat of exposing our children to the profound homophobia that still permeates our society hovers over us as we write. For when we write about our lives as mothers we write about our children as well. Whether they want us to or not, we come out for them, forcing them to cope with the reactions of their peers. For some women, these risks were too great, and, despite their desire to write an article, in the end, they had to decline. Others have chosen to write under a pseudonym, sometimes because of their jobs, more often to protect their children. While I abhor the homophobia that has forced them to seek anonymity or to withdraw their articles, I have understood all too well the reasons that lay behind those decisions.

Work on this book has occurred mainly in the tiny spaces between the other parts of my life — composing letters to authors on Sunday mornings, reading faxes in the early hours of the morning. There were times when I thought I was completely crazy for taking on this book, and times when I thought it would never see the light of day. After over a year and a half of publicizing the project, I had only a handful of articles. But slowly, through word of mouth, news of the book began to travel. A call at work — was I still accepting articles? Another brown envelope in the mail. Each time, I would rip open the envelope, eagerly anticipating the story that lay inside. It was incredibly exciting to hear from lesbian parents all across the country, to realize once again how many of us there are, and how many roads we have taken to lesbian motherhood. This is a book of our stories, a book about our lives as lesbian mothers. Writing about our lives as lesbians and as parents, represents an act of bravery, and I salute the courage of all the women and children who have done so.

During the course of the compiling of this book, the government of Ontario introduced a piece of legislation designed to eliminate discrimination against lesbian and gay families in Ontario. The struggle over Bill 167, the government's last minute decision to succumb to opposition attacks by removing adoption from the legislation, and the eventual defeat of the bill, galvanized the lesbian and gay communities. Demonstrations, petition and letter-writing campaigns, and lobbying reached a fever pitch in the brief period during which the legislation was debated. Watching the vicious attacks against our families pushed many lesbians to enter the public eye for the first time, granting television and newspaper interviews, holding family picnics on the lawn of the legislature, proudly proclaiming the rights of our families. The defeat of Bill 167 angered many people, both in Ontario and elsewhere in the country, where lesbian and gay activists had eagerly anticipated the passage of the most sweeping anti-discrimination legislation in North

America. In its aftermath, many lesbian families have continued to push for legal rights for non-biological mothers, and a number of second-parent adoptions are now proceeding through the courts.

While the defeat of Bill 167 is only one event in the long march towards equality for gay and lesbian families, in many respects it epitomizes the historical moment we have reached. Across North America, we are witnessing right-wing efforts to resurrect and reinforce the patriarchal, heterosexual nuclear family. From attacks on lesbian and gay adoption and foster parenting to the repeal of anti-discrimination laws, right-wing forces are targeting lesbian and gay communities. For many in Ontario, lulled into complacency by an apparent attitude of acceptance, the defeat of Bill 167 was a wake-up call. While support for the bill from many quarters of the province was tremendous, the viciousness of the homophobia unleashed by the debate reminded us all that we have a long way to go in gaining acceptance and rights for our families.

The articles in this collection document many of the victories that we have achieved and the struggles that remain. You will find stories of second-parent adoptions and namings, of custody victories, and of important legislative initiatives. You will read about parents and grandparents, neighbours and teachers who have learned to reach out and embrace our diverse families. You will also read about the continued inability of lesbians to adopt as a couple, of lesbian mothers' treatment by homophobic judges, and of the prejudice and discrimination faced by our children. Our struggles are far from over. But surrounded by the love of our children, our families and our friends, we are fighting, with pride and prejudice. This book begins to record some of our lives and, I hope, to inspire us to keep on fighting.

Many people have contributed to the success of this venture. First, my thanks to the women at gynergy books, who have supported this effort enthusiastically over its three-year gestation. In particular, I would like to thank Lynn Henry, my tireless, endlessly patient editor at gynergy books. Lynn put up with my worrying, responded politely and promptly to my endless faxes, and turned her fine editorial hand to every article in this collection. My research assistant, Jennifer Quaile, assisted in compiling the bibliography, making sense of the boxes of articles and books on lesbian parenting that I have collected over the years. And, of course, to the thirty-eight authors who contributed to this collection — thanks for taking the risk to write about your lives, for managing to meet tight deadlines, and for hardly ever getting mad at me. Finally, I wish to thank my family, who are, in the end, the reason I undertook this book. Our conversations, our struggles, and our daily lives provided me with endless inspiration for this book.

Notes

1. Del Martin and Phyllis Lyon, *Lesbian/Woman*, (New York: Bantam, 1972), pp. 140-1.
2. Ellen Herman, "The Romance of Lesbian Motherhood," in *Sojourner: The Women's Forum*, 12 (March 1988). Other estimates range as high as six to ten million lesbian mothers.
3. April Martin, *The Lesbian and Gay Parenting Handbook: Creating and Raising Our Families*, (New York: HarperCollins, 1993), p. 6.

*Choosing
Parenthood*

Dykes, Donors & Dry Ice:
Alternative Insemination

JANE BERNSTEIN & LAURA STEPHENSON

OUR DAUGHTER WILL SOON CELEBRATE HER SECOND BIRTHDAY AND IS, BY HER very existence, an A.I. "success" story. As two women in a committed lesbian relationship, we fulfilled our dream of starting a family by conceiving through alternative insemination with an anonymous donor. Our experience was contrary to the experience of many other women — our daughter's conception was relatively uncomplicated. To the outside observer, the circumstances of our life are equally enviable. Laura has a professional career outside the home, while Jane runs the family business and provides child care during the day. We have a cat, a station wagon and a mortgage. In short, we are precisely the kind of family journalists seek out when writing stories about how "normal" gay people are.

The reality of first conceiving and then raising a child in a lesbian household is, however, anything but "normal." The recent debates over same-sex spousal benefits in Ontario have served to underscore how different our world is from that of other parents — how thin is the blanket of security we have attempted to weave around our family. We comfort ourselves by saying that we don't want to be seen as the same as everyone else, that if the yardstick for a "normal" family includes the abuse and dysfunctions found in heterosexual households, we are grateful to be excluded from hegemonic definitions of "family." Such bravado does little to assuage our fears, however, as we watch our daughter, an infant no longer, march with growing determination toward an inevitable head-on collision with a society all too ready to condemn and reject her.

In this article, we will discuss our experience with alternative insemination from two angles. First, we will describe the technological circumstances of conception — our "how to" guide for getting pregnant. We will then examine the social issues surrounding this technology, and how society's preoccupation with the mechanics of reproduction has diverted the debate around reproductive technology from what we feel should be its major focus — the babies themselves. It is our contention that while vehicles such as the Royal Commission on New Reproductive Technologies have drawn attention to a multitude of new ways of creating life (ethically or otherwise), very little attention has been given to how these children will be accepted once they arrive. The gulf between a proclivity for alternative methods of reproduction, and society's capacity to accept them, becomes a chasm when a lesbian moves from discussing pregnancy to choosing a gynaecologist in her second trimester.

But first things first ...

Finding a Donor

In the twenty years or so since we were teenagers, something quite unexpected happened to our bodies. At fifteen, a surreptitious kiss, or even the illusion of misbehaviour, would cause our stomachs to swell and our reputations to be ruined — or so we were told by well-meaning teachers and our equally misinformed friends. Lesbians in their thirties, it would appear, have dramatically different reproductive capacities. We now seem to have a better chance of surviving Niagara Falls in a barrel than we do of becoming pregnant.

Not only is there an immediate conflict between our sexual orientation and the desire to mother (no small issue within the gay and lesbian community, whose membership has been known to condemn heterosexuals as "breeders"), the alternatives for becoming pregnant are fairly unsavoury, at best. The option of the one-night stand with a faceless stranger has been all but eliminated with the reality of AIDS. Finding a compatible and willing male friend to act as a donor continues to be difficult. Whether they are straight or gay, many men are unwilling to be tested for the virus causing AIDS, or even for a variety of genetic diseases. More problematic, however, is the question of the involvement of the prospective "daddy." While many men may happily indulge in countless sexual encounters without a thought for the possible repercussions of their actions, they become inexplicably concerned when pregnancy rather than passion is the desired result, and what may begin as a selfless act of friendship often ends in bitter quarreling over naming and visitation rights, even before the time of the child's birth.

It is precisely to avoid such physical and emotional quagmires that many lesbians turn to the medical profession for a "clean," nameless, and undemanding donor. The medical profession, however, can be highly unprofessional. In Canada, gaining access to clinics providing services for alternative insemination can be erratic, complex and frustrating. Almost all give preferential treatment to heterosexual married women whose spouses are infertile. Those that do cater to single women may balk at inseminating lesbians, using a plethora of lies, deceit and double-speak against those brave enough to take on the system. In addition, the waiting lists are long, and the costs often prohibitive. The formation of support groups for lesbians attempting to be alternatively inseminated through such channels testifies to the enormous stress such an undertaking generates for both the mother-to-be and, in the case of a couple, her often-unacknowledged partner.

In response to the limited accessibility that lesbians have to such clinics, a few individual doctors have set up private insemination services that vary only slightly from those provided by mainstream programs. These doctors have their own "bank" of anonymous donors, often medical students, who provide sperm for prospective mothers. The record keeping and selection process is controlled by the doctors, who perform the insemination at their place of practice. As in the case of the clinics, the "patient" has almost no input at any stage of the "procedure."

By determining not only who gets inseminated but the very process of insemination itself, doctors have completely mystified and over-medicalized what is, after all, a very simple act. In addition, by determining *when* a woman gets inseminated, the medical profession is, however inadvertently, helping to determine the sex of the fetus. Male sperm swim faster, but female sperm live longer in the uterus, so if a woman is inseminated only when she is at her most fertile, that is, when she has already ovulated, the chances of bearing a male infant are substantially increased. In order to increase the chances of conception, doctors will often insist on testing for ovulation prior to insemination — hence the imbalance in the number of male offspring born to women through alternative insemination. Inseminating slightly prior to ovulation will not increase the chances of bearing a female infant per se, but it will redress the balance to that found in the general population — an option available only to those using a "private" donor.

Cross-border Shopping: The Catalogue Option

Faced with such a wall of discouraging facts and well-versed in the negative experiences of others, we began our foray into the world of motherhood in the only way we saw fit. We started watching a lot of daytime television. On one of the finer talk-shows, we heard of a feminist clinic in Atlanta, Georgia, that provided insemination services specifically for lesbians. Our request for information brought a thick packet of pamphlets, questionnaires and application forms. While we were prepared to go to Georgia, we were completely unprepared for the rigorous questioning and counselling that the program demanded of all its participants. However feminist in its philosophy, the insemination program still demanded that women make an application for motherhood, with acceptance dependent on the successful completion of a series of counselling sessions. However great our desire to have a child, we simply couldn't bring ourselves to justify our suitability for something that teenagers achieve every day in the back-seat of their parents' station wagon.

Finally, through a series of happy coincidences, we found a doctor in Vermont who was willing to act as a go-between for us with the Sperm Bank of California. In the United States, any doctor who registers has access to the services of two privately run sperm banks located in Oakland and New York City. The doctor acts as the initial contact for any woman wishing to use the bank, and all subsequent arrangements are made directly between the bank and the "client." The relationship then ceases to be one of doctor/patient and becomes, rather, a service-for-payment proposition. By distancing the procedure from the medical profession, power over decision-making rests squarely with the client, as it would with any woman or couple considering parenthood.

Upon request, the sperm bank provides the client with a list of prospective donors. Only the most basic information on the donor is provided — ethnicity, height, weight, hair and eye colour, and blood-type. In addition, information is provided as to whether the donor is open to the possibility of having his name released to any offspring. Part of the bank's policy is to allow a donor the option of either releasing his name, address and social security number to the child when he or she reaches the age of majority, or choosing to remain anonymous. In either case, the donor never receives any information about the client, and in the case of a "yes" donor, only the child may make contact, if he or she wishes, at age eighteen.

After reviewing the full list, clients choose five or six files they think may be suitable and request an information sheet for each numbered donor. This sheet provides additional information including profession, education, age, religion and a brief medical history. On the first day of her menstrual cycle, the client orders the sperm by telephone, specifying on which date she would like to receive it, and in what quantity. In this way, she is able to control the timing and frequency of her inseminations. The sperm is delivered in dry ice, which may be easily replenished and thus allows the sperm to be preserved indefinitely.

The courier-delivered package can be collected from any airport, but discomfort with the prospect of facing Canadian customs officials prompted us to pick up our box in Vermont. Driving home, we stuffed the cooler with Ben and Jerry's Cherry Garcia ice cream and explained to the nice customs agent that we just couldn't find anything quite as good in Canada. When our "ice cream" baby arrived nine months later, we were a little disappointed that she hadn't acquired red hair and a creamy complexion.

Instructions for performing the insemination at home are provided, along with a needleless syringe. Contrary to what most doctors will have you believe, the procedure doesn't require a medical degree, past experience or even assistance. We heard one story of a friend whose partner happened to be out of town when the right time came, and lacking a mirror, she performed the insemination herself with the help of a reflection from a toaster. If a woman is lucky enough to conceive the first time, the entire procedure will cost about $300 (U.S.), a fraction of the cost of proceeding through the regulated Canadian system. The cost becomes prohibitive only if it takes months or years to conceive. Our strictly unscientific observation of others would indicate that women are conceiving in fewer attempts at home than in a clinical setting, thus further decreasing the potential cost involved in alternative insemination.

Once into her second trimester, the client can request that the sperm bank send her the donor's complete family medical history, which covers all major illnesses in family members for three generations. This is a comprehensive document that the donor himself fills out, and includes such information as daily diet, exercise habits, and even a brief personal message. In addition, the donor indicates whether or not he has had any same-sex sexual encounters. In order to ensure that the donor is free of the AIDS virus, the frozen sperm is held for two years before being released and the donor is tested every six months. In this way, gay men are not excluded from participating in the program and may well make up the majority of those wishing to be contacted by their offspring in later years. This is the last contact the client has with the sperm bank, other than to send the bank notification of the birth of the child — strictly for the purpose of keeping accurate records. This is particularly important as each donor is limited to ten offspring, several of whom must be out-of-state. The information is then kept confidential in perpetuity.

Negotiating the New Arrival: A Dose of Reality

No amount of thoughtful discussion, anticipation or political awareness can prepare a lesbian couple for the experience of pregnancy, childbirth and parenthood. Just as heterosexual couples find their lives changed beyond all expectation with the arrival of a newborn, so, too, do lesbians find their world turned upside down in a sea of diapers, breast-pumps and pacifiers. The difference is, however, that in addition to all the usual discomforts of sleep deprivation and altered schedules, lesbians must face an often disturbing and always unexpected reception from friends, family, and virtual strangers. The first and perhaps most important lesson we learned as prospective parents was to never anticipate how someone would react to the birth of our child.

We are very fortunate to have a wonderful family doctor who, as a lesbian herself, greeted the news of our recent conception as she would any other change in our medical status — she prescribed crackers for morning sickness, a competent gynecologist, and a dose of good luck. At the end of the first trimester, we went to meet the specialist with some hesitation, having made it through the first three months without having to deal with the "straight" profession. Again, we were lucky. Having explained the unusual circumstances surrounding the pregnancy, we were treated as though we had pulled off some kind of minor miracle — conception without the assistance of a trained professional. This seemed to elevate Laura, who had performed the insemination, to the status of a peer, and for the next six months the doctor treated her as though she had some specialized knowledge of the workings of the female body. Unfortunately, when Jane went into labor, reality hit.

Due to some late complications, the birth had to be induced and we spent some sixty hours in the delivery room and sixteen days in the hospital. This meant that we had to deal with approximately thirty doctors, nurses, medical students and assorted other interested parties. Throughout the ordeal, Laura was acknowledged as the labour coach but never as the other parent, and every change in shift brought new inquiries as to the whereabouts of the father. Finally, in desperation, Jane insisted that there was no point in waiting for the father to show up before the decision to induce was made because she had never met him! All questions then came to an abrupt and uncomfortable halt. While no one at the hospital made any overt remarks about Laura's presence, her constant visits in the days preceding and following the birth were clearly deemed unusual and the nursing staff commented on how lucky Jane, as a single mother, was to have such an attentive "friend." This set the stage for what has been a repeating theme ever since — Jane is a single parent with a good-hearted friend who helps with the baby.

By and large, we have encountered many conservative heterosexuals who have been joyful, unjudgemental and fascinated with our new infant. When it became clear that Jane was indeed pregnant and not just gaining a few pounds, we decided it was time to talk to our nice, middle-class, white, Catholic, churchgoing neighbours. At first, Ruth and John looked extremely uncomfortable. When we explained that Jane was alternatively inseminated, they were greatly relieved and extremely supportive. It dawned on us that anyone who has experienced parenthood can instantly understand why a "single" woman would want to have a child. More importantly, however, A.I. is totally "sexless." Our neighbours would have been far more shocked had Jane been sleeping around and been "caught" than they were by what they imagined to be a clean, odourless, clinical procedure. (The fact that Laura performed the insemination herself remained our little secret.) We both have "unenlightened" relatives who also took the news in stride once they were assured that no sexual act had actually taken place. Laura's first visitor was her eighty-three-year-old grandfather who, we suspect, was curious to see whether the baby would look like everyone else's. Much to his relief, she looked just like him.

(Re)Naming: The Role of the "Other" Parent

Many lesbian parents choose to fight being labeled "single parents" at every turn, seeking to educate and further a political agenda through the birth of their child. Our own decision to maintain our privacy and allow others to think what they will has led to accusations of "selling-out" and "internalized homophobia" from within the lesbian community. Ironically, it is among gays and lesbians that we have found the least support for our decision to parent. We have gay and lesbian friends who, having suffered discrimination and abuse themselves, have told us without hesitation that we have no right to subject a child to the ridicule and shame that must surely accompany life within a lesbian family. Others suggest that by having a child, we are profiting from a kind of heterosexual privilege by "passing for straight." Still others were simply unprepared to cope with this great change in our lives, and have drifted away since the pregnancy. For whatever reason, we have had to seek out new friends who are child-centered or parents themselves — just as heterosexual women tend to build new support networks with the other mothers at the park or playground.

The most difficult challenge we have had to face has been with what we describe as the "Heather tyranny." Banned in several states in the U.S., *Heather Has Two Mommies* is a children's book by Leslea Newman that depicts a lesbian family with, as the title suggests, two mothers. It reflects an orthodoxy in the way gay people are supposed to parent, at least according to certain paradigms established within the gay and lesbian community. It underscores the fact that even gay-positive literature reinforces the ingrained notion of "mommy" and "daddy," leaving unchallenged the assumption that a parent must be either one or the other. When our daughter was born, for instance, Laura was asked by several friends what her role in child-rearing would be, questions phrased in terms of "mommy" or "daddy." It is always assumed that if a child has two female parents, they must both be "mommies."

Our daughter, however, has only one mother. Only one of her parents carried her for nine months, gave birth to her and breast-fed her. Only Jane is able to fill out health forms, receive government benefits, and claim the child tax credit. Only Jane is called "mommy" by both our daughter and by the state. This leaves Laura hanging in a vacuum without a label that would affirm her equal role in nurturing, caring for and loving our daughter. While she is not our child's mother, neither is she her father, her aunt or a close personal friend. She is her other parent, and as such needs a special, distinctive name that both binds her to our daughter and reflects the unique bond they have with each other. At home, Laura has such a name, one that our daughter is coming to recognize is especially for the two of them — something personal that they share. It is not a name that replicates the power and prestige accorded to "mommy," however, and so, to others, Laura continues to be unrecognized and invisible.

What may appear to be merely a problem of language goes much deeper when the labels define such socially constructed roles. Put plainly, if you are not a "mommy" or a "daddy," you are unacknowledged in the public life of a child. It is a problem common not only to the non-biological parents of A.I. babies, but to those who "inherit" children in new relationships. Often, these children simply call their new parents by name, but again, this does not acknowledge the particular and unique part they play in these children's lives. However strong and empowering it may be to know that your child does not play favorites at home, at some point every parent wants to be recognized as the central figure in their child's world — by teachers, neighbours and, yes, total strangers.

Our roles as parents need to be redefined in lesbian relationships, beyond the "two mommies" approach to naming. Ultimately, this becomes as important for the identity and security of the child as it does for the adults. If society at large does not validate the position of a parent who is neither "mommy" or "daddy," the place of the "other" parent becomes confusing for a child who is trying to establish her or his own position in a "non-traditional" family. If our daughter is to continue to acknowledge and validate Laura's central role in her life as she grows older and more astute, she must receive external acceptance for her love of both her parents. This will only happen if we can collectively find new definitions for the roles we share as the guardians of our children.

A.I. & the State

Our successful and positive experience with alternative insemination is, unfortunately, all too rare for lesbians wishing to conceive with an anonymous donor. Far more common are stories of endless waiting, intimidation and insensitivity from doctors who care far less about the well being of their patients than they do about technology, morals and ethics. We firmly believe that it is through the exploitation of our fear, and our own ignorance of the options available to us, that clinics and individual practitioners continue to dictate how, when and even if we conceive. There are no advertisements or pamphlets in Canadian clinics for the services provided by the U.S. sperm banks, and no comparable services in our own country.

Perhaps the most disturbing development in the short history of A.I. in Canada has been the insistence on the part of those controlling the technology on blurring the boundaries between the simple insemination of a fertile woman, and the host of other medical procedures lumped under the heading of "new reproductive technologies." By discussing issues surrounding A.I. in the same context as procedures like in-vitro fertilization and gender selection, the possibility of further government intervention threatens even the few avenues for conception presently available. While it will continue to be impossible to halt the thousands of private arrangements individual lesbians make with male donors, it is our fear that well-meaning attempts to control new reproductive technologies will close the door on alternative insemination with anonymous donors. As with the debate over legalizing abortion, denying women access to "safe" sperm forces us to take unnecessary risks with our lives in order to control our own bodies. The added terrors, however, are the threats that inadequate testing and incomplete medical histories pose to the lives of our unborn children. It is imperative that lesbians continue to contextualize alternative insemination as just that — an alternative to insemination through sexual intercourse. We must support and seek out services which attempt to demedicalize the procedure, and return decisions concerning conception and pregnancy to those who will ultimately be responsible for the lives they create.

Several years passed between our first conversations about parenthood — tentative probings on dangerous ground — to the day we actually conceived a child. We felt that we needed to explore every possible outcome of such a venture before taking even the first steps toward insemination. We needed to be sure, beyond any doubt, that we could raise a son. We felt we had to agree on everything from education to bottle-feeding to the use of cloth diapers. Before either one of us was prepared to say we were ready, we tried to anticipate every turn our lives would take, every argument that might arise and every unpleasant situation we would encounter. These efforts were, in hindsight, brave but embarrassingly naive endeavours.

Every day, we make decisions, large and small, concerning the well being of our child. We deal with problems we never even knew existed and find solutions we would never have thought possible. Every one of our preconceived ideas of how life would be has proved at best misguided, at worst destructive. We have had to learn to be patient with the ignorance of others, open to the endless mysteries of our child, and gentle with ourselves. Above all, we have learned to listen for the questions before coming up with the answers because, in spite of our age, our size, our wallets and our education, our lives are ruled by a small third party who cares little for the carefully constructed and hard-won logic of her parents.

In the end, all lesbian parents find a way to negotiate the minefield laid by centuries of patriarchy and homophobia. We adapt as we go and compromise when we must, seeking support for the choices we have made while delighting in the joy our children bring to our lives. But what about our children? It is they, after all, who need our greatest love and strongest encouragement. In our effort to ensure that our right to reproduce remains intact, we naturally concentrate on the beginning of the process — the donor, the sperm, the technology and the medical profession. It seems, however, that once the deed is actually done, the parade moves off and leaves behind a newborn infant, shell-shocked parents, and advice literature that fails miserably to deal with anything other than physical aches and infant fevers.

Then what? How do we begin to unravel the stereotypes and social norms our children must confront as they try to make sense of a world that condemns everything they find familiar and comforting? As we strive to gain equal access to alternative forms of insemination, we must strive even more fervently to ensure that the lives created through our efforts, and the alternative families they join, will be equally well received.

Biddy & Libby in Minusland:
Adventures in Reproductive Technology

DEBRA SHOGAN & GLORIA FILAX

THIS IS THE STORY OF OUR ATTEMPTS, AS TWO LESBIANS IN A COMMITTED relationship, to have a child together, and what transpired to change our minds. We began talking about having children together early in our relationship. We were already co-parenting Gloria's birth child, who was six when the three of us began to live together. Although we try to make it clear to those we encounter that we are both invested in parenting this child and that he (even now, as a twelve-year-old) actively engages in undermining perceptions of who counts as a parent by, for example, making us dual Mother's Day cards at school, we have not been able to overcome the identification of Gloria as his mother by those outside our home — in part, because of expectations established prior to the three of us living together.[1] By sharing the parenting of a child from birth, we hoped to have both of us recognized as parents, if only by friends and family.

At the beginning we had grand plans: we wanted to both be pregnant and to give birth at home at the same time so that we could each lactate both babies, who for the time being we referred to as "Biddy and Libby." We would be mothers of both babies and we would refuse to identify babies with birth mothers. Not only did we see these alternative ways of mothering as important for our future interactions with each other and these children, but we saw these choices as transgressive of culturally normative notions of mothering.

As we soon learned, it was not going to be easy to accomplish this reconceptualization of mothering. We gradually modified our plans: only Debra would birth the child, since she had not yet had an experience of birthing, but we would both be the child's mothers. Later we modified our plans again and, for reasons described in this essay, now refer to the aftermath of our encounter with "experts" in reproductive technology as "Biddy and Libby in Minusland." Here's how it happened.

For about a year after making the decision to have a child together, Debra charted her cycles, using the Justisse Method for Fertility Management.[2] We were able to locate a doctor who was willing to help us conceive and we began to look for ways of finding what we preferred to call "genetic material." We learned from our doctor that a female gynaecologist appointed to a university reproduction clinic was prepared to impregnate lesbians.[3] We contacted this clinic and were placed on a three to six month waiting list. In December of 1990, we were informed that we had an appointment on Monday, January 21, 1991, at nine o'clock a.m.

We had plenty of time to talk about life with Biddy and Libby as the three of us — two adults and a child — drove the several hours to the clinic. Debra went into the appointment alone and underwent a physical exam. She then had an inter-view — which was more like an exam — about why she wanted to be a mother.

"Why do you want to be a mother?" the doctor inquired. Debra spoke about her desire to experience pregnancy and the birthing process; her interest in sharing this important life event with her partner; the excitement of having a growing, inquisi-tive young human life in our home; and the challenge of engag-ing in dual mothering in the context of this culture.

"Yes, but why do you want to be a mother?"

Debra thought that she had misunderstood the question. Perhaps the doctor was not, after all, asking, "why do you want to be a *mother*?" but "why do you *want* to be a mother?" Or maybe it was, "why do *you* (a lesbian) want to be a mother?" Could this doctor be wary of lesbians, despite indicating that she would "help" lesbians?

The doctor persisted with another line of questioning: "What do you do at the university? Are you an activist? I wouldn't want a story about this clinic appearing on the national news."

Finally, the conversation shifted to details of the procedure, including the doctor's observation that there would be no need to match up characteristics from the genetic material to the other parent in our case, and an indication that in order to be accepted for the procedure we would be required to undergo a psychological assessment — apparently a standard procedure with this "infertility" clinic.

On the drive back home, we reviewed our options and decided to send the following letter when we returned:

> Dear Dr. A:
> We are writing this letter to outline why Debra did not phone to confirm the appointment with Dr. B. We do this with the hope that you will nevertheless continue to consider us as participants in the insemination by donor program.
>
> We understand that there is a protocol which is expected of participants in this program and we are poignantly aware that our decision not to participate in further screening of our psycho-social appropriateness as parents jeopardizes our chances of future involvement.
>
> The purpose of this letter is not to ask to be considered as exceptions to your screening procedures but rather to request that you consider the effects of these screening procedures on those required to participate in them. We believe that decisions about fertility must be made by those whose bodies are most intimately affected. We don't doubt that there are certain pathological situations in which a woman is coerced into having a child or in which a woman's psychological health is such that parenting would be inappropriate and over which some discretion would be advisable. (We are aware that when these circumstances are apparent outside clinical settings there is no interventionist strategy available and that there is certainly never any intervening in the choices of individuals when these circumstances are not present.)
>
> The seriousness with which Debra has charted her cycle for the past nine months; our commitment to travelling a long distance to your clinic; and our decision to share the parenting of a child born to us even as we live in a culture which will not make this decision in any

way easy for us, are indications that our decision has neither been lightly made nor coerced. We believe that further requirements that we demonstrate our "fitness" to be parents of a child conceived by donor insemination not only undermine our choices over our fertility, they bring into question our fitness to be involved in our present parenting of a young child. We are not willing to be complicit in this.

We would like you to respect that our decision to have a child has been considered over many months. We want you to respect this because we do still wish to be part of your program.

Sincerely,

We received no response to this letter, which effectively terminated our involvement with this program. Although we had realized that this could be an outcome of our letter, we were angry at the cavalier way in which we had been dismissed.

In April of 1991, we learned of a private company that provided "cryopreserved" genetic material to physicians and did not screen recipients. Both we and our doctor wrote to this company to determine procedures and costs, neither of which became apparent to us even after four months of correspondence. Response to our inquiries was very often highly technical, sometimes in the form of abstracts of current literature in reproductive medicine or charts outlining, for example, "summary of cumulative probability of pregnancy." Information about the "characteristics" of the donors was provided, however. A characteristic common to all donors was that they were Caucasian.

One of our questions did prompt a personal response from the president and medical director of the company. Because we were already parenting a boy child, we had decided that we wanted to birth a female baby. We wrote inquiring about a "spinning" service which selects for X or Y chromosomes. In his reply, the director indicated that the spinning procedure is not performed "unless there is a medical occasion for this procedure to be done (X-linked disorders)." We thought that the reference to X-linked and not Y-linked disorders reflected an assumption that sex selection always entails selecting out X chromosomes and thus ensuring the birth of a male. The following reply sent by Debra notes and (ironically) attributes noble motives to this assumption, while attempting to make the point that selection of traditionally undervalued babies — those who are female and/or nonwhite is not the same as selecting for male and/or white babies:

> Dear Dr. C:
>
> Thank you for your May 7 reply to my inquiries of April 19. I gather that your reference to X and not Y-linked disorders in your response to my question about sex selection reflects your concern to combat the still prevalent tendency in this (and other cultures) to select for male children. I commend you for taking this position. It is necessary that those working in "reproductive technology" be vigilant to ensure that babies reproduced when utilizing the technology not be exclusively those already privileged and valued in a culture — those who are white and/or those who are male.
>
> Because the inclination is to use these technologies to reproduce those who are more valued rather than less valued in a society, I do not believe there are the same ethical or political implications in using procedures to select for a nonwhite baby or a female baby as there are in using them to select for a white or male baby. I see selecting for girl children, when the procedure is almost never used to do this, to be affirming of a group less valued in our culture.
>
> You may wish to note that your procedures do, however, pre-select for other characteristics. Since your donors are all white, I am, as a white woman, in fact, selecting by race.
>
> Sincerely,

Finally, there were just too many unanswered questions for either our doctor or us to have any sense of either the projected cost of many applications or the probability of conceiving. We chose not to proceed with this method.

In the meantime, we continued inquiries about the possibility of local donors and we began formulating stories about

Biddy and Libby happily playing in Minusland. The three of us had recently read Roald Dahl's *Charlie and the Great Glass Elevator*, a fantastic story about space travel in a giant glass elevator. The story culminates in the near disappearance of many of the characters and the complete absence of one of them as a result of swallowing wonka-vite, a youth serum. The person who disappeared went to Minusland, a place where one waits it out until one becomes "a plus." The more we talked about it, the more it seemed all right for Biddy and Libby to be in Minusland — a place, at least as we construed it, that seemed much more pleasant than the "Plusland" we were often forced to confront.

In the months since our decision to leave Biddy and Libby in Minusland, we have continued to reflect on the implications of our attempt to have a child together. We are well aware that it is never possible to completely break away from the dominant culture — that one is always complicit in it, even as one may be critical of it. Since one cannot avoid complicity, some people might question why we didn't go along with some of the demands of the "experts." After all, we would now likely be living with the child we had wanted, a subversive result that would more than offset having to go along with the beliefs of those administering the technology. As actively political lesbians, however, we often find ourselves in the position of having to decide when a situation demands so *much* compliance that it makes effective criticism or subversion impossible. For us, this was a situation in which compliance with "the experts" did not give us enough room to exert ourselves as lesbians. We felt that compliance would have undermined our sense of how we wished to embark on our shared lesbian motherhood.

From the beginning, we wanted to question the desire we had to share in the birth "of our own child." After all, we were already mothering a child and certainly fully "engaged" in the institution of mothering — even while attempting to subvert expectations from schools, other children's parents, and our own birth families. It seemed to us that even though our desire to have a child complied with the dominant cultural notion that women need to birth their own children in order to be "fulfilled" as women, wanting to birth a child as lesbians had the potential to undermine the notion of the heteronormative pregnant woman. Moreover, since, for many, "lesbian mother" is an oxymoron, we anticipated that our both being mothers of this child would be even more disruptive of sexual norms than our present arrangement with the child in our care.

As we engaged with the reproduction clinic and business, we were aware that utilizing reproductive technologies is not a neutral undertaking, given that the effectiveness of many technologies has been tested on women's bodies;[4] that the race for development of these technologies often makes or breaks the careers of the (most-often male) doctors working in this area; and that these technologies have the potential for screening for white and male babies. These are serious concerns.

Yet, like other technologies, reproductive technologies have political uses. The reproduction of a human embryo from an egg, for example — technology which was described on the front page of the *The Globe and Mail* more than a decade ago[5] — has obvious political ramifications, not missed by those developing this technology. The newspaper article indicated that the embryo was destroyed because the scientists said "they wanted to study only the early stages of growth and ... because they had to follow medical guidelines which forbade them to continue the experiment." Certain technologies, even mainstream technologies, can be taken on for subversive purposes. Utilization of reproductive technologies by lesbians has the potential to be disruptive of expected processes of genderization. Lesbians having babies disrupts a notion of "true" womanhood in which one's success as a heterosexual woman culminates in giving birth. Moreover, lesbians can utilize reproductive technologies to undermine expectations that there will be a continuity in skin colour between parents and children — an expectation which contributes to ways in which we are all racialized. For example, a recent postcard with the caption "lesbian mothers" has a representation of a white lesbian and a Chinese lesbian holding their Black child.

While lesbians must not be oblivious to the implications to women generally of reproductive technologies, to us the issues are those of control of the technologies and whether these technologies can be utilized to undermine dominant cultural notions of the "good" mother.

We will have to leave this to others, since we are now at a point in our life cycles where birthing a child is no longer viable. Meanwhile, however, we continue to mother the child in our care while engaging and subverting those institutions which are not constituted to acknowledge us.

As for Biddy and Libby — we think of them happily playing in Minusland.

Notes

1. While the three of us are "out" in many contexts, he is not "out" as the child of a lesbian couple in every situation he may encounter. Since we believe that how and when he does "come out" is his decision, we are hesitant to say more about him here.

2. The Justisse Method determines ovulation based on changes in cervical mucous.

3. Although our experience with this clinic turned out to be negative, we are not prepared to name the clinic because we do not want to jeopardize the chances for other lesbians to conceive utilizing these services.

4. At a reproductive technology conference in Edmonton, Debra heard a medical researcher in *in vitro* fertilization indicate that women are used to test this technology because apes are too expensive.

5. The headline reads, "Human egg becomes embryo without fertilization by male." (*The Globe and Mail*, May 27, 1983).

Having a Baby?

MARY-WOO SIMS

PAT AND I HAD BEEN TOGETHER FOR ALMOST A YEAR. WE ARE ELEVEN YEARS apart in age, and when we first met, I was thirty-six and Pat forty-seven. The age difference didn't mean much to us, as we both knew when to have fun and when to act like sober adults. One of the many things we shared was our notion of "family" — our respective families are important to both of us, and we believe that we are a family ourselves, in spite of what society and laws say about gay and lesbian domestic partnerships.

Very early on in our relationship we talked about having a child together. When we looked for a house, we specifically looked for one that would have room for a baby, even though our minds had not yet been completely made up about having one. Once we were settled in our house, we finally had time to think about it. Should we start a family together? We thought that the decision about whether or not to have a child would be rather simple. It did not turn out that way, mainly because we are in a lesbian relationship, and the law treats our relationship and intended family differently than it treats heterosexual relationships and families. In this article, I will describe our efforts to have a baby.

First, we thought about adoption. However, this was made more complicated by the fact that, under current family law in Ontario, only one of us could adopt. Either of us could adopt a child as a single lesbian but we could not adopt as a couple. Thus, only one of us would be the official parent; the other would have no legal status. Our child, presumably, would not make these legal distinctions and, to him or her, we would both be mommies. But, if I were the adopting parent, Pat would have no legal status. What would happen if I were to die? How would the law treat Pat's relationship with the child? Pat, having no status under the law, would not have any rights to the care of our child. How would our child feel? The death of a parent would be bad enough, but how would the child deal with the possibility of losing both parents because of the unfairness of the law? Yes, there are legal ways around the dilemma of adopting as a couple. We could push the system to allow us to adopt as a couple and file a complaint of discrimination if we were turned down. This would involve years of potential litigation and legal fees. In the end, we decided against this course.

Pat and I decided to be creative. Let's have our own baby, we said. Suddenly, all of our male friends became potential sperm donors. We started looking at them all in a brand new light: Was he good looking? Was he healthy (of course, he would have to agree to an HIV/AIDS test)? Was he smart? There were other questions, too: How do you ask your male friends if they would agree to donating sperm? What if they asked about co-parenting or being the male role model? Did we want a three-way parenting arrangement — potentially four-way, if the donor was in a relationship and his partner wanted some role in raising the child? It was complicated, but we were determined to look further.

We then thought of going to a fertility clinic. Heterosexual female friends of mine who were having reproductive problems were going to fertility clinics. I took them into my confidence and talked about my interest in having a child. They were very excited for me and Pat. They told me all about how the clinics guarantee "clean" sperm. That is, all the necessary health-related tests, including those concerning HIV/AIDS, are done before donors can donate sperm. You can even choose the racial background of the donor, height, weight, hair colour and whatever else you might be interested in knowing about the donor, other than their identity. One friend lent me a book on the procedures. It covered many points of interest about artificial insemination. Pat studied it thoroughly and briefed me.

Finally we thought we were ready. But no, there were still other issues to consider — legal issues. Under the law, the birth mother would still be the only one with status. The other partner would still have to establish a legal co-parenting relationship. We also had medical considerations. I was thirty-six. This was not too late to become pregnant in terms of the biological clock, but I have hereditary high blood pressure, which would not be very good for my health during pregnancy or for the health of the baby. Pat was forty-seven. For her the biological clock's alarm had struck, although she was in perfect health to carry the baby to term. It was now that we became very creative.

Pat presented the situation to her doctor and asked for a referral to a fertility specialist. We wanted a referral to a specialist who would consider the following radical action: fertilizing my eggs and implanting them in Pat. If she could then carry the fetus to term, our medical dilemma would be solved.

And what of the legal implications? "Very interesting and very mischievous," said a lawyer friend of ours who volunteered to take the case. The legal question would be: "Who is the mother?" Genetically, the baby would be partly mine because my egg would be used. Pat would be the birth mother. We would still have to establish the co-parent relationship in court, but what a strong argument! Pat's doctor, a lovely woman, was most excited for us and set about finding us a specialist who would be interested and able to help.

Pat and I couldn't wait. We were so excited at the prospect of having the baby together. This was the best way to ensure that the child was the product of both of our bodies and of our love. It was also a way of challenging discriminatory laws that would not recognize our relationship or our family unit. We waited impatiently for Pat's doctor to call us. The call finally came and an appointment was made for two months later. We talked excitedly about the necessary changes to the baby's room, which we had turned into a library when we first bought the house. We talked quite seriously about the impact that raising a child would have on our life style. We were making a commitment to another human being for the next sixteen years, at least, of his or her life. We were ready for it.

Finally, the day of the appointment arrived. The car ride to the specialist's office was filled with conversation punctuated by nervous anticipation. The office was a long way from home, and the ride took about an hour. At last we reached our destination. The waiting room was packed. There were many women, some children and some men. The men were nervously waiting with their partners, and to me they seemed uncomfortable — after all, this was about women's bodies; this was about getting pregnant. Some men looked as though they were asking themselves why they were there. I looked around the room again. "It's obvious," I said to Pat, "that we're the only lesbian couple in the room." I was nervous. Pat held my hand.

Then the call came: "Pat Dewhirst? The doctor will see you now." We went in and met the doctor. (Pat and I both agreed later that he met our donor criteria.) We explained why we were there, and he confirmed our medical assessment. Pat, in his words, was "over the hill." "Your eggs are no good," he told her. I could get pregnant, but my high blood pressure was an issue. He told us that he had helped out other "gals" who wanted to have a child together. (He later changed his reference to us from "gals" to "guys." Whatever made him comfortable, I thought — he might be messing about with our bodies. We also were more comfortable with "guys" than "gals.")

We presented the doctor with our preferred scenario. What about my eggs being fertilized and implanted into Pat? He had never received such a request, he said, but it certainly could be done. There were no medical reasons to prevent this from happening. There were, however, some ethical considerations. Was this akin to a surrogate mother situation, except that Pat would not be a surrogate? He would have to talk to his lawyer before he could give us an answer. He also asked us if we had thought of the ramifications of this decision should the details of our child's conception become public. We had indeed considered this and agreed that we would not initiate any publicity — this was a private affair. However, if the matter went to court, we were ready for it. The doctor concluded our conversation by saying that he would consult with his lawyer and we agreed to set another appointment.

Initially, we were a little disappointed that the doctor felt he had to consult a lawyer. However, as we looked at the issue a little more rationally, we thought that it was probably a good idea, and certainly in the doctor's own self-interest, to look into the legality of being the physician of record in this instance. If the matter became public, his name would be public along with ours. He needed to be prepared for the range of enquiries or comments that might be directed at him.

The day of our next appointment arrived. What would the doctor tell us? We anticipated disappointment. "Hi guys," the doctor greeted us. He smiled. "I talked to my lawyer. She tells me there is no problem if you guys want to go ahead. I'm ready. It will cost some money and involve some medical procedures." We explained that we were both covered by good medical plans and costs not covered by our plans were not a problem.

He then went on to explain the medical procedures: "Mary-Woo, you will have the hard part and Pat's part will be a piece of cake." He explained that I would require a full medical. They would "harvest" some eggs and conduct some tests to determine what shape they were in. I would then have a series of hormone treatments which would stimulate egg production. This involved coming in daily to the doctor's office for injections of the hormones. My vaginal temperature and blood samples would be taken on a daily basis. The procedures would have to take place first thing in the morning (before any breakfast, including coffee! Unfortunately, the doctor's office was located twenty-five miles from home, which would make all of this even more uncomfortable.) All these procedures would help to determine when I was ovulating and, therefore, when the best time would be to harvest my eggs for fertilization. "We fertilize four eggs and hope that one will take," the doctor explained. "We repeat this process until we achieve success."

"How many times will it take?" I asked.

"Don't know, but there are times when multiple harvests are necessary before we achieve success."

Pat said, "Sounds more like luck than science."

"More like a blend of luck with science," the doctor replied. He went on to say that, after we had achieved success with fertilization, Pat's turn would be next. Pat would have to undergo an examination as well. In particular, her womb would be checked out and scraped to ensure that nothing would interfere with her ability to carry the fetus to term. Once that was done, the fertilized egg would be implanted in Pat. Nine months later, we should have a healthy child. Of course, Pat would have to go for regular check-ups during the pregnancy, but, as the doctor repeated, "Her job is a lot easier than yours, relatively speaking."

I remember thinking, "What an understatement!" The doctor suggested that we take some time to think about it some more, as usually people are quite surprised at the medical procedures. Furthermore, although he understood that cost was not an issue with us, he wanted us to give some more thought to the costs associated with the whole process. We made another appointment for a month down the road.

During that month, Pat and I had long discussions about our decision to have a child. We again explored our rationales. We reconsidered the change in lifestyle, the costs associated not only with getting pregnant, but with raising a child, and the commitment we were making to the child for the next sixteen years. The legal and medical considerations were no longer as great a barrier as we had thought. The issue had now become more ethical and personal.

I had just read an article on reproductive technologies and realized that we now had the capacity to make sex selections. We could now examine the physiology of the fetus to determine if there would be any genetic deficiencies. I asked myself: What are the social, moral, ethical implications of reproductive technologies? I learned how the Nazis experimented with reproductive technologies on women during the 1930s and '40s. And I discovered that Germany, in the wake of that experience, now bans any form of reproductive technology. I also learned that the majority of reproductive specialists are men experimenting with women's bodies to help them give birth. If Pat and I decided to proceed, we would be part of the experiment.

Our personal dilemma was two-fold. I am a very private person — prudish even. I share my body intimately with my partner, and no one else. Change in public? Not me. The very thought of the medical procedures my body and my psyche would have to endure sent chills through me. As a friend who was going through the process told me, "Forget any thoughts of modesty you might have. It's all out the window. The probing, the examinations, the injections. You really must want to have a baby badly."

The other personal consideration was age. Pat was now forty-eight. A commitment to a child for sixteen years meant that she would be past retirement age by the time the child was legally able to leave our care. We were also fairly new in our relationship. We had celebrated our first anniversary a few months earlier. We really enjoyed each other's company. We wanted to travel. We wanted to play together. What impact would a child have on our energy, on our relationship and our need to spend time together?

In the end, we decided not to have a child. The doctor was disappointed. He really thought "you guys would go through with it."

A little over a year later, we still have no regrets. We make fine babysitters and we have my niece and nephew — who are eleven and nine, respectively — stay with us for holidays. We know we would have made great parents. However, as they say, "it's all in the timing." For us, neither the time nor circumstances were right in the end.

Another Kind of Baby Story

YVETTE PERREAULT

᯽

I WOULD GIVE ANYTHING NOT TO BE HERE. IT'S FOUR-FIFTEEN ON A MONDAY afternoon and I'm sitting in the fertility specialist's office waiting for the results of my final endometrial biopsy. This is the last test in a long series of progressively invasive procedures attempting to answer my question: "Why can't I get pregnant?" At least, that was the question two years ago, but after a grueling stint on fertility drugs and the horror of two miscarriages, the question has now become: "Why can't I *stay* pregnant?" My palms are damp. I recognize this as an effect of nervous anxiety and I am humbled by my longing for a baby ... a healthy uterus could mean another try ... all the other parts are checking out okay so far ... I still have good eggs, Ed's sperm are fine, we're genetically compatible ... why can't this dream be mine?

The doctor comes in with my chart and I search her face for some small sign of hope. She doesn't speak yet, and takes a very long time to read the lab reports.

I remember her open, laughing expression during my first visit: "We'll get you that baby," she had chirped, full of the confidence that appears to come with a medical degree. I had so wanted to believe her — to silence the gnawing edge of awareness that I might never raise my own child. Desperation had led me to the ritzy office on the seventeenth floor. As I had walked into the office that fall morning so long ago, I had glanced quickly at the dozens of photographs of deliriously happy mothers and new babies on the bulletin board. I had imagined my picture up there, a beaming face nestling my newborn, and my lover holding both of us. Ed would be taking the photograph. I remember my acute relief upon discovering that this doctor wasn't weird about lesbians who wanted to be mothers.

I was hopeless and without options — I simply couldn't summon the internal resources to respond to any overt homophobia. My decision to visit the fertility specialist was a last resort after years of Chinese herbs, homeopathic tinctures, herbal teas, stress reduction techniques and the very best self-care I could manage. How I clung to the doctor's words! In saying "we'll get you that baby," she had held out the promise that the numerous tests, the unwanted effects of fertility drugs and the anguish of monthly disappointments would eventually all be worth it.

I flush at the realization that I would have tried *anything* she suggested — my "good/passive patient" persona symbolized the depth of my hopelessness. I would even have allowed someone else to take charge, if it would get me my baby.

Hope is an incredible gift — I had lived so much of the past three years dreaming and planning, measuring most of that time in two-week cycles. What excitement I experienced when the ovulation predictor test told me I was having an LH surge and would release an egg within twenty-four hours! The wetness of ovulation had once meant strong sexual desire, and, in the old days, I would make "play time" with my beloved. But for longer than I had ever thought possible, my fullness and juiciness meant "maybe-baby time" and I did not feel my sexual hunger in any familiar way. My poor lover ...

Debbie didn't, and doesn't, want children in her day-to-day life. When I met her twelve years ago, I didn't think I did either. After all, if I was meant to be a mother, I would have somehow found a way to keep the infant son I had given up for adoption twenty-two years ago. I still recognize that scared, lonely but determined teenager in the part of me that sticks out my chin, pulls back my shoulders and marches into a confrontation. That tough-kid bravado guided me through the terror of being pregnant at eighteen with a boyfriend I simply wouldn't marry. I didn't know what else was out there, but I knew that settling down with this man in a small prairie town would have surely meant the death of my soul. It was 1972. Abortion was not an option for a small town girl with no money. So I gave my son away, hoping for a better life for him and for me. With that event, I closed the door on motherhood. No one talked about the grief of birth mothers then. I sealed my sorrow and my tenderness for children in a room so hiddenwithin me that I forgot it even existed.

My decision not to be a teenage mother gave me the courage to find my way out of a predictable life: I left psychiatric nursing and moved to the west coast, where I joyfully embraced a world of loving women with my body, my heart and my politics. I used my developing feminist sensibilities as an activist in the war on violence against women and children. Over the years, I continued to trust my intuition and follow my passions. By 1985, I was on the front lines in another battle — working with a Toronto community-based AIDS organization, helping people live with, and die from, HIV disease. For years I was immersed in a sea of grief with no preparation for dealing with its impact. And one day, with dozens of deaths behind me, I found myself weeping uncontrollably during a bereavement counselling session. I let the client believe that I was a particularly empathetic counsellor, but I knew I could no longer really hear him. Some scab had been ripped off an ancient place deep inside of me and a raw wound oozed pain in my chest.

My therapist asked me: "What other loss have you experienced in your life? How did you deal with it?" I came to appreciate how grief has no timetable — the hurt was about a baby lost eighteen years ago. My son was now the age I had been when I had birthed him. It was time to unearth that loss, so that I could be more present to the new grief of my friends dying of AIDS. Digging around in that old sore meant facing my shame at handing over my son to strangers and expressing my rage at not having real options about being a single mother. But as I did my work, I also had to come to terms with my fierce desire to be a mother — in the present. It came as quite a challenge to my perception of myself and to my life with Debbie. I could never find a satisfactory explanation as to *why* I wanted to be a mother — my words sounded clever but couldn't convey much about the core part of my identity that needed to express itself as "mother." I once described my desire to be a mother as similar to my discovery that I wanted to be a lesbian: "It's a part of me that needs to be lived out in order for me to be complete." Taking care of other women's children became an increasingly inadequate way to fill my mother-hunger.

Debbie and I struggled hard over my desire to bear and raise a child. For over a year, in and out of therapy, we fought and raged and almost left one other. We were torn apart by "either/or" choices: *either* we could stay living together without children or I could pursue this dream to have a baby but Debbie would leave. Even with lots of help, we never came to "one decision." I passionately wanted what I wanted —a baby *and* a life with Debbie. With equal passion, she wanted me as a lover and no daily life with a child. We both knew our relationship would never survive if either of us gave in on something so fundamental. So we each stuck to our turf and cautiously started looking for something beyond "either/or" — at least we were searching together. Eventually an idea from Marge Piercey's book, *Woman on the Edge of Time*, gave us a glimmer of a third option: in that science fiction tale, children were raised by at least three adults who chose to share the responsibility of bringing an infant into maturity. It was not necessarily biological affiliation or sexual intimacy with the mother that determined the childrearing relationship.

Deb and I stayed together, as lovers sharing the same house — an arrangement that suited the bond between us. I looked for others to help raise my child. We joined a "Dykes and Tykes" group with other lesbian couples trying to have babies. It was vital for us not be struggling alone.

Still, there was an essential element missing — sperm! Several men had offered, but none of them "felt right." I didn't want the anonymity of a sperm bank, nor, given the reality of AIDS, did I want a quick pick-up in a bar. I vividly remember the night I chose my baby's father. It began with a list of criteria:

1. a gay man who knew the reality of the AIDS world I was immersed in; someone who would understand the delight of bringing life to a death-saturated environment;

2. someone who was willing to be known as the father. I already had one child in the world who didn't know where he came from!;

3. someone whose politics I respected — someone who could offer a child a perspective on gay and lesbian activism I would be proud to share;

4. someone I could trust not to take a child from me and whose biological family would never be in a position to attempt something similar.

As I created this list, Ed's face came swirling into my mind. He wasn't a friend; he was a colleague and a kindred, working-class soul from the farmlands of New Brunswick. My heart felt satisfied — he was the right choice. I approached him the next day at work and to my shy delight, he was willing. Over the summer, Deb and I continued to fight while Ed and I got on with the practicalities of medical tests and contracts. I told my family I was going to have a baby and entered yet another battle with their homophobia. What is it about lesbians being mothers that drives people wild?

By that winter, I was ready to start inseminating. I'd heard it could take as long as two years for someone my age, but I'd gotten pregnant once before without trying and many of my friends had conceived within a few months, so I had no reason to think this was going to take long. I began the monthly routine of charting, trying, waiting and watching for any little sign: were my premenstrual breasts more swollen than usual? Was this a real period or only spotting? I'd sit up long into the nights, the rush of anticipation keeping me awake when my period was a day or two late. I'd try the pregnancy test and be fiercely disappointed when there was to be no baby this month. I'd be so sad when the bleeding would finally start. People close to me, including my staff and co-workers, became familiar with my monthly highs and lows. A week after my period, it would all begin again: I'd watch my temperature, mark down the consistency of each day's cervical mucous and note the position of my os. I grew to love this part of the routine because it gave me such awareness of my body's hormonal cycles and a strong connection with my fertile female self.

In the fourth month, I had some spotting but no real period. I redid the pregnancy test just to make sure that there was a definite blue line. It took forty-eight hours for the doctor's office to confirm that I was really, truly pregnant! It was impossible not to tell people.

I had ten weeks of blissful pregnancy before I woke up one morning just "feeling different." Something was not okay. There was no bleeding, but I called the doctor and begged to be seen that morning. "Things look fine," my doctor said. "Your cervix is closed and there is no bleeding, but I'll send you for a beta blood test and an ultrasound just to reassure you." I raced to the lab, alone. I didn't try to control my crying; they took me in right away so I'd stop disturbing the other women in the waiting room.

I'm lying on the table in the darkened room, my legs spread open for the transvaginal ultrasound. Still the tears won't stop. The technician is an older gentlewoman. I know she isn't supposed to tell me anything, but I ask anyway. She sucks in her breath, "Well, take a look over here." I strain to make sense of the little grey and white blotches on the screen. "See, the amniotic sack is already detached from the endometrial lining ... you're going to lose this pregnancy ... I'm so sorry. And this looks like a fibroid tumour."

I somehow make it back to my doctor's office; she sees me right away. My beta counts have plummeted and I am going to lose the baby. Because it's early in the pregnancy, I may not need a D&C, so I make a decision to go home and just wait for what my hormones already know. Deb is with me as the cramping and bleeding start. I look at the bloody tissue and clots on the pads and wonder, "Is this you, little being? Why couldn't you stay with me?" The baby already had a name.

Three days later, the doctor told that me my cervix was closed. She reminded me that twenty-five percent of pregnancies end in miscarriage. "Give your uterine lining a few months to build up and try again," she said. "The fibroid shouldn't be a problem yet."

I had been utterly unprepared for a miscarriage — all the women in my family had children without really giving it any thought; there was no family history of this type of baby loss. How was I supposed to deal with this?

I took a few days off work then threw myself back into the "baby project." I researched fibroids and their impact on pregnancy. I purchased Chinese infusions and an assortment of herbal teas to strengthen my uterus. Coffee became a thing of the past. I worked very hard to put the pain of the miscarriage behind me and to focus on a positive baby-filled future. I began to fill the basement with baby clothes, books, toys, a playpen. The unthinkable had already happened with this miscarriage; I would certainly be granted my wish now.

The months went by. I didn't notice how everything had become planned around my insemination schedule. I would drive for hours to connect with Ed when I was out of town and ovulating. I was determined to do whatever it took to get pregnant again.

I couldn't help but notice internal changes — my cycle was becoming increasingly erratic, ranging unpredictably from twenty-one to thirty-five days. Often there were only seven days between ovulation and a period. I could feel the other changes in my body — my hair was greying and thinning, there were noticeable lines on my face, my skin had a strange, "old" texture. When had I suddenly started aging?

A long, hard year passed by, measured in two-week chunks. Everything else in my life receded in importance. I thought I was pregnant at least a dozen times, but no ... I became sadder and sadder and began to see my hopelessness reflected in Debbie's searching eyes: "When will it be enough, Yvette?"

"I don't know," was my only reply.

I slowly began to talk to friends who had visited fertility specialists. I was ready to do something I once swore I would never do — try medical intervention. I got a referral to a woman doctor who, I had heard, was okay about lesbian mothers. I needed to know what was happening with my body.

"We'll get you that baby," the doctor said during the first visit. "The tests tell us that everything seems to be in good working order with one exception — your progesterone levels are low, which is normal for a woman your age moving into mid-life, but there are drugs to deal with this type of infertility."

The label was a shock: *infertile*. The possibility had never occurred to me! "What exactly does that term mean?" I asked. My mind raced as the doctor cheerfully explained about the inability to get pregnant despite prolonged attempts. I remember the sheer horror of the word. A protest surged from my depths. That would *not* be me. "Put me on the fertility drugs — the high dose you were talking about."

The drugs made me utterly crazy, with intolerable hormonal shifts. I had wild mood swings, with little pause between elation and sobbing; my skin broke out like a teenager's; my breasts were sore all the time. But all this was a price I was willing to pay, in order to stay in the place of hope and possibility. I added another element to my monthly routine: after the grief of my period, a trip to the doctor's office for a clomid check; then more drugs, the morning temperature, the mucous watch, the charts in the bathroom, the ovulation predictor kits, the negotiations with Ed around insemination time. I was vaguely aware that my head and heart were completely consumed by "the baby project." I didn't even know I had a lover. I had no idea about my sexual self. Everything became tinged with my frantic desire to be a mother. "When will it be enough?" Debbie asked again. I had no answer. I was ashamed of my desperation.

I was working in a remote area of the province when my period started — then stopped! My heart soared with hope for three days, until I had access to a drug store pregnancy test. My joy at watching the blue line fill in was indescribable. The drugs had worked! My body had worked! My swollen breasts and queasy stomach weren't just "wishful" this month — it was real! I floated through the days on a "high" and welcomed my time alone late at night, listening to tapes of nature sounds, feeling connected to the earth and to all living things. Reproduction — it's basic, animal, utterly physical. I was awed by the protection this pregnancy offered me from the pain of relentless

AIDS deaths and mounting work-related stress. I could cope with anything. What really mattered had shifted — I had a baby to take care of. I took long walks alone, talking to my baby. I knew this baby's name, too.

I passed the ten-week mark — the point at which I had lost the last pregnancy. It was a milestone, and afterwards I let myself rejoice in what felt like certain success. I made work plans to take maternity leave. Morning sickness was a welcome sign that this baby was continuing to grow. I loved the fact that my aching breasts demanded that I sleep in a bra. I welcomed every subtlety, every change. I began to make preparations for a home birth. My lover and I visited the mid-wife ... I was so ready for this baby. And I was so happy to be off the roller coaster of "trying."

I decide to undergo a routine ultrasound because I need the reassurance that everything is okay. My sister is visiting from Chicago, so I bring her with me to the lab. I had asked the doctor to send me to a different lab — it was bad luck to go back to the place where I'd heard about my lost pregnancy. My mood is quite different this time as I lie happily on the tiny table in the darkened cubicle, my bladder close to bursting from my recent intake of twenty ounces of fluid. But suddenly my awareness is drawn to the technician. She is taking a very long time with this ultrasound — she runs the wand outside on my belly then another back inside my vagina. This is different. She stops and clicks at the keyboard, talking measurements into a microphone. There's a tension in the room and I feel sick. A huge cold lump is beginning to make its presence felt in my chest. I crack a desperate joke, "Are the fibroids getting in the way?"

The technician doesn't laugh. I push for any information I can get. "Can I see the baby on the screen?" I know how much should be visible at this stage of development. The technician won't look me in the eye. "The radiologist needs to read this, then your doctor will give you the results. That's the policy," she says. She can't get out of the room fast enough. I know some-thing is very wrong but I can't believe it — my body isn't telling me there's a problem. I trust the wisdom of my body. My sister sees my face and takes me home. I begin to shake and the tears start to flow before I can even get into the car. I am so afraid.

My doctor calls: "The radiologist won't be in for three hours. Try to stay calm." She reassures me, "I'm sure everything is fine — your blood levels are good. Maybe you just got a really bad technician." Please, please promise me this baby will be okay. But she doesn't. My sister and I stay at the kitchen table, silently making a Mystery Puzzle, trying to fill the long spaces between minutes. I put pieces together without knowing the final picture. I plod ahead with the puzzle in good faith that whoever designed this will give me all the clues I need to solve the mystery. It all feels too damned symbolic.

The doctor finally calls. With a frozen heart, I catch her soft tone and I know her news will not be good. "The fetus is not developing properly." What exactly are you telling me? What kind of problem? Spina bifida? I've read about that — I'm ready to deal with a disability. "Your baby has no heartbeat." No heartbeat. I'm pregnant but there's no life inside of me.

"What do I do now?" I ask from some frozen, coping place inside me.

"You could wait for a spontaneous miscarriage like last time, although it may take awhile as your Beta levels are still really high." My body doesn't know yet that there is no life inside of me. How long could cells go on dividing and developing without a heartbeat? "Or I could arrange a D&C."

"Do that," I direct, taking control where I can. The doctor will call me tomorrow morning with details. I hang up; everything goes into slow motion. I hear the sound coming from my belly — a long howl, the protests of a mother-wolf calling for her pup. My sister quietly and respectfully stays with me in my grief. Debbie comes home. Ed is informed. I go alone to my room, trying to find the escape of sleep, but I wake up screaming. I hold my belly, trying to find the piece of the puzzle that answers the question, "Why couldn't you stay with me?" The ground opens up and I am lost in the pain. I am not even sixteen weeks pregnant yet.

The next day the doctor calls me: "It's a Friday and there won't be a hospital bed for a non-emergency D&C until

Tuesday." I can't live for four days with a dead baby inside of me. We make a decision to go to an abortion clinic. My doctor faxes the ultrasound results to the clinic so that they are prepared for me. The appointment will be the last one of the day so that I won't be faced with a room full of women who don't want their pregnancies. Debbie knows the dyke nurse who works there. I am so grateful that this place exists.

We approach the office and I see the placards of the anti-choice picketers. "Don't do this," they yell as we come up the walk, "your baby wants to live. Your baby already has a heartbeat."

My knees buckle as I shriek, "My baby has no heartbeat. Who are you people?" My sister and Deb are bodyguards, protecting me until I'm inside the clinic. The dyke nurse gives me drugs to take the wild look out of my eyes. She holds my hand throughout the procedure, softly telling me what the doctor is about to do. As he reads the ultrasound report, the doctor asks, "You wanted this baby, didn't you?"

I taste the tears. "So much, so much." Then I feel the metal probes suctioning and scraping my insides, taking away my tiny baby's body-with-no-heartbeat.

"Fetal tissue to pathology?" the doctor queries. Yes, I want to know what happened.

It takes days for this pregnancy to fully leave me. I embrace the shift in my hormones, carefully watching my body bleed and feeling my breasts subside. If I can't have this baby, I don't want any remnants of its brief presence. The light has gone from my heart and I know this grieving will be profound — there will be no rushing past this loss. I search for rituals to bring some closure to this pregnancy. A therapist friend offers to help, and I invite Ed, Deb and my sister to the ceremony. I have bought a lovely magenta box, shaped like the gay triangle. My sister helps me gather my "baby-making stuff": the pregnancy books; the "congratulations, mother-to-be" greetings; the fertility goddesses; three years of temperature charts; my positive pregnancy tests; the bags of herbal teas; the little brown tincture bottles; all the insemination equipment — the symbols of my baby-journey. As we each speak about our connection to this baby-story, we place the objects in the box and say goodbye.

During that ceremony, I find a place in my being that dares to whisper, "No more. This is the end of my baby-journey."

Sobbing, crying jags overtake me for weeks after that. I am on my back in the bottom of a pit of despair with walls of pain so high I know it's impossible to crawl out. So I lay there and choke on my tears and rage bitterly at a god I don't even believe in. For the first time, I know the bleakness of wanting to take my life. My swollen eyes and unclean hair frame an unrecognizable face in the bathroom mirror. I don't wash my body for days. I don't care. Something more than a baby has died — my world as I expected it to be has ceased.

My sisters help Debbie make sure I'm getting the basics of food, sleep, exercise and space to grieve. I see on their faces how much of a strain it is to be around me — I know I exude a sorrow unfamiliar and terrifying. I can't struggle at work anymore and I can't help other people through their losses. I want to run away but instead I visit friends out west for awhile. I am moving through life at a snail's pace while everything around me is rushing along. I notice that spring is here and I am so resentful. How dare leaves burst forth and birds build nests when I still need the cold comfort of winter? I finally find enough courage to buy books on baby loss and infertility. If that label is to be mine, I need the survival stories of women who have been there before me. In one of the books, there are eight lines mentioning lesbians and infertility. I don't find my whole self reflected in any of the others.

I give my body a few months to heal and it's a shock when I start dreaming about trying again to get pregnant: maybe now that I've left a stressful job; maybe if I try stronger fertility drugs; maybe ... I'm clearly not finished.

I go back to the fertility doctor with questions: "Why do I keep losing babies? Can you fix it?" I don't want this "no baby" state of affairs to be my truth. I do not want to adjust to a life with no child of my own. That's what has brought me to this office on a Monday afternoon at four-fifteen.

I'm still watching her face — the face of this usually perky fertility specialist. I'm sure she doesn't know anything about my distress. She has her babies — I've seen their pictures on her desk. She finally begins to speak. She can, at least, look me in the eye. The only way I can hear her words is to completely disconnect from the ball of fear in my chest. Why didn't I bring Debbie with me to remember what she's saying?

"Your uterine lining isn't building up sufficiently, even with clomid. You're really unlikely to ever maintain a pregnancy past the twelve- to sixteen-week mark." She takes a breath, "You can keep trying — it's your choice."

I stop hearing her. My hormonal levels, even with drugs, aren't going to make this a reality ... "Other options ... surrogate motherhood ... adoption ..." Don't they ever just say, "This is *not* going to happen for you in the way you want" — then help you get on with your grieving?

In my frozen, coping state, I politely leave her office. Home. I have to get home. It feels like someone has stepped on my chest. The cold sun is low in the afternoon sky and casts shadows of the stark bare branches; I smell the fallen leaves. It's almost twenty-one years to the day since my son was born. Winter is coming soon — a barren time. Is that to be my life? I keep waiting to wake up from this nightmare.

That last visit to the doctor was seven weeks ago. I don't yet have the luxury time brings to dull the intensity of grief, nor do I have the comfort of a well-developed analysis in which to frame the impact of infertility on my identity and sexuality. But as I move through this life transition, I do know what helps and what doesn't. I don't want to hear one more hopeful baby story: "My sister had seven miscarriages and then her son." Nor do I want to answer questions: "Have you thought about going to Peru for a baby? Adoption? Fostering?" Yes, I am registered with Parent Finders in case my son is trying to find me; no, the likelihood of adoption for a lesbian without large amounts of money is not great; no, I do not want to foster an abandoned child dying of AIDS; no, babysitting your daughter once a week won't help this pain right now.

Clumsily, I am also saying, "No, I don't want to be distracted." I want to scream at well-intentioned people, "Stop giving me advice. You can't take away my hurt. When you ask how I am, be willing to listen to my pain. I am raw with my searching, and yearning. I go to Loblaws and fantasize about stealing another woman's baby from its stroller. No, I am not happy that two members of my family are pregnant, again, without trying. I can't move through this any faster than I am. I don't want to be hurried through this time. This is not about problem-solving. This is about the tremendous pain of losing babies *and* losing hope that I will ever have another baby from this body. Give me your arms and a tender heart. I am adjusting to the reality that I am a childless mother, that I will live childless, *not* by choice. This is the end of a part of my life, and, to make meaning of it, I must experience it fully. Learn a little about grief before you try to help me."

I've looked for role models during these months. My call to an infertility group did not result in a lesbian-positive experience. Where are the infertile dykes? I don't have the strength right now to create that group, but I sure could use it. I have continued to search for strong women, toughened by infertility but not bitter or disconnected from their bodies; two heterosexual women well into their own journeys have offered their support. I have let them in — a little.

Where is the solace? Every TV commercial has a baby. There is so little respite. Even on a walk in the woods, I am confronted by cute baby animals and budding plant life. It's unbearable. I sometimes hate my lover — she was the one who never wanted children. What kind of god gives her what she wants but cannot find the compassion to grant me my simple wish? What's the point in being a lesbian if I don't have access to my lover's uterus? Will I ever make love again with passion and abandon? Will I ever like this barren body which has failed me so cruelly?

I have cleaned all the baby things out of the basement, and given them away to a battered women's shelter. I am trying hard to make space for whatever will come with this emerging, "child-free" identity. I can once again see my friends who have children, although I can't yet spend time alone with their kids. I can think about work with genuine enthusiasm and energy. I have planted things in the earth and I anticipate the buds and blooms next spring. Occasionally I have days where the absence of a baby is not the first thing on my mind. And occasionally there are painful surprises. Spending time with Ed can still tear open the hurt in my heart. I look into his eyes and watch the curve of his cheekbones, having thought a thousand times about those features reflected in the faces of my babies. We would have made such beautiful children. I would have loved to watch the changes fatherhood would certainly have brought this man.

This story is not complete. I do not know yet how these wounds will alter my core and shape my choices. I do know that I will honor my baby-story — and I will make something wonderful from this sorrow.

Adopting Sami

AMY GOTTLEIB

✺

I'M SURROUNDED BY LISTS THAT ARE A KIND OF MAP OF THE LAST FEW WEEKS. Many of the scribbles are crossed off, but not all — not this article. I find my focus is hard to come by. I fly from one thing to the next, cleaning and organizing up a storm, but I can't settle into a good book. I'm expecting, but I'm not pregnant. If all goes well, my lover and I will be adopting a newborn child sometime very soon. The baby is over a week late and we are both on leave from work, enjoying our unexpected time at home. This is the crazy calm before our lives are turned upside down and inside out, before we experience the wonderment and innocence of a newborn child and the punishment of sleep deprivation and mushy brain syndrome.

This child has been a long time coming. Although this latest possibility has been on the horizon for two and a half months, we've been trying to adopt for almost two years. Before that, I struggled to get pregnant for five years. I'm writing this article to make sense of the struggles that led, through a combination of luck, effort and circumstance, to our present state of happy expectation.

For many years, Maureen and I have developed and nourished four specific relationships with other people's children. Until now, when I've been asked if I have children I have often hesitated. Sometimes I have said no, and sometimes I've explained that I have four children in my life, ranging in age from two-and-a-half to twenty-four, but that none of them are mine biologically and none of them live with us. It has only recently become a bit easier to claim some parental identity. A few years ago, Maureen, who I refer to as the Queen of Relationships with Other People's Children, filled out an application for a "family" credit card at Ikea and said she had four children. We both laughed at how subversive this seemed and at how wonderful it was that she felt at ease to make this claim, even on a silly little application.

Our four "children" have a central and integrated place in our lives. They are part of my worries as well as a source of constant joy and learning. They show up on our phone bill, test my ability to think of wonderful birthday presents and are part of daily and holiday life. Most of all, each one of them is lodged in my heart forever.

There is a balancing act in having relationships with other peoples' children. We parent, but we are not their parents and they are not "ours." We embrace the verb "to parent"; but the noun "parent" does not describe us. There is a precariousness about these relationships, a sense of uncharted waters. And there is a sense of getting a lot of the "goodies" of parenting — the play times — and less of the troubles.

Maureen would have been fine to just continue as we were, growing with these four children (one of whom is now a young woman) and maintaining a significant freedom in not having full-time care for any of them. But I wanted to have a child, to give birth to a child, to raise a child with Maureen. Friends asked us why. Weren't our other kids enough? I still puzzle over that one, though I know that I feel the need to be a parent, to be part of the intimacy that is created with the daily task of raising a child.

Whatever the motivation, naive and/or wise, I tried to get pregnant for five years. My infertility has been a source of grief, and sometimes of despair. Sometimes I thought it was a plot by the goddess of Relationships with Other People's Children, so that our energies would be focussed on the children we were already parenting. But as much as I have mourned not being able to give birth to a child out of my body, that failure has somehow been softened by my relationships with our network of children. I am infertile, but I am not childless.

After being diagnosed with scarred fallopian tubes, which I discovered was likely caused by surgery to remove ovarian cysts eight years ago, I decided to stop inseminating. I felt that there was no justice. Maureen, on the other hand, who did not identify with the process of trying to get pregnant and felt that the experience had become too painful, with its dramatic ups and downs, was relieved to be off that roller coaster. She had already talked about fostering or adopting, but I had never sustained these thoughts — I could only hear my own body's desire to become pregnant. I took a year to sit with the thought of adoption, to think things over, half-heartedly pretending that I was interested but still hoping to find a way to get pregnant.

Finally, a year after my diagnosis with scarred tubes, I was ready to move on, and symbolized this in a ritual that I created with Maureen and some close friends. Over a period of time we had both come to a similar place, by different routes. Maureen had always been more inclined towards adoption because she felt that there would be an equality of potential bonding right from the beginning. And I reached a point where the most important thing to me was raising a child, not the act of carrying and birthing it. In retrospect, adoption seems quite an organic development — from our relationships with other peoples' children to adopting a child who is to begin with, and, in some sense, remains forever, someone else's child as well as your own.

In making the decision to pursue adoption, both Maureen and I agreed we wanted to be open about being lesbians. We were not willing to misrepresent our lives or conceal our relationship. We wanted to lead with what we identified as one of our major strengths for raising a child — our relationship. We also wanted as open an adoption as a birth mother (or birth parents) would agree to.

Our first experience with a social worker, whom we approached to do the home study required for anyone trying to adopt, was pretty disastrous. It occurred before I had really iven up trying to become pregnant. So while I pretended to be interested in adopting, I was really checking it out more than I was letting on. I think the social worker sensed this, though she never said anything to me. What I did come up against was some subtle and not so subtle homophobia and anti-semitism. During one of the interviews, I expressed incredulity that a birth parent would request that Maureen and I — a non-practising, lapsed Anglican and a secular Jew, respectively — raise a child as a Christian. The social worker announced that not agreeing to this would result in two strikes against me: that I was Jewish and that I was a lesbian. The valid but inadequate adoption procedures, which insure that white, middle class, heterosexual couples develop some consciousness of the birth mother's racial, cultural and/or religious background, were being used against me. We never saw this social worker again.

Maureen and I both assumed that a private adoption was our only option. But when I heard from a friend that the Metropolitan Toronto Children's Aid Society (CAS) was in the process of changing their longstanding policy of excluding lesbians and gay men from openly adopting through CAS, I called them. The intake worker seemed unimpressed by my situation and basically said that until the provincial law changed regarding the definition of a spouse, we would not be able to apply to adopt as a couple through CAS. In fact, we already knew that we couldn't legally adopt as a couple anywhere in Canada — a situation that angers us. What we were trying to do through CAS was adopt with the acknowledgement, at least, that I am a lesbian and in a relationship.

After these experiences, our central concern became getting the word out that we wanted to adopt. A year after meeting with the social worker, we printed up postcards with a photo of Maureen and me on the front and a message to a potential birth mother on the back. When I went to pick up the postcards, the woman at the front desk in the print shop said she thought it was a great card and wished me luck. And as I was about to leave, another woman who worked there ran up to me and told me she was an adoptee. She loved the card and hoped that we would be successful in our search. I left the store feeling high and sure once again that we had made the right decision and that we could find a birth mother who would be entirely comfortable with us as adoptive parents for her child.

We distributed postcards to our network and to people who might come in contact with a young, pregnant woman who might be considering adoption. Trying to adopt at this point was a project for me, but my heart still wasn't completely in it.

Maureen carried more of the load of thinking about it and strategizing.

Six months after printing the postcards, I found a flyer from an adoption support group about an adoption fair they were organizing. At the adoption fair, Maureen and I made our way to most of the tables, asking the same questions: "Hi, we want to adopt. Do you have any familiarity with lesbians adopting? We want to adopt domestically, do you have any information that would be helpful for us?"

The fair was a turning point for us. We found a straightforward, supportive social worker, who later conducted a very energizing and expansive home study. She assured us that the home study, which included both of us even though legally I am the adoptive parent, would be approved by the Ministry of Community and Social Services. Our job was to find a birth mother, and she seemed confident that we could. The home study interviews created an even stronger commitment to adoption between Maureen and me. One of the wonderful and unexpected bonuses of the home study was reading the supportive reference letters that our friends wrote for us.

At the fair, we also met a lawyer from Buffalo who had a very aggressive and refreshing approach. She recommended advertising in local or national newspapers, which was how she had found a birth mother and had helped others to do the same. She clearly endorsed a more open approach to adoption, with potential contact between the birth mother and the adoptive mother or parents. And she was willing to work with us. She offered us a lot of hope, a greater sense of agency in this process and the assurance that we would be able to adopt a newborn within six months or less if we advertised in the United States.

In giving us hope, the adoption fair fueled our efforts. We contacted other people who had adopted and began researching some of our options in the U.S. We contacted a gay man in New York who had adopted, and talked with him about agencies that are supportive of lesbians and gay men adopting. A woman who had adopted a number of children put us in touch with the Jewish Children's Adoption Network in Denver, Colorado.

Our desire to adopt now seemed to have taken a front-row seat in our lives. It demanded time and focus. We were faced with many pressing questions raised by these new possibilities. Would we be willing to adopt an older child — a two- or three-year-old? Would we be open to adopting a child with a disability? Or a child who had survived incest or assault? Would we be willing to adopt in a situation where we had no contact with the birth mother and where she had twenty-four hours to make her decision? These are all questions faced by anyone who adopts. We were forced to continually reassess our bottom line. We had many discussions and came up with a common approach: we preferred a newborn, though we would gladly adopt a child up to twelve months old; we felt open to and aware of our responsibilities in adopting a child of colour or mixed race, but didn't feel that we had the capabilities to raise a child with a disability, though we felt fine about a "correctable" condition or a slight disability; we felt open to adopting a child who resulted from rape or incest. These were difficult decisions that made us both feel uncomfortable.

As lesbians, we were faced with another set of questions: were we willing for the sake of convenience and expediency to hide our identities, or would we be hopeful and patient enough to find a pregnant woman who would choose us to raise her child? I make no judgement about either choice. Both Maureen and I felt most comfortable with the latter option. We wanted to give the birth mother the necessary information about us, to facilitate our future relationship with the adopted child and the adopted child's access to as much information about their birth identity as possible. As a result, we decided to reject the possibility of a closed adoption of a child from Arkansas or South Carolina — two possibilities presented to us by the Buffalo lawyer.

In July 1994, we went to New York to celebrate the twenty-fifth anniversary of the Stonewall riots. This was a great opportunity to contact lesbians and gay men who had adopted. We particularly wanted to talk to anyone who had adopted openly as a lesbian or a lesbian couple, either privately or through a public agency. We expected to find lots of women to talk to; after all, this was The Big Apple. To our surprise, we weren't able to contact even one lesbian couple who had adopted openly, in spite of meeting and talking to a number of women who had adopted. We did speak with a gay man who, with his partner, had adopted an infant girl through a public agency five years ago. When we spoke with lesbians who had adopted, we found that all of them had adopted as single women because they had no other choice if they wanted to adopt, or, in some cases, because they *felt* they had no other choice. We started to feel less excited about a U.S. adoption, partly because the costs were astronomical, but also because we didn't feel comfortable with the possibility of a more closed adoption. We wanted to continue to pursue the course we felt most strongly about — an open adoption.

We began to feel that there might be an opening in Ontario for lesbians who wanted to adopt. In addition to distributing our postcards, we decided to advertise to find a birth mother in Ontario. At around the same time, the struggle over Bill 167, the legislation dealing with same-sex spousal rights, was heating up. While it made us feel a common cause with other lesbians and gay men, particularly those trying to adopt, becoming more familiar with the adoption "community" also made us aware of how we were different from many lesbians. Adoption is a very middle class, class-bound activity and will continue to be so until access to public agencies is opened up to lesbians and gay men. Private adoptions, whether international or domestic, cost a lot of money — anywhere from five- to twenty-thousand dollars, depending on the country from which you adopt or whether you cross provincial boundaries. One's ability to get through the system and receive a positive assessment as potential parents also depends upon a class privilege.

In the end, the NDP government in Ontario watered down its bill and excluded adoption from the legislation, only to have it defeated. Although we were angered by the NDP actions, we were just as angry at the opposition parties — the Liberals and Conservatives — and we demonstrated against the bill's defeat and the political climate this had created. With the debate about Bill 167 swirling around us, there were moments when we faltered in our conviction that it would be possible to arrange an adoption in which we could be open about our lives. But with the support of lesbian and gay activism and our friends and colleagues, we plodded on. We decided that Ontario might not be a great place to advertise for a birth mother for awhile. So we picked a place where we thought the political climate might be more favourable: British Columbia.

Before placing our ad, we went away for a few weeks. While we relaxed in the country, we received a call from a friend who was just arranging an adoption from a Central American country. It looked like we could adopt as well, possibly at the same time or several months later. Beyond the shock of a new and little-considered option, we faced the moral and political dilemmas of an international adoption. Though it definitely was not our first choice, largely because we wanted an open adoption, we decided we were willing to pursue it. Most of all, we were ready to adopt. If this was how it was going to happen, we thought, then so be it. We were beginning to approach a zen state about adoption: we would roll with the punches, we would learn, we would take from every situation a new piece of the puzzle, hoping and sometimes knowing that all of this was leading us to a child.

While on holiday, we started to do some of the preparatory work for an international adoption. By far the most humorous adventure was my trip to RCMP headquarters in Ottawa to be fingerprinted. I am the daughter of communists whose files I had retrieved from the FBI and whose employment opportunities and promotions had been affected by membership in "the party." Now here I was, wilfully submitting to surveillance by the RCMP! My parents were both rolling over in their urns, but I assured them it was necessary.

On a more serious note, our social worker had to change the home study for our international adoption application. Maureen was now relegated to a "friend," and mentioned in only one paragraph. The social worker said she was making the changes out of necessity, but she wanted us to know that it was extremely hard for her to write Maureen out of the home study — it just didn't feel right. This, of course, was difficult to hear because it mirrored our own feelings, but it also made us feel good about our relationship with our social worker.

When we returned to Toronto, we decided to go ahead and place an ad in an alternative newspaper in B.C.: *Lesbian in a loving relationship seeks to adopt a child under a year old. Please call 1-800-261-3550.*

Two women responded. One was eighteen and said that it didn't matter that we are lesbians. According to her, "having a man around didn't guarantee anything." The other was in her early thirties and, as it turned out, really just needed some help creating a support network and developing more self-confidence about her parenting abilities.

A month later, after talking on the phone a number of times with the eighteen-year-old birth mother, we went out to B.C. for a visit. The visit didn't go well. It was obvious from the beginning of our meeting that she was changing her mind, but was finding it hard to communicate that to us. Her friend, at whose house we all met, told us that she was wanting to get back together with the child's father, who was also the father of one of her other children. It was a hard trip.

Meanwhile, the Central American adoption was not looking good. Maureen and I prepared an ad for *NOW* magazine in Toronto, thinking that the worst of the post Bill-167 anti-gay backlash had subsided. The week before putting the ad in, we received a call from a friend of a friend to say that *she* had a friend whose sister was pregnant and wanted to have the child adopted. We quickly sent her our postcard and a letter. The pregnant woman wrote back. She told us that, for her, sexual orientation has nothing to do with one's ability to parent. Our hearts sang when we heard that.

Over the past three months, we have had long talks on the phone with this woman. She has sent us a letter and a photograph for the child. As I write this article, she is in labour — or maybe giving birth to her child, who will then become ours as well. Our bags are packed and we're ready to leave. We are overflowing with anxious excitement, with joy and, *oy vey*, some trepidation. We are literally going out of our minds.

There are a number of significant lessons that I can tease out of our story. First of all, adoption will remain a possibility only for lesbians who are middle class and/or have financial resources, unless the law changes with regard to who can adopt. More specifically, this means that the definition of spouse must be changed to include same-sex partners. Lesbians must have access to public adoption. Politicians are lagging behind majority public opinion and even, in some cases, the courts.

Across Canada, there is a movement towards more open adoption records. In part, this will have an impact on adult adoptees who want information about their birth parents. But it will also have an impact on how adoptions are conducted in the future. This growing openness has been fueled by research into the importance of adopted children having access to information about their birth parents, as well by a movement of adoptees demanding that records be open and accessible. Part of these changes within the adoption community must be to embrace lesbians and gay men who adopt, and to support the principle of lesbians and gay men being open with birth parents about who they are.

Looking back at our process of adopting, it's clear that going after and succeeding in an open adoption as lesbians is more unusual than we had ever imagined. The irony of our own impending adoption is this: adopting a newborn child in Canada is rare. So how is it that we, two lesbians, find ourselves in this situation? Is it luck or class privilege? It is probably both of those things, in combination with our strong coast-to-coast network as lesbians.

Postscript

Maureen and I are now the mothers of a wonderful baby boy, who came into our arms just eighteen hours after his birth. We still cannot believe the miracle of our Sami, even though we believed that there must be a birth mother out there who would choose us to raise her birth child.

Sami has been welcomed with overwhelming enthusiasm and excitement, by friends from different communities and by our families. We feel blessed to have him in our lives, and clearly we are not the only ones who feel this. Sadie, who is almost three, is exuberant about her love for Sami, whom she sees almost twice a week. She calls him "her baby." Jesse, who is twelve, lives in Ottawa and has just spent ten days with us. Much of that time she spent feeding, rocking and holding Sami. Anta, who lives a few blocks away, is eager to be Sami's official babysitter. And Cindy, who is about to turn twenty-five, is flying across the country in a few weeks to visit this latest addition to her family. A longtime friend brings supper once a week and spends the night, getting to know Sami and beginning to fulfil her role as one of his special aunts. Sadie's mothers come once a week to be with Sami and have welcomed him into their extended family. Another friend's children have already named Sami their cousin, and are thinking of all the things they will teach him. He has been cooed at and sung to in English, Arabic, Spanish, Hebrew, Yiddish and Twi. We are joyous about this latest addition to our created family.

Adopting New Lives

JAN RADFORD

MY PARTNER AND I HAD BEEN TOGETHER FOR ABOUT FIVE YEARS WHEN I started thinking about having a baby. I was thirty-five and she was forty-three. When I first mentioned the idea to my partner, she really wasn't too keen. She had never really considered parenthood as a possibility for herself before, so the whole idea came as a bit of a shock. She worried that perhaps she was too old to take on a project of such magnitude. After all, she'd been around enough people with babies and young children to realize that parenthood is not easy nor is it cheap. We'd both read the stories projecting the costs of raising one child to adulthood and the figures were rather daunting. It would most certainly eliminate any possibility of early retirement for her. It caused both of us to do a lot of soul searching. Could our relationship take the strain? Did we really have what it takes to be good parents? What would it be like for a child to grow up in a lesbian family in a middle class suburb? Who would stay home to care for the baby? Who would get up with the baby at night? Could we afford living on one salary? Did we really want to give up sleeping in and weekends away? I don't think we were able to answer all our questions or concerns but finally my partner and I agreed we should at least explore our options.

I ploughed ahead in my usual fashion. Very quickly, I found a very nice doctor who agreed to artificially inseminate me using donor sperm. He met with my partner and me and surprised us by stating that he thought any child born into a lesbian family was twice as lucky as they had two mothers. I've since come to realize how fortunate we were to hear about this particular physician and start out our pregnancy project with such positive energy. I got to know him very well over the next couple of years and, without a doubt, he was someone special. However, after trying A.I. unsuccessfully for almost a year, my disappointment and frustration were mounting. He suggested numerous tests and procedures to determine if there was some reason I wasn't getting pregnant. I would have tried anything at this point. My determination to become a mother had only increased with every passing month. After enduring various diagnostic tests, drugs, hormones and two laparoscopies, I finally resorted to tubal surgery followed by another year of artificial insemination — all with no success. The two-and-a-half-year emotional roller coaster ride was hell for both my partner and me. I was crying and depressed much of the time and my partner felt like she was left helplessly on the sidelines, watching me go through some painful inner struggle in which she really had no part. Finally, with much sadness, we decided to end our pursuit of parenthood.

But it was not meant to be! It was only about three months later when a lesbian couple we knew arrived home from overseas with a beautiful baby girl. We knew that they too had been trying to get pregnant for some time but didn't know that they had also been exploring the possibility of international adoption. We were shocked to find out that it was possible to adopt an infant internationally, as we had been led to believe that only toddlers and older children were available. We had always had our hearts set on having a newborn so we had never even pursued this option. I remember holding their baby in my arms for the first time and looking at my partner. The instant our eyes met, we both knew what we had to do.

In a frenzy we began the process of completing all the necessary paperwork. Our friends were particularly helpful and supportive, having just gone through the process themselves. We had to have a home study done, apply for permission through immigration to sponsor a child into Canada, obtain police clearance, letters of reference and statements from my employer regarding my job security and from our bank regarding our financial assets. We knew we had to hurry as there was some talk that the overseas government was thinking about stopping foreign adoptions.

In approximately three weeks, we had everything we needed. After exploring the costs of airfare, accommodation, food, a translator and possible legal costs while abroad, it was obvious that it would be too expensive for both of us to go. As it might be necessary to be away for as long as three to four months to complete the adoption, it seemed more reasonable for one of us to stay at home and keep on working.

I landed in Bucharest in the middle of October feeling very much alone. The inside of the airport was very dark and smoky as I was led off to customs. My eyes were burning and my head was hurting as the custom officials went through every piece of my luggage and all my baby clothes piece by piece. It was obvious to everyone there that I had come to their country hoping to adopt. They kept looking at me and then speaking to each other in their own language. No one appeared to speak English. Finally, after well over an hour, they stamped my passport at least a dozen times and indicated that I could pack up all my things and go. I quickly threw everything into my duffle bag and headed out through the double doors only to be greeted by a crowd of people, all gathered together to hustle the tourists as they arrived. The air was thick with cigarette smoke and I thought I was going to be sick.

A woman approached me and in very broken English asked if I needed a place to sleep. Given that the remainder of the room seemed to be filled with men, I immediately leapt at the opportunity to go with her. As we headed out into the cold air I was pleased to be able to breathe again. She took me to her car and we drove off into the dark. The streets were all narrow with tall stone buildings on either side and suddenly I realized how precarious a position I was in — off in the darkness in a strange country going god knows where with some woman — and me with seven thousand American dollars in cash stuffed inside my pockets, socks, panties and bra.

We seemed to drive around for hours and after making several stops, we finally pulled up in front of what looked like tenement housing. There were rows and rows of tall white apartment blocks desperately in need of a coat of paint. We rode up on a rickety old elevator which only held two people and had a door that consisted of a lattice work screen. It all seemed like something I had seen in a black and white movie somewhere. The hallway to the apartment reeked of urine and was lit by only one low watt lightbulb suspended by a cord hanging from the ceiling. When my guide opened the apartment door to what I presumed to be her suite, I gasped. Inside was the most opulently carved rosewood furniture and the plushest carpets I had ever seen. She showed me to a similarly furnished bedroom and indicated that I could sleep here for thirty dollars a night. Based on my previous travelling experience, this seemed a little steep for a developing country, but who was going to argue at four in the morning. I climbed into the bed and slept soundly until seven.

Upon awakening, I found my hostess, Adina, already in the kitchen. She apologized in halting English for the lack of food in her small refrigerator. Indeed, inside there were only two hard boiled eggs, a piece of very dry crusty bread and a small bottle of a foul smelling clear liquid which I later learned had been purchased from the local bootlegger. Fortunately, I had brought a pound of coffee from home and set out to brew us a cup. During our "breakfast," Adina explained that her cousin who spoke English was coming soon. He would be my translator and take me around the countryside in his car to find a baby — all for only another thirty dollars a day! (By now I was beginning to wonder how many times she had done this before.)

When Adina's cousin Max arrived, I was pleased to find that he did speak English fairly well. He was probably in his midthirties and spoke in a very brusque manner. After exchanging a few brief words, he insisted we set off. We jumped in his little car and spent all day racing up and down narrow cobblestone streets. Periodically, he would stop the car, tell me to wait and run into some tall dark concrete building. After a few minutes, he would come out, get back in the car and without a word, we would start driving again. After this scenario had been repeated a few times, I gently asked him what was happening. He abruptly cut me off and said that I had to trust him. He asked me for some American money to buy "gifts" for the doctors and nurses. I gave him two hundred dollars and we drove to a "dollar store" in one of the large American hotels. He very quickly spent it all buying imported whiskey, American cigarettes, coffee and nylons, which we loaded into the trunk of his car. I was feeling very uneasy at this point but was reluctant to speak up for fear of what might happen.

By this time it was starting to get dark. We drove out into the countryside for miles and miles, down long deserted dirt roads. He said we were going to see "Pig Man." I had given up all hope of making sense of this bizarre day so I waited patiently to see what would happen. We finally pulled up in front of a small cottage and parked. In the yard I could see two large pigs and some chickens running around. Then out of the darkness came a middle aged man and woman. They seemed very happy to see us and the woman came over to me and, speaking non-stop Romanian, ushered me inside their home. Before I knew it, I was sitting at a small table with a bowl of homemade cabbage soup in front of me. It was the first real meal I had had since the airplane so I dug in eagerly. Even the dry bread tasted good as I soaked it in the soup.

My driver and hosts talked loudly amongst themselves while I ate. When I was finished, the dishes were quickly cleared away and out came a bottle of clear liquid like the one I had seen that morning in the refrigerator. Shots were poured all around and it was clear that I was expected to drink this unknown liquid. I raised the little glass to my lips and the smell was quite overwhelming. I tasted it carefully as my lips burned and my eyes started to run. Everyone laughed and they all drank their "tuica" down in one gulp. Not wishing to offend, I followed suit. Then Max indicated it was time to go and out we went into the cold dark air. We drove for what seemed like hours. I must have fallen asleep. I awoke to Max shaking me and telling me to go in to bed. We were back in front of Adina's apartment. I looked at my watch and it was three a.m. Max said he would be back in the morning and would honk when he arrived. I climbed out of the car and stumbled up to what I hoped was the right apartment block. I rode the elevator up to the eleventh floor and found the door to Adina's apartment. Not having a key, I knocked gingerly on the door. Within a few seconds, Adina opened the door and let me in. I couldn't tell if she was waiting for me or if it was her usual habit to stay up all night.

For the next several days, Max and I repeated this same little scene with only minor variations. We did start driving further and further out into the countryside — sometimes for three to four hours — before we would stop and go into some building. By now I had figured out that some of these dimly lit buildings were medical clinics while others were apparently orphanages. I stood by passively while Max interacted loudly and at length with various men and women who seemed to be doctors or nurses. Max told me little of what was going on and every time I asked, he got very annoyed. "Don't you trust me" he would yell. I felt very intimidated and quite scared at times. I would see him discreetly hand a bag of "gifts" to each of the doctors or nurses he would talk to. I was sure we must be running low on whisky and cigarettes by now, though I never saw inside the trunk again.

Every night after dark, we would stop at "Pig Man's" house to eat. I don't know how it was that "Pig Man's" house was always on the way home, but it was. "Pig Man" and his wife were always expecting us and a hot meal was always ready. I couldn't recognize much of what it was they fed me — different kinds of spicy sausage, pickled cabbage and a coarse corn-like mixture that resembled porridge. As a long-standing vegetarian, it certainly wasn't my choice of menu, but as it was the only meal I got to eat every day, I became more and more appreciative of their generosity with each passing day. The meal was always followed by a drink of hot "tuica" before we headed home.

Finally, Max seemed to have made some headway. We started revisiting some of the clinics and orphanages we had been to before. The staff were much more welcoming to us now, largely, I suspect, because of our earlier "gifts." We were allowed to make it further than the lobbies and offices of our previous visits and were led through room after room filled with young children in white metal cribs placed end to end. It was very disturbing to see so many children crowded together like this. They were all very thin and pale, and lay passively in their cribs staring into space. There were no toys for them to play with and most of the children could not roll over or stand up although many of them appeared to be well over one year of age. I was struck by how quiet it was — none of the children were crying. Their blank empty eyes simply stared straight ahead and few of the children seemed to notice we were even in the room.

The older preschool children were also kept together in large groups in cold, poorly lit rooms. They were all dressed in layers of wool clothing and wore woolen hats even when in bed. The rooms where they spent their days were empty except for a few stuffed animals placed along the windowsills and the odd hard backed chair for a staff member to sit on. When we entered, all the children came running towards us with outstretched arms, crying to be picked up. It was incredibly heart wrenching! My first impulse was to scoop them all up and bring them back to Canada, but I knew that I had to be realistic. My partner and I had talked about this. We knew the risks associated with adopting an older child and had agreed that we would not adopt an infant over four months of age. I was starting to feel desperate, however, and had to fight the urge to adopt almost every child I saw.

I found myself crying for hours late at night when I got back to Adina's apartment and was alone. My partner, who had been telephoning me weekly up till this point, now started calling me daily. I remember one call from her at six a.m., when I sobbed for forty-five minutes straight. I was emotionally devastated seeing so many needy children and being absolutely powerless to do anything about it.

For some strange reason, newborn baby girls seemed almost impossible to find. We continued our search daily but often arrived to hear that the only baby girl they had at the orphanage had been adopted the day before by an American or German couple. Max told me not to get discouraged because he was sure he would find me a baby soon. I was not so confident and was beginning to express my doubts to my partner. By now I had been away from home for six weeks but it seemed like very much longer. To lift my spirits, my partner arranged for my friends and family to take turns calling me early every morning. It was so strange to pick up the phone and over crackling telephone wires hear familiar voices who spoke English! I was so lonely and depressed that the calls really helped to keep me sane.

We stopped visiting the orphanages and started going directly to the maternity wards in the local hospitals. The Romanian hospitals were certainly very different from the hospitals at home in Canada. They were dirty and dark. Many of the windows were broken. Large cracks were apparent in the concrete walls — from the latest round of earthquakes I was told. To keep warm, all the hospital staff wore coats that looked like flannel bath robes over their uniforms. I couldn't tell who were the doctors or nurses or cleaning staff. Everyone was smoking and drinking instant coffee in dimly lit offices. I could hear lots of babies crying in the background but had no sense that anyone was looking after them.

We met a young woman who seemed to be a doctor. Max started giving her "gifts" every time we saw her. She was very friendly and seemed flattered by all of Max's attention. They spent hours talking to each other while I sat quietly drinking *Nescafé* and writing in my journal. The doctor would frequently look at me and I would put on my best smile. After several days of this behaviour, suddenly I was hustled down a hallway to a little office. Max had told me that this doctor knew of some twin baby girls who might be available for adoption. I tried hard not to get my hopes up because I knew I couldn't take too much more disappointment. My heart was pounding as I sat there — not sure what I was even waiting for.

Suddenly, in walked a woman all dressed in white, carrying two little white bundles — one in each hand. They looked like two little sausages and couldn't have been any more than twelve inches long. I stood up and could see a bright little face peeking out of each of the little bundles. It was love at first sight! They were the cutest little faces that I had ever seen, with the tiniest little noses and a dimple in the middle of each chin. I nervously asked Max if these were the twins that were up for adoption? I was giddy with excitement and when he said yes, both he and the doctor started to laugh happily at my joy.

By this time I was crying. I asked if I could hold the babies. I wasn't even sure if they were girls because they were swaddled from head to toe. They were so tiny that it was easy to hold them each in one hand. I asked if I could undress them so that I could see their little bodies. I gasped with disbelief as I unwrapped first one and then the other. They were so scrawny and malnourished and their bottoms were bleeding and raw. It was obvious to me that they were premature infants, just recently born. The umbilical cords were still attached. I was very distressed by the sight of infection around their cords and little sores all over their bodies. I asked Max again if these babies were up for adoption. Were they really to be mine? He said yes, but indicated that we must first get some papers signed by the birth mother. She lived several hours away in the mountains so we would have to drive up there to see if we could find her. I quickly wrapped up the babies and reluctantly handed them back to the "nurse." It was so hard to part with them after so brief a glimpse but I knew we had to go.

We jumped in the car, the doctor in tow, and drove up into the mountains. The scenery was incredibly beautiful and there was a light sprinkling of snow on the ground. As Max and the doctor talked and laughed together, I was left to my thoughts in the backseat. I was filled with a mixture of excitement and fear. What if the birth mother said no? What if she didn't like me? I suddenly became conscious of my appearance and wondered if my jeans and sweater would make her think I was too young or not wealthy enough to raise her babies. We stopped somewhere along the way and the doctor got out and made a telephone call to the midwife in the village. Apparently, she asked the midwife to let the babies' birth mother know we were coming to see her.

After what seemed like an eternity, we arrived in the most lovely little mountain village. We drove up in front of a small office building of some kind. There, sitting out front on a wooden bench, was a handsome older woman wearing a shabby yellow coat and "babushka" on her head. I hardly looked at her at first because I had no idea who she was. The doctor rushed over to her and they began talking. She motioned to me to come over and introduced me to Maria. I was struck by this woman's kind but tired face. Her hands were worn from a life of hard work. She smiled at me and I could see her eyes twinkle. I knew immediately that she had agreed to let me adopt her babies.

I could hardly wait till my partner called the next morning. I grabbed the phone on the second ring. It was a terrible connection. Apprehensively, she asked how I was doing and how the previous day had gone. She knew that we had been "courting" this female doctor for several days in hopes of seeing a baby girl. Trying to hold back my excitement, I blurted out, "So how do you feel about having twins?" She screamed with delight and, in disbelief, told me to tell her everything. I recounted the story of the last twenty-four hours as best I could and tried to describe the babies in minute detail. I was crying with happiness and so was she. We kept telling each other not to get too excited because the adoption could still fall apart. We needed to wait till we had gone to court and signed all the papers. Having said all that, our minds were racing and our hearts were filled with hope.

We had to wait almost two weeks before I could go to court and finalize the adoption. Each day, Max and I drove the three hours out to the hospital so that I could spend time with "the babies." I wanted to stay at the hospital all the time but there was still so much paperwork to do in town. The night before our court hearing, I was so nervous and excited that I could hardly sleep. I remember lying in bed trying to think rationally. Was I doing the right thing? Would we really be able to manage twins?

Finally, morning came. Max and I arrived early at the courthouse, which was in a small town several hours' drive from the village where the babies had been born. I worried that Maria, the babies' birth mother, wouldn't show up. I could hardly sit still I was so nervous and then, finally, I saw her step off the bus. She was wearing the same coat and scarf she had worn on the day we had met. She spotted me and came right over and gave me a big hug. She started speaking to me in Romanian and kept smiling over and over at me. I couldn't understand a word she was saying but somehow I think she was thanking me for agreeing to adopt her daughters and give them a good life in Canada. We spent the day together in the courthouse waiting for our number to be called. Not being able to talk to Maria frustrated me dreadfully. I knew that this might be our only opportunity to communicate, but with Max nowhere in sight, conversation was impossible.

The adoption went through without a hitch. The judge spoke French so I was at least able to generally follow what was going on and answer all his questions appropriately. My papers were all in order so we were in and out in less than thirty minutes. It all seemed so unreal. Maria hugged me outside the courthouse and I asked Max to take a photo of us together. Maria handed me a piece of paper with her address written on it. She seemed to indicate that she wanted me to write to her and I promised that I would. With that she left on the bus and we headed to the hospital to get the babies.

I'll never forget that moment — taking all the little baby clothes out of my bag and starting to get my babies dressed. They were so tiny that the newborn diapers I had brought from home came up to their armpits. The sleeves of the little sleepers had to be rolled up four times to find their little hands. I carefully wrapped them up in their matching little wool blankets, said goodbye to the hospital staff and walked out to the car. It all seemed so unreal. The three-hour drive back to the city was the most blissful time of my life. I sat in the backseat holding the two tiny infants and staring at them as they slept. I was already deeply in love with them and was sure that they were the most beautiful babies in the whole world.

Max dropped me outside Adina's apartment and I arrived to find the apartment empty and cold. I quickly took the babies into the kitchen, shut the door and lit all the burners on the gas stove. With no central heating, it was the only way I could raise the temperature in the apartment to something that was liveable. Thus started my first night of motherhood. Huddled around a gas stove with two delicate little creatures, who were totally dependent on me, in a little basket.

Between the two of them, they cried most of the night. I was exhausted by the time the sun came up and I was beginning to wonder if I was really cut out for this parenthood stuff. Both babies seemed to have stomach aches after they ate and I now knew why their bottoms were so red and sore. They seemed to have non-stop diarrhea and I was wondering how long the disposable diapers I had brought from home would last.

When Max arrived at nine o'clock, I packed up both babies and we headed off to the local hospital. It was necessary for both babies to pass a medical examination before I would be able to obtain their visas from the embassy for their entry into Canada. We waited at the hospital for several hours before our turn to see the doctor finally came. There were lots of other foreigners there with their newly adopted children and it was wonderful to be able to spend some time together, swapping stories and sharing in each other's happiness. Finally, we were ushered into the examination room and, as I undressed the first baby, I heard the doctor gasp. She started yelling and waving her arms up and down. I couldn't understand a word she was saying but I knew instantly that she was horrified at how small and undernourished the baby was. She lifted the baby up onto the scale. Curiously I leaned forward to read the scale. I had been told how well the babies were doing at the other hospital, but at that moment I could see the truth. My new daughter weighed all of 1500 grams — or just over three pounds. My other daughter weighed scarcely more. Max tried to calm the doctor down. She refused to sign the medical certificates, explaining that these babies were just too small to travel. Suddenly another bag of "gifts" appeared from under Max's jacket. The doctor protested only slightly then signed the medical certificates and accepted the gifts. With an incredible feeling of relief, I quickly dressed both babies and we hurried out of the hospital to the car, clutching the necessary papers.

Max recognized that I needed help in caring for the babies. He took me to another apartment, where a very nice family of four allowed the three of us to move in. It was ten days of hell for all of us as both babies were now very obviously sick. The diarrhea and stomach aches continued and it was all that Christina, the matriarch, and I could do to try to keep both babies fed, clean and dry. How the seven of us managed in that small three-room apartment for those ten days with two crying, sick babies is still a mystery to me.

In spite of severe sleep deprivation, I managed to run around to the various embassies and obtain passports, visas and airline tickets. My partner and family were anxiously phoning every day trying to determine when we might get out of the country. The political tensions in Romania were starting to mount again and there was talk of another revolution. The streets were filled with soldiers carrying machine guns, and tanks were strategically placed throughout the city. Max reassured me that he had an escape plan for the babies and me and would get us out of the country if trouble erupted. It was reassuring to hear that, although my heart was set on flying out under less frightening circumstances.

Finally, on a sunny cold December morning my new friends drove my daughters and me out to the airport. In the daylight, the airport didn't seem as oppressive or smoky as it had some nine weeks earlier. The customs officials barely glanced at the three passports I presented to them or the two little bundles I carried in my arms. Before I knew it, I was walking out across the runway and up the stairs into the airplane. I tried to keep my excitement under control until the plane was actually airborne — I kept expecting something to happen that would shatter my dream.

We landed in Canada after a rather uneventful seventeen-hour flight. Much to my surprise and delight, my partner, friends and family were all waiting with balloons and banners as we came through the doors at customs. I was on such an adrenalin high I could have skipped across the airport floor except for the two little beings sleeping soundly together in the Snugli wrapped tightly around my waist. My partner came towards me and after a quick hug and kiss said, "Let me see them? How do I get them out?" I helped her lift first one baby and then the other from the Snugli and cradle them in her arms. It was one of the happiest moments of my life and all the weeks of hardship quickly became a distant memory.

After a short period of socializing with friends, my new family and I headed home. I knew that the babies needed to go to the hospital but I just had to go home first so we could all be alone together for just a little while. My partner was overjoyed with the babies and once we got home, she just kept smiling at them and kissing them all over. That short time together stands out vividly in my memory. Then it was time to pack up our daughters and head for the hospital. They were admitted immediately.

We spent the next month getting to know our daughters in the artificial environment of the hospital. We spent long days at the hospital as a variety of doctors, interns, residents and nurses trooped through asking us what seemed like the same questions over and over again. The hospital staff were generally awkward with our relationship and were unsure what to call us. At various times we heard ourselves referred to as the mothers, the caregivers and even the foster mothers! They asked us things like "which one is yours?" They struggled with the idea that we called ourselves a family, and yet no one was openly homophobic or discriminatory.

At night, my partner and I made the hour-long drive home so we could sleep in our own bed. For the first week or so, I would wake up in the middle of the night completely disoriented, clutching my pillow and in a panic yelling, "Where are the babies? I can only find one. Where is the other one? Help me, help me." My partner would calmly reassure me that the babies were safe in the hospital and encourage me to lie down and go back to sleep.

It was an exciting moment when our daughters were finally able to come home from the hospital. They now weighed just over four pounds each and had lost their gaunt little looks. My partner took some holiday time and we nestled into a comfortable routine of feeding, changing and bathing our two little darlings. Neither my partner nor I ever felt left out because, with two babies, there was always something for both of us to do. We took turns doing the night shift, and with feedings every two hours, the days and weeks passed quickly. It took several months, however, before my heart would stop pounding every time there was a knock on the door. I was so anxious that we might open the door to find some official standing there ready to take our babies away — telling us perhaps that Maria had changed her mind or my papers really hadn't been in order. Even though the girls' birth mother was at least ten thousand miles away and I knew that our adoption was perfectly legal, it took ages before I could shake this irrational fear.

When the girls finally weighed about ten pounds, we dared to venture out into the real world. We were completely unprepared, however, for all the attention we attracted. Complete strangers would approach us and after the usual "oohs and aahs" would come the question "Are they twins?" and then the inevitable "So which one of you is the mother?" At first, caught completely off guard and still extremely proud of our newfound motherhood, one of us would blurt out, "We both are." This response was usually met with blank looks and then followed nervously by a series of new questions. Things like, "Did you know you were going to have twins? Was it a vaginal delivery or a caesarian birth?" or "Why aren't you breastfeeding?" Not wanting to stand and discuss our entire life story with strangers, we soon became adept at deflecting such prying questions. We also realized that our daughters' adoption story was something private and that it would be up to them to share their story with others, if they so wished, when they were older. To reduce the constant detection in public, we decided then not to dress our daughters alike.

Once our life had settled down into somewhat of a routine, we decided to explore the possibility of joint adoption. In retrospect, I realize we were pretty naive. It had just never dawned on us that lesbians and gays in Canada were not, as yet, able to adopt as a couple. We were extremely disappointed to find this out but on the advice of our lesbian lawyer decided to try instead for joint custody and joint guardianship. This was particularly important for my partner, who up to this point had no legal relationship with our daughters. Much to our surprise, even joint custody and joint guardianship had never been awarded to a lesbian or gay couple before. Our lawyer asked if we were prepared to be a test case and we agreed. Nervously we waited while all the necessary papers were submitted to the court. Within a few months, our lawyer called to say that we had been successful in our application and our relationship as a family finally seemed legitimized.

I went back to work when the girls were five months old, and my partner (the one who had never contemplated motherhood!) became the stay-at-home parent. Over the months, I became much more understanding of the plight of fathers in our society. It was often very difficult and a bit surreal to arrive home after a hard day and a long commute to enter the "world of babies." I was longing for some peace and quiet and my partner was longing for an extra pair of hands to help feed, change and entertain increasingly mobile twins. No wonder some men choose to work late and come home after the kids are in bed. We processed this (and each little hurdle of parenthood as it arose), learned to make compromises, and gradually began to adapt to life with children.

Although the girls were always delighted to see me, more and more, they looked towards my partner as their primary caregiver. That is, they were always happy to have me participate in their care but when the chips were down and they needed comforting, only my partner would do. As the one who had longed to be a mother, it was ironic that things would turn out this way. I felt hurt and rejected every time one of my daughters would reach out preferentially for my partner. Although intellectually I understood that for the first year of life children are intensely attached to their primary caregiver, emotionally it was very hard to bear. I had to reassure myself frequently that it didn't mean that the children didn't love me nor did it mean I wasn't a good mother.

I struggled for many months trying to define my role in relationship to our daughters. I realized that my partner and I were treading in unknown territory. We certainly had no socialization regarding the role of the "second mother" — the one who goes back to work full time, and, yet, wants to be an equal partner in parenting. I sometimes felt quite excluded from the "inner triangle," consisting of my partner and our two daughters, and had to aggressively pursue my individual relationship with each of the girls.

Sometime before the girls turned three, their relationship with me began to change. I started to notice that they snuggled up to me first when we all sat together on the sofa. When one of them fell off their trike, it was just as likely that it would be me to whom they would turn for comforting and hugs. It was wonderful and exactly how the books said it would be! Although I knew from my study of child psychology that the intense attachment to "mother" begins to decrease after one year of age and that children start to show multiple attachments to other people important in their everyday lives, experiencing it firsthand was very different. For me, it finally feels like the girls truly have two mothers — both with different skills and very different parenting styles — but participating equally in the day to day activities of our daughters' lives.

The girls are now four and into the whirl of birthday parties, bicycle riding and dancing lessons. They call us both "mommy" or "mama" but when there is a need to differentiate between us, they refer to us by our first names. When we overhear them talking between themselves, they usually refer to us as "the moms." The staff and other children at their daycare have taken the lead from our daughters and seem equally comfortable referring to us as "the two moms."

The girls know they are adopted. We have always talked openly about the fact that they grew in Maria's womb and then "Mama Jan" brought them on a long airplane ride to Canada. Not wanting to confuse them, we have only recently started to refer to Maria as their birth mother and their four half-siblings as brothers and sisters. We have an open adoption and exchange regular letters with Maria and send small gifts to her and her other children for birthdays and Christmas. We have put together a "life book" for our girls that contains photos of my trip to Romania and their early days in hospital, as well as copies of all Maria's letters and cards. (To protect against loss or damage, the negatives and originals of all Maria's letters are safely locked away in our safety deposit box at the bank). We maintain regular contact with other Romanian people here in Canada and try to incorporate aspects of the girls' culture into our home. We talk about going back to Romania someday when the girls are older — but, of course, the ultimate decision will rest with our daughters.

Parenthood is everything we'd hoped it would be. I have learned more about myself in the last four years than I ever thought possible. No one can adequately prepare you for all that it has to offer. It truly is a personal voyage of discovery — one that I'm glad I didn't miss.

Apparently a Parent

ANTOINETTE REED

WHILE WE WERE IN THE HOSPITAL JUST AFTER OUR SON WAS BORN, WE HAD TO fill out his birth certificate. A square gray woman dropped the paper off with us and then returned at hourly intervals to see if we had finished it yet. In between calling the relatives, entertaining friends and taking turns gingerly holding the baby, we debated whether or not we were allowed to be honest. We figured it couldn't hurt to try, so we crossed off "Father" and wrote in "Other Parent," then my name, and my date and state of birth.

It felt really important to be writing these things down; I loved it that some state agency cared where and when I was born. I know — and knew then — that other things I had done were far more important: holding my son's tiny head and neck in my hands while his legs still lay in Dey's womb; murmuring to him — while the doctors cleaned out his meconium-stained lungs — the same melodies I had sung to him through her thickening belly; being with him in the nursery during his first experiences with soap, water, combs and pyjamas. But there is something about filling out an official form that makes things seem more real, and this felt like my first big commitment to Harper in his *ex utero* lifetime.

The square gray woman returned very shortly after having taken the form away. "You can't do this," she said with the first color I had seen in her face. When she understood my partner's particular situation — not just that Dey didn't want the father involved — she said, "Oh, in *those* cases what you are supposed to do is put 'A.I.' in place of 'Father' ... for 'Artificial Insemination,'" she simpered. And that's how his birth certificate came back to us, with little ugly lines filling the spaces where I had put my birthday and birthplace.

I had been forewarned — by books and by other people — that something that was going to be potentially very difficult for me as the "non-biological parent" was feeling legitimacy as a parent. And in fact, despite all my preparation, the first few days felt especially difficult. I wanted — needed — all the time in the world to hold Harper, to hold Dey. I needed a quiet still space in which to accept this new identity of mine as a parent. It still all felt unreal to me. Every time a different friend came over to meet the baby, I felt displaced, as if some very important piece of work were being interrupted, as if I were trying to grow a new arm and it needed all my concentration and energy. Every time the door would open and close to admit a new person, my fragile sprout could not withstand the draft, and I would have to start over.

I didn't want to feel this way; it made me feel selfish and petty. Another part of me was grateful for the meals people brought, the sleep they sometimes let us have. But when they were done holding the baby (or when Harper was done being held), there was always a reason for him to go to Dey, always a legitimate reason for her to hold him: breastfeeding. It took me quite a while to feel that my holding him was as legitimate in its own way. I had many different dreams about Harper's birth, in which hundreds of people would come to celebrate with us, and they would all turn out to be Dey's friends, and I would lose both Dey and Harper in the crowd. I think these dreams partly emerged from my new insecurity around Dey, too: now that she had this child, now that this powerful, biological mother-son force breathed between them, where would I stand? In fact, I needn't have worried. Most of the reason I have ultimately been able to feel so legitimate is that Dey is so firm and strong in her belief in *us* as his parents, and so entirely free of jealousy about my developing my own relationship with Harper. And from the beginning, Dey has encouraged me to adopt Harper, understanding that adoption is one symbolic (yet also very concrete) way to solidify that feeling of legitimacy.

We started the adoption process shortly after Harper's birth. Our lawyer — who specializes in cases like ours and has successfully adopted her partner's two children — told us that things have changed a lot in California over the last few years.

The Department of Social Services still routinely recommends against allowing lesbians to adopt their partners' children ("They are a lovely and loving couple, but ..."). But just five years ago, said our lawyer, she would have counselled against us initiating the adoption until: our child was older (three or four at least) so that we could have documented good parenting; and we had been together as a couple longer (preferably ten or more years — we've been together two) so that we could have documented unimpeachable stability. Now, she says, it doesn't matter so much. The experience in our county has been that, following the Department of Social Services' "No" vote, one of the county judges has always overturned their recommendation and allowed the adoption to proceed.

Obviously, things are different from judge to judge, county to county, state to state. In the state of Washington, for instance, a bill is currently being debated that would make illegal all adoptions by homosexuals, bisexuals, transsexuals or transvestites because "there is a legitimate and compelling state interest in ensuring minor children are placed ... in sound female with male married households (House Bill 1171)." And in Nebraska, gay couples may no longer become foster parents, much less adoptive ones.

It was very exciting to see our petition to the court in its final form. Sentences like "Petitioner Antoinette Elsa Reed acts in all respects as a parent to the minor child and the child considers Petitioner to be his parent" did much to assuage the ugly feelings of having been crossed off his birth certificate. And again, something about seeing it in writing gave it all a dizzying feeling of reality.

The next step involved filling out forms and more forms. Mine were pretty interesting, though a little scary. After all the reams of questions about where I've ever lived and worked and to whom I've ever been married, there were several pages of essentially psychological questions about my perceptions of and relationship with my parents, presumably designed to evaluate my likely parenting abilities. It was very difficult. Our lawyer said her most important piece of advice was to be honest — that no adoption she had seen had been refused because the

petitioner was the child of an alcoholic, or had taken anti-
depressants, or had been in psychotherapy — that adoptions
were refused rather for disingenuousness on the part of the
petitioner, for *lying* about psychiatric history or income or
family details.

The questions about my parents were things like "How
would you describe the way your father was when you were a
child (check all that apply)?" and then thirty or forty adjectives,
things like "Hostile," "Fun," "Creative" and "Demanding."
Or "How did your parents resolve their differences (check all
that apply)?" There were, of course, many questions about my
relationship with my "spouse." And many about how I would
discipline my children (they actually offered "Tying the child
up" as a choice!).

My partner's forms were much more frustrating because
there are no forms designed for us. It would make the most
sense for us to be given the same forms that are given to married
couples, when one spouse wants to adopt the children of the
other. Instead we are given the same forms used in "stranger
adoptions," i.e. when the biological mother is giving up the
child and will have no further contact. So Dey responded to
twenty pages of questions with "Not Applicable."

Along with the forms, I had to submit various testimonials.
My physician had to assert that I am healthy, my employer had
to confirm that I am gainfully employed and earning what I say
I earn, the Department of Justice had to establish that my
fingerprints are not connected to any crimes (particularly of the
child abuse variety), and four people of my choosing had to fill
out more forms attesting to my skills as a parent. Our lawyer
counselled me to choose a good balance of people — male and
female, straight and gay — but preferably all parents. It is
worth noting that straight couples in the identical circumstances do not have to provide testimonials.

Nor do straight couples have to go through a home visit,
which was our next hurdle. The rules of a home visit are
apparently few: Harper has to have his own room, whether he
actually sleeps in it or not; we have to have fire alarms and
escapes; and we have to have locked away all toxic chemicals,

guns, and keys to the well, swimming pool, etc. Beyond that, the home visit is basically as intrusive as the social worker. Our lawyer (who was the adopting parent in her petition) was asked if she had ever slept with men; other people we know were treated to a lecture about the inferiority of two-women house-holds. We were fortunate — our social worker seemed embar-rassed to be putting us through a visit at all, asked us hardly anything, and gave our house the most cursory once-over, without recommending any changes (this, of course, after we had spent hours cleaning, childproofing, and removing our more *risqué* refrigerator magnets).

I wish I could say that we have experienced the whole adoption process and come through to the other end. But in fact, we are still waiting to hear back from the Department of Social Services, still waiting for our day in court. There's no reason to think that day won't be a happy one, but I'm none-theless impatient to have it come. I would love to be Harper's official parent by his first birthday and I look forward to seeing — finally — that updated birth certificate with both of us there as his parents and no ugly blanks or cold abbreviations. But the reality is that — eight months into Harper's life — I have other, more tangible, proofs of my legitimacy: the half-chewed crusts of bagel in my pockets; the white spit-up stains on the left shoulder of every nice shirt I own; the feel of his little hands climbing up my leg when he's ready to be cuddled by someone he "considers to be his parent."

Defining
"Family"

Legal Aliens: An Alternative Family

JANE ROUNTHWAITE & KATHLEEN WYNNE

THIS PIECE WAS WRITTEN BY JANE AND KATHLEEN IN TWO VOICES. WE wanted both voices to be heard clearly but to blend the tones into one story. What you hear is the same story from two vantage points.

This is not an academic analysis: it's a story about an affluent middle-class family living in a particularly well-off white, middle-class uptown neighbourhood. The dominant mythology in North Toronto is that it is a homogeneous community of perfect heterosexual families, built around educated couples in their original marriages. The fact of the neighbourhood differs from this ideal in that there are many single mothers struggling to stay in the marital home so their children can have the advantages of this type of neighbourhood; there are families struggling with alcoholism, job loss, and insecure incomes, and there are many small "l" liberals who are characterized by their open-mindedness.

While we have attempted to give the essential elements of our transformation into a family unit, we have not described in minute detail the process we have undergone. We also recognize that there are options open to us because of our affluence that are not open to others. However, we believe that the spirit of our story has more to do with creativity and open-heartedness than with privilege. That is the piece of this story which we believe can give hope to others who have reached the same decision points, even if they do not have the financial resources that we did.

Lesbian and gay parenting are currently topics of hot interest as our society struggles to decide whether it will move forward on human rights issues or attempt to retrench and move back into a mythical past of "family values." We tell this story in an attempt to illustrate that for the health and well-being of all our children, it is only rational and right to move forward. While we still do not have any answers on how to do this, we want to share our story in the hopes that it may help other lesbians who are struggling with some of the same issues in similar or different situations.

Jane's Story

I never thought I would ever be a parent. And when I fell in love and got involved with Kathleen, a married woman with three children, three-and-a-half years ago, it was still the farthest thing from my mind. I was so fixed on pursuing the woman of my dreams and the love of my life that it never occurred to me that the kids would be a revolutionary factor in my life.

Kathleen and I had been best friends since we lived in the same residence in 1973, our second year of university. We shared each other's deepest secrets and supported each other's choices unselfishly and with enthusiasm. Kathleen was the first person I came out to when my first relationship with a woman broke up. She saved my life by not dying of shock and by letting me know that she still supported and cared for me even though the dread secret was out! Over the years I returned that caring by listening to her secrets and standing firmly behind her in dealing with the men in her life. And, in fact, it was through me that she originally met Philip, the father of Kathleen's children and the other significant adult in this story.

As the years passed, we considered each other a "lifeline" to another world that compelled us but which was not to be ours. When Kath was a young mother at home in North Toronto with three small children, I lived downtown and represented the excitement of urban professional life. My house was a bastion of quiet, adult-only living space. Kathleen had often been held up to me by my own mother as the model for how I should be living my life. For my part, I always felt that Kath was my alter-ego — that had it not been for my inability to suppress my lesbianism (after several years of trying), I would have had a life very much like hers.

The key difference between us was our sexual orientation — or so we thought!

Given the intensity of our friendship — both in its close sharing times and its strained hurtful episodes — it was always odd that we had such difficulty being physically close. In my terror at losing Kath's friendship because I was a lesbian, I had promised her that she would never have to worry about me coming on to her. At the same time as I made this promise, she was hurt that I did not find her attractive enough to want to make a move. Over the years of our respective "marriages" — hers to Phil and mine to Gail — we only had veiled conversations about how those relationships were not working for us emotionally or sexually. When we did start to have those explicit conversations about six years ago, the power of our feelings for each other were very strong although contained. It was not until the late fall of 1990 that the lid came off.

The next few months were a wild combination of joy and sadness as Kath and I finally acknowledged what we really meant to each other and the implications of that naming. Once Kathleen and I started to be lovers, I knew that there was no going back to my old safe, settled, and not-too-challenging relationship and home. I was ready for more in my life and I was clear that my path lay with Kathleen.

My journals at this time are full of wonder at this new life that had opened up for me and my commitment to pursue her at all costs. Each day seemed to produce another step forward to the inevitable conclusion about what to do next — I wanted to live with Kathleen. And I still did not really understand what it would mean to live with her children.

By the spring of 1991, my living situation with Gail had become intolerable and Kath, Philip, and I decided that I should move into their house. Phil would move to the third floor while a finished room was created for him in the basement. All six of us — Kath, Phil, their three children (aged eleven, nine-and-a-half and seven), and I — lived together in that house for one-and-a-half years. On January 1, 1993, Phil was ready to move out into a house that Kathleen and I had bought right around the corner, the backyard of which connects to the original family home.

My reason for outlining in such detail the steps leading up to actually coming to live with Katheen and her kids is that it is different from all the other stories we have heard. It is unusual that the children retained the daily presence of both their parents during this transition at the same time as they acquired a new grownup in their daily lives, albeit one that they had known since they were infants. And it was unique that the adults could build on the strength of a long friendship and much deep caring to produce such a creative solution to what, on the surface, looked like an impossible situation. Kath and I could live together; Kath and Phil could both live with and continue to co-parent their children; and we could stun our neighbours and familes with our boldness.

However, this alternative family structure was also confusing for all of us as it involved multi-levels of change and different dynamics. For me, I was moving in with (and in the eyes of the world, breaking up) that sacrosanct social structure, the nuclear family! This meant living with five people instead of the one that I had been used to for fifteen years. I also had to live with Kath and Phil as they worked through their separation and figured out what they were going to be for each other. Kath struggled with her conflicted feelings about wanting to be with me and not wanting to hurt the children. The kids were not quite clear how their parents were separating or why, given that they were not acting the way that other kids' parents did when they separated. Phil learned about sharing power and control with yet another adult with strong ideas about how things should be done.

Before Kath and I became partners, I had spent many hours with this family in a variety of settings — at home, at the cottage, on vacation. I would characterize my relationship to the kids as that of a tourist or visitor, somewhat "aunt-like" but always their parents' friend. While Kath and Phil looked on me as nearly family, the children did not. And moving in with them under these new circumstances was not exactly the best way to win them over. They were furious, particularly the older two, at not being asked. The eldest (a boy) dubbed me the "new resident" and would goad his mother when someone strange came to the door, asking her whether it was someone else who would be moving in too.

As the new resident, I quickly learned a few facts about my new life that had conveniently escaped me in the heat of court-ship. First, the children and their needs were all important, huge, and the central focus of the family's life. Second, the assumptions I had made about how decisions would be made — that the adults would decide and the kids would adjust — did not hold up under fire from the kids. Third, there would be no exclusive adult space for Kathleen and me, not even our bedroom, as the children had to have access to her whenever they wanted or needed her. Remember those tales of the risks of getting between a mother bear and her cubs? Believe them!

In the months to follow, I often felt like an observer in the life of this volatile, energetic, and hardworking family. Watch-ing everything and everyone, trying to figure out where and how I could fit in as a full-fledged family member. Needless to say, being Kathleen's lover did not afford me any status in the eyes of the children. I had to prove myself as a driver, cook, school volunteer, homework helper, etc. In the early days, I was clearly second rate on all fronts, and no substitute for their parents, regardless of how hard I tried to do it just the way their parents would.

One role that I assumed quite early was to comfort the youngest (a girl), and to a lesser extent, the middle child (also a girl) during the loud and inevitable conflicts that erupted as this family dealt with its collective grief at the fact that their world had changed. Other overwhelming feelings from this time centre around my own angst in the face of openly expressed, red hot anger. When I comforted the youngest, I was also telling myself that the conflict was necessary and healthy and that we would all be okay, that it would be better in the morning.

My relationship with the children during this phase, which lasted for about eight months, was quite polite. As I was still in their minds a visitor, they did not feel they could get mad at me directly or tell me how they felt about anything significant. In order to get this information, I had to listen to numerous hard conversations with their mother, who continued to shoulder the load as the dumping ground for all serious problems. They, lke others in our neighbourhood, did not understand Phil's role in this transition and blamed their mother and me for the change. This is still true.

The question of "who I was" in their lives came up early at home and in public as we began to move out into the community that spring and summer. How would they describe me to their friends? Would they even bother? Why was I living with them? Was I an aunt? A family friend? Their mother's partner? Their mother's friend? A stepmother? Their friend? All of these were options but none of them really fit. It has taken three years to realize that there is no easy answer to the naming of this relationship. And we have not named it yet. The kids know that I sometimes refer to them as my "stepchildren," as shorthand in situations where a full explanation is not appropriate. The middle child called me the "legal alien" as recently as six months ago. For the youngest, I am "one of her grownups." For the oldest, I range from being "the nag" (or worse) to an advocate for additional rights and responsbilities that his parents can be reluctant to grant.

The girls told their friends about us — the middle child volunteered the information and the youngest would say something when someone asked. The eldest has never felt that he can tell anyone and in fact, during the early days, he made up very elaborate stories to explain me which all ended in me moving out. In other words, my presence in his life and this family had an end.

Throughout these difficult months, I held on to a feeling of being privileged to be part of this venture, forging this new vision of an alternative family, of being allowed to "parent," even in a limited way. The fact that I was living with Kathleen and her children was such a gift and something that I had never expected to experience. And yet, it felt so fragile, as none of it was mine and hence it could all be taken away if I did not behave.

This uncertainty around my right to remain and the confusion about my status in the family contributed to lots of anxiety about whether I would ever belong and whether I could ever call this place home. Often, the only place of belonging was at night, lying with Kathleen in our bed, after the chores were done and the kids in bed. When we connected behind closed doors, then I knew I had come home and we could both understand why we were doing this hard thing.

It is important to say something about Philip as he was and is a critical member of the family unit. Phil and I had been good friends in our own right for nearly fifteen years and had an almost fraternal affection and understanding of each other. Building from this base of trust and mutual respect, we have made room for each other in our adult lives, much to the disbelief of the onlookers. Other lesbians warned me to be careful of what Phil might do if and when he got mad. Yet Phil was often the person I turned to for a hug in the middle of a rough day. And I quickly learned to appreciate the freedom that his presence afforded Kathleen and me as a couple.

For his part, Philip has been incredibly consistent in his unwavering commitment to make the new family work as a unit. In contrast to my tenuous position, Phil had all the rights, status, and power that comes with being the father of the children, the primary breadwinner, owner of the house, and just an all-round nice and competent man. His continued and constant presence meant there was no immediate hole for me to fill, as there often is for another grownup in a single mother household. In this evolutionary separation, his constant presence was both confusing and comforting for all concerned, especially Kathleen who was juggling the demands of two adults, as well as the three children. Things became much clearer for all of us when Phil moved into the other house.

This journey has taught me many things about parenting and step-parenting which, in my opinion, are two very different roles. My experience of being a "step-parent" is as a lesbian in a relationship with a woman who has children from a heterosexual marriage. This is not the same as being a lesbian parent who is part of creating a family and has lived with the children from birth. My observations about the role of "step-parent" have been gleaned from incidents, experiences, and moments too numerous to mention and are offered here to help another unsuspecting lesbian who finds herself living with her lover's children.

First, I am not a parent although I am an excellent caregiver. The two terms are not synonymous and when I have thought for a second they were, the kids have set me straight immediately. It is not uncommon, even after several years of living with this family, to have one of the children crying for their mother or father at the end of a day totally given over to meeting their demands. My offer of help is rebuffed with a phrase like "I just need Mom" or even "You're not good enough." A thick skin at such times is a definite asset!

Second, my relationship with each child is different as they are distinct individuals and cannot be approached as a group entitled "the children" although their behaviour may be "packish" at certain times. I believe that the nature of each relationship is influenced by the age of the child when I moved into their home, the compatability of our temperaments, and the freedom allowed by the parents for the relationship to develop. It is also no different than building any other sort of relationship, except that the stakes in doing it successfully are incredibly high and the motivation for doing it is because of my relationship with Kathleen. I am absolutely committed to making it work because I know that Kathleen would have difficulty living with me if I could not get along with her children.

I have had to learn that my relationships with each of them will evolve over time, and the child's needs or inclinations will set the pace as they come to realize that I am not leaving, that having me here makes their lives better because their mother is less "hyperactive" (to quote the middle child) when I am there, and that they really do enjoy my company and my energy. Conventional wisdom on step-families say that it takes about three years for the new unit to form, a timeframe that has been validated by my experience.

My ability to make a successful transition from adult-only living to being part of a family with kids depended on enormous flexibility and my readiness to respond to whatever came along. Certainly in the early going when everyone was taking stock of one another, the kids had an uncanny ability to find all the hot buttons of resistance and push them. Rather than putting up a fight over one of these issues, it worked better to back off and take the long view of the situation. This took an enormous amount of self-control and I was helped in these moments by going back to the basic premise of why I was trying to fit in to this family — that I wanted to live with Kathleen and would do anything to make that work.

However, my need to have Kathleen's approval in order to ensure that I could stay has led me to make a major mistake in how I have been with the kids when Kathleen is not there. I have assumed that my job was to try to set things up with them in the way that I thought she would want if she were home. Although my need for control over their every movement is much less than hers, I have ended up "nagging" them to do things how and when I think their mother would want them done, rather than how I think they could be done. This has become an acute problem with the oldest child, who has rebelled strenuously against being told how to order his evening. In his words, "What do you care what order I do it in as long as I am in bed by ten-thirty?" I agree with him: it is up to him and he needs the space to learn how to manage his own time. And I need to support him in this and not be cowed by my fear of his mother's displeasure.

Our kids, like most, are very conscious of their public image and what the world knows and thinks of them. I have been very conscientious about how visible I am at their public events. I ask them if I can attend school games, parents' nights, etc., and am usually rewarded for the courtesy with a "yes." However, there have been a few "no's" and that is part of the lot of being the "other" grownup. And respecting that they have their own lives and rights as to how they wish to be seen in their own lives.

Honest discussion, and lots of it, has been a key ingredient of making this alternative family work. In this context, "discussion" can mean anything from a civilized family meeting sitting in the living room having tea, to roaring around the house, trying to get everyone to come back to the table to finish a difficult conversation. It also means being genuine in each interaction and answering uncomfortable questions directly and truthfully as they relate to the children.

I add this last qualifier as there are aspects of our complex adult lives and relationships that the kids will not understand, nor do they need to be exposed to the intimate details of their parents' private lives. And, in our experience, there are decisions which need to be made by the adults, often after consultation with the children but not always, about how the family will function. For example, we instituted a twenty-five cent penalty on swearing and putdowns, a decision that was supported by two of the children but rejected by the third in the most colourful language!

As a step-parent, I find discipline and its opposite, the right to grant privileges and freedoms, to be an area of potential frustration and even conflict with the "real" parents. The frustrations around discipline stem from my questionable and varying authority to discipline the kids myself and, in the event that I cannot, having to watch their parents do the disciplining, often differently than I would because of my nature and temperament. On the other side, taking the authority to change a plan that has been set up by a parent, usually Kathleen, is also problematic.

My greatest strength in these two areas is the consistency that comes with not being as emotionally tied to the children. As I am not making up for some transgression committed when the child was two, I can often deal with the incident that is on the table with more clarity than their parents. As a result, the children often ask me to override their parents when it comes to privileges, under the assumption that my answer will be more rational. However, when it comes to discipline, they want to opt for the potential irrationality of the parental, especially the maternal, response, which often translates into a punishment that is removed or reduced.

My authority on the discipline side varies from child to child, consistent with the degree of trust and respect in our relationship as well as the age of the child. My freedom to act on the positive side — the granting of privileges — is also greater with the youngest child than it is with the oldest. In short, I am able to "parent" much more completely with the youngest, who was just turning seven when I moved in, than with the eldest, who was already eleven. My authority with the middle child, who was nine when I started living with her, lies somewhere in between.

Issues of authority always lead to discussions of entitlements and rights. And this trips us into homophobia, gay-baiting, and all the negative stereotyping that is directed at gays and lesbians. It is very hard for our kids to keep the world's opinions of their alternative family separate from their own experience of living with their lesbian mother, her partner, and their father. The brunt of this gay-bashing is felt most keenly by Kathleen, who is still struggling with her new identity as a "deviant" — her word, not mine. The vehemence of the attacks diminishes as time passes and it becomes harder to blame every family conflict on our relationship. However, that dark place still lurks and our periodic forays there remain for me the most painful part of our life.

On the positive side, I have never been so alive, involved, overwhelmed, and challenged. Our life is rich and variable, every day. And the best part is that I get to live with this wonderful woman for whom I now know I waited twenty years.

Kathleen's Story

> I worry that I will split in two pieces, unable to live a double life. I worry that I will choose to live with Jane. I cannot leave my children. I must leave my children. This is my prayer: *Please let there be another way for me to feel whole. Please let me create a picture for my children that allows them to live and grow and be free.*
> — journal entry, February 1, 1991.

For the first thirty-seven years of my life I lived with all the privilege of a white, middle class, heterosexual woman. In 1991 I fell in love, changed my life and began to live in a committed relationship with another woman. I learned the meaning of heterosexual privilege in the losing of it.

Jane and I have lived together for nearly four years now. She and I parent my three children, along with their father. We all live together in two houses on adjoining lots in the North End of Toronto. We share meals and outings and the trials and tribulations of being six over-achieving individuals with strong personalities. Jane and I live in the former family home with the children, but they move back and forth across the garden to sleep where they like, as the spirit moves them. Their dad lives in the smaller house on his own, but the grownups use both houses for work, storage, meal preparation and meetings. This family configuration is not one that any of us had ever before encountered and it was not one that was easy for our friends and neighbours to recognize or accept. It is an arrangement that was twenty years in the making.

Jane, Phil and I all met about twenty years ago in 1972, at Queen's University at Kingston. Jane and I met when Jane, as the head proctor in one of the residences, was interviewing prospective floor proctors. I was an applicant for the position. Once we met, we became friends, attended some of the same history classes, came to know each other's families. I was Jane's primary confidante as she grappled, throughout her twenties, with her sexual orientation, and loved a woman who subsequently married. I watched her date men and finally proclaim to me and her family that she was a lesbian. Jane was my strongest support as I attempted to establish myself in a happy heterosexual relationship, and found only unhappiness and instability. It was she who introduced me to Phil and in the end applauded our marriage.

Throughout those early adult years Jane and I were best friends, and Jane vowed to me, who had never before known a lesbian, that she would never compromise our friendship and that I was "safe," that we would never be lovers. I was always drawn to the women's community. I participated in women's events, attended concerts with Jane and was generally woman-identified. It was quite simply not a part of my conscious thought that I might ever be in love with a woman. The longer I knew Jane, the more I imagined that a relationship with a woman would have a quality of understanding that I had never been able to achieve with a man. Still, I never explored the possibility for myself. Our story is a classic lesson in "never say never."

I always assumed that I would be married. I always assumed that I would have children. I never questioned that I would live "happily ever after." I was married from 1977 to 1991, and for the last five of those years I realized — we realized — that it was not working as we both wished. Philip was discovering that he had a strong need to be on his own and we were moving away from each other physically. What was missing for me was the physical and emotional connection that I knew made a happy relationship. Phil, by his own admission, could not meet those needs and I could not accommodate his growing need for space and a less intimate relationship. I had grown up in a family where my parents were closely connected to each other. I wanted that connection myself and I wanted to be able to show it to my children. Throughout my marriage, Jane was an important part of my life. She and her partner, Gail, spent a lot of time with our children and with us. In fact, they were one of the most important couples in our lives in terms of social contact. My children were always aware of lesbian relationships and I was increasingly woman-identified as years passed. They were not, however, prepared to have a lesbian as a mother.

My personal "coming out" process will last me a lifetime. To the world, however, and to my children, the feat is accomplished. There is much talk in the literature around lesbian identities about the diversity of meanings of the label, of the need or lack of need for a label, of lesbian psychology separate from sexual practice. In North Toronto, as the mother of three children, living in a committed relationship with another woman, that talk is academic. I am a lesbian and as such must be coped with, reviled, accepted or avoided.

By transforming our relationship in 1991 to accommodate Jane's and my need to be together and Phil's need to be alone, we introduced a family model into our neighbourhood that confused many of our friends, our families, and our children. At the core of the model was our commitment to meet the emotional and physical needs of our children to the best of our ability. We moved quickly in that first year, probably too fast for the children. They say now that they did not even know that Phil and I were contemplating a change. We talked and talked with them as we went through the change and they railed at us, rejected Jane and gradually saw that they were not losing everything but that the change was here to stay. In rare moments, at first, my daughters would acknowledge that there was less bickering among the adults than there had been in the past.

My sense of what happened in that first year of separation was that we all decided to stay very close to each other until we could figure out what had to happen. It was a highly stressful, tense time. We felt disapproval from outside, from friends and family and community. One of the ways I attempted to cope was by seeking out the support of a lesbian and gay parents group through the Toronto Board of Education in an effort to find someone else in the city who had experienced a similar situation. I had come out to the principal and vice-principal in my children's school so that they would be alerted to the issues with which my children were dealing. I was on extremely good terms with both of them and felt that they were very supportive as I told my story. A few months later they called me into the school to discuss an incident involving my son when he had been disruptive in class and had not listened to his teacher's requests for quiet. At that time the administrators said that they thought that perhaps it had been a mistake for him to be in this female teacher's class because he was having trouble with women at the moment and needed a male role model. It was not until I was relating this story in the support group that I realized that my son's behaviour, which was well within the normal range for a twelve-year-old, was being attributed to the fact that his dad and I had separated and he was living with two women. Even though his dad was in his life every day, the school line became that my son was more at risk because he was living with Jane and me, two "strong" women. This interpretation did not stop my interaction with the school, but it heightened my awareness of my new problematic status.

We also felt the weight of our own disapproval of ourselves as we dealt with the feeling that we were navigating uncharted waters. We were making up the rules as we went, all of us living in the family home, Phil in the renovated basement. In lighter moments we three adults laughed about taking out an ad or putting up a billboard on the front lawn announcing that "Phil really loves his newly renovated basement apartment. He chose to do it this way!" Much of the overt feedback we got from people came in the form of "Is Phil okay?" and "How's Phil?" Jane took to referring to herself privately as the "lesbian homewrecker." My own identity was often just a dark, ill-articulated self-hatred for doing this horrible thing to my children. It was a year of long, late night talks as the adults found their way. It was a year of intense family meetings where the kids, especially my eldest (son) raged at us for what we had done. It was a year of intense conversations between Phil and me as we attempted to separate with honesty and integrity and truly transform rather than destroy our relationship. It was a year, for Jane and me, of intense intimacy as we found each other at the end of the day. Thankfully our relationship is a strong and nourishing one that has been worth all the chaos it has wrought.

Since we transformed our family, I have felt, as the mother, as though I am at the hub of the energy generated by the family. Especially at the beginning I was balancing the complex emotional needs of the children, myself, Jane and Phil. I was the person who knew all members of the family most completely and have had to work to let all the personalities establish themselves in relation to each other without the assistance of my interpretation. Jane's role with the children had ranged in the children's language from "legal alien," to "step-parent" to "one of my grownups." To this day, when Jane is out of town the children and I often need to process the discussion of how unfairly they fear that they have been treated, how I have ruined their lives. In their minds, especially the minds of the older two, I have created this situation. We process, we vent and in the morning we move on. All of my children are high achievers at school. They are involved in sports and extra-curricular activities. They have friends whom they bring home, whom they keep home for sleepovers. None of them acts as though he/she is ashamed of life at home except in the dark moments of those conversations, often late at night, where they voice their fears of rejection and ostracism.

My relationship to my neighbourhood has undergone a radical transformation since our situation changed. It is in this arena that I feel the loss of status the most acutely. In my former incarnation, I was one of dozens of mothers balancing part-time volunteer and paid work, or part-time academics with being a mom at home. When our children were young we took part in playgroups, baked muffins for each other, dropped in for coffee, worked on committees together, sorted out neighbourhood politics, organized impromptu shared meals; we knew each other well, in that circumstantial neighbour manner. As soon as I changed my life and it was known that Jane had moved in, I realized that the morning coffee was happening without me.

Conversations became strained with former friends. To those closest to me I described what I was going through, but in at least three cases, my friends were obviously uncomfortable and a chilly silence ensued over the following months. First signs of a thaw began to appear when Phil moved into the other house and people could relax and believe that we had moved closer to a "normal" configuration. At least now Phil was okay. It was essential to people to know that Phil was not suffering at the hands of either me or Jane and of course that the children were being treated well. The shock for me was that people who knew me very well, who had spent hundreds of hours with me, did not trust that I would do the right thing.

I came to understand that people around me would have been relatively comfortable had Philip and I entered into an acrimonious separation when I came out. What was difficult for people to understand was that we wanted to reconfigure our family to allow Jane and I to live together as a couple, for Philip to be alone or in a new relationship as he chose, for Philip and me to be friends and co-parents, for Jane and Phil to remain good friends and for the children to have both their parents in their lives every day.

The initial chill in the community is passing as we have proven that we are still upstanding citizens and that we will not embarrass anyone unduly. In fact we are "old news" now. Personally I have never regained my sense of belonging and I miss the easy friendships that I enjoyed as a neighbourhood mom. I know that I have isolated myself in the past three years, justifying to myself that I am too busy for much social contact. In my heart I know that I still hold myself back from heterosexual social situations for fear of feeling on the outside. We are less alone than we were three years ago but it is a slow process to build a new community. We have begun to meet some other lesbian families with children, and neighbourhood friends are less wary of us. I have recently decided to run for political office on our local school board and I know that for some parents it will be impossible to vote for me because I am a lesbian. I am prepared to deal with that attitude as one of a long list of prejudices that infuse our community and am encouraged that it seems to be by far the minority opinion.

When people ask about my life I describe my family as "alternative," and, depending on the circumstances, I am apologetic or proud. In my heart I believe that I have done the best that I could to create a situation that allows my children to live, grow and be free, surrounded by the adults who love them most in the world. And I am a lesbian. Jane and I do not live a double life. We share one life in love.

A Good Mother

KAREN WILLIAMS

FOURTEEN YEARS AGO, I BECAME A MOTHER. DETERMINED TO BE A GOOD mother, I went to prenatal classes, kept my newborn infant in my room instead of in the hospital nursery, breastfed him, and read parenting and child development books so that I could be sure he was meeting or exceeding his developmental milestones.

Seven years ago, I became a mother again. I wasn't as anxious about being a good mother. I didn't go to prenatal classes, and I didn't read as many books. I quit breastfeeding my daughter at four months because I was finishing my degree. When my daughter walked for the first time I was excited, but I didn't write it down in a little baby book. I used to jokingly say that I'd transcended the good mother guilt-trip.

Six years ago, when I was in graduate school, I came out as a lesbian. Like everything I do, I wanted to do it well. So I read books by lesbians, and listened and watched other lesbians, to figure out how a good lesbian talks and thinks.

Four years ago, my lover, Pam, and I moved in together with my two children. Again, I wanted to do this lesbian family thing well. I tried to figure out our roles with the children, how to divide the housework, how to balance togetherness and independence, and when and how to "come out."

These events in my life have created a collection of very personal memories. The memories are about individual struggles, couple arguments, family issues, and feelings about my family's place in our neighbourhood, and the place for me and my partner in the feminist lesbian community in our city.

The dominant accounts of lesbian women who care for children rest on heterosexist assumptions. They describe us as "deviants," with children who are pathological products of that deviance. Counter-accounts of lesbian mothering often present fairy tale versions of our lives in which we are all happy individuals, partners and family members; or they present an analysis which demands that we "evacuate motherhood" altogether. These accounts, I believe, have come to analysis too quickly — and, as a result, are based primarily on political agendas rather than reflection about the daily life experiences of lesbians caring for children and children living with lesbians.

One strategy to change such accounts is to begin telling our stories to each other, with all their contradictions, embarrasments, pride and shame. This article is my attempt to present a part of my family's story, as a jumping-off point for animated truth-telling about our lives. My partner, Pam, has added her own words about her experiences, and together we have attempted to recount the children's stories as they have told them. Still, this version is saturated with my biases. I am the biological mother of the two children so I tell these stories from that point of view. I am also middle-class, educated, white, and have the privilege of being safely "out" at work and with some members of my family. I do not risk losing custody by writing this article and I am relatively more privileged than most custodial mothers because the children's father exercises visitation rights and monthly child support payments are regularly deducted from his pay cheque. Like other mothers, I am exploited by motherhood, and, like other lesbians, I must daily negotiate through a heterosexist minefield.

In order to present this account of two lesbians and two children living together, I have divided our stories into two sections. The first section, entitled "The Good Mother," is an attempt to "step back" and see how my story and my partner's story are affected by our relationships to motherhood. In the second section, "The Good Lesbian," I have described feeling marginalized in the lesbian community and discussed how this marginalization relates to motherhood.

The Good Mother

In our society most women choose heterosexuality and motherhood. Increasingly, lesbians are also making the choice to be mothers. Ann Ferguson believes that one reason women still have children is because our society psychologically rewards women for mothering — it is seen as a mark of successful womanhood. In addition, society has constructed a psychological need for us to belong to a family — usually one with two adults and children. Thus, despite the societal devaluation of women's mothering, and the exploitation of women through their mothering labour, motherhood becomes for many women — including lesbians — a central aspect of their gender identity, positive self-image, and psychological need for a sense of belonging.

These positive aspects of motherhood are granted to women only under certain conditions, and only to those women deemed to be "good mothers." Every woman, when she gives birth to a child or chooses to care for children, will enter a set of societally determined practises, concepts, and relationships which she cannot totally escape. Our stories reflect both the inevitability of being linked to the social construction of motherhood as well as the individual ways in which we have tried to resist the negative aspects of that code:

Karen: I was a mother before I was a lesbian, and when a conflict arises between those two identities, I'm a mother first. When I left my husband, I was using all my energy to fight against the feeling that I had become a bad mother by becoming a lesbian. I was taking the kids away from their father — changing their schools, their neighbourhood, and their friends. I knew I had a right to do it for myself — but I had lots of guilt. When Pam suggested anything that I felt made me choose between being a good mother and a good lover — I got angry at her. Over stupid things — like who should choose their bedroom first in the first place we lived — I was feeling guilty so I wanted the kids to choose but she thought we should be able to choose. It was hard not to think of her as not understanding what was really important.

Pam: I never had any desire to be a mother. I don't know if I even thought about it — I didn't want to take responsibility for other people. I was always careful to say that women worked inside or outside the home, but I thought my job was to work outside the home. I was a feminist at age ten and I thought then that I had a choice to be a mother or be someone who could follow my dreams. I saw motherhood as a trap — something that didn't allow me to be a person. I thought Karen being a mother wouldn't affect our relationship. I kept telling her that she and the kids were a package deal. But what I meant was that I thought they were her kids so she should take care of them. The reality of her motherhood, however, did and does affect our relationship. It isn't just the two of us. There are four of us. It was one night when we were having a fight that the whole thing became really clear for me. Karen would always come first for me; but the kids would always come first for her.

Karen: Being a mother is always there for me. When Pam wants time alone as a couple and the kids want time with Mom — I get angry at her for needing me. I expect her to understand that kids come first. I have to admit that I expected that she would just jump in, love the kids instantly and split the work with me. But, instead, she thinks about how hard the work is, how much they cramp our style — and when she talks like that it's hard not to think she's less of a woman because of it; it's hard not to think of her as just self-absorbed. And I'm not sure why, but it bugs me that she doesn't come to caring about the kids because she always wanted kids — I guess I don't know why anyone would stick with it if they didn't have an overwhelming urge to have children. At the same time I know that she pushes me to think of myself first — and with all the guilt of divorce — I have needed that. Like going shopping — and not heading for the children's clothing department first. I guess I thought I was pushing the limits enough by being a lesbian mom — so I wanted to be the best lesbian mom on earth so I could still be a good mom.

Pam: Karen was struggling to take care of the kids and still have time for us and for herself. And, with some embarrassment now, I must admit she was doing most of it by herself. I moved in and continued my activism and she was the one who made the sacrifices. She'd argue that caring for children should be organized differently so that raising kids is more of a community thing. I took that to mean that I should take responsibility so she could do what she pleased. The bottom line for me was, "They're your kids and your responsibility." When I began to understand that she couldn't work full-time and do all the kid stuff and have time for us and herself, I got angry at the children's father and at Karen. I thought she should fix it. Either she should expect and demand more help from him or she should stop expecting so much of herself. It took me a long time to realize that Karen is held responsible for their care, and even though she has joint custody with their father, the psychological costs to Karen and the kids of trying to make him live up to that were too high. She couldn't send them to his house when he was neglecting them. She couldn't refuse them when they didn't want to go or wanted to come home early.

Karen: I felt caught between everyone's needs. The kids wanted more attention from me because they were insecure. Their father wanted total freedom from responsibility. Pam wanted to spend time with me, and I was trying to take time for myself as well. Over time, the kids have calmed down and Pam has accepted that I can't do this all by myself. But it still pisses me off — I can't demand that Pam take an equal share of responsibility for the kids because they aren't "her kids." And I can demand it from their father but I can't make him do anything. He never has to miss a day of work. He never has to change his plans. He simply does what he pleases, and thinks that the child support pays me to do the parenting. Pam had to choose to take responsibility for the children out of her love for me — there's no societal mechanism that would make her want to and no societal rewards. If I were a man, society would expect her to mother my children, but society makes her invisible.

Lesbian women complicate the status quo when they struggle to bring one woman's biological children into the equation of their shared lives. They invade it from both the heterosexual viewpoint and the lesbian feminist viewpoint: mothers aren't lesbians and lesbians aren't mothers. Conflict inevitably ensues. The biological mother may believe that female partners, like male partners, should share in the care of children in order to solve the unfair distribution of labour. Although her past male partner did not likely take fifty percent of all the responsibilities, she may believe that a woman will understand motherhood intuitively. The mother's partner, who has not internalized society's demand to become a mother, can be seen as "selfish" or "insensitive" by the biological mother because she is concerned about her own individual needs first. Biological mothers, like myself, can be seen to be unnecessarily "tied to their children" — adopting some kind of societal Superwoman lifestyle.

From the partner's point of view, the responsibility for raising children belongs to the biological parents. She didn't choose to have children so she shouldn't be saddled with the responsibility. Her work and her political action is also important and shouldn't be sacrificed for children she didn't choose to have. When she chooses to live with a mother she is faced, however, with the realities of mothering. She may expect the father to help out but can see why this, in many cases, is not realistic. When she becomes fully aware of the mother's struggles to juggle kids, work, relationship, political action, and individual interests — she may begin to understand that the biological mother is doing the best she can, but the workload is unwieldy. She may also be drawn to understanding because she sees that her partner, because of her mothering, is very limited in her ability to pursue her individual interests or be involved in political action — not because she is "overinvested" but because the demands are unreasonable:

Pam: I didn't want to change and become more responsible for the kids. I wanted their father to take on his parental responsibilities, or Karen would have to do all of it and leave me alone. But that wasn't going to happen. I knew that if Karen was going to have time to play, I'd have to help with the kids. After all, she did help me with some of my individual projects. And I liked some aspects of being a family. I guess I started to see myself as a family member over time and when I did that — I thought that if you're going to be part of a family, you have to do your share of the work. When I didn't get involved I felt peripheral and I didn't like that feeling.

Karen: I remember watching Pam start to involve herself more with the kids. And the more she did, the more she wanted to be recognized as the other mother. For instance, when I broke my ankle she took Heather to daycare sometimes and the teachers got to know her and treat her like the other mother. Phil's school called her because they couldn't reach me and she got involved. We went to Heather's open house together and she felt like she also wanted to come out to the second grade teacher. It seemed like helping me pulled her into this, but once she was in, she found that she was invested in it. For instance, she put the kids on her benefit plan and took a neighbour on when she thought the woman was treating Phil unfairly.

Our understandings of each other are rooted in the societal code of motherhood. This code requires mothers to care for children without support from society, without financial reward, and without complaining. Mothers are not expected to need help. They are expected to make whatever sacrifices are necessary, even if that means staying home from work when a child is sick or taking part-time instead of full-time work. Women who do not give birth to children, unless they are caring for their husband's children, are not expected to contribute to children's care. Therefore, it makes sense that we would think of each other as we do. We have each taken our place in the socially constructed dichotomy. I am the mother — held totally responsible. Pam is the non-mother — held totally non-responsible. I expect her to leap outside her socially constructed role and she expects me to leap outside mine. Arguments ensue as we attempt to negotiate, each of us attemping to keep the positive aspects of our position while also attempting to create a situation fair and equitable for each of us.

Our couple strategy to deal with the overburdening of the mother has been to share the care for the children somewhat more equally between us, though all of us (including the children) resist it. I want to have help, but I am used to being in charge of the mothering and don't want to give up that authority. The children are used to my mothering and resist change. My son doesn't want to deal with another authority figure and my daughter, at first, wanted only Mommy to read her books at bedtime. Over time, Pam has been able to take a primary role in some of these tasks, especially with my daughter since she has lived most of her life with Pam. In this way we have challenged the notion that only biological mothers are responsible for children because Pam has taken on the role of the other mother for children she is not biologically related to. We have also partially challenged the notion that lesbians are bad mothers every time a neighbour or teacher is impressed with our commitment and our parenting abilities. We have not challenged society's notion that one or two adults should be responsible for the children who live with them. Similarly, we have not challenged the notion that the credit or blame for their development belongs only to us.

Until there are societal structures which support the shared care of children amongst many adult caregivers — and shared credit or blame — biological mothers will continue to be "over-responsible," as society requires them to be, and non-mothers will continue to expect freedom from child care. When they are challenged to step outside this role, resistance will ensue. Although lesbian women can bring a challenge to society's model, their brave and relentless efforts of resistance cannot erase the societal realities or the guilt which they experience when they don't live up to its standards. Even if our neighbourhood school accepts Pam as the other mother, and we carve out a more equitable child care arrangement, the notion that two adults who live with children are entirely responsible for their care will not be challenged.

The Good Lesbian

Discussing various analyses of motherhood is not top priority within the lesbian community I interact with. It's only when a lesbian couple raising children bumps up against certain "taken for granted" assumptions, practises, and reactions to children that the subject arises. These stories are about the ways in which my partner and I and the children have bumped into our lesbian community.

Karen: I came out in 1989 while I was in graduate school. It's kind of embarrassing now. I had ideas about how lesbians should dress, how short their hair should be, and what kind of relationships they should have with men that I wouldn't admit in public now. It was being a mother that jolted me into a different space — led me to look for different images and writers and places to be in the community. Until then my lesbian identity didn't have much room for children — it was only about me. And for awhile I enjoyed that — spending time on my own needs — but after several months, I began to feel the split. I wanted to feel close to my kids again. And that's when I noticed the separation between the lesbian community and kids. Some lesbians reacted negatively to my son just because he is male. Some lesbians only wanted to see us when the kids weren't around. And I was expected to be as involved as before in political organizing — having to stay home with the kids or wanting to stay home with the kids was either suspect or a cause to have sympathy for me.

Pam: I felt that being a good lesbian meant denying my union activism, my working class identity, my lack of education. It meant wearing the costume and acting like what was expected of me as a lesbian. I hated that. I like to wear skirts and dresses.

The lesbian community didn't seem to take my family life into consideration either. Everyone said that the kids were welcome to come to events; but they asked questions like: Will the kids be there? Translate that to read: I hope not. Before I was involved with children, I didn't feel this additional separation from the community. Now, both Karen and I wanted to find a way out of having so little freedom and so much responsibility, but the other lesbians — who would also benefit from the work the children do in the future — didn't have to worry about kids.

The hardest thing for me in the beginning was having no one to talk to about being a co-mother in a lesbian family. I read lots of things about heterosexual step-mothering because that was all that was available to me; but it is different. A step-mother who lives with a man rarely has the children full-time and therefore her relationship to her partner's kids is less intimate and less time consuming. But when you are a partner of a mother and a woman yourself, there is much more expected about how you need to be part of the kids lives. I found the role very confusing and difficult. I didn't know how to be. And I didn't know any other co-mothers at that time.

Karen: I think my solution at first was to become more involved with mothers in heterosexual couples — moms in the neighbourhood. Sometimes I would come out to them, sometimes I wouldn't. We'd talk about stuff about the kids — and sometimes about our relationships. I wanted a place to socialize where I knew I could drop in with the kids and we'd drink tea and expect to be interrupted. Then I wanted to be more political about it — and I wanted to be able to talk about being a lesbian mother — and sometimes these moms couldn't personally relate to those struggles. So we started looking for lesbian moms more seriously. We went to a Gay and Lesbian Parents Coalition International conference. Then we started to spend more energy on gay and lesbian issues — like Bill 167 and developing a group for lesbian moms. The biggest support for me is when we have a pot luck or something and we have a house full of moms and their kids — we moms sit around and talk and the kids play together.

Pam: When we didn't have connections with lesbian moms it was very difficult. It wasn't until we had a group of friends who care for children that I found a place to be validated as a co-mother. I wasn't part of the heterosexual community raising kids. So I couldn't find support with heterosexual moms. Being involved with other lesbian moms validated a life with kids — I understood more the problems around fathers and the struggles of mothering because I heard other mothers and co-mothers talking about it. So I didn't think it was just Karen's problem. And the thing that surprised me was some women looked to me sort of as a role model — they'd ask me things about living with kids — it made me feel like I was doing okay and it made me feel normal because they also felt angry and frustrated with their partners in some of the ways I did.

Some of our struggles are changing — the lesbian community we identify with is becoming more and more inclusive of children. More lesbians are choosing to have children. As a result, more books are published about lesbian and gay parenting and there are more support groups and informal networks for lesbians who share common experiences with children. Lesbian mothers are more "out" as well because they are able, more and more, to get custody of their children.

These actions are not to be taken lightly. Supportive lesbian communities and political action to fight for "equal families" can go a long way toward making lesbian family life a little easier. The movement towards inclusivity has created the possibility that lesbian mothers can meet each other, and our needs have become more visible. But, the division created by society of women into "mothers" and "non-mothers" will continue to hold sway. As a result, I believe lesbian mothers will continue to create networks primarily with other mothers — lesbian mothers or heterosexual mothers. Mothers share a common thread in their experiences. They know their task is onerous and so are more willing to provide each other emotional and child care support. They know that children take up a lot of psychological energy and they expect to talk about kids in many of their conversations. They also know that children make lives unpredictable and they expect interruptions and changes in plans.

A lesbian co-mother may care for children but her labour is invisible to most people in both the heterosexual and lesbian community. In order to find a place in the heterosexual community of mothers she will have to come out and will be dependent on their willingness to recognize her status. Her membership will always be dependent on their good will. Her membership in the lesbian community may cause her also to feel that split if she identifies herself as a member of a family with her partner and her children. She, too, is likely to choose a place in a community of other lesbian mothers with their partners so that she can find some validation for her role and share her experiences with others who also live with children.

Just like the "good mother" struggles were played out in our relationship and felt like individual or couple problems, so the good lesbian struggle can be seen as a problem of the lesbian community — either instigated by lesbians who demand space for children or instigated by lesbians who do not live with children and demand that nothing change.

Until women who give birth to children are not held solely responsible for caring for children, and until the structures of society no longer divide human beings into the groups, "parents" and "non-parents" — lesbians with children will live different daily lives and have different relationships to social messages and institutions. Mothers and co-mothers will resist and challenge this division as will communities which try to be more inclusive and fight for legislation such as Ontario's failed Omnibus Bill on Lesbian and Gay Rights, Bill 167. But the division will remain until our society supports a different model of caring for children.

I have discussed our struggle against society's "good mother" code and "good lesbian" code. We have attempted to resist the good mother code by sharing in the child care, and we attempt to resist the good lesbian code by involving ourselves in a lesbian community of mothers, co-mothers and children so that we can bring lesbian and mother identities together.

The injustices we suffer as mothers, lesbians and as a family are obvious. And we must continue to fight against them on every level — even if our struggles provide only partial relief and do not significantly unravel heterosexist and anti-mother relations.

If we want the social structuring of motherhood to change, I expect we will have to come together with all our various and contradictory concerns and talk together for a long time. That sounds like a naive suggestion — but I believe it is a radical one. Truth-telling together requires us to break the silence created by the code of motherhood which affects all women and makes many women feel like failures or divided from each other. Reflective truth-telling requires us, in the heat of the moment, to stand inside our experience to find societally constructed patterns, without being duped into believing that our thoughts and feelings are simply a product of our own imagination and effort. Cooperative truth-telling requires us to engage in reflection together — attempting to find a balance between letting go and holding on to our own meanings and interpretations. Active truth-telling requires us to move into action without losing what we've gained so far in the process. Before I can imagine a different world, I imagine much more truth-telling will need to occur.

The Other Mother

PERRY ADAMS

TODAY THE SKY IS SOFT AND PEARLY, THE WIND COOL AND FRESH. AFTER nearly a month of cold and snow, this December day feels like early spring. I walk into the health food store where our older daughter works. She's on cashier duty but she stops what she is doing to give me a warm hug and say, "Hello Mother Number Two!"

After twelve years, she knows how that warms my heart — not only that she thinks of me as a parent but that she is willing to publicly announce that she has two mothers. Winning that accolade from her has taken a lot of years. For me to trust that, after all this time, she would still be in my life has taken a long time, too.

I return the hug and say, "Hello Daughter Number One."

This is the story of my circuitous journey to parenthood, and the different children with whom I was involved along the way. The journey began twenty-five years ago, when I was eighteen and telling the trees in the neighbouring orchard the sad tale of my confused sexual identity. Where else could I reveal that I was in love with my best friend? Finally, after six months of angst and indecision, I shared my first passionate kiss with a woman — and discovered she loved me, too. Thus began my checkered career as a lesbian. At the time, there was only one sad part to this otherwise delightful revelation — I didn't believe I could be a lesbian *and* have children. And I wanted to be a mother.

My own family was "different," even a little bohemian in the blue-collar, Republican New York town where I grew up. Dad was an artist and designer who taught three days a week in New York City; Mom loved people, plants, books and challenging the accepted social order. My two sisters, my brother and I were close. For over a decade, we rented a small house on a large estate and had the run of 360 acres of fields, orchards, meadows, woods, old barns, and a large pond. This particular upbringing helped me to feel good about being different, to accept my lesbianism easily despite a notable lack of role models. And it made me want to have a family just like mine.

In 1969, I headed off to university. For awhile, thoughts of family and children were lost in a headlong exploration of myself as a social, sexual and political being. Five years later, after a brief stint in graduate school in Montreal, my lover and I set out for Vancouver. We settled into a large house, and, within a year, our numbers had swelled to eight women. Through this motley assortment, I soon met a fair number of lesbians with children. These women had all conceived their children in heterosexual relationships. The idea of choosing to have children relatively independent of men, by artificial insemination for example, hadn't yet caught on. Watching these women made me want to think about parenting again.

In the spring of 1976, our lesbian household exploded into its separate pieces. My partner and I moved to the Gulf Islands, where we found a log house and settled in for the winter. Perhaps it was the fresh island air or the salt water or those womblike saunas — my partner began thinking about having a baby. While she began the search for a suitable sperm donor, I thought about parenting with her. At last, the possibility felt real and close.

The following March, our savings ran out. My partner went off to the big city to work in a fish plant and came home only to tell me she'd fallen in love with someone else and was moving back to Vancouver. The abrupt end of our dreams of having a child proved as devastating for me as the end of our three-year relationship. Then, miraculously, a woman and her two-year-old daughter appeared on my doorstep. They had been sent by my conscientious (or guilty) ex-partner. The woman had left her husband on a northern island to experience the wild lesbian life in the big city, and now she needed a little peace for herself and her child.

I remember standing by the house in the spring sunshine, discussing living arrangements, when the daughter started to wander down the driveway. "Don't go down to the road!" warned her mother. Within seconds, she was as close to that road as she could get without being on it, laughing an unencumbered belly laugh. Defiance may not be an easy trait in a two-year-old, but it won my heart.

Over the next months, that little girl and I found kindred souls in each other. She had a kind of quiet seriousness, the ability to be companionably silent, that I have always valued in a friend. We understood each other. I knew how important it was to find that last bit of blanket silk for her to rub as she drifted off to sleep. I knew when she needed to do a thing herself. And we both loved books. She often woke me in the early morning by dropping a pile of picture books on my chest and commanding me to "Read!" I loved the feeling of sharing things important to me — an essential part of my parenting dream. Not everything was sweet and quiet, though. We went through a portion of the terrible twos together — toilet training again (the change of scene had upset my small friend), the "I do it myself!" stuff. I surprised myself with my patience.

We lived together as a strange little family for only three short months and then, at my encouragement, my housemate went back to her husband. I had met him and liked him and could see how much they all missed each other. But losing my little friend and, in a sense, my first child, was hard. I missed her terribly. I hadn't known it could hurt so much. I had opened my heart to her without fear or caution. Now I had no claim to time with her. That northern island might as well have been the Arctic for all the access I had to her. They visited once or twice — but it was living with her, parenting her, that I missed.

The next spring, I finally reconciled myself to the failure of my attempts to support myself on the island. Regretfully, I went off to find work in Vancouver. I found a four-month job and settled into yet another lesbian communal house. During this short and rather miserable stay (I spent most of it missing the island desperately), I fell in love with a woman with a four-year-old son.

In retrospect, I think I felt both drawn to and a little afraid of the fact that this woman had a child. Was he part of the attraction? I know I felt some eagerness to parent again. By summer's end, we knew we wanted to see more of each other. I packed up my belongings and settled myself into my new partner's life, and more slowly into her son's.

As I became closer to my partner's son, I discovered inside me a wall of caution I had not experienced before. Losing my first child was still too fresh, the ache still too powerful. I wasn't ready to lose my heart to a child again so soon. In time, however, this kind, clever, curly-headed little boy slipped under my defenses and I grew to love him. I remember him swimming naked on the island, massaging my tired shoulders as I walked him on my back from the bus stop, slumped wearily against my chest at the end of a long day of play. I remember, too, stroking his small face to help him sleep. I began to want him to be part of my life. I took a certain pleasure in the daily tasks that meant I was "looking after" him. Again, I liked reading to him, teaching him to read the words himself. There were times, of course, in so new a relationship, when I was less kind and wished he wasn't there to demand of our time, to take energy away from just the two of us. I was learning that my fantasy of family involved easily as much work as fun.

In late September, too soon after I had begun my new job and my new life, I went for a routine gynecological examination. The doctor discovered a cyst on one ovary. A short time later, I woke in the recovery room to discover that I had been given a complete hysterectomy. I was devastated. Any hopes I might have had of giving birth to my own child were now irretrievably dashed. I was twenty-eight years old and I was "barren."

I cried often during that long week in the hospital. My partner visited frequently, bringing me healthy food and tender support. Her son was too young to be allowed to visit and I found I missed him. At last, I went home to rest and gather my strength for my return to work.

My partner was as patient as she could be with someone going through surgical menopause, but my mood swings and weariness took their toll on our young relationship. We seemed unable to talk about the hard things — my childlessness, her increasing distance. She quit her job and devoted her energies full-time to her musical group. I worked all day and she most of the night. I was still firmly in the dream of family, wanting a stable and warm home life, filled with my partner and our son. She had begun to discover freedom — a freedom which paradoxically I provided by being dependable. One terrible night she didn't come home and when I called later from work, she told me she had spent the night with one of her fellow musicians. A month or so later, we decided to go our separate ways.

In as final an ending as I could manage, I divested myself of all responsibilities except one small kitten and found a small attic apartment in Vancouver. I had been so certain that this was to be a long relationship that its demise after only one year caught me unawares. I was still very much in love and grieving. I needed some time on my own. My ex-partner and her son came to visit me now and again, and sometimes her son came alone. He and I enjoyed each other's company but I was still too sad to be a lot of fun. I think now how utterly confusing for his young mind all of this must have been.

That fall, my ex-partner fell in love with someone else, and a few months later they all moved to the Kootenay region in southeastern British Columbia. I missed both her and her son terribly. I hung on for a few more months in the big city, growing increasingly tired of the dirt and noise, of the opening and shutting of hearts all around me in some manic dance, of my own heartache. Then I learned that my first child and her mother had also recently moved to the Kootenays. In May of 1980, in my twenty-ninth year, I joined them all, moving with two friends into a house perched on a mountainside. I had found a place to heal myself.

After two years in the valley, my housemates and I found a house closer to Nelson. Within the first year of moving there, major change overtook me. I fell in love.

She was a tall and striking woman with two daughters, five and seven. We became tentative friends, she being shy and I cautious. I visited her house once and felt myself drawn to the art and literature lining her walls, to her blend of humanitarianism and imagination.

During this early phase of our acquaintanceship, her husband and children were back East visiting relatives for a month or so while she took some time to decide the fate of their marriage. One weekend, we both happened to be in Vancouver at the same time — she was attending a workshop, I was visiting friends. I offered to show her around what was a new city for her. I took her to her first Japanese restaurant and watched as her beautiful long hands wrestled with the chopsticks. I took her for a walk along False Creek. Her long black hair blew around her high cheekbones and her clear gray-green eyes looked down at me with interest from under her fine intelligent brow. We talked and walked for hours and I can't remember anything of what we said.

When I got back to the Kootenays, I knew I had to tell her how I was feeling. With unusual bravery, I invited her out to tea and told her I believed myself to be in love with her. She grinned and said she was "whelmed." I didn't know what to think. A few days later, however, she called and asked to "have a talk." My heart sank. The talk, however, ended in our first kiss and our first night together.

Two blissful weeks followed, in which we were appropriately crazy and irresponsible. We went out for breakfast at two in the afternoon after staying up all night talking and making love. We took long walks in beautiful places and mostly noticed each other. I watched her swim in the cold water of Kootenay Lake, her strong body pushing a silver phalanx into its dark surface.

Then her husband and children came home. Everything abruptly and quite naturally changed. I began the slow and difficult process of forming a separate relationship with her children and learning to share her with them. She began the painful process of separating from her husband — a process begun before we met, but now in its rough final stages.

Both girls initially exhibited a natural caution and resistance to incorporating me into their lives. Too much was changing in their young lives to take in yet another element to which they would have to adjust. My partner called me her "triple best friend" — a concept their young minds could understand far better than "lover."

I remember the first time I met them — two serious and closed little girls absorbing the tension around them. I had them over for dinner and made a rice casserole which they both didn't like and didn't eat. The eldest looked like a small version of her mother, creamy English skin, dark hair. The youngest had lighter hair and a sturdy little body. I decided, probably unwisely, that I'd have to court them a little.

In 1984, still not ready to move in with my new partner but needing to escape an increasing tension in my living situation, I found a little duplex of my own. I made sure there was room for the girls to stay and they did, visiting me often by themselves. I watched them as they coloured, played with my cats, built lego constructions, slept the sound sleep of children who have played hard. I read to them and listened to them laugh. I began slowly to know them for themselves.

I began also to feel impatient to parent, to act out what was still largely a fantasy of warm and cozy family interactions, despite my few doses with reality. My partner suggested I try to be a kind of special adult friend to them instead. I felt shut out and wondered aloud how different it would have been had I been a man, someone who could be, in the eyes of the world, a legal and identifiable second parent.

Years later, a friend whose grown daughter had weathered several lesbian relationships said to me bluntly, "Forget trying. You will never be an equal parent to them. You can be a friend and supporter to all of them, however, and that's nothing to sneeze at." This was not, however, an easy realization at the time. Only later when my friend enlightened me was I ready to match my experience to her words and understand. In the intervening time, I found my own way to parent — by being neither mother nor father but a little of both and something else altogether.

In 1986, we finally decided to buy a house together. The girls had to embrace another series of changes and, although my partner and I found our rhythms worked well together, tensions were thick around us as we all tried to adjust to a wholly different living situation. Eventually, we settled into something like a nuclear family — two parents, two kids. I began, at last, to learn the real demands of parenting.

My partner was and is first and foremost the mother — the one who bears the heaviest financial and emotional responsibility for them, the one they knew would always be there no matter what. I was and am an adjunct to that central unit of family — a supporter, a friend, and sometimes, at my worst moments, an extra child. At the same time, I remain my partner's lover and mate and so am integral to us as a couple. This dichotomy — of being in both a supporting and a starring role simultaneously — creates a tension in me that is sometimes difficult to maintain. Then I fall back on solitude, on myself as the only unit, for a time. This tension has decreased as the girls have become young women.

I have grown into many responsibilities over the years — learned to cope with crises, talk about school and boyfriends with the girls, live with a lot less money even though I am earning more than I ever have. I survived the eldest daughter's first car accident — and the loss of my car in the process. I survived the dramatic teen years of both daughters — the vocal expressions of angst, and the silent ones, the tempestuous relationships with girlfriends and boyfriends, the struggles with a school system that could not accommodate much less stimulate them.

I remember thinking that our youngest had found the essence of co-parenting after one of those typical teen interactions where Mom says, "Wouldn't it work better if you did such and such?" and the teen says, "You don't know anything about it. Why can't you just stay out of my life?" My partner hugged our youngest and said, jokingly, "But I'm the best Mommy you've got!"

"You're the only mother I have," was the dry reply.

"Well, what about Perry?" my partner asked.

"She's not my Mommy, she's my *Perry*," our youngest explained in a matter-of-fact tone. In the next room, I smiled to myself. She was saying, I think, that her relationship with me has importance, special status — but it's not the same as what she has with her mother.

I survived, not always gracefully, my partner's thorough involvement in her work, her distance when the collective burdens became too much, her personal crises, her sometimes very different relationship needs. And, miraculously, my partner and her children survived me and my growing pains — learning to drive at thirty-four, giving in to temper and frustration, sinking myself into my job until I could barely swim out, withdrawing into myself when the stress of family became more than my limited tolerance could endure.

An important element in our continued survival has been the support and acceptance by our families of our relationship and our family. Mine knows and recognizes the nature of our relationship as I have been "out" with them all for years. Presents are sent at Christmas for my partner and the girls, photographs and visits are exchanged. All of them have visited at one time or another. My partner's family has a less defined recognition of me as part of her immediate family. Her elderly parents liked me and wrote that they were glad for the support and friendship I provided for all of them. They included me in their Christmasses and in visits. We were sure they knew the truth, but our relationship wasn't labelled. There seemed no need to define it any further.

Most importantly, we are still together, still muddling through. Our oldest lives on her own now and will head off to Vancouver next year for some higher education. Our youngest has graduated from high school and is casting about for a career in which to invest her considerable talents. We are beginning to prepare for an "empty nest." Even though one daughter still lives at home, her life is more and more independent of us — and ours of her. We plan trips, evenings out, changes to the house between ourselves. We are increasingly aware that it is time to create our life — the life we'll live for the next thirty years without children.

We are also facing ourselves, each other and the nature of our relationship in a way we haven't in years. We're talking more about the hard things, the things you only show to someone you trust — learning to look at ourselves and each other as whole and different people. At the same time, I think we are also seeing our daughters more as whole people, as people independent of us even as they remain irrevocably tied to us. I am, of course, more ready to let go of them than my partner — they are hers in a way that they will never be mine.

I am mostly not afraid of the coming years, mostly looking forward to them eagerly as a time to put energy into those things put aside during child-rearing. Only occasionally do I look back wistfully on those days when the children were little and sweet and depended on me. And only occasionally do I feel wistful about my wilder, younger years, realizing even as I do that the freedom I imagined I had then was largely illusory. There are things, after all, that bind us at any age.

The first presentiment of spring, that raw freshness in the air, the earth emerging in dark stains through the snow, the snow drops up, the buds swelling and ready to unfold. I want to toss my head and gallop for no good reason across a field, to run up a tree after nothing in particular, to stretch my wings on the softening wind and fly over the gentling mountains.

My partner, no fan of winter, walks with me in the mornings again. We hold hands and lean against each other's shoulders when we feel safe to do so. We talk about our daughters, who are suddenly young women, about their relationships and futures. And about our own. Even in the sap-running spring, I feel content.

When I look back to my adolescent dreams of mothering, I see that very little of what I dreamed has come true. I have not created a family just like mine. I have not been able to share all that I wanted to share with the children in my life. I have never given birth.

I *have* found a home in the country to share with my odd and wonderful little family. I have given them my love and my support when I could. I have taught them what I could and what they were willing and able to learn at various times. I have touched them with my values, my passions, my beliefs, my critical view of the world.

My proudest moments come when I look at them and see what fine people they have all become. And, sometimes, I can see in these two girls whose lives I've shared for twelve years, some of me — good traits and not-so-good ones — but me nonetheless. Perhaps that is all the posterity we can ever expect.

On Being a Family

JANICE CZYSCON

~~❦~~

WE WERE AT THE TOY STORE, DOING OUR CHRISTMAS SHOPPING, AND STOPPED at the dollhouses. A pretty dollhouse was on our daughters' lists to Santa. The display dollhouse, furnished with little beds and tables, lamps and bathroom fixtures, also included two children and a mother and father. Without speaking, my life partner, Crystal, and I turned to each other. There was a twinkle in Crystal's eyes as she replaced the father doll in the dollhouse we were buying with the mother doll from the display house. We then proceeded to the checkout counter. We found this to be very affirming, as well as hilarious, and somehow knew that it wouldn't be long before the gay dads' dollhouse found a couple of ebullient customers. On Christmas day, the girls were delighted with their present. They never asked for a father doll to make the family resemble a traditional family. The dollhouse family looked like our family.

Being a family for the past fifteen years is something we four have worked hard at. I had no idea of the types of difficult times that were in store for us when, early in our family life, I wrote a song called, "We Four Have a Lot to Look Forward To." In the song I wrote about birthday parties, camping trips, and bike rides that we would share. I wrote about all the goodness I knew we could enjoy as a family. I believed that my total commitment to the girls and my caring and love for them would provide them with enriched and happy childhoods and the foundation for happy adult lives. There would be no doubt in anyone's mind that I was a parent to Carmen and Miranda (Nanda) and that we four were a family. I could not envision what type of person would find wrong in giving the girls another caring adult to provide for them.

At the same time, I knew there was a lot of hard work ahead

for me as a parent. What could be more difficult than guarding, nurturing and guiding two precious little girls, five-year-old Carmen, and two-year-old Nanda? I knew, when Crystal told me "It's a package deal, dear," that there would be sleepless nights rocking sick children, sibling arguments to referee, homework and piano practice to hound the girls about, and bruised egos to mend. I was willing and ready to accept the full parental rights and responsibilities that Crystal gave to me. Crystal and I gave official status to my role as parent by creating a notarized authorization from Crystal that gave me authority to consent to medical, surgical or dental examination or treatment for the girls. It also expressed Crystal's wish to afford me the visitation rights afforded to her should either minor child be hospitalized.

In 1980, the terms "alternative family" and "co-mom" were words our community used to describe our relationships to the world. We used these words with our children. We explained that I was their co-mom, who was just as committed to them as their biological mom. I firmly believed that my actions would help them believe and appreciate that I was their parent. We talked about what really made people family. Was it only blood and marital relationships? Or was it more? We stressed commitment, love and caring as the critical elements of a family unit.

Crystal and I believed that our family could be a democratic family. We did not want to use our parental status to coerce the girls into cooperation or obedience. Instead we hoped that through honest dialogue the girls would understand why we had the rules of our house. We encouraged critical analysis and encouraged the girls to "question authority." We had several long discussions with the girls about the hypostatized forces in society, the cultural construction of gender and the deceptive possibilities of language.

There was a price to pay for choosing democracy over autocracy. Our daughters often challenged us and questioned our authority. We spent many hours discussing and explaining to Carmen and Nanda how we had to reconcile our parental responsibilities with being fair to the girls and giving them a voice. In the end, it was definitely worth it. Carmen and Nanda have grown into thoughtful, assertive young women.

Within our democratic household, Crystal and I equally shared the role of disciplinarian. We had comparable ideas about discipline so that we generally agreed with the course of disciplinary action each of us had taken. In situations where we were not sure about the best approach to take we would consult with each other and reach agreement about how to deal with a specific situation. We were clear with the girls about the limits we set for them and the consequences for overstepping those limits. We believed that it was important for the girls to know that we agreed on discipline; otherwise, they would be confused. They would question our values. It did not take the girls long to figure out how aligned Crystal and I were on disciplinary matters. In fact, Carmen and Nanda believe that Crystal and I share a mind. So there were only a few times when Carmen and Nanda asked either me or Crystal for something and, if denied, went off to ask the other parent.

We were honest about our relationship with the girls from the outset. We introduced the word lesbian into their vocabularies early in their lives. We felt it important to hug and touch in front of our daughters so they knew being physically close was okay. There were many times when, as Crystal and I were hugging, one of the girls would wedge her little body between us to be part of the embrace. We believed it was important for our daughters to know that we did not think there was anything wrong with our relationship. How could they feel good about their family if we had any reservations? So we did nothing to hide who we were. We did not put away things in our home that would identify us as lesbians. We did not try to make visitors think we slept in separate bedrooms. And the girls, bless their hearts, never asked us to pretend we were just roommates.

Although Crystal and I both knew that the girls needed ways to describe our family, it became clear to us how children might have trouble understanding our family when Nanda came home from pre-school one day and said that one of her little friends asked if I was the maid. We asked her to describe me to her friends as her co-mom — something like a step-mom.

At this time there were no books, such as "Heather Has Two Mommies," available to give the girls support or to introduce to the schools. So we were pretty much on our own figuring out how to do this. During the early years of our relationship, we participated in the local lesbian moms' support group that met for monthly potlucks. The meetings allowed Crystal and me to share our experiences with other lesbian moms, to vent our frustrations, and to consider solutions to problems. We took the girls to these meetings. There they were able to play with other children from lesbian families. There they could see that they were not the only children in the world with an alternative family. They made some long-term friendships with a few of these children. As teenagers, Carmen and Nanda have asked more than once if there are any potlucks to go to.

Although attending these potlucks was valuable, all of us (lesbian moms, lesbian co-moms, and our children) were breaking new territory coming out as alternative families. We felt like pioneers. So Crystal and I just naturally presented ourselves to the world as family from the very beginning. In our interactions with school personnel, doctors, dentists, our daughters' friends and their families, we introduced ourselves as Carmen and Nanda's parents. We explained that Crystal, the girls and I lived together and that I was fully responsible for the girls as a parent. We felt no need to present ourselves as Carmen and Nanda's lesbian parents. First, there was always the fine line to walk between coming out to the world and protecting the children from the negative consequences of choosing to do this. Furthermore, Crystal and I believed, and still believe, that our sexual orientation is just one part of our relationship and really is nobody's business. After all, how many heterosexual couples go to parent-teacher conferences and announce, "Pleased to meet you, Ms Frances. We're a heterosexual couple and the parents of Tracy?"

However, during the past fifteen years, we have come out to the City of Madison several times. As members of a grass roots organization that worked to secure a city domestic partner/alternative family ordinance, we were publicly vocal about our family. We spoke at public hearings and delivered many outreach presentations to raise public awareness about the issue. We were interviewed by several reporters who published newspaper articles about our family. When Carmen was in fifth grade, one of these articles appeared in the city's special weekly paper. Nanda, who was in third grade, was excited to be in the paper. She asked if she could take the story to school. Upon hearing this, Carmen went ballistic. She did not want Nanda to take the article to school, because some of her schoolmates had already been making fun of her and her dyke mothers. We explained this to Nanda who seemed to understand that at this point in time Carmen did not want to draw attention to her family. We were impressed that Carmen, who didn't want to hurt us, had not told us about these episodes earlier. She said it didn't matter because she "didn't like these kids anyway." We told Carmen and Nanda that we wanted them to share such experiences with us — we did not expect them to deal with this alone. To our knowledge, neither Carmen nor Nanda were subjected to much ridicule or rejection because they had two mothers.

Both Carmen and Nanda regularly had friends over to our house to play, to celebrate birthdays, and for sleepovers. During her high school years, Carmen threw several large parties at our home. She attended virtually every school dance and brought her dates to our home prior to the dance. She decided in her freshman year to "come out" as the daughter of two lesbians. Her rationale was that she would beat any homophobic schoolmates to the punch. It seemed to pay off. In her senior year, she was elected to the prom court. This year Carmen and a group of her friends met us at the Ten Percent Society's Harvest Ball and thought it was so cool to dance with us. We recently took Nanda (now sixteen) and her friend to a lesbian performance. We had a great time.

The schools, health care providers, and families of our daughters' friends seemed to have accepted us as a family. They made me feel that being an alternative family was nothing to take issue with. They made me feel that our sexual orientation was none of their business. I attended all parent-teacher conferences with Crystal and took the girls to doctors' and dentists' appointments. I was invited by the schools to participate in parental activities (field trips, graduation planning committees, career days, etc.). Crystal and I were Girl Scout troop leaders for two years. The year we had planned to resign, we could not do so, because at the end-of-the-year awards ceremony, the parents presented us with tokens of their appreciation and begged us to continue as leaders for another year. As people got to know us they could not deny that we were a close family. The kids were great about asserting our identity as a family, too. I can't remember one Crayola family portrait without me in it. I can't remember one homemade Mother's Day card that didn't have me on it.

However, there were a few times when Carmen and Nanda said to me, "You're not my mother." Knowing that this comment went for my jugular, they said it to let me know that they were very angry with me. They used it when I reminded them that I had expectations of them and would not let them wriggle out of meeting them. Although I knew that the girls knew that this comment would change nothing about what Crystal and I expected of them, it left me wondering if Crystal's biological bond with the girls did in fact provide her with some intrinsic quality that garnered her recognition as a parent that I could never hope to garner as a non-biological parent. This caused discussions that often led to arguments between Crystal and me. After many years, we concluded that any distinction the girls drew between me and Crystal as parents was not caused by biology, but by society. We believe that society strongly instills the belief that a birth parent is more important than a non-biological parent. It was often frustrating trying to help the girls understand that the dominant definition of parent as a biological entity was a social construction, not an unchangeable truth.

But, as I had hoped, as people in the outside world saw how involved I was in the girls' lives, they recognized me as the girls' parent. In fact, there were numerous times when teachers and doctors could not figure out who the biological mom was because they saw that we were both so involved with the girls. They certainly couldn't decide who was the real mother based on our intimate knowledge of Carmen and Nanda — knowledge that comes from day-to-day parenting. More than once we have had a good laugh when people have commented that the girls resemble me.

Recently, one of the teachers at the after school daycare program our girls attended more than six years ago told us that we were her first experience with an alternative family and lesbian parents. She said she learned much from us and from our daughters, who were so open about their "alternative family."

My family of origin has been kind and loving to Crystal and our daughters. My mother and Aunt Anne routinely sent the girls cards and gifts for their birthdays and for every holiday (including Hallowe'en, Sweetest Day and Valentine's Day) from the very beginning. They too loved and cared for these precious little girls. (Who couldn't? They were cute, fun little darlings.) We visited my family of origin and they visited us often. My mother and aunt remembered the girls' favorite foods and toys and indulged them. They took the girls to fun places (Chucky Cheese's, Hard Rock Cafe, the oceanarium, the museum and Bloomingdale's, for example).

Our daughters have established interesting relationships with the members of my family of origin. But I believe that these relationships may have been richer or deeper, if, in the beginning I had asked my family if Carmen and Nanda could refer to them with the traditional titles used to designate family relationships. Despite the kindness and generosity of my family of origin, they seemed to tacitly communicate that my alternative family was not quite as real as my two brothers' traditional families. In fact, this past Mother's Day, during my phone call to my mom, she ended it by saying, "Tell Crystal I wish her a happy Mother's Day." I didn't say anything to my mom, but I was screaming in my head "What about me?"

Had we used traditional family titles or some derivation of them, my family of origin may have had an easier time understanding and accepting us as a real family. I think these titles may have given all of us permission to expect more from each other and give more to each other (demonstrations of affection, expressions of concern, declarations of advice). By not using traditional family titles we may have unintentionally communicated that even Crystal, Carmen, Nanda and I did not consider ourselves a real family. If we want society to recognize us as a real family we must use the words that currently validate family. Society is not ready to identify families based on the nature of our relationships. Society definitely attaches greater significance to family then to close friends. Using traditional family titles would have made it easier for Carmen and Nanda to relate to my family of origin as members of their extended family.

We are certain that the most difficult struggles we have had helping the children accept me as their real parent and us as a real family were caused by our daughters' father. None of the struggles associated with parenting (children and their rebellious nature, their sense of indestructibility, their moods and their confusion) have been as difficult as dealing with the girls' father and the problems he has created. Crystal and I have often said that his involvement was comparable to having a third and evil child to deal with. Although our daughters have called me Janice from the beginning, about three years ago I started referring to myself as Janice-mom, when I felt that the negative talk of their father may have been affecting the girls acknowledgment of me as a parent. I cannot be sure, of course, whether doing this was necessary. But the girls are consistent in identifying me as their parent, so I guess it didn't hurt.

My partner had been married for nearly five years (the girls were one and four) when we fell in love. In 1982, eighteen months after we made our life commitment to each other and established our household together, my partner nervously went to divorce court, which stipulated joint legal custody/joint physical custody. She agreed to the settlement, concerned that if she requested anything more, she would only lose. Her attorney concurred, and so did I. Although there was no legal custody battle, we spent the next ten years in an on-going battle with the girls' father.

To make a long story short, the father has been a nightmare. When the kids were younger, he failed to parent them. He was more interested in turning them against us. He didn't keep them, his house, or their clothes clean; he didn't instill in them a respect for school; he kept them out late on school nights; he took them to violence-filled movies; he didn't attend to their medical needs until situations were more serious than they had to be; he left them alone at home often; he referred to us as "sea hags" and "control freaks." He'd ask his two little daughters if they had their hard hats on when he brought them to our home for their time with us. The list of neglect and incompetent parenting by "father" goes on and on.

During the days of joint physical custody the girls were actually with us about sixty-five percent of the time and with their father about thirty-five percent of the time. Whenever there was something he personally wanted to do and the girls would be an impediment, he felt just fine about letting the girls be with us even though it was "his time." However, when we pointed out that it made no sense for the girls to be at his house when he wasn't there, he told us to butt out. He's been totally irrational, mean-spirited, manipulative and has wreaked emotional/psychological abuse on the girls and us. We also found out that he had been physically abusive on occasion with the girls. He has always put his self-interest before the best interests of the girls, although he would never admit to this. He has put his energy into revenge rather than parenting. He has been a constant negative aspect in all of our lives, and a stress on my relationship with my partner and the girls.

Both of our daughters decided, when they each turned thirteen, to live with us full time. Since then, neither child has been genuinely interested in maintaining contact with "father." Our older daughter has not communicated with him for one year. She recognized how he was laying guilt trips on her by phone and mail and decided not to concede to this sick behaviour. Our younger daughter maintains a superficial relationship with him, agreeing to spend time with him on her terms — at most, one day each month.

A lesbian mom I met on the Information Superhighway said that her ex-husband thinks of his children as poodles — they're only useful to him if he can be showing them off, parading them around town, establishing his heterosexual identity. I couldn't agree more with her, since Carmen had often told us that this was how her father made her feel. However, she didn't use the poodle analogy. She said her father made her feel like a piece of furniture he could show off.

Although the girls appear to be fairly well-adjusted, they have some serious issues to contend with, which I believe could have been avoided had they had a mature, child-centered father, instead of a misogynous, homophobic, egotistical sperm donor. In addition to creating stress, hardship and confusion for our daughters by denying our family status, the father further damaged our girls by promoting values that were in direct conflict to ours. He encouraged behaviours, through his personal example, that we were attempting to discourage (lying, using and manipulating people, disregarding and ignoring peoples' requests, blaming others for situations caused by his irresponsibility). If our daughters had had limited visitation with him, all of our lives would have been happier. We cannot deny the excessive misery he created for all of us.

Many times during the past fifteen years I had to bite my tongue when the girls told us about things they did with their father or about comments he made. We knew that if we brought the issues to his attention he would take it out on the girls. However, I did not refrain from telling our daughters when their father's behaviour toward them sounded abusive to me. The situation that disgusts me the most is when Carmen told me that her father told her to cut his toe nails, and she did because she did not want to get in trouble. I told her this was perhaps the most overt way he could show her how he viewed their relationship and that she did not have to put up with that kind of treatment. If anyone would interpret this as trashing their father, then I did trash him, and I'm glad I did.

Although we often thought about going after full custody, we knew, based on the legal climate at the time, that the courts would not consider him an unfit parent. It's a shame that parental rights often take precedence over children's rights. So Crystal and I tried to compensate for the rough times Carmen and Nanda experienced at their father's house. We tried to make our home a safe haven, a peaceful place for them. And they recognized this.

The father never acknowledged my parental status and tried to instill in the girls the concept that family must be defined by blood or marriage. When he denied my parental status to my face, I often let the anger get to me and railed against him. My anger was justified and intense, because it was obvious to anyone that I was more of a parent to Carmen and Nanda than he could ever hope to be. But I resent those times I gave in to my anger, because that is exactly what he wanted — to get a rise out of me.

Knowing that hindsight has 20/20 vision, Crystal and I do not beat ourselves up for how we dealt with this man. Given what we had to deal with, we believe we've been generally successful. The girls chose to live with us full time, after all. We do believe, however, that we should have dealt with his refusal to recognize me as parent by refusing to give him his way when he said he would only talk to Crystal because she was the girls' mother.

In defining ourselves as a family in the face of the father's self-declared war to invalidate us as a family, we each became stronger and wiser individuals. We have weathered many storms. Because we worked so hard at being recognized as a family, I think we have a greater appreciation for our family than we would have otherwise. We take nothing for granted, and we respect one another. We are also grateful to everyone we know who sincerely accepted us as a family.

Crystal and I have put our hearts and souls into providing our daughters with happy childhoods and the basis for happy adult lives. We hope they will always be caring and honest people. I will love them forever.

Sixteen-year-old Nanda is very open at school about her family. She recently gave a presentation on the gay and lesbian movement in her speech class. In her family issues class she gave a well-received presentation about her "alternative" family. Nanda told her class that she tried to think of all the ways being in her family was different from being in any other family and could not identify any differences. She told her class that she had curfews and got grounded and that her moms went to parent-teacher conferences — just like any other family. Nanda said she wouldn't want any other family, but wished it was easier for Crystal and me and people like us.

Carmen, now nineteen and a college freshman, also makes us feel good about our work as parents. She sports a button on her backpack that reads, "Two moms are better than one." Recently she told us that she believed all moms should be lesbian moms.

A *"Blended"* Family

BRYN SHERIDAN & KATHERINE STUART

Our family consists of two moms and seven children. Jeanne, twenty-seven, is Katherine's birth daughter. Hope, aged eighteen, was born to my former husband and me, and we adopted Ben, now sixteen, when he was fifteen months of age. After Katherine and I had been together for ten years, we adopted Daniel, currently eight, and then, a year later, five-year-old Delayne, three-year-old Connor, and Ethan, aged two. Ben and Ethan have fetal alcohol syndrome (FAS), Daniel has severe learning disabilities, and Delayne has a problem with speech. Each of our adopted children has the kind of emotional problems that are normal for children who have experienced trauma and too much change. Each of our birth children has the kind of emotional ups and downs that go with growing up. They are all beautiful, wonderful, funny and ours.

With all of the issues we have had to confront, our family story is similar to something that might have been found in a soap opera script: we are a blended family; Katherine was a teen mom and now we are both older moms; we have had to make choices between career and family; we have lived through tragedy (like the one terrible year when Katherine's mom died, Hope and Ben's father succumbed to cancer, a favourite uncle died unexpectedly and, finally, the family dog died just before Christmas). We have also adapted to the special needs of our children and to their normal life transitions. Jeanne has grown up, established a career and recently bought her first home in a nearby town. Hope just finished high school and is beginning to take her first steps into real adulthood. Ben, who has so many struggles with FAS, has reunited with his birth grandmother and is trying to find his identity as an adopted teen with special needs. Some of these issues have almost destroyed our family, others have made us stronger.

The first hurdle we faced was in trying to blend our two families. For many years, Katherine had been raising Jeanne in the context of relationships in which her partner was childless and barely tolerated Jeanne. Most of the other lesbians in Katherine's social circle were also childless, and so social events, while inclusive of children, were rarely focussed on the children. As well, Katherine and Jeanne had lived a fairly unstructured life. Katherine worked in a demanding profession and owned her own home, but beyond that their daily life was spontaneous and had few rules. On the other hand, my married social circle was made up of couples who lived very child oriented lives. I was, and continue to be, an organized and structured person who likes to plan a spontaneous moment six weeks in advance.

We were both willing to change, and knew that we had to do so if we wanted to stay together, but it was not easy. Jeanne, who was in her teens at the time, reacted the most negatively to the blending process. She felt betrayed by her mother's changes and, as is the way of teens, made it clear that she would not participate in them. We tried to help her adjust, and she made her own attempts from time to time, but it never seemed to work. Now that we have gone through two more teenagers, we have learned not to expect children to adjust to external changes when they are caught up in their own internal change process. Not that we should have given up on, or excluded, Jeanne but I think we would have done better if we had understood how long the blending takes and if we had placed our expectation of a successful outcome much farther into the future.

Hope and Ben also had to make harsh adjustments when their father was diagnosed with cancer shortly after our marital separation. The illness devastated him physically and emotionally and he was never again well enough to be as involved in their lives and their activities as he had been in their early years. We watched them lose him, bit by bit, over the years, as the illness took away his ability to parent. There was little we could do to help them with their pain. We had to learn to accept how powerless we were to help the children when they needed us the most.

Throughout the years of blending, we also had to contend with Ben's problems. Alcohol related birth defects have only recently begun to be understood and properly diagnosed, but when Ben was growing up, the long-term behavioural disorders that are part of this condition were still considered to be short-term, or, even worse, the fault of the child. We know now that the learning and behaviour problems never end, and that the child has no control over the parts of the brain that have been permanently damaged by the prenatal exposure to alcohol. But nobody knew that when Ben was little, so instead of helping him to learn to cope with his condition, we all kept trying to find the magic answer that would change it. There are still very few support services available for teenagers with fetal alcohol syndrome or fetal alcohol effects, and Ben keeps getting bounced from one resource to another as his behaviours wear out those who try to help him. My only consolation is that he is able to keep trying, and he and I have a very close relationship. He knows that I love him and that his family never gives up on him. What he does not know is how angry we get — angry at his behaviours, angry at the unfairness of it, angry at the world for not making a place for him, and angry at ourselves for not being able to fix it all. We have not stood idly by and watched Ben struggle. We have instituted changes in the way professionals in our community understand and treat people with this condition, and until recently I travelled extensively lecturing on the topic. The changes and the increased knowledge have given us a reasonable expectation that Ethan will have an easier time in his life than Ben has had, that he will be given help to learn to cope, and that no one will expect things from him that are beyond his abilities. Being the parents of a child with defined special needs is all about learning to advocate and learning to live on hope. Hoping that the next resource will work, that the newest technique will make a difference. And learning to advocate for even more resources and more techniques as each falls short of what the child needs. We are far more skilled in those areas than we ever expected to be, more than anyone should ever have to be.

The decision to increase our family from the original three children to the current seven was one of those struggles that almost broke us up but ended up making us stronger. In other words, it was an awful process. I had never felt finished in terms of having children and when I was in my late thirties I began to get the dreaded sense of now or never. At that point, Jeanne was grown up and Hope and Ben were both in their early teens. I could see my years of actively raising children coming to an end and it horrified me. All I ever really wanted in life was to raise children, and, being a feminist and having a successful career did not alter that desire in me. Katherine, on the other hand, saw it as a welcome change. She had been a mom since she was eighteen and was looking forward to paying off the mortgage, travelling, and not always watching her needs finish in last place.

We talked about the pros and cons of having another child until we were all talked out. It became obvious though, that the issue was going to destroy our relationship if we did not reach some kind of agreement. It was finally Katherine who made the decision when she agreed to one more child. For her, it was a matter of knowing that she was capable of doing the job of child-raising, and being willing to continue with her life as it was. From then, it became a matter of getting the child.

Artificial insemination was not something either of us wanted to undertake. We had each brought a child into the world and did not feel that it was right for us to bring in any more. Adoption, though, was something that we were both comfortable with as it was part of our life experience with Ben. We did not have any particular need to have another newborn, and as we had learned over the years, all children have special needs, whether they are defined as such or not. Therefore, as we saw it, any child that we might adopt was already in the world and would likely have some kind of special need that we could meet.

The problem, of course, is that adoption is never simple and becomes even more complicated when it involves a same-sex couple. We considered an international adoption because there are some countries that adopt to single parents and we had a friend who is a registered social worker and who was willing to do a home study on one of us as a single parent. But that did not feel right. One of the many things we have learned from our children is that the parent cannot lie, and starting our life with a new child as the result of a lie seemed wrong. Many adopted children love to hear the story of how they came to be part of the family, and telling our child that we had lied and deceived people would not likely enhance his or her self-esteem or sense of moral character. We decided to just go ahead and apply through the normal channels, however slim the chances. That way, if we did not get to raise another child, I would at least know that we had tried the only viable means for us and I would have to live with the grief. Katherine did not believe we had any chance of adopting in this manner but she agreed because she could not think of any other way that would work for us. So, without any real hope, we got an application form and sent it in.

To our delight and our surprise, the application was processed and whatever discussions or decisions were made about our situation were never revealed to us. All we knew was that the application was accepted and we were assigned a social worker to do our homestudy. The adoption application process is long and arduous, involving many forms, and many, many home visits and office visits with a social worker. The worker assigned to us was a bit confused by our application at first because she did not have any role models to fall back on. The forms are designed for heterosexual couples and her extensive training in adoptions had assumed that applicants would be married and heterosexual. She is a creative social worker, though, and decided to take our application in the same manner as a common-law heterosexual couple, which meant that only one of us would be the legally adopting parent and the other would be the adopting partner. There was no deception in this, as the first line of the completed homestudy began, "This same-sex couple ... " There is the potential for problems, however, as it means that Katherine has no legal rights to the children. We have included her last name on their birth certificates and made certain custody arrangements in my will, but she is not a legal parent.

In order to go through with the adoption in this way, we had to be very clear about our commitment to each other, not just as a couple, but beyond any breaking up of our relationship. Of course, like most couples, we assume that we will always be together, but the responsibility of having children precludes any comfort in assumptions. What we have relied on is our firm belief that custody battles destroy children and settle nothing. Katherine has to trust that if we break up, I will not hurt her or our children by depriving her of full access. I do not believe that I would do this: I did not do it with my husband and I would not do it with her. But she had to believe me in order for it to work. More importantly, we had to be very sure that we were committed enough to our relationship and to raising the children in a two-parent home, that we would do everything possible to stay together. Neither of us has a history of infidelity or leaving in the hard times, and it has helped to know that about each other. It has also helped to know that we stayed together through the early blending years and through so many life transitions, and that we are still in love with each other after more than a decade. As we considered all of these factors, we decided that such a method of adoption, while not right for everyone, would work for us.

The social worker made it clear that acceptance of an application did not mean that we would get a child, and she made sure that we understood that the mandate of the social services is to find families for children, not to find children for families. In other words, the social worker must get to know the adopting couple so that she or he can determine what they have to offer a child even though there may never be a child who needs what a particular family has to offer. This state of affairs is not because we are lesbian, it is the way of adoption. The history of adoption shows that for centuries the process existed for the convenience of the adults, and a great many of the children suffered from this position. In the last twenty years, however, the growing knowledge about the needs of children and the lack of children available for adoption have combined to make "the best interests of the child" paramount. Adoption services now do everything they can to understand the needs of each child and to find a home that is the most likely to meet those needs.

Knowing that we may never be chosen for a child, no matter how wonderful anybody thinks we are, made it slightly threatening to open up our lives for public record. To our amazement, we found the process of letting the social worker get to know us both unusual and exciting. She made us examine facets of our relationship and of our values that we had never before put into words, let alone discussed with someone else. She wanted to know about our weaknesses as much as she wanted to know about our strengths, and we had to listen to our children tell her what it is like to grow up in the family we have created. We had to consider who we were as individuals and as parents from a perspective that was new and challenging. And it was good. At the end, we felt strong in our decision to adopt, and re-committed to our family. We then sat back to wait, perhaps forever.

We were fortunate, though, because the adoption workers decided that there was a little boy who needed some of the things we had to offer. Ours was not the only home considered for him, but his worker felt that we were the ones most likely to meet his unique needs over the long term. So, one year later we welcomed Daniel, then five, to our family. He was a joy right from the beginning. We had expected it to be a more difficult adjustment than it was, or maybe it was just as hard as we thought it would be but we did not notice. However, it worked, and Daniel brought us into a new world. He entered kindergarten and, because I was home, not working, for a few months, I became re-involved with the school and social life of the five year old. It is an exciting time in any child's life, but for Daniel, not only was he trying to adjust to a new family, but he had to adjust to a new school and new friends. He managed well and his determined and gregarious nature helped him to carve his own place in our home and in his school. Soon there was the delight of birthday parties and hot dog days, and the dilemma of trying to decide whether it was safe for Daniel if we came "out" to the teacher and the other parents. At first, we decided that while we would not lie if asked, nor hide the fact that Katherine and I lived together, we would not make it explicitly clear until after the adoption was finalized. Since then, we have told some of the other moms, and just continued on as before with the rest. The fact that one of the mothers pointedly moved away when I sat next to her at a Christmas concert made it clear that most of them had figured it out and some did not like it. Our contact with the dads has been positive albeit more focussed. Most of the dads I talk to are involved with the children through coaching sports or leading groups like Beavers and so our conversations tend to be task oriented and not very personal.

Our decision to expand the family yet again came about when we realized that the age gap between Daniel and the other three was so wide that he was virtually an only child. I am an only child, as was Jeanne for many years, so we are able to see many positive aspects to that status. However, we were worried about his being the only child of lesbians and what it could be like for him without allies. Also, Daniel had grown up in foster care with lots of other young children around him, and he missed the kind of interaction and activity that having peers in the home provided. Yet we knew it would have been wrong to have more children just to be a companion for one we already had. Dogs can be acquired for companionship, but little human beings deserve to be wanted for better reasons — and we had better reasons. To be honest, I was thrilled with the fact that it looked like Daniel needed siblings, because I still felt eager to have more children. Whatever it is that causes the urge to experience mothering, it had not been fully requited in me. Therefore, after Daniel's adoption was finalized, we re-applied for one more child, preferably around the same age. Shortly after, we were joined by Delayne, Connor, and Ethan.

Neither of us ever expected to have so many children, and being offered a sibling group of three, when we asked for one, took a great deal of thought, at least on Katherine's sensible part. We also had to consider our age because the youngest was born when I, the younger of the two of us, was forty, which means that we will be actively parenting through menopause and into our late fifties. We also had to consider the quality of our relationship, and whether there would even be time for us as a couple with so many little children to care for. After much deliberation, we decided to go ahead, and after meeting the children it seemed like there could never have been any other decision. They, too, have carved out a place in the family and made themselves the center of our world. Getting used to diapers, midnight wake-ups, and having our house fill up with high chairs, cribs, pull toys and riding toys, has re-energized us far more than it has tired us. People are always quick to remind us that these truly wonderful children will someday be teenagers. And we are quick to remind them that we know that, we have had three teens already. Adolescence is not new territory for us and we have learned to take each child, and the way each child navigates through each life stage, one day at a time. As for our relationship, it has become even stronger. There is something very comforting about believing that we cannot break up because of the damage it would do to the children. They make us feel bound together more deeply, and more lovingly, than we ever anticipated. Nothing has ever happened with our children the way we thought it would; they have turned out very differently than we expected and we are delighted with who they are. So we will love these little ones without dread for the future because we have learned that the future is always too much of a surprise for us to accurately predict the things we should fear.

We have certainly noticed some differences between having young children in our twenties and having them now, in our forties. When we were younger, both of us were still more concerned with our social lives and our careers. Katherine was either going to university or working full time from the time Jeanne was born. I did not work full time until the children were in school but I took courses and was active in a variety of community organizations. I was also busy taking the children to every type of lesson I could find. It seemed important to me then that they be exposed to the larger world of culture, regardless of where their interests or talents lay. Once I began working, I focussed on my career and it seemed that I was always trying to find a balance between home and work.

Now, our careers are established and I have reduced my work to only two days a week and have no intention of increasing it in the future. I have been lucky enough to have fulfilled all of my professional ambitions, and my past needs to accomplish things outside of the home have been fading away for several years. Katherine still works full-time, but her day ends at four-thirty and her interest in her work is now based on personal fulfilment rather than advancement. We are also far more relaxed about everything. We do not expect the children to be little superstars and we only enrol them in things in which they show a clear interest and talent. It helps, too, that we are financially comfortable at this stage in our lives. Money may not be everything but it helps to take away some of the stress and worry that we both experienced twenty years ago. The biggest difference between our parenting when we were in our twenties and our parenting now is our ability to enjoy the children as they are, rather than pushing them to ensure that they reflect well on us.

When I first took Daniel to kindergarten, I had expected to be older than most of the other moms. Certainly with my first two children, most of the parents had been around my age and that was some time ago. It seems, however, that lots of women are having children in their late thirties and early forties because, to my surprise, I still found that most of the parents were my age. Many of these women had also made the same choices I had in that they had either let go of careers or had put them on a much lower priority. I found a real bond with some of these moms, much like the bond I had experienced when I Iope and Ben were young, and I was amazed at how much I enjoyed experiencing that kind of relationship again. It felt good to talk with other women who had chosen to stay home either full time or part time, and it felt wonderful to swap "cute kid" stories with people who actually wanted to hear them. As a lesbian I have been more in the company of women than men for many years, yet there is something different, and special, about the kind of bond that is shared between mothers of young children, and I had not realized how much I have missed it.

The ways in which our being lesbians has affected our parenting and our family life is more difficult to sort out because I am not certain of all of the ways that being a mother and being a lesbian are related or are separate. Katherine and I face the same problems as every type of parent and, like most others, sometimes we handle the difficulties well and sometimes we handle them poorly. Sometimes the fact that we are two women makes it easier, and sometimes it makes it harder. Our big concern is that since we are different from the majority of society, we have an obligation to teach our children how to handle the negative reactions they may get from others. We have to help them learn to cope with any potential teasing, and to feel strong about themselves regardless of what others say about them. This is not unlike what we must do to help them cope with the special needs that are a part of our children's lives. The difference is that we did not cause their learning or behaviour problems and so we are more easily able to remain objective and supportive on those issues. The fact that they can be hurt because we are lesbians makes it harder for us emotionally because it is something that has come from us.

One of the unexpected things we have noticed is that as our family has grown, our social circle has shrunk. The research literature is quite consistent in its findings that lesbian families are often isolated from the rest of the lesbian community, and that has become true for us. We no longer have much in common with our friends. The ones who are mothers are the same age as us so they are at the empty nest stage of life and enjoying it. They are looking forward to grandchildren and they are spending their time and money on interesting hobbies and exotic vacations. Our younger friends, and those who do not have children, are focussed on their careers or they are exploring fascinating post-graduate programs. Not many people consider our preoccupations with speech therapy, diaper rash, and the merits of vacationing at Disney World versus Disneyland to be interesting dinner party conversation. We also have trouble staying up late enough to go to dances because we know that our three pre-schoolers will all be up by six or seven at the latest. And getting a competent babysitter is difficult. Hope used to babysit for us quite regularly but now she is out of high school and working full time, mostly evenings, and planning on going to college soon, so she is rarely available. We are fortunate to have a wonderful nanny who cares for the children in our home the two days a week that I work, and comes back on Friday evenings so that we have one night out together. But if our friends are busy on that night, as is frequently the case, then we do not see them. We also do not have the time to go to the coffee house, or to join the baseball team, or to actively support lesbian political causes, and so we pull back from joining things that used to keep us in touch with the lesbian community. I once complained to the lesbian mother of one child that I felt that putting the yearly lesbian ball on Hallowe'en night was an incredible faux pas because it meant that those of us with children could not attend. She then suggested that we do what she does — she takes her little girl out trick or treating and then drops her off at a friend's house for the night. Good idea, but it does not work when there are four!

Several years ago I attended a workshop on adoption, and the speaker stated that adoptive families have more in common with each other than with their peers or their own families. My experience as an adoptive parent for fifteen years confirms that statement, and so the natural place for us to go for support and friendship is to adoptive parent associations. In our community, there are support groups available to adoptive families with special needs children and when I was still with my husband we found that many of our friends and our social activities revolved around these groups. Yet Katherine and I have not connected with the support groups because, as far as we know, there are no other lesbian families in this network, and we are not interested in the potential problems that could result if we joined. We do not want to expose the children to the negative publicity that could result if the membership had issues about our lifestyle, so we stay away from the people with whom we have the most in common. We may be unfairly characterizing these groups, but we are not political activists and we are not willing to challenge our own stereotypes in the same manner in which we ask others to challenge theirs.

This is not to say that we are without any friends or any support. We do still have some lesbian friends, we just do not see them as often as we used to and we have had to adjust to the loss of the larger network to which we used to belong. As well, Katherine's heterosexual colleagues at work are a wonderful group who provide enormous support and friendship. Our church (Unitarian) has been very accepting and have made it clear that our family is welcome there. We have also found my family to be caring and supportive. My mother gives us great support in practical ways, like coming to our house to wash and change the bedding every week. That is no small task in such a large family. And my cousins and I have all reached an age where it is okay to be best friends with the same relatives with whom one fought all through childhood. My family had many initial problems with our lesbian relationship, but they have either worked through or forgotten them with the years, and our children have become part of the large network of cousins that has always held our extended family together.

We are like most parents in that we want to pass on our values to our children. Yet we tread a thin line trying to teach them the difference between being strong and being defensive, and rejecting intolerance in others without feeling that they have to take on the problems that an intolerant society attempts to create for us. We want to teach our children to see us, themselves and others as whole people, not just sets of characteristics. We are lesbian, we are successful professionals, we are good parents and we live a committed family life. All of those things are part of us and those are all things that we want our children to learn to value in us.

In turn, we want our children to value the characteristics that are unique to each of them. So far, they are all happily heterosexual. Jeanne and Hope are both hard workers, and both are quite creative. Jeanne is a self-taught seamstress who makes the most wonderful outfits and jackets for her little brothers and sisters. Hope is a budding writer who plans to make a career with her ability to manage words and tell stories. Ben does not have any particularly outstanding talents, but he has shown an ability to survive, despite the odds, that is remarkable. Daniel is a singer and entertainer with the most wonderful imagination. Delayne is a strong, determined little girl who loves pretty clothes and Barbie dolls. Connor is shy, steady and sensitive, and probably the most intelligent child we have ever met. Ethan is bubbly, curious, and can climb over any obstacle or into any space.

We are still discovering the many talents of all of our children and we can see the potential that lies within each of them. And we will do our best to see that their potential has the opportunity to be realised.

Postscript by Katherine

Bryn is the writer, but I have a few comments to add. I have been lesbian for a long time and I have noticed how attitudes towards children have changed within the lesbian community over the last three decades. At different times there have been periods of greater or lesser acceptance of children in our community. In my experience, children were welcome at the dances and social activities of the 1970s, but this welcome seems to have decreased over time. The seventies were, at least on the surface, a more child-inclusive decade — although it cannot be said that this was a truly inclusive time, as there were heated debates about whether the dances were appropriate environments for the children, and whether older male children were welcome. Certainly, though, there were activities for families. I think that this is something we must still work on creating.

As well, I think it is important to know that Bryn and I have come from very different backgrounds. She is from an upper middle-class family and I am from a working-class background. Her family was conventional and respectable, and mine was neither. We have struggled over standards and expectations in our relationship, our living situation and our parenting. It has not been easy, but we seem to always find something to "work on," and the result is usually a synthesis that is stronger than either of the positions with which we began. Having more children creates greater pressure and more areas of difference, so we always have lots to talk about. It is a fortunate characteristic of parenting that the positive experiences make the struggles worthwhile.

The "Second Mother"

LOUISE FLEMING

~~◦~~

EVERYONE ALWAYS THOUGHT THAT I WOULD HAVE CHILDREN — LOTS OF children. As the oldest girl in a big family, I was involved early on in mothering my five younger brothers and sisters. This was not only a responsibility that was imposed on me, it was a responsibility that I embraced gladly. To this day, my mother and siblings still refer to me, tongue-in-cheek, as the "second mother."

But life didn't unfold in the prescribed heterosexual manner for me. Even before I came out, I knew that I wanted meaningful and career-oriented work, and that I wanted the world to be a place with more choices for women. When I headed off to university in 1970, the Women's Liberation Movement was becoming an important political force and I was overjoyed to discover that there were like-minded women who wanted to challenge the status quo. Twenty-five years later, we're still at it.

Throughout my twenties I was involved with a series of men, yet I managed to avoid marriage and family. Just after my twenty-ninth birthday, I took the plunge and came out as a lesbian. It was a euphoric time in my life — I felt at peace with myself and I had connected with a lesbian community that felt like home.

Then my biological clock began ticking very loudly. I wrestled with the "to have or not to have a child" dilemma. In my practical way, I decided that if it hadn't happened by the time I was thirty-five, I would turn the biological clock off. I do remember thinking that I would be open to becoming involved with a woman with children, although it didn't seem likely at that time. My life wasn't deprived of children — I was the aunt and godmother who spent regular time with several children and gave their parents a much-needed break. I knew that I didn't want to be a single mother and I also knew that not every woman in the world wanted to have children in her life on a daily basis. My thirty-fifth birthday came and went. I mentally struck children off my life list.

This was not to be.

In 1989, my job was getting in the way of my beliefs and my integrity, so I left my well-paid career in the boy's club and purchased a publishing house. I redid my budget, pulled up my sleeves and applied myself to the task of learning how to be a businesswoman and a publisher. Then, an old friend and former lover, who had had a baby the year before, decided to visit me. I borrowed a crib, checked out highchairs, laid in a few toys and diapers, and was ready for the visit.

Sibyl and I had been in regular contact over the years and I had known that she wanted a child. When Sarah was born, I was thrilled for Sibyl and looked forward to meeting this child who had "stolen" Sibyl's heart. Shortly after they arrived, my own heart was stolen, not just by Sarah but by Sibyl as well.

Like most single mothers, Sibyl was running on empty most of the time; she also didn't have much support as a mother. Throughout their visit, I got up with Sarah in the morning so that Sibyl could catch up on her sleep. Sarah and I spent lots of time together and she honoured me by taking her first steps in my house. There were two more visits that gave all three of us the time to be together and to feel what it was like to be a family. Sibyl lived at the other end of the country, so we spent much time on the phone and wrote each other several times a week. After several months of astronomical phone bills, loneliness and weighing all our options, we decided we wanted to be together. I was very happy to have another chance to become involved with Sibyl — this time, when both of us were ready. It seemed best if Sibyl and Sarah moved to be with me. We wanted to live our lives openly as lesbians and that was more likely to be the case in the town where I lived. Also, Sibyl was more likely to find work in my area of the country than I was in hers.

As best we could, Sibyl and I tried to figure out what kind of a family arrangement we wanted. I was willing and able to take on a significant role in Sarah's life, but I also wanted to protect myself from getting hurt. I thought that if I slowly eased myself into the parenting responsibility — accepting thirty percent of the parenting to start — I could spare my feelings until it became clear whether our family arrangement would actually work. Well, I soon discovered three things: it took me no time whatsoever to feel total love for Sarah; all my "looking after" children did not equate with the reality of being a parent twenty-four hours a day, seven days a week, fifty-two weeks a year; and there is no such thing as giving thirty percent, because there is no such thing as giving one hundred percent when it comes to looking after a young child.

Sarah was twenty-one months old when she and Sibyl moved in with me. A child at that age gets sick often, has high fevers in the middle of the night, never stops until she sleeps, needs constant supervision and stimulation, goes through diapers in a big way (yes, we did the cloth diaper routine), needs to be fed at odd hours, etc. Sibyl and I spelled each other off as best we could. Sibyl had suffered from sleep deprivation since Sarah was born (Sarah didn't sleep through the night until she was well past three years), so I tried to give her as many opportunities to catch up on her sleep as I could. My relationship with Sarah flourished as we spent lots of time together.

I admired how open Sibyl was to letting me develop such a close relationship with Sarah — I'm not sure, had our positions been reversed, that I would have allowed such a primary relationship to form — and I appreciated how much she recognized my positive influence on Sarah (under my tutelage, Sarah, at two-and-a-half, could do a complete rendition of "On The Good Ship Lollipop") and my parenting abilities. But the more attached I became to Sarah, the more vulnerable I felt. What would happen to my relationship with Sarah if Sibyl and I split up or, worse yet, if Sibyl died?

Occasionally, Sarah's biological father would make contact with Sibyl. He was a non-starter in Sarah's life but liked to try to wield power over Sibyl every once in awhile. There had been a custody battle — the usual "I don't really care about my child but let's make her mother's life more difficult" — but it wasn't about Sibyl's lesbianism, thankfully. He knew nothing of me and he remains an anomaly in my life — the only person with any rank in Sarah's life with whom I have no communication.

All of this pushed Sibyl and me to address the imbalance of power in our relationship with Sarah, and led me to express my need for Sibyl to act to protect my role as Sarah's parent. Sibyl took up the challenge and responded to what I needed. She can't always appreciate my position, but she came to understand what was hard for me.

We have been a family for almost five years. Sarah calls me her "Lulu" and so do all her friends. We went through the daycare system as openly lesbian parents and are now out in the school system. Sarah began French immersion this year and explained to the class that she had "deux mamans," because, as she told me, she didn't know how to say Lulu in French. The neighbours who have children Sarah's age know that we are lesbians and one couple has even given us positive feedback for being openly so. We live in a small town, and small town friendliness has so far been the standard reaction we encounter. Sarah thinks we are the best parents in the world and, like all parents, we puff our chests and feel honoured with the compliment.

There are definitely hard parts for me as the non-biological mother. There isn't a word to describe who I am to Sarah or who she is to me. I'm often asked who she is, and when I respond with "Sarah," I know I'm not answering the question that is really being asked. My biological family has been very accepting of me and my chosen family, but Sarah's role with them isn't named either. She calls my mother "Mrs. Fleming," which I find difficult, especially when all the grandchildren are together and she's the outsider. My sisters and brothers treat Sarah very well — but I feel that if I had been with a man, Sarah's status in my family, and I guess in the world at large, would have been clearer and more legitimate. When it comes right down to it, it's about authenticity — what makes our family authentic to the larger world. We have a way to go in our immediate families, and a much longer way to go in the world.

Mother's Day is a loaded holiday for me. I want to honour Sibyl's role as Sarah's mother, but there is no recognition of my role because I'm not the mother. We all recognize that I'm *like* the mother and that a Lulu is a parent but, to the world, Sibyl is the mother and I am the other. There are still all those times when I am invisible unless I choose to explain my position, or when people refer to me as the babysitter or the aunt. Fortunately, I have a good sense of humour, which gets me through many situations. It doesn't change the fact that my status in Sarah's life and our status as a family aren't recognized in the ways they should be, but a sense of humour keeps me and Sibyl sane and we hope it will help Sarah to cope with some of the difficult moments ahead for her as the child of lesbian parents.

I still have no legal rights to Sarah, and I probably never will. In the event of Sibyl's death, we face the big unknown. The longer Sarah and I are family, the more likely it is that a court would award custody to me, especially with the support of Sibyl's family, who recognize me as the other parent.

We have done what we can to give me rights in our family. Sibyl and I have a written agreement which spells out our moral commitments to each other and to Sarah in the event of the breakup of our relationship. This agreement includes seeking the help of a facilitator. We both know that Sarah's needs come first and we are committed to making sure that anything we decide as a couple will not be at her expense. Sibyl has a good will which addresses her wishes for guardianship for Sarah in the event of her death. Sibyl has also solicited the support of her family, who would help me if I needed to fight the biological father for custody of Sarah. We have lots of life insurance, to cover the legal costs. I am the executor and major beneficiary of Sibyl's estate, which would allow me to maintain an ongoing relationship with Sarah even if I didn't win a custody battle.

We live our life openly as a family and we believe that this would help me if ever there was a custody battle. We don't live openly for that reason however; we do so because neither of us wants to live in the closet. And we want Sarah to grow up proud of who we are.

We have actively cultivated an extended lesbian family. My sister Lee (also a lesbian) is Sarah's "Aunt LeeLee," who takes her overnight every week. Through the years, we have had many friends who have cared for Sarah in many ways. Sarah's life is full of love from many different people and, as a result, she too is full of love. She is an extremely insightful child with a flare for the dramatic and a sense of what's important. Like all children who are loved and cherished, she enjoys life and doesn't hesitate to take her place and speak her mind. As an only child, she is used to having an attentive audience but she is also able to entertain herself with her crafts for hours at a time. She loves to be with people and already she has one best friend at school, one in the neighbourhood, and a good friend in the country. All this is to say that she is a well-adjusted little girl who is doing just fine in her lesbian family.

There are still things we must do in our family to help each other and protect ourselves. It's not easy for me to acknowledge to others how difficult it is to feel invisible, but it's only by doing so that others will understand. We have talked with Sibyl's mother and sisters about the support I would need in the event of Sibyl's death, but we still need to be more specific with them and to involve her brothers in that support. We know from other lesbian family experiences that there will be difficult times for Sarah with her peers and we must prepare her for them. She understands, as well as a six year old can, about discrimination and prejudice, but she hasn't felt them yet. It saddens me to think about our sweet loving girl being treated badly, but it will happen and she has to be ready.

In conclusion, I guess this time around I really am the "second mother," and I am honoured to have this chance to mother and to co-parent. A friend of mine in her sixties, who came out in her fifties and who has several children and many grandchildren, summed it up very well when she told me that parenting was the most heady experience of her life. Sarah is the only person in my life who is so pleased to see me that she will run across a room screaming my name at the top of her lungs and fling herself into my waiting arms. She can make me feel on top of the world just by telling me how much she appreciates the smallest things I do for her. Having a child in my life is one of the most wonderful things that has happened to me; so is co-parenting with the woman I love.

Protecting Our Lesbian Family

SIBYL FREI

~❧~

As a teenager, I did not have a big role to play in helping my mother with my younger siblings. Nor was I interested in babysitting, given the world of possibilities open to a precocious youth. In spite of little experience, by the time I reached twenty-five I knew that I wanted to have or adopt a child.

I came out as a lesbian at eighteen. By the time I was in my mid-twenties, I was living in the far north of Canada. For my survival, I lived very much in the closet. After all, "feminist" was a dirty word in my small mining-town home, and I took enough flack for that! When my lesbian lover left, I thought my only option was an emotional relationship with a man. The one relationship I tried did not last, but it firmed my resolve to have a child.

So there I was, thirty years old, ready to be a mother and willing to be a single parent. I had a good job, with maternity leave benefits that included job protection. To me, that meant that I could afford to raise a child on my own. Because adoption was difficult for a single woman, I set out to get pregnant. The easiest option open to a northern woman was "the old fashioned way."

As it turned out, I had sex with the man with whom I had been involved once after we broke up, and I got pregnant. I was thrilled! Because the father was an aboriginal man, I felt it would be important for my child to know that she, too, had an aboriginal heritage. Under the influence of wildly swinging hormones, I tried to recreate a relationship with the father, but within a few months of Sarah's birth I gave it up as a bad job.

For the next year-and-a-half, I was the single parent of a happy, curious, hungry, non-sleeping bundle of energy. Sarah's father had only sporadic contact with her during that time. He didn't look after her overnight or do anything but play with her when she was clean and fed.

When Sarah was fourteen months old, I visited an old friend, Louise, who lived on the other side of the country. We fell in love. Over the next few months, we explored our commitment to each other and decided that we wanted to live together. We also decided that we could not live together comfortably in the north, where we would be in the closet, and that Sarah and I should move to join Louise.

This brought the question of custody of Sarah to the forefront. I was considered to have "practical" custody of Sarah, as I was her full-time caregiver. But I had to either obtain legal custody of Sarah, or take off and face the potential consequences.

I did consider running away, for two powerful reasons. First, Sarah's father had not wanted to hear about my lesbian past and, for my safety, I had stayed in the closet. I was not sure that human rights protections would stop lesbianism from becoming an issue in the custody case. Second, there were recent Canadian cases where non-native mothers who wanted custody of their aboriginal children had been forced to stay in the geographical area of the father's family in order to preserve the child's cultural access. Although I had actively supported Sarah's connections with her aboriginal culture and heritage, I strongly believed that it was in her best interest to live with me on a full-time basis. I did not have faith in the justice system doing the right thing for Sarah.

Eventually, friends and a good lawyer persuaded me to let the father know we were leaving and settle a custody agreement. A short legal battle with Sarah's father resulted in court-ordered joint custody. I was allowed to continue to have Sarah live with me for much of each year. Her father was given one month's access each summer. This was a very difficult time, as I struggled with a system that would award joint custody of a child to someone who could do nothing more than play with her once in a while, and that would force a child to spend one month a year with a relative stranger.

With the battle behind us, Sarah and I flew off to live with Louise and make our new family. For the sake of my mental health, I was committed to living as a fairly out lesbian in my new community; but for our family's safety, I did not tell Sarah's father that I was living with a woman and I stayed in the closet with my former community.

The first few months of living with Louise passed in a blur. I was exhausted from being the single parent of a baby who did not sleep through the night, ever! And Louise and I had all of the new love delirium and new living/working arrangements craziness that moving into "*the* relationship" brings. Louise told me within the first week that she was committed to doing thirty percent of the child care — a commitment that startled me but never did materialize as planned. After all, she did three-quarters of the care for Sarah while I recuperated under her tender ministrations!

From the beginning, I was very open to Louise's involvement in parenting Sarah. I was committed to our relationship, I recognized Louise's parenting skills, and I couldn't help but see the depth of the relationship that was forming between Louise and Sarah. I have always been glad, and, yes, a little bit proud, that I was able to truly let go of being Sarah's only parent and embrace Louise's role in our family. I did sometimes feel jealous of Sarah's love for Louise. But mostly I celebrated the large amount of love in Sarah's life — love that came from Louise and me and from our small but supportive lesbian community.

One of the issues that came up right from the start was the legal non-recognition of Louise's relationship with Sarah. Louise was investing love and care and time into a relationship where she had no legal standing — particularly if we split up, or if the biological father decided to play more games.

Within six months of Louise and I being together, we set down a written, loving agreement. It was our commitment ceremony, made with only each other as witnesses, on the anniversary of falling in love. In the agreement, I promised Louise that I would support her relationship with Sarah even if we broke up. We hung onto that promise as we faced the challenges and fears of the next few years.

Nine months after I moved to live with Louise, Sarah's biological father made some waves about custody. I got advice from a lawyer about how to live up to the custody order while protecting Sarah, and ourselves as lesbian parents. We were to offer him the access provided by the custody order, but to insist on a certain amount of notice if she was to be away for one month (as it turns out, he never has made that access happen for Sarah). We were also advised not to rock the boat for as long as possible. The longer Sarah lived with Louise and me in our new home, the better chance we would have if it came to another legal tangle over custody.

That custody scare was enough to prompt me to make a will which named Louise as Sarah's guardian. I also bought life insurance to pay for any custody fight and to give Louise money to raise Sarah if I died. Another part of my strategy about custody was to keep track of all contacts by Sarah's biological father, to show how little interest he had in her. I had done this since she was born, and it had helped in the first custody battle. After about two years of our family living together, I added this detailed information about the father's non-involvement to my will, and I have continued to keep track of it ever since. Lots of information about the daily role Louise plays as a parent to Sarah was also included in my will.

At about the same time, I approached my family about my wishes if I died. I made it very clear that I expected them to support Louise in any custody fight. I talked with one brother, who is a lawyer, about being the person who would telephone the biological father. And I asked all of my family to bear witness to Louise's role as one of Sarah's parents. As well, I again increased my life insurance.

After four years of being together, Louise and I asked a lawyer if we still needed to be worried that Sarah's biological father would learn of my lesbianism and sue for custody. The lawyer said that the length of time during which Louise had been Sarah's parent was on our side, but we would be better off if the father didn't find out until Sarah was in school. Although lesbianism is not supposed to be an issue in Canadian family law, "why test it?" has continued to be our approach.

Still, no matter what we have done to protect Louise and Sarah's relationship, a simple phone call from the father can trigger our fears about custody. We have tried to support each other. I have regularly reaffirmed my commitment to Louise's continued relationship with Sarah. And, whenever we can, we strengthen the legal and family supports for Louise's role as Sarah's parent.

With some relief, and a great deal of trepidation that our daughter had moved further outside our sphere of influence, Sarah started school this year. We registered as co-parents with the local department of education (we think we are the first same-sex parents to do so in this area). We showed up together or in rotation at school, and joined the home and school association as a family. The school had to deal with an openly "lesbian family." It appears that all of the teachers have been informed, as at least one of the teachers was prepared to tell other parents that a lesbian family had a child in grade one when the subject of alternative families came up.

We did feel that Sarah should be at least somewhat prepared about the lesbian issue before she started school. It was brought to a head the day last spring when Sarah danced around the house singing Alix Dobkin's line, "Every woman can be a lesbian." I talked to her about how some people wouldn't like it that her parents were lesbians. After an aside about what a lesbian was and whether she knew any (although Louise and I have been openly affectionate all along and Sarah really is raised in lesbian culture, we're still working on that one, at least outside of her immediate family!), we talked about discrimination. This was not a new concept, because we had talked about how some people would discriminate against her because she is aboriginal. Sarah was not very interested in pursuing the topic, but it was a start.

From the time Sarah and I moved in, Louise and I were out as lesbian parents in the lesbian and feminist community. But we have come out much more slowly in the community at large. This is partly because we don't mingle a lot in the larger community (we have our own business with female employees who are mostly lesbian) and also because we live in a very traditional community where you can be quite comfortably lesbian as long as you don't name it.

That slow pace has contributed to undervaluing and failing to recognize Louise's role in Sarah's life, and failing to affirm that we are a family. It is only after four years that the woman who cuts Sarah's and my hair understands that Louise is much, much more than a "great babysitter." It is only in the last year that the neighbourhood families, whose daughters have played with Sarah since we moved here, have grappled with the word "lesbian" with respect to us.

In hindsight, and despite all our intentions to protect Louise and Sarah's relationship legally, I continued, inadvertently, to contribute to Louise's invisibility. A classic example of this occured when we were at a party and Louise's lesbian sister, who by that time had had an ongoing relationship with Sarah for over three years, wanted to know what word to use to define her relationship with Sarah. I had to struggle to call her Sarah's aunt! Another example: at a recent local women's festival, two other lesbian mothers and I put on a workshop about lesbian parenting. We didn't understand the importance of including at least one non-biological mother as a workshop facilitator. No wonder Louise feels invisible, if I, too, hide her role in Sarah's life!

Although I still have work to do in order to live up to my commitments to Louise regarding Sarah, I do believe that putting legal support for Louise's relationship with Sarah in my will, and buying life insurance to protect that relationship if I die, were very constructive and positive steps to take. Yet these options, which also include consulting a lawyer when we get really scared about custody issues, are only available to us because we can afford them.

There are many other steps that we have taken to acknowledge and support Louise's role in Sarah's life and to honour our family. I made a clear commitment to Louise that her relationship with Sarah will continue even if we break up. I talked to my family about my expectations that they will support Louise's custody bid if I die. We show ourselves to be a lesbian family in our lesbian/feminist community, in the neighbourhood, in our political/social volunteer activities and at school. These are inclusive ways in which we can support Louise's parenting role and celebrate the love we share — in our lesbian family, and with the friends around us.

Still Family After All These Years

KATE WALKER & JESSICA WALKER

Kate

SHE DISAPPEARED FROM MY LIFE WHEN I WAS TWELVE. SHE HAD BEEN PART OF our lives for five years. She taught me how to sketch, took me horseback riding. We had fun together. She cared about me and I loved her.

My mother and I stopped seeing her and I wasn't told why. When I asked why we couldn't see her, the answers I was given were from that part of the adult world that a child comes to know as off limits, part "you are too young to understand" and part "this doesn't concern you." I didn't find her again until I was forty-two, the year I came out.

My mother met Joyce in a foreign country in 1954. They met at a party, and had a sudden and powerful attraction for each other. Returning to North America, they divorced their husbands and moved to the west coast, each with a young daughter. We all shared the next few years, living together or near each other, spending summer holidays at a lakeside cabin, mothers working, daughters going to school, lives entwining. Then, suddenly, it was over.

According to 1950s conventions, women were supposed to be devoted wives and perfect mothers who raised model children. They weren't supposed to be overcome with lust for each other and fall into bed at every opportunity. Women without men could live together as girlfriends, but wouldn't they have separate bedrooms? I haven't had enough time to talk with Joyce yet about how she and my mother managed to live together as lovers for five years in the straight fifties. But I want to know what they told friends and family. Did they have to hide their love from everyone, or were there some people they could confide in? And what did my family think, particularly my grandmother?

Joyce has told me that it was pressure from my grandmother that finally forced an end to their relationship. As the daughter of an old, established San Francisco family, my grandmother had had a conventional upbringing that placed great value on propriety. She must have been concerned about "appearances." Was she also concerned about how her daughter's behaviour would affect *her* granddaughter? Was she worried about my sexuality?

Divorce wasn't common among my mother's friends in the mid-1950s, but my mother had already been married twice before she met Joyce. When those marriages ended, the grown-ups talked about "divorce," and explained enough for a child to understand that their world would continue, but under new conditions. But the separation from Joyce was not explained to me, just as our relationship to each other had never been explained to me. I had to wait until my late teenage years to discover the word "lesbian," and until the middle of my life to reconnect with that world of women loving women.

Sometimes I imagine what it would have been like to grow up in a household where the primary relationship in my mother's life was acknowledged and given a name. There are photographs of Joyce and my mother together. I can tell from the look in my mother's eyes that this was perhaps the happiest time of her life. It's those photographs of the two of them, and of all of us together, that make it possible for me to remember when we were a family. Had that model been openly there for me, perhaps I would have followed it sooner.

I never heard from my mother herself about the true nature of her relationship with Joyce. It was years after my mother had died, and I had fallen for a woman myself, that I found Joyce again. She told me what I suspected — that yes, she had loved my mother. I remembered the great compassion and caring this woman had for my mother. But had her love been returned? That's what I wanted to find out.

Joyce told me what my mother never did: that they had been lovers, and that even though Joyce had loved other women, my mother had been the big love of her life. I had called her one summer evening, desperate to find confirmation of what I suspected about the two of them as a way to help myself. I'd had little previous contact with lesbian culture, and no one else to talk to. I was head-over-heels, truly, madly and, as it turned out, deeply in love with a woman for the first time in my life, and wanted to find someone to tell me it was okay.

Joyce reclaimed a bond with me that night as we talked on the telephone. She was totally *there* for me. Through the telephone wire, I could hear that she knew exactly what I was feeling. She told me about the joy that such a tremendous love had brought to her, but also about the division her lesbianism had caused within her own family. I had not seen her since I was twelve years old and had only had one previous telephone conversation with her in thirty years, yet, here Joyce was, sharing everything with me, illuminating parts of my own life history that my flesh and blood family had kept hidden.

It would have meant a great deal to me if my mother had taken me into her confidence, and told me about Joyce — even years later, when she could have talked to me as adult woman to adult woman. But, as a dear friend who is of my mother's generation reminded me, it would have been extremely difficult for my mother to talk to me about being a lesbian, and she most likely wanted to protect me from having to carry the burden of that knowledge. My mother chose not to tell me for reasons now known only to her. She took her own life, ending a third and very unhappy marriage. I don't think there was any one particular event during her sixty-three years that made her choose to end her life. There were probably layers of unhappiness. Losing Joyce was one part of it. My mother lived many years after their separation, but I don't believe she was ever truly happy again.

I wasn't going to keep my mother's sexuality a secret from her grandchildren, however, particularly my two older daughters, who knew their grandmother. They knew that she was often unhappy and difficult, especially during the daily "cocktail hour," when her misery found solace in socially accepted drinking. Maybe knowing something of her real life would help them understand her better. I wanted them to know that she hadn't always been miserable, and I wanted them to see what I saw in the photographs of the two lovers together in the 1950s.

Not sharing my own new-found lesbianism with my own children wasn't an option for me. I couldn't imagine lying to them or trying to hide something so wonderful. Coming out later in life has been compared to having a second adolescence, and my children would have known something was up during those giddy, heady days of romance! They have also made it so easy for me to tell them, and have never been anything but accepting of who I am. Most important, there aren't secrets between us, and they know that I trust them and trust myself.

During my three-year relationship with a woman, my young son formed a bond with my lover, much as I had, as a child, with Joyce. But this time the now-absent lover hasn't disappeared into a void without acknowledgement. The morning we told my son that my lover was going to be leaving us, he cried and we all stayed home from school and work that day and spent a lot of it in tears. Now, when he tells me he misses her, I can sympathize with his loss. When he tells me he wants to see her, I feel I have the right to ask her to take him into account. She may not be part of his life forever, but at least he will know that the bond between them was valued, and she can ease him into a different kind of friendship with her.

Meanwhile, Joyce and I are making time to get to know each other again. Even though many miles separate us, I have a wonderful "connected" feeling knowing she is part of my life again. We still need more time to talk about the years we were part of the same family. I have yet to get to know Joyce's daughter, but I'm pleased to know that we both still like the same cereal we ate as children. Childhood memories I had lost have started to come back — times and places and events. That's what families do. They remind the kids of what they were like when they were little, telling stories about them to help them hold on to those memories.

Joyce is coming for a visit soon. We'll have time to work on the revival of our family. I want her to get to know my children, to come to my son's soccer games and go trick-or-treating with us on Hallowe'en. I want her to go hiking with my dyke friends, go dyke-watching on Commercial Drive, and take her dancing at the *Lotus*.

I presume a familial responsibility exists between us, and that we have the right to ask for certain things from each other. She was my co-mother for a time, and I was her daughter. Now that we have found each other again, I want us to include each other in our lives, and I feel tremendously grateful that she feels the same way.

Jessica

"Your mother is a lesbian" sounds like a schoolyard taunt akin to "your mother wears army boots." If things were really bad, your mother would be a lesbian who wears army boots. It's hard to say what my reaction would have been if my mom had come out when I was a child or a teenager instead of an adult. I like to think I would have accepted it with aplomb and understanding, but I feel that there would also have been a fair amount of panic at the prospect of somehow being different from my peers at a time when conventionality is a prized trait. I also think that I wouldn't really have understood what such a declaration meant for her: to what extent her identity and her life would change and to what extent they would remain the same.

As it was, I became aware of my mother's lesbianism in a most natural way: I watched her fall in love. As her friend became more and more a part of family dinners and other events, I felt that there was more to their relationship than friendship. They were never publicly intimate before my mother told us, but there are gestures — a look, the way a hand rests briefly on a shoulder — that are particular to love no matter what one's sexual orientation. Several months earlier my mother had told me of my grandmother's relationship with Joyce, and we had cried over the tragic way that they had been forced apart. We both felt that their parting had repercussions throughout my grandmother's life and contributed to her eventual suicide. I wondered if, at least in part, my mother was trying to correct this past injustice, having a woman lover just to prove a point.

When my mother asked if we could have a talk one day, I knew what she wanted to tell me. I also knew by then that she was happier than I had ever seen her and that her relationship was more than a means of identifying with my grandmother. I wanted my mother to be with someone who loved her and whom she could love, and beyond that I felt that her life, particularly her sexual life, was her own. Our relationship as mother and daughter could only be strengthened if she was otherwise happy and content.

Directions for Research
About Lesbian Families

MIRIAM KAUFMAN & SUSAN DUNDAS

LESBIAN CHILDBEARING IS A PHENOMENON THAT HAS CHANGED GREATLY IN
North America and Europe in the past two decades. Until
approximately fifteen years ago, most lesbian mothers conceived their children in the context of a heterosexual relationship. When they left those relationships to live as lesbians, many
kept their sexual orientation secret. Those who didn't often
faced custody battles. Many of these women mobilized politically around legal issues. Since that time, a number of factors
have shifted the emphasis in lesbian child rearing and lesbians
are having children openly as lesbians, usually within relationships, but sometimes as single parents. Politically, the gay rights
movement engendered a climate of openness among gays and
lesbians. Secrecy, which was a major barrier to accessing reproductive technology, became much less prevalent. "Gay pride"
led us to challenge previously held beliefs that we were less than
"real" or complete women, and led us to a recognition of the
urge to parent as a legitimate feeling for lesbians. At the same
time, the technology of alternative insemination by donor
sperm (A.I.) became demystified, partially as a result of the
women's health movement. In centres where A.I. was not easily
available to lesbians through clinics, women learned how to do
it themselves and created networks to disseminate the information.

The legal issues now are those of the rights of a donor,
anonymity, the legal role of the non-biological mother, and
custody issues when lesbian relationships break down. As
families diversify in these and other ways in the next decade,
legal and public policy will also be evolving. Research into child
development in this changing situation, attachment, self-esteem

and family stress will be valuable in facilitating public policy changes. Research will also help us find the knowledge that we crave as parents: What do other people tell their children? How do lesbian parents help their children deal with homophobia? In what ways do our children develop differently from mainstream children?

Research to Date

Canadian statistics on the number of parents and children in lesbian families are difficult to find. Statistics Canada does not gather information regarding sexual orientation. In 1981, it was estimated that there were over two million lesbian mothers in the United States (Hanscombe, 1981). More recent estimates from the U.S. suggest that there are between three and eight million gay and lesbian parents in the United States, raising between six and fourteen million children (Martin, 1993). So, using the ten percent rule, we would guess that there are about a half million gay and lesbian parents in Canada, raising a million or so children.

Activists have challenged researchers who denigrate home environments that differ from the traditional family by virtue of race, ethnicity, income, household composition, and/or maternal employment. It has become clear that many types of families can foster the healthy psychological development of children (Patterson, 1992). "The lesbian and gay baby boom is creating a culture of its own, evolving new definitions of family relationships" (Martin, 1993).

Parental influences are critical in psychosocial development. To the extent that lesbians may provide different kinds of influences than heterosexual parents, the children of lesbians can be expected to develop in ways that are different from children of heterosexual parents. Whether any such differences are expected to be beneficial, detrimental, or nonexistent depends on the viewpoint from which the phenomena are observed.

The idea that homosexuality constitutes a mental illness or disorder has long been repudiated both by the American and Canadian Psychological Association and by the American and

Canadian Psychiatric Association (Blumenfeld & Raymond, 1988). The 1973 version of the DSM, a listing of criteria for mental illnesses, was the first that did not refer to homosexuality as a mental illness. Still, many psychological theories are negative. For example, many emphasize the importance of children having both male and female heterosexual parents for normal psychosexual development (Freud, S., 1905; Mussen, 1969). There may be an assumption that children reared by a lesbian mother have an increased risk of poor peer relationships and of psychiatric disorder because teasing, ostracism, or social disapproval will adversely affect the child. Another assumption is that gay relationships (whether as a result of their nature or of societal disapproval) are more likely to prove transient, and the children will suffer from family disruptions.

Although systematic study of these issues is just beginning, results of research to date have failed to confirm any of these fears. These studies suggest that children usually develop an appropriate psychosexual identity and a typical heterosexual orientation (Green, 1978; Hoeffer, 1981; Kirkpatrick et al., 1981; Golombok et al., 1983). Transience has not been any more characteristic of lesbian relationships than of women's heterosexual relationships (Kenyon, 1970; Golombok et al., 1983). There has not been any evidence to date of increased psychiatric, emotional or relationship difficulties in children raised by lesbians (Golombok et al., 1983).

We could not find any research studies done in Canada. As Canada is distinct from the United States in its politics, culture, and level of acceptance of differences, there may be significant differences in the experiences of lesbian families.

Why More Research?

Despite the lack of evidence for pathology in the development of children raised in lesbian headed families, the legal and political systems in the United States and Canada have been slow to establish laws and policies that protect lesbians and our children from injustices. In the U.S., judicial and legislative assumptions about adverse effects of parental homosexuality on children have often led to lesbians and gay men being denied custody of and/or visitation with their children following divorce (Editors of the *Harvard Law Review*, 1990). In Canada, custody cases are directed on the premise of "the best interests of the child." A great deal of discretion is left in the hands of the judges. There is little to protect lesbian and gay parents and their children in Canada or the U.S. from subjective and arbitrary decisions.

Children may grow up within a two-parent same-sex relationship all of their lives and have no legal status to protect them from losing their non-biological parent if the parents separate or the biological parent dies. To date, no precedents have been set in Canada for second (same sex) parent adoption. There have been some precedents in the U.S., but there are still no regulations guiding these proceedings. Similarly, Canadian children have no right to the estate of a non-biological parent who dies without a will. These issues become even more complex when the biological father is involved or when the nature of the lesbian relationship is kept secret.

There has been important research in the area of the nature of a child's attachment to a parent or "caregiver" (although none of it is focussed on lesbian families). The quality of a child's attachment influences the child's evolving adaptation to the environment. A secure attachment to a primary caregiver, biological parent or not, can have a powerful positive influence on the social, cognitive, and emotional development of that child (Bowlby, 1988). Loss of that important attachment due to separation of the parents, loss of custody or other factors, can have an equally profound negative effect (Bowlby, 1980). In many custody situations, this important research is being taken into account. However, in some provinces and states a child's attachment may be discounted if a parent is homosexual.

Progress is being made in the area of human rights, but successes are slow and sporadic. The defeat of Bill 167 in Ontario made it clear that these decisions will be made in the courts, not legislatively. Recently in Ontario, the *Leschner* decision (1992) affirmed the right of lesbians and gays to receive family benefits from employers. Federally, the *Lorenzen* case (1993) has also affirmed this. Lesbians and gays have been granted the right to marry in some countries. However, rights in Canada have not extended to things such as equal access to reproductive technology, or the ability to qualify as a foster parent. The Income Tax Act defines a spouse as a member of the opposite sex. Therefore, non-biological parents cannot deduct child-care expenses, and a stay-at-home parent cannot be claimed as a dependant of the working parent (LEAF, 1993).

The sporadic and inconsistent nature of these changes reflects society's ambivalence and resistance to acceptance of gay men and lesbians and our contribution to society. The confusing mix of laws and policies serves to emphasize the need for more studies that examine the development of families headed by same-sex couples, most of whom are female. What messages are being given to us and our children? In many cases lesbians still feel forced to keep their lesbian identity a secret; this raises the question of how this secrecy affects their children. Alternatively, how does a lesbian parent's openness about her sexuality influence her children in a society with so many negative or confusing messages?

Internalized homophobia can have a negative effect on self-esteem. Oppression as a woman and as a lesbian, the resultant sense of powerlessness, combined with rejection by relatives or fear of losing employment, may result in a personal feeling of worthlessness or helplessness (Lyons, 1983). Secrecy can result from fears of rejection or from real threats to a homosexual who is "out." Pragmatically and psychologically, a child of a parent who harbours such a secret is not left unencumbered: "Family therapists have examined the family rules surrounding a 'family secret' and the ways in which the sense of something terribly wrong (but unspoken) in the family can be internalized by the child as his/her own defect" (Haley, 1977). Depending upon the degree of secrecy and unconscious guilt surrounding the mother's lesbianism, the child may internalize a sense of shame or "wrongness" without consciously knowing the cause (Lyons, 1983).

Few studies have examined lesbians who have chosen to have children within the context of a lesbian relationship. These families should be the focus of research. There has been little systematic research looking at the development of children of lesbians who have used A.I. Much of the research on lesbian families has been short term and has looked at a narrow range of children from latency age to late adolescence. These studies have not examined infant and preschool development — a time when much of a person's gender and sexual development occurs. In addition, the "father absence" literature looks only at children raised by single heterosexual women. The impact of "father absence" on children of lesbians may be quite different.

Society has not been ready to redefine the family, but new definitions must be developed to protect the children involved. The "natural history" of the lesbian family must be understood. Most studies thus far have attempted to look at myths surrounding potential pathology in lesbian parents and their children. No studies examine children's identity development or their understanding of the role of the biological father in their lives. Other than simple examinations of the differentiation of parental roles in terms of caregiving or housework, there are no published studies of the role of the non-biological parent in the child's life. Finally, the important issue of secrecy regarding sexual orientation hasn't been systematically examined to determine its effect on family or child development. It is not known how families have negotiated this issue in a society which is just beginning to acknowledge their existence.

Little has been done to help lesbian parents and their children sort through the unique questions that face us psychologically and legally in our society. The important theoretical questions that we are beginning to ask about lesbian parenting will contribute to the literature on attachment, father absence, child care, psychosexual development, family law, biotechnical research and civil rights. More importantly, they will give those of us in lesbian families an idea of what other families are experiencing, and advance knowledge of what is to come.

Direction of Research Into Lesbian Families

Research into lesbian families might include:

1. An examination of the "natural psychosocial history" of the lesbian family. This should include a wide variety of family structures, socioeconomic backgrounds, cultures and races. Questions to be addressed include: is there a particular stage in a relationship when lesbians consider parenthood? what decision-making processes are used? what is the impact on the parents of having children? is this different for biological and non-biological parents? what happens to the sex life of parents? what are the common stages in a family's life when the relationship is at most risk? if the relationship ends, how do the parents deal with custody? do single lesbian parents tend to stay single? and many others.

2. A look at the psychosexual, social and emotional development of children reared in lesbian families. This needs to be looked at, not from a point of view of "how are they different from kids in straight families?" but in a way that compares the commonalities and differences amongst lesbian families.

3. An examination of the many models that exist in the lesbian community with regard to fathers. Some families have anonymous donors, others have known donors who are like uncles or friends, and some donors actively co-parent. We should examine these models and the nature of the children's concept of "father." For those children who have no identified "father," are there any effects of father absence? Do they feel significantly different from kids who have fathers? Do they wish they had fathers?

4. An examination of how lesbians with children decide how "out" to be, to the world in general, to those who interact with their kids as teachers, coaches and childcare workers, and to their children. Does this depend on their own self-esteem, how much control they feel they have over their lives, or personal experience? We need to identify any relationship between the degree to which parents are "out" as lesbians, and their own and their children's self-esteem, development, social relationships, family structure and locus of control (the degree to which someone feels that her life is controlled by external versus internal factors).

5. The key role of attachment in the first year of life. This has been studied extensively in heterosexual families. Are non-biological mothers' attachment styles similar to those of biological mothers or fathers, or do they have a unique style? In families where both mothers are biological and nonbiological parents, are there differences in their attachment to the children? Do things like sharing feeding of an infant modify attachment styles?

6. A look at the community or communities with which these kids identify. Do they see themselves as part of the gay or lesbian community, or do they identify more with the groups their families are affiliated with through schools, neighbourhoods, politics, or religion?

7. An examination of the effect homophobia, both the blatant and the more discreet varieties, has on the children in our families. Does it affect how they view themselves? Does it make them more concerned about justice?

8. An examination of the paths that children of lesbians follow towards their knowledge of their own sexual orientation. Is it harder or easier for those of them who are gay to come out than it was for their parents? Can it be difficult for them to "come out" as being heterosexual? Are the rates of teen pregnancy different in lesbian families?

9. A study of the parenting styles of adults who were raised by lesbians. Do males brought up in women's households act more like "mothers" than "fathers"? Do they identify any advantages in having been brought up by lesbians? Are our sons, in some sense, going to grow up to be lesbians?

All research should involve lesbian mothers from a variety of backgrounds in the planning. Participants can be kept informed of the progress of the research, and should be given an opportunity to see any material before publication.

Finally, this research will be best done by teams of researchers, with team members bringing a variety of skills and viewpoints to the research.

It is essential that the results of research into lesbian families reaches those in lesbian families, and those who deal with us regularly (teachers, doctors, nurses, child-care workers, etc.). The results also should be shared with the scientific community at large, as this research will contribute to the body of knowledge about the family. Research results should be easily available to those lobbying for legislative changes regarding families.

Research must be made available to the gay and lesbian media. Individual research projects could also develop newsletters to convey their findings to the broader community. With luck, the mainstream media (read by many gays and lesbians) will pick up on these reports and have stories based on the findings.

An international symposium on lesbian families would be an ideal way to disseminate this information, and would also lead to a third generation of research. While policy makers could be invited to the symposium, lesbian families should be the major participants.

Lesbians and their children are looking for information about lesbian families. So are educators and law makers. Lack of available research may have been a key factor in the defeat of Bill 167 in Ontario. Governments fighting for equality legislation must have readily available information. Research can be done in a way that it is inclusive of gay and lesbian families, recognizes that there is no one norm for lesbian families, and is respectful of their experience and input into the research.

The importance of this research is clear: the more information we have, the easier it will be to raise our children, answer their questions about what the future has in store for them, and involve all of society in their (and our) fair treatment.

References

Blumenfeld, W.J. and D. Raymond, *Looking at Gay and Lesbian Life*, (Boston: Beacon, 1988).

Bowlby, J., *Attachment and Loss*, Vol. 3: Loss, sadness and depression, (New York: Basic Books, 1980).

Bowlby, J.A., *Secure Base: Parent-Child Attachment and Healthy Human Development*, (New York: Basic Books, 1988).

Freud, S., "Three Essays on Sexuality," in *The Standard Edition of the Complete Works of Sigmund Freud, Vol. VII*, J. Strachey (ed.), (London: Hogarth Press, 1905), pp. 125-43.

Golombok, S., A. Spencer and M. Rutter, "Children in Lesbian and Single-Parent Households: Psychosexual and Psychiatric Appraisal," *Journal of Child Psychology and Psychiatry*, 24, 4 (1983), pp. 551-72.

Green, R., "Sexual identity of 37 children raised by homosexual or transexual parents," *American Journal of Psychiatry*, 135 (1978), pp. 692-97.

Haley, J., *Problem Solving Therapy*, (San Francisco: Jossey-Gass, 1977).

Hascombe, E. and J. Forster, *Rocking the Cradle: Lesbian Mothers, A Challenge in Family Living*, (Boston: Alyson Publications, 1981).

Hoeffer, B., "Children's acquisition of sex-role behavior in lesbian mother families," *American Journal of Orthopsychiatry*, 51 (1981), pp. 536-44.

Kenyon, F.E., "Homosexuality in the female," *British Journal of Hospital Medicine*, 3 (1970), pp. 183-206.

Kirkpatrick M., C. Smith and R. Roy, "Lesbian mothers and their children: a comparative survey," *American Journal of Orthopsychiatry*, 51 (1981), pp. 545-51.

LEAF (The Women's Legal Education and Action Fund), "Litigating for Lesbians: LEAF's Report on Consultations with the Lesbian Community," (Toronto: LEAF, June 1993).

Lyons, T. A., "Lesbian Mothers' Custody Fears," in *Women Changing Therapy*, Joan H. Robbins and Rachel J. Siegel (eds.), (New York: Haworth Press, 1983), pp. 231-40.

Martin, A., *The Lesbian and Gay Parenting Handbook*, (New York: Harper Collins, 1993).

McGuire, M. and N. Alexander, "Artificial insemination of single women," *Fertility and Sterility*, 43 (1985), pp. 182-4.

Mussen, P. H., "Early Sex-role Development," in *Handbook of Socialization Theory and Reseach*, D.A. Goslin (ed.), (Chicago: Rand McNally, 1969), pp. 707-31.

Patterson, C. J., "Children of Lesbian and Gay Parents," *Child Development*, 63 (1992), pp. 1025-42.

Raising
Children

lesbian/motherhood

CHRISTINA STARR

I AM A LESBIAN, I AM A MOTHER, I AM A WRITER. IT MAKES SENSE THAT I SHOULD write about being a lesbian mother. However, when I sit down to consider what it is I want to say, where it is that these identities intersect and what's important about that, I find they don't.

Well, of course they do in a number of unintentional, unavoidable, day-to-day ways, the way pick-up sticks will randomly lie across each other once you toss them on the floor. But what is the container? I ask myself. What is the box that holds these different pieces of identity together, side by side, organized, picked up, contained? If I am going to describe it, make some insightful and useful comments about it, try to better understand the situation of lesbian motherhood for my own benefit and the benefit of others creating their own containers for the various and colourful sticks of their identity, what will I say?

I ask this because I find my lesbianism and my motherhood don't necessarily intersect. I don't parent the way I parent because I am a lesbian. I wasn't a lesbian when I chose to become a mother; rather, my daughter is the product of a long-term heterosexual relationship that ended when she was two-and-a-half years old. She was young enough at the time of this separation not to look back at the way things were as the way things are supposed to be. She also has enough friends whose parents live in similar situations — whether they are a separated straight couple, a gay man and lesbian woman, or two lesbian women no longer in a relationship — for it not to seem very strange. And because nobody's ever told her it's not "normal," she does not think it an issue one way or another that her mommy prefers the company of women, loves to kiss and hug women, and that sometimes they stay overnight (in fact, she's developed the courtesy of sometimes asking them to stay before I do). Given the number of women-only events we attend, the woman-centred feminist work I do, the woman-celebrating festivities that are part of our lives, I wouldn't be surprised if she thought that being with women was the only natural choice.

She has some political awareness. She knows women need to march together to declare our right to be safe ("and children too" she adds); she knows that as a woman she should have the right to abortion and she knows that women and children have an unusual risk of being hurt. She knows that women can love women and men can love men. But I have not yet much pressed the political nature of lesbian identity with her because so far I am enjoying the luxury of taking it for granted, of living with someone who never questions its rightness, who has not yet — in her short life — ever considered the possibility of questioning it at all. Not that to map out the political nature of lesbian identity is to question it, but it is to acknowledge that others will question it and that the "truth" for some out there is completely different from the reality she lives at home. As a mother, I have to face the necessity of letting her explore her own truths (while guiding her); of letting her tell me some days, "You're wrong mommy"; of letting her find out what the right-wing, homophobic agenda is and decide for herself its validity. I know, as most parents do, that sometimes it's the things you sound the most sure of that become the points of disagreement, become the opportunities for children to stake out independent opinions, no matter how ridiculous or impossible.

And because I'm her mommy, and there's no one else in the world who could be her mommy, no one else she would want to be her mommy, she would not toss the slightest bit of credibility towards a position that de-legitimizes my motherhood because of my sexual orientation. How do you discuss something that doesn't make sense? To identify the contentious, political, or controversial nature of the intersection between lesbianism and motherhood is almost irrelevant since I cannot imagine not being her mother and she could not imagine not being my daughter. And in my fortunate case, my being lesbian has not been cause for any controversy with others who are close to us — not with her father, her father's family, nor my own family. As a lesbian I am happier with myself, with my life and with my freedom, and this certainly must affect the way I behave as a mother. But I still find no immediate, intentional, pressing or unavoidable way in which my being lesbian directly affects my being the one to open up my arms and catch a running flight of flesh and bones colliding with the impact of love.

Do my lesbianism and my motherhood not intersect because I happen to be fortunate? Because I've not been through, at least not in a painful way, the fight of having to justify being a lesbian while being a mother or justify being a mother while being a lesbian? Because I've avoided making an issue out of it, the way feminist mothers may avoid talking directly about sexism to their daughters because they want them to be purely strong, unspoiled by any idea that the breadth of their horizons or the limits of their identities could be questioned? It's like not telling her about the war because you don't want her to run off and be killed. Of course, we leave our children in ignorance at their peril, or at least at the mercy of their own uninformed and unguided curiosity.

Perhaps I'm the one who's trying to live the life of unquestioned existence, who's trying hard not to see how being a lesbian has any impact on being a mother: I would like to live in a world where anthologies on lesbian motherhood are not politically necessary. I do not question, and could not conceive of questioning, my right to be her mother; I do not question, but could conceive of questioning (or at least could conceive of the question), my right to be a lesbian. I do not have to defend my choice to be her mother (or to be a mother); I do, of course, have to defend my existence as lesbian, but not to my daughter. I have not, so far, except in a broader political way, had to defend my existence as a lesbian mother. And I have not been pressed to explain to her, nor have I taken the initiative to explain to her, why defending my existence as a lesbian mother might be necessary.

But I do not feel that my being lesbian much informs my motherhood, nor that my motherhood much informs my lesbianism. I remember reading sometime, somewhere, that Nicole Brossard felt a compelling and urgent need to be in touch and in intimacy with women after giving birth to her daughter. I did not feel that. If anything, I stuck through two more years of a very unnurturing relationship because at first we shared the joy of our daughter and then because I struggled with the social expectations that I should work it out with her father so we could all stay together. My choice to explore relationships with women had nothing to do with being a mother; it was propelled by my own needs and desires, which I am certain would have surfaced regardless of motherhood. I am a mother, and I hold strong beliefs and philosophies about motherhood which have been formed out of being a mother, not out of being a lesbian. I am a lesbian, and I hold strong beliefs and philosophies about lesbian existence, which have been formed out of being lesbian, not out of being a mother. The one identity which informs both more than anything and which keeps them connected, like thread running through two disparate pieces of fabric, is that I am also a woman.

As a woman, I know what it means to be oppressed. I know what it means to be convinced that I belong to a lesser class of human being, that I am not capable of achieving much, that I do not have much right to take up space in the world. I know what it means to have my self-esteem humiliated out of me, to be ruthlessly critical of myself for not meeting some oppressive standard of beauty, charm, thoughtfulness or compliance. I know what it means to feel that love is conditional on some erasure of myself. I do not want my daughter to feel any of this.

It is feminism, then, which most informs my motherhood and, perhaps, which most informs my lesbianism. Since my daughter was very young, I have endeavoured to parent by putting her above social conventions, unnecessary restrictions, and my own internalized expectations. I'd much rather have her offend, annoy, or uncomfort other people than circumscribe her behaviour, and this is sometimes amusing, sometimes challenging. I have not instructed her not to "bother" or impose herself on others; she considers it a matter of course to communicate with those around her and I am proud of her assumption. Sometimes it means we stop to talk to a woman sitting quietly in a park so my daughter can share the fact that she has the same sandals. Sometimes it means not silencing her interest in the difference between herself and a person with a disability. Sometimes it means allowing her to insist on a response from someone on the subway to whom she's posed the question "What's your name?" If she hurts herself or loses her patience in a park or other public space, I check the urge to silence her so that other people don't have to hear her cry. And, though sometimes it's hard, I try not to get caught up in wanting to win an argument with her, in forcing her to comply because it's so much easier for me.

Our society is not set up to nurture kids or to take into account their needs or desires. When I am asking her for the third time to get dressed in the morning so that she can go to daycare and I can go to work, I have to remember that she is not maliciously being petulant or uncooperative. She did not choose this system of work that pulls her mommy away from her every morning and throws her back at the end of the day when we are both tired and sometimes grumpy. Because the child's world of immediate emotions, immediate pleasures, and self-centredness so often collides with the adult world of repressed emotion, delayed pleasure, and concern for our impact on others, it's easy to forget that we are the ones with all the power. We often feel impatient and thwarted but we are our children's agents in the world, without whom nothing can happen, not a glass of milk, not a scrap of love.

My approach to parenting, then, to mothering, is based on always acknowledging my daughter as an individual, due respect, concern and attention the same as any other individual, from myself and from everybody else. The catch is that this is much harder work since children do not repress their emotions, their needs, their frustrations or their right to demand your attention. And it is terribly rewarding since they also do not repress their pleasures, their joy, their wisdom or their folly. But such an approach has nothing, or very little, to do with the fact that I am a lesbian. Heterosexual or bisexual mothers could also practice it; all those who believe in social justice might want to parent this way, to treat their children with compassion and respect so that they learn to treat others this way, to break the cycle of domination and oppression that so permeates all our social, cultural, political and religious institutions.

But my parenting remains unshaped by my lesbianism in another crucial way. I have, at present, no permanent partner. And this is, I think, how my being a mother affects my being a lesbian. In the time-consuming, draining and make-your-head-spin world of child-rearing, work, daycare, volunteerism, political activism, and keep-up-with-your-friends, there's not a whole lot of time or energy left to meet new people. When new people do come along, schedules are often so conflicting as to make it hard to get together more than once every two weeks. And then there's the cost — both financially and emotionally — of babysitting. I do have considerable non-parent time when my daughter stays with her father; I am often exhausted, doing chores or errands, trying to fit in time with a friend, or trying to finish what I've started writing.

Which poses the question: how do those of us with children meet new lovers? Many lesbians I know who have children decided to do so within a committed relationship. But those don't always last. Some of us end up single with children, and finding a date also means finding someone responsive to our needs as mothers and to the existence of our children. Being a single mother (even with a supportive co-parent) means not necessarily being interested in the bar scene, or if interested, not going often or staying late. It means not having the time to get involved in social, political or cultural groups, where new faces might be expected. It means trying to fit a love life around the demands of child-rearing, and when children get sacrificed for so much else — work (paid and unpaid), fatigue, time to oneself — it can get hard to justify.

I've recently joined the Out & Out club of Toronto (a leisure and recreation organization for gays and lesbians) with the hope of diving into some activities and surfacing in the company of other women. However, I've just read that though the membership count for 1994 is a healthy 925, less than one-third of those members are women. Very few pictures in the newsletter, teasingly flaunting the fun and games of Out & Out activities, capture the smiling faces of women. Most of the contact names for scheduled activities are men. Though the promotional brochure promises that the club is "a great way to meet new people" (nudge, nudge), I'm not necessarily on a mission to increase the number of my gay male friends. And I am willing to bet that a very small percentage of these people, including the few women, who are jumping from a white water raft to a vertical rock face to cross country skis to the twice monthly Saturday afternoon book club, have children.

Should it be possible to make that special connection with someone, the rest is not easy. As mothers we already have (at least) one intense, demanding relationship. It's also unpredictable. What if you're on your way out the door for a date, and your kid gets sick? What if you bring your date home, see the babysitter out, start together towards your bedroom, and the little one wakes up? What if your daughter wants to sleep with you, all night every night? And when you get it all organized, have a perfect date and a perfect night of love making because it's your co-parent's turn and you have your house to yourself, you're exhausted, crabby and short-tempered when you have to be a mom again because you haven't had enough sleep and because you won't see *her* again for three more days. A perfect set-up for strain at both ends, with the resulting tear down the middle.

But I don't want to stay dateless, loverless, celibate. That's not fair. Even as a straight woman (even as a twelve-year-old girl witnessing the unhappiness of my mother) I did not ever think it a reasonable arrangement to expect only one, or even two, adults to be responsible for the care and demands of children. As lesbians we are often not expected to have children, despite the growing frequency with which lesbian women are choosing to become mothers. And we are still expected to be responsible for those children ourselves. I want to share this joy and this burden. I want my daughter to feel safe — and I want to know she's safe — with another caregiver when I'm dizzy about some woman and can't wait to be with her alone. I think the work and pleasure of child-rearing should be a shared responsibility in the gay community, not only amongst the women but also amongst the men. We women — even lesbian women — still do so much of the caretaking in the world, it's high time that gay men, who are often without children of their own, throw a little energy our way.

So a solution occurs to me. I will become an event leader for Out & Out and organize a day at the Royal Ontario Museum for gay men in the company of the children of lesbians. We will do a training weekend first (as is usually offered to those new to certain "sports") including: the rudiments of first aid, negotiating skills, bathroom and/or diaper management, nap time, places to go, explanations to give, allowable treats, times to say yes, and ways of saying no without saying no. It can become a regular event, like the bookclub, the bingo night, or the movie outing. We'll charge a fee, too, because the economic burden of raising children should be shared, and because becoming a child's friend and caregiver is an important and transferable skill that many gay men would not otherwise have the opportunity to gain.

We'll start it out as an afternoon, increase it to a day, and eventually to a whole weekend, so that we lesbian mothers can go off canoeing in the wilderness secure in the knowledge that our children are well and competently cared for. There can be overnight visits during the week so that we know we have one extra night to ourselves. The lives of gay men will be enriched immeasurably by the relationships they form with children, the children will mature with matter-of-fact acceptance not only of woman-to-woman but of man-to-man relationships, and we lesbian mothers might just be able to have a love life.

And this, finally, may be how my lesbianism and my motherhood integrate. As a public and visible organizer for shared child care, I will no doubt be pushed to defend the right of homosexual people to interact with and be the parents of children. As a lesbian with a lover, I will no doubt have to defend my daughter's right to be exposed to, enmeshed in, lesbian lifestyle. With such attention drawn to us, I will no doubt be pressed to explain to her why some people think I cannot love both her and another woman. Never again will my house be the non-political haven of lesbian parenting that it is today. My best hope, however, is still to preserve her unquestioned acceptance of who I am and who I love. If I can do that, I know, by the strength of her love, that I will have a fierce and unfailing ally beside me for the rest of my life.

Gender, Sexuality & the Schoolyard

ELISE CHENIER

~~~

> Throughout her childhood the little girl suffered bully-
> ing and curtailment of activity; but nonetheless she felt
> herself to be an autonomous individual. In her relations
> with family and friends, in her schoolwork and her
> games, she seemed at the time a transcendent being: her
> future passivity was only a dream.
> — "The Young Girl," Simone de Beauvoir, *The Second Sex*

IT WAS A QUIET AFTERNOON, JUST THE TWO OF US AT HOME ON THE FIRST WARM
day of spring. The sun was beating a path along my green shag
carpet, tempting me to do something completely wild.

I loaded my camera with film.

Using the dining room table, a stool and some white sheets,
I built a small throne. From the back of my closet I retrieved a
pink satin nightgown, and from the bottom of Natasha's play
basket I gathered two strings of fake pearls. And just because I
had some, I brought with me a tube of pink lipstick. Mommy
wants to play photographer. And Natasha's going to play dress
up.

At the age of three, putting on a nightgown was not Natasha's
idea of fun. Sitting on the table, however, was the thrill that kept
her still long enough for me to capture her on film. But I know
now, as I knew then, that this wasn't so much about capturing
her as it was about capturing myself in a moment of intense
conflict: what I was doing flew in the face of everything I wanted
parenting to be. I was reconstructing oppressive Western codes
of femininity, and documenting it. I was being bad, and I knew
it.

That was in the heyday of my feminist parenting practices
when Natasha did not challenge my choice of clothes, games,
and television programs. Back then, she could move easily from

butch to femme and back again without a second thought. But, not unlike the feminist movement itself, there eventually came a time of reckoning with the real world. For us, it happened in senior kindergarten.

Natasha and I went head-to-head every morning from mid-September to November. No longer content with Mommy's choice of day wear, my daughter jockeyed for position on the issue of dress each and every day. But you can't climb trees in a dress, I insisted, and you will scuff your knees. No matter. She had to wear a dress. Lulu, after all, said so. And Lulu knows because she wears dresses every day. My opponent was a four-year-old. The hierarchy of power was shifting beneath me and all I could do was curse as I tumbled downward to the bottom of the heap.

Ironically, all this occurred at a time when I was beginning to tire of my own butch persona in the lesbian community, and began reclaiming my "Rocker Chick" past. Partly motivated by Joan Nestle, the resilient New York femme, and partly as a result of my adventures into s/m sex, I refused to devalue the very qualities that had got me through the minefield of hetero-sexual youth culture. After all, part of the appeal of the lesbian sexual economy was that I could continue to exert agency without the moral baggage that had been utterly oppressive to me as a young heterosexual woman. But agency in my peer group meant Doc Martens, loose tee-shirts and belted jeans hooked on the cusp of your hips, a real challenge for my post-natal physique. Natasha and I both wanted something different. Playing with feminine roles was *exactly* what we were doing. The question then was, how would I keep Natasha from ever taking it seriously?

But it was serious. The battle over Natasha's desire to wear dresses to school and my refusal to allow her to do so more than once a week profoundly affected our daily lives. For the first time, she waged a sustained campaign of resistance against my arbitrary and unjust use of power over her. She refused to cooperate. My commitment to non-coercive parenting was pushed to the wall. I constantly re-evaluated my position, swinging from intense emotional turmoil over our growing dislike of each other, to a kind of firm militancy that refused to capitulate to the tantrums of a four-year-old. Finally, I relinquished control and gave Natasha almost full reign over her wardrobe choices. She was in her glory. And Natasha and Lulu were inseparable for the rest of the school year.

Shortly afterward, Natasha turned her attention towards me. She began to police my behaviour and appearance. You wear boys' shoes, she insisted, and your hair is too short. I refused to engage in any more intelligent discussion about the issue. You dress the way you want, I retorted, but don't try to tell other people how they should look. Her response was interesting. If she couldn't dress me the way she wanted, she could draw me the way she wanted: with triangle skirts and a Doris Day "hair do," Natasha's mommy blended well with all the other mommies proudly displayed on the senior kindergarten walls. Why does she do this? I asked my own mother. Because, my mother said matter-of-factly, that's the way mothers look. Oh.

In that year, almost everything became gendered. There were boy toys and girl toys, boy clothes and girl clothes, boy colours and girl colours. It was hard to believe that barely a year had passed since Natasha sat crying in a grocery cart after two children had taunted her for having a "boy's haircut," and here she was doing the same thing. Well, almost. Shortly after the school year began, her best friend refused to play with her anymore.

"Why won't Francis play with you?" I asked.

"Because all he wants to play is Dick Tracy, and they say that only boys can play it."

"Well, what about Lulu and the other girls?"

"All they ever play is puppy."

"What," I was dying to know, "is puppy?"

"You just pretend you're a puppy! It's so boring." She looked up at me in sheer desperation. It took everything to keep the smile from my lips. Finally, a light at the end of the tunnel.

God forbid I should be called a liberal feminist, but I have developed a deeper respect for my "foremothers." I spend my life theorizing difference, attending to complex struggles over representation and sites of (potential) resistance. I know, for example, that there is nothing intrinsically wrong with dresses, but that it is the way dresses function symbolically in white heterosexual North American culture that is problematic. Pro-choice and anti-censorship is not only about abortion and pornography; for me it is the right to choose and the right not to have your choice narrowly defined or legislated against. Which is why I labour over these seemingly insignificant issues. My peers might disagree, but they at least know what I am talking about. My kid, on the other hand, has no idea what lies ahead. She can't see the patriarchy for the frills.

My daughter's pleasure met with danger the following spring. It was a classic scenario, the kind de Beauvoir knew best. On the first warm day of spring, floral cotton wraps hit the playground like a Paris runway. Natasha was not to be left in the cold. I pushed images of gritty sand sticking like glue in the folds of her tender labia to the back of my mind, and put away the tights. Francis moved in for the kill.

"The boys made us show them our underwear," Natasha reported.

Now, most parents, I think, would immediately wonder where the teachers were while the boys were up to their not-so-original tricks. But not I. Fresh from a reading of Susie Bright's *Sexual Reality: A Virtual Sex World Reader*, I scrambled for the road in to this one. Natasha offered no clues: she appeared nonplussed. But obviously it was important enough for her to want to tell me — no doubt this was only one in one hundred events that day.

I checked my initial reaction of overprotective horror, and wondered how I could turn this into a positive opportunity to empower my daughter as a sexual being with private parts who is at liberty to expose them at her own will, while at the same time attend to the very real danger she might face for having the particular set of privates she does. I paused, and finally, approached with caution.

"Did you want to lift up your dress?" I asked.

"They wanted to see our underwear," she said in a very matter-of-fact tone.

Still no clues. I thought about this for a minute and finally it began to dawn on me what this was all about. What my daughter was learning was not about sex, or about bodies, but about the way girls and boys, and women and men, see each other. For example, that spring she informed me that "breasts, Mommy, are called sexies." It wasn't the name that was important, because it was obvious that she didn't know what sexy meant. But she did know that it was something that you said with your eyes cast down and a sheepish grin on your face. Breasts are a body part. "Sexies," however, are the things that boys talk about, point out and make silly about. Two entirely different things. Ordering her not to show her privates would only contribute to the way in which her school chums coded their, and others', bodies. Natasha was looking for a bridge between the way our bodies (hers and mine) are treated at home, and the way her body is treated at school.

"Yes, I know, honey," I persisted, "but did you want to show them?"

She shrugged her shoulders, and was beginning to tire of the conversation. Or maybe, I thought, she was uncomfortable with the way the focus was on her. How could she possibly think that I would be angry or upset with her? Was this like getting cross-examined at a rape trial?

"What matters," I explained, "is that you only do things you want to. If it feels bad, or if someone is asking you to do something that isn't what you want, then you shouldn't do it. And you should get away from them no matter what they say, and tell me or one of the daycare workers about it. It's okay to show your underwear," I reassured her. "But it's not okay for someone to make you do something you don't want to do."

My kid is doubly street proofed; she gets it at home and at school. But this isn't the street, this is the playground. Francis and I both occupy a place in Natasha's life, and are competing for more than meanings. Natasha is hardly able to negotiate the vast chasm that lies between Francis and me — or Lulu and me, for that matter — on her own.

My ability to apply my politics to my parenting style was fine-tuned over the dress issue, and I was ready for sex, which not surprisingly emerged as the spring topic. Sex was *the* issue, in fact, from what it is to who can have it. In order to participate in senior kindergarten culture, Natasha had to unlearn a lot of things that had appeared as obvious truths at home. The first item under attack was same-sex sex. Because I had been out since she was two, I thought I had that covered. Yet despite the supportive queer visibility her daycare teachers provided, the word on the monkey bars was not homo-inclusive.

To combat lesbian invisibility, some friends of mine took an interesting approach. Accompanied by our children, we spent one mild fall afternoon wandering through High Park, a popular spot for families, lovers, and, of course, wedding photo shoots. In fact, as we neared the gardens, we could see a newly-wed couple posing by the petunias. Natasha and I both became excited, she and I being equal and unashamed lovers of wedding gowns. Our friends, however, abruptly steered us in the opposite direction. I looked quizzically at my walking companions.

"We see enough of heterosexual culture," they explained, while literally shielding their daughters' eyes. "We don't need to go looking for it."

My tactics, on the other hand, were lifted from the pages of *On Our Backs*. I wasn't interested in censoring heterosexual culture, I was interested in finding my own pleasure, on my own terms, in whatever garden I might find them. I reluctantly read my daughter lesbian books for kids, but have yet to feel that my lifestyle is accurately represented. And besides, they aren't good stories. With Natasha, reverse discourse is often the most effective tool to challenge some of her monkey-bar notions.

When Natasha was three, a terrifically sporty looking couple walked by the family cottage where my lover, Natasha and I were staying. I screamed "*Lesbians*," from the front room and my lover raced out with tea towel in hand. Where, where? she wanted to know, and I pointed eagerly out the window. We debated their sexuality for a minute or two, until we were interrupted by Natasha. What, she wanted to know, are lesbians?

When people grow up, I explained, they pick a special person to spend time with. Sometimes they live together, I continued, inserting appropriate examples from our roster of friends and family, and sometimes they don't. Sometimes they get married, and sometimes they don't. And sometimes — finally! — they are a man and a woman, and sometimes they are two women, or two men. I am a lesbian because my special person is a woman. It was one of my most eloquent moments, but it was lost to the faulty and inconsistent memory of a three year old. In senior kindergarten, I had to explain "lesbian" so many times that I eventually gave up. It was a word, and she was dealing with concepts. Which is why she responded so violently to my rewriting of one of the most insidious of all children's rhymes: the tree song.

"Lulu and Francis sitting in a tree, k-i-s-s-i-n-g ..." she began, as if I had never heard it before. To me, it had been a vicious weapon used by girls against girls. To Natasha, it was cute. I let her finish, and sang back my own version: "Natasha and Maria ..."

"No!" she screamed. "It has to be a boy and a girl."

"Says who?" I demanded.

"That's what Francis said."

"Oh yeah? Well, who do I kiss?"

"Pauline."

"Is Pauline a boy or a girl?"

Natasha hadn't always been sure. Pauline was my second significant lover since I came out. Natasha had spent the last two years surrounded by young university dykes, and had had no trouble with their gender. Pauline was different. She walked, talked, dressed and looked like a man. Out alone with her one afternoon, Natasha asked her if she was going to be her dad. About a month later, Natasha returned from the park with Pauline to inform me that "Pauline isn't the type of woman to wear a dress." That was during the fall, when I could have strangled her. But by the spring, she was pretty clear on the topic of Pauline's biological sex.

"Pauline is a girl," she replied.

"So? Does it have to be a girl and a boy?" I teased.

The nice thing is that Natasha and I are mother and daughter, not just theory and practice. Natasha is genuinely curious about sex. She has an intimate relationship with her own body, but when she finds out it has a name, and that it is in fact sex, she will probably still want to know about "real" sex. I was up late one night, unable to fall asleep. A sure-fire remedy is those late night news magazine programs, the kind that appeal to that monkey-bar sensibility that exists in all of us. Well, most of us anyway. Natasha woke up in search of a glass of water. Not surprisingly, the "s" word came flying out of the television and landed smack in the middle of our living room.

"What is sex?" Natasha asked, as though she was fed up with the empty euphemism employed by her schoolyard chums.

"Well, it's like a special massage. It makes your body feel good."

Not too long after, we were walking through a shopping plaza, and Natasha, trailing twenty feet behind, shouted: "Mom, do you have sex?"

I blushed of course, and repeated what still seems a pretty good explanation.

She paused for a moment, and asked, "Do we have sex?"

"No, honey," I answered. "But we have lots of love, which is the best thing in the world you can have."

"But Mommy," she cried, grabbing hold of my legs, "it's not fair."

I used to joke with my family and say that when Natasha is prime for rebellion, she'll become a cheerleader and throw her pom poms at me during a dinner party. Boy, am I slow. The same fall that we spent head to head over dresses, she announced over Thanksgiving dinner that when she grew up, she wanted to be "the lady who turns the letters on TV." I wasn't sure which annoyed me more, that she idolized Vanna White or that someone was letting her watch *Wheel of Fortune*. But either way, my kid is going to end up having to figure out how to get from here to there on her own. If she doesn't know Vanna White now, she'll know her later, no matter what vision I may have of the world.

It was my own mother who practised the valuable skill of respecting your children's choices, so long as everyone was safe. Somehow I managed to find my way through the minefield of sex and love and boys and girls. And sometimes the best thing I can do is loan Natasha the map.

Do I Have a Dad?

LAURA BARRY

~❦~

"YOUR DAD IS MY DAD, RIGHT, MOM?" RACHEL, OUR THREE-AND-A-HALF year old, asked.

I let out a huge sigh and wondered how to tackle the situation. "Uh," I said (great beginning), "my dad is your grandpa." I waited. It was enough for her at that moment. Whew, another sigh.

The time had come. I had been presented with the question I had worried about since my daughter was born. Her family does not have a "daddy." I knew I would have to have a more complete explanation ready for her when she decided to pursue the topic. I needed to be able to present her with an answer that she could understand.

The next week, we were sitting at the dinner table at my parents' place when Rachel addressed the subject again. Right out of the blue, she seemed to pick up our previous conversation.

"Grandpa was your dad when you were a little girl, right, Mom?" she asked.

"He still is my dad," I answered.

"And Nana is your mom." She pointed to my mother. Then she looked at me and continued, "And you're *my* mom."

"Right, dear." I waited and watched as she processed all the information. Would she ask who *her* dad was? No, she was distracted from the dreaded question with some more food. Still, I knew that the question would come soon. Was my answer ready?

Some days I felt confident that I would be able to handle "The Question," and other days I would feel that I was not quite ready yet. As Rachel continued to grow, she also presented me with another question — that of (her) creation. And so I realised that the subject of fathers must be addressed in the context of how our children are made.

I always knew that I wanted children — more than one, I was sure of that. When I was a bisexual suburbanite in my mid-twenties, I knew a bit about artificial insemination. However, I opted for a much more acceptable solution (in my family's eyes) to having a child. A brief relationship with a selected father resulted in the quick conception of my baby. During the caesarean section procedure I was fully awake, and I eagerly awaited the doctor's declaration of the baby's sex. "It's a girl," he said. I felt my cheeks crinkle up in the biggest smile imaginable. I had been more anxious about providing a father, should the baby have been born a male, than about being a single parent. At this same point in my life, I came to the realization that I was a lesbian.

My daughter and I lived with my father for three years after Rachel's birth and my father was her male role model for those early years. I call him Dad, and Rachel has followed suit, just as a heterosexual couple's child will sometimes call the father by his first name — the child copies the mother's expressions. Often, I would reinforce to Rachel that my father was her grandpa. She would block that word out. To her, he was "Dad." And, for most purposes, he served as such.

I am now in my thirties, and have settled down in a relationship in which both my partner and I assume co-parenting responsibilities. Rachel is four-and-a-half years old. During most of her early life, I was involved with a parent-child centre, toy-lending library, babysitting cooperative and a cooperative nursery school. Over that time, Rachel and I came to know the other parents quite well, and she saw some of the fathers of her classmates. There they were: those glorious men, doting over their daughters or rough-housing it with the boys. I watched as Rachel tilted her head in awe at the fathers of her friends. They gave great piggyback rides, they indulged in candies for the kids and let them stay up later. I ached when I watched her, wide-eyed with wonder at these men. Nothing I could have said would have altered her observation that dads were neat. And they were something she didn't have.

When I view other families, the mom-and-dad kind, I find myself staring, too. I sometimes see the man, a snugli with a sleeping infant strapped to his chest; or I watch a father wheel a stroller down the street, perhaps accompanied by a dog or an older child on a tricycle. Of course I stare. It's not often that you see men involved in their children's lives so attentively. Most men I've met find kids neat, and, sure, they want them in their lives, but they often leave the bulk of the work to the women.

I remember my weekly trips to the library with Rachel when she was about two years old. In the beginning, I would choose the books to take home and read. Later, when Rachel began asserting her independence, she wanted to make the selection herself. And I found that books I had once taken for granted now made me uneasy, because they had daddies in them and because of how they portrayed families. Occassionally I tried to intervene. "Why don't you want that book?" Rachel would ask me, head titled.

I would pause before answering, "It's just not quite the book that I want to read to you."

"Why not?" Rachel would persist.

"Well ..." I would hesitate. She had me cornered. What could I say? That I didn't want to answer questions about her own daddy?

As my partner and I struggle with basic parenting issues, we have also asked ourselves: What is a dad? What is a father? Are we talking about the man who raises the child alongside the mother? Or do we mean the man whose sperm created a being? Is this person active in the child's life? And, as I rehearse my lines for our talk about dads, I feel that I have come up with a pretty basic explanation for Rachel: Parents are the most important thing. No matter what title you give them, these are the people who will guide and teach the child. I will give Rachel examples of how the world is full of variety — I will point out the great numbers of different animals and also the differences between human beings: the various colours of our skin or eyes; the different types of clothes we wear, houses we live in or cars we drive.

In the past year or so, we have weathered many more questions and comments about dads. Rachel continues to call her grandpa "Dad" on occasion, and I feel my back stiffen in response. Sometimes I correct her word, sometimes I let the issue slide. When I correct her, the insistence in my voice collides with her stubbornness. In the end, I'd like her to know that I am proud to offer her two parents — both women, both lesbians.

With the progressive change from the nuclear family, I feel today's children need to be educated about the different ways of constructing a family. Our feeling is that Rachel doesn't have a "dad" (a term I see as referring to a male parent). We haven't talked about our being a "two-mommy" household since my partner came on the scene when Rachel was two-and-a-half years old. Instead, Rachel refers to my partner by her first name. I am not out to all members of my community, and this gives me some security since the biological father, a man with a criminal past, could jeopardize our situation with a nasty custody battle.

I used to think that the words "father" and "dad" were interchangeable. Now, in the days of gay couples with children, two-dad households exist. A man can father a child, providing the sperm for procreation, but that does not automatically make him a dad, although some men do choose to be involved in the child's life. What about lesbian couples who have a male friend donate sperm for the child? What if he remains involved in that child's life? Is he a dad? A biological father only? To be referred to as "uncle"? There are so many questions for parents of a child without a dad. Even now, cases of donors fighting birth mothers for rights to "their" children are being brought before the courts. It is frightening that these men who helped us create our children would challenge us for parental rights.

Nineteen-ninety-four was named "The Year of the Family." It was a year when gays and lesbians held their breath while the courts voted on whether to grant us equal access to family and spousal benefits. It turned out not to be our time, but we remain hopeful that in some not-so-distant future our families will not only be tolerated but accepted by society. In the meantime, we see ads on television featuring various celebrities talking about the "family": all those wonderful captured moments of Mom, Dad, the kids and the dog frolicking on the beach are enough to make a lesbian mom sick at heart. We must provide our children with positive reflections of our lifestyle.

My partner and I went for the longest time without contact with other lesbian couples with children, so were unable to provide our daughter with positive role models outside the home. As Rachel tries to fit our family into what she sees in her books and in the world around her, I must reinforce the fact that a family with two moms is okay. I don't want to tell her that we don't *need* a daddy, or that we're different.

When Rachel was three years of age, I began my search for some support as a lesbian mother. I phoned the gay community centre, contacted a counselling centre and checked bookstores for information. I could find little help. Eventually, my partner and I found a lesbian mothers' support group in downtown Toronto. We were excited at first about meeting and talking with other women in similar circumstances, but our joy faded when, out of the enormous population of our city, only one other couple and a single mom showed up. Due to the lack of interest, the moderator was forced to cancel our meetings.

Then we joined a lesbian businesswomen's group in our area. We were sure that, out of the thirty women in the group, someone would be a mother or know of a friend who was a lesbian mom. As luck would have it, the co-ordinator of the group passed my phone number on to three other women. Within two weeks, I felt like I had hit the jackpot. I set up meetings with the other moms at McDonalds and then attempted to start a social group for us and our kids. Unfortunately, everyone's needs were not similar and soon this small group disbanded as well. It seemed I was destined to just hang out with the straight moms, and I became discouraged that we would ever be able to provide proper and necessary outside role models for our daughter.

When Rachel plays with her dolls, she often says that there should be a daddy. I gently tell her that a daddy isn't required, giving her the example of a single mother friend of mine. "Sarah and Kathy don't have a daddy, and that's okay."

Once, my partner and I sat in the living room while Rachel and a friend ate their snack in the next room. We overheard their discussion about dads.

"Where's your dad?" Rachel's friend asked.

"I don't have a dad," replied Rachel.

"Of course you do. Everybody's got a dad," her friend insisted.

"I don't." We waited for Rachel to explain that she had her mom and Dawn (my partner). Silence. The continuation of the munching of crackers. I guess the other child hadn't encountered such a situation before. Later we discussed what the child may have asked her parents when she went home (they are friends of ours who know we are lesbians). We were proud that Rachel could stand her ground, but still concerned that we hadn't filled her in on how she came to be.

Just a short while ago, Rachel sat at the kitchen table as I prepared dinner. Again, right out of the blue, she asked, "How are babies made?"

I took a deep breath, put down the paring knife and sat at the table with her. I had to tell her. I couldn't put it off any longer. So I explained, while my brain was spinning, that babies are created from a tiny egg inside a special place in the mommy's tummy. I kept the explanation short and to the point.

Looking back later, I wondered why Rachel was thinking about babies again. Then I recalled my father and me discussing the soon-to-be-born baby of my brother and his wife. I was very proud of myself for being able to give her enough information to fulfil her curiosity at that moment.

Sometimes, I wonder if my daughter cares that she has no daddy. It could be that she just wants to have it all sorted out in her mind — just like she knows she has blue eyes and I have brown. Similarly, "Susie" has a dad and she doesn't. Though the grass may seem greener on the other side of the fence, at least Rachel has two people to whom she can turn. She receives all the attention from my partner Dawn that a father might (and I stress, might) provide. There's fishing, T-ball, cutting down tree branches, car washes and fixing the lawn mower, to name a few of their bonding moments. I provide the domestic touches — baking cookies, bathtimes and gushy cuddling.

All I ever wanted to do was have children. I am not a man-hater. I just don't want a man involved with the raising of our child. And as I watch Rachel grow up, I pray that she doesn't feel that she is being raised as a second generation lesbian. I would like her to be able to choose her sexuality for herself and I want to be able to provide her with an appropriate explanation for lesbians choosing to have children, who, like her, grow up without a dad.

No Easy Answers

CHRISTINA MILLS

> I am thankful that one of my children is male, since that
> helps to keep me honest. Every line I write shrieks there
> are no easy answers.
> — Audre Lorde, in "Man Child: a Black
> Lesbian Feminist's Response"

WHEN I WAS PREGNANT IT NEVER OCCURRED TO ME THAT I MIGHT HAVE A BOY. I called "her" Margaret throughout my pregnancy and hadn't even thought about a boy's name. This had nothing to do with being a lesbian (I didn't even think about coming out until a few years later), but much to do with knowing that I would be raising my child alone. I had never imagined myself involved in a permanent relationship with a partner (male *or* female), but I had a fantasy of the bond I would have with my daughter. We would have none of the communication problems so common between parents and children: she would be open, affectionate, confiding in me about her every hope and fear; I would be wise and supportive, never losing my perspective or sense of humour. As she matured to womanhood, the closeness of mother and child would turn into that of best friends. This idealized relationship depended on her being a girl; there was just too much I didn't understand about men. And I knew, or thought I did, what I could teach a girl; I had no idea what lessons from my life would be of value to a boy.

Nothing happened as planned: the natural childbirth I had prepared for turned into a Caesarean section with epidural anesthetic, and when the doctor said, "It's a boy!" my response was "*What?*" In that instant I had to begin to reconstruct my vision of what my life as a mother would be. It was an adjustment that took some time, despite the fact that I loved him from the moment I touched his wet, bruised head, cone-shaped from my long labour.

Between Alexis' third and fifth years I had an arrangement with another single mother to alternate sleepovers on weekend nights, so each of us would have a night to herself. The other child was a girl the same age as Alexis. Aisha was petite, pretty and highly verbal, with a keenly developed sense of how to use her tongue as a weapon. From the kitchen I would hear a one-sided conversation in the living room, Aisha needling, taunting, goading ... until there would be the *thump* of Aisha's bum hitting the floor, a brief silence and then Aisha's wail as she ran to the kitchen to show me her tears: "Alexis pushed me! He pushed me and I wasn't doing *anything*!" I would tell Alexis to "use your words" to resolve differences (my generation's version of "hitting's not allowed") and I would tell Aisha to deal with Alexis directly without appealing to authority (my generation's version of "don't be a tattle-tale"). I was chagrined by how neatly their temperaments seemed to fit the stereotypes I had rejected in endless undergraduate nature-versus-nurture debates. When Alexis was being particularly rambunctious I would have to bite back the words, "Why do you have to act like such a *boy*?"

When I came out, the year Alexis turned five, it occurred to me that the Michigan Women's Music Festival would be a great way to celebrate, and started making plans to go there with my friend, M., who had a daughter the same age as Alexis. My dreams of sapphic splendour in the grass wilted when I found out that, while M.'s daughter would have the run of the land and be able to go anywhere with us during the week, Alexis would have to stay in a special compound for boys, outside the main campground. Apparently it was essential that this women's space be safe from the oppressive masculinity of five-year-olds.

I was assured that the compound was a happy, friendly place where nurturing caregivers provided the boys with lots of stimulating activities. Still, I couldn't help but think of the boys' compound as a miniature concentration camp. Moreover, as a single working mother, I looked forward to holidays as a chance to spend more time with Alexis; to forego those precious hours was unthinkable. It was immaterial whether I left him with friends in Toronto or parked him in the care of strangers (feminist though they be) every day and evening. I could not face his inevitable question: "How come S. can go and not me?" I resigned myself to missing the quintessential lesbian cultural event. What I had more difficulty accepting was M.'s blank incomprehension:

M: We need it to be a women-only space, for women to feel safe. So many women have suffered abuse at the hands of men.

C: I can understand not wanting to deal with male teenagers, but he's only a little boy. How much of a threat can he be?

M: But he's still male. He represents patriarchy.

C: The fact that patriarchy has made little girls feel second-class for centuries doesn't make it right to treat little boys as second-class.

M: You're making a big deal over nothing. He'll have so much fun, he won't even miss you.

C: That sounds like some southern redneck in the '60s defending Jim Crow. "Really, they're so much happier with their own kind ..."

And so it went, me not understanding how Alexis and his little penis could intimidate grown women, M. not understanding why I felt so passionately that we had to find a way to give little girls an unassailable sense of being at home in the world, without taking it away from boys. It soon became clear that there was no common ground from which to discuss the issue: for me, theory faltered at the point where my child became defined as Other, as Enemy, as a symbol rather than a child. M.'s child was female and so to her the theory was clear and inarguable. I decided not to pursue a debate that could only be divisive. *Oh well*, I thought, *I can go in a few years when he's older and can go to camp.*

When Alexis was six I left the city I had called home for most of my adult life to do a training program. Faced with the task of building an entire social support network from scratch,

I contacted a lesbian mothers' group. My first encounter with Dykes 'n' Tykes was at a softball game; there were enough moms and kids to field two complete teams — ironically, almost all the kids were boys. During the many potlucks we had over the next two years, we talked about co-parenting, dealing with homophobia in school, discipline, homework, chores and allowances, but I don't recall ever discussing whether having boys was any different for us than having girls. It's not as if we were entirely without a basis of comparison — two of the group had daughters. We would joke about testosterone poisoning, but sometimes it seemed too true to be funny. Did we avoid discussing it seriously because we were afraid of where the discussion would take us? I don't know about that, but I do know that I've never heard the mother of a boy support the strict nurture side of the nature-versus argument. For us the question is not whether it's nature or nurture, but *how* to nurture the best that is in our children's natures.

Audre Lorde said that her son represented as much hope for our future world as did her daughter. Surely that hope can only be fulfilled if we find ways to help our boys grow up as whole and proud as our girls. I sometimes envy my friends who have daughters — not that I'd trade, but it seems to me it must be easier to give a girl positive models than to teach a boy what his possibilities are and counter the negative models that are so pervasive in our culture. With girls, we have the lessons in our own bodies and lives; with boys, we have to work entirely from theory.

My son is bright, funny, creative and affectionate. He is also stubborn, rebellious, sarcastic and a master of passive resistance. Now fourteen, he is taller than I am and subject to sudden excesses of energy which seem to compel him to jump, run, throw things or make loud noises. Unfortunately, these attacks seem to happen indoors more often than not and my patience frequently wears thin. I am sometimes overwhelmed by the sheer energy and out-thereness of him. I still find myself thinking (but manage to keep from saying), *Why do you have to act like such a BOY?*

My partner, who has never had the remotest desire to be a mother and whose synonym for "men" is "jerks," has even less patience with what she regards as male behaviour. I accuse her of stereotyping; she accuses me of coddling him. I worry that because she is so important to him, her comments must have much more weight with him than they would coming from an acquaintance or a stranger. As a result, they might convince him that he cannot escape becoming the male jerk. My fears for Alexis and my partner's negative feelings about men are played out almost daily in our struggles about household chores and responsibilities. She feels his chores are too few and that I am not hard enough on him when he doesn't come through, so he will never learn to take responsibility. I compare his housework load to other children his age, boys *and* girls, and try to make the consequences fit the "crime" when he doesn't do what is expected — since I don't judge myself by the quality of my housekeeping, I have trouble seeing it as a moral flaw when the bathroom isn't cleaned perfectly! When she commented recently that her brother "got away with murder" (i.e. didn't have to do chores, much less housework) as a teenager because he was a boy, I suddenly understood that when she calls Alexis a lazy bum, she's expressing her resentment and hurt that she and her brother were treated differently and unfairly because of sexist assumptions about their roles. I want Alexis to understand the origins of those feelings and to be respectful of women's experience without becoming ashamed of himself for being male. If he feels guilty about being male, how can he help but resent women? I want him to value himself so he can find worth in others, male and female.

I grew up in a welfare family; everything in my experience until well into high school taught me that no matter what I did, I would never be good enough — because *who* I was, was, *by definition*, bad. At forty-five, I'm still dealing with the effects of that training. Countless women have had the same sense of intrinsic inadequacy ground into them, whether because of poverty or abuse or being lesbians in a homophobic world. As a feminist I work to unlearn and help others unlearn this most central and hateful lesson of patriarchy. As a mother, I refuse to have it transposed and turned against my son.

Boys & Us

CATHY KING

My partner, Maureen, and I are doing something a little unusual for a couple of formerly urban, active, and slightly wild women. We are smack in the middle of raising three young boys. That's three, as in a houseful, and I've scarcely had a moment until now to even think about it.

Maureen and I had been together for about a year when I began to mention that I must, must have a child. So we made some arrangements and set some strange wheels in motion, and by the grace of diligence and great good fortune we became parents of our firstborn, Adrian. We were transported. We were in yet another new life, the one that often follows being in love. Our dream was coming true. We were focussed, we were committed, and we had a wonderful "easy" baby who was doted upon by our large, loose circle of lesbian friends. This baby had changed us — but not for a moment had he restricted us. On the contrary. We brought him to dances, we brought him to meetings, we brought him to poolhalls and we brought him on long car trips to meet far-flung friends.

And then ... then, with all the pride and enthusiasm of the newly converted, we decided to do it again. Well, why not, we thought — we're already here. If one is so wonderful, why not two? Take the pressure off Adrian, give him some company, keep a good thing going ...

Hah! Hubris, I call it now. Because within a couple of months of making that decision, we found we were expecting — twins!

Our two new baby boys were just as wonderful and special as our first, but by now our heads were spinning. We entered a personal Dark Ages, in which I stayed home with three babies and Maureen tried to keep the whole thing afloat, and we almost lost sight of one another. I know many of our friends used to come over to help out, but, to tell the truth, I can't really remember much of those early days.

Somehow we made it. We are a family now, a family of two lesbian women and three little boys. It's an unusual configuration, but it has a certain balance to it. Our boys, being so close in age — Adrian is six, Paul and Jeremy are four — make up a little gang, and they tend to pay far more attention to one another than to us. They are bright, boisterous boys who love to tumble around and play in what I can only call "boy" style.

I must mention that before I had kids, I was convinced that much of what we characterize as male or female behaviours was a result of pummelling and pounding by external forces. I really believed that gender identity was shaped by parental expectations and other social pressures, either subtle or overt. My own gender-neutral children, raised in a non-sexist environment, would of course never display any gender-specific behaviour whatsoever. But now I have three boys, and although they are all very different in personality, there is a quintessential maleness to each one of them that I find difficult to fathom. I certainly do not feel akin to it. At their young age this "boyness" manifests itself as chaotic squealing, rolling physical activity. They are drawn to one another like magnets and cannot restrain themselves from constant physical contact. This way of being is alien to me. As an adult woman, I find it at best irksome and at worst totally intrusive. But I'm determined to resist my own impulse to squelch this behaviour precisely because it does seem so central and instinctive to them. I cringe, I set limits and I do damage control, but I never really call a halt. Because I feel it's a crucial thing I'm dealing with here, a crucial and delicate thing, strange as that may sound. It has to do with their basic sense of identity. I cannot stand to think of these children growing up with the suspicion that their most natural way of being is something abhorrent to their parents. On the other hand, I suppose it's entirely possible that my own perception of my children's maleness, of their difference from me, is affecting my attitudes towards them and so I am actually contributing to this shaping of their male identities. But at least I am confident that these boys have not built their vision of reality along "us and them" lines. They are being exposed to heavier than average doses of questioning the status quo by their parents. Well, their very existence is a flouting of the status quo, so they can't really escape that! I only hope they will always have the courage and energy to resist complacency.

I know that as people we are all constantly in the process of developing and refining our views and values. But I think that when we become parents, this process accelerates. Sometimes we encounter shocking and unusual things in this occupation. One realm in which I found myself totally unanchored was that of the current Kiddie Culture. This is a starkly black and white — or should I say pink and blue — world, and one that demands a surprising amount of soul-searching. It makes us examine our attitudes towards such things as censorship, values, peer pressure, commercialism, and the very foundation of our society. The "blue" side of this Kiddie Culture appeals strongly to any boy past babyhood, who has begun to identify himself as such. It is designed to be this way. It abounds with symbols and themes that are blatantly male, instantly recognizable and utterly seductive for little boys. It is also the direct antithesis of many values that we as lesbians and as feminists hold dear. This is a very complicated issue. We do not want to shield our children from their society; nor can we, short of keeping them totally under house arrest. But neither do we want them to fall so far under the influence of that enticing world of action heroes and scary monsters that they become little aliens in our world! We instinctively despise the war toys which encourage a mindset that, brought to its ultimate conclusion, results in worldwide death and destruction. At the same time, we sympathise with our boys' urges to bond with things male. It seems to now be our monumental task to unravel these issues for ourselves, communicate our findings to our boys, and then let them make their own choices. Even as I'm tripping over Mighty Maxes, I do have an implicit faith that I will be able to live with those choices. But this is not an easy assignment. In the meantime, I suppose we should be relieved that we aren't tripping over Barbies and dealing with the pink side of Kiddie Culture. I'm sure that must be even more difficult.

Our family is viewed as an anomaly by outsiders, and I'm sure many would consider our boys to be disadvantaged since they do not have a dad. I believe our children enjoy a distinct advantage in having two women as parents. For one thing, Maureen and I are very different from one another. The boys see the workload involved in running a home divided according to interest and ability rather than traditional gender roles. There is no danger of them acquiring stereotypes of a woman's "position" in the home, since we are both women holding all the different positions required. We hope this will teach them that necessity and skill, in that order, are what determine the work split in any home. Our boys will know that women can do it all. And, we are determined that they will also know that men can do it all. We have a fear and loathing in this family of spoiled little boys who grow up to become spoiled men. Without wanting to blame all mothers for our men, I do want to say that I think we as lesbian mothers are in the unique position of interrupting a predictable cycle of attitudes about mothers and sons. What I'm trying to say is that our reverence for the male undoubtedly falls somewhere short of the norm, whereas our respect for the male — and this we must cherish and preserve, for the sake of our sons — remains healthy and intact.

Some of our family's values are downright traditional despite our intrinsic nonconformity. There are behaviours I insist upon which I once considered superfluous but now see as the basis of respect for others. Yes, we are insisting on manners. We expect our boys to be polite and considerate towards one another, us, and everyone they encounter. It's a learning process of course, but we definitely do not want to turn out three more teenage boys who leave the toilet seat up, hog the handicapped spaces at the store, or speak sarcastically to their girlfriends. We have high hopes for our boys, but reasonable expectations.

I hope this doesn't convey the impression that our lives are entirely serious and principled. Mostly, like any other family, we just do the best we can and try to have fun doing it. It is fun having three little boys in our lives. This feeling seems to spill out all over. I've had other mothers approach me at our kids' after-school program to say "my son is crazy about your boys — I think he wants to join your family!" This makes me feel very proud. There is something giddily satisfying about having our particular family being the envy of all the kids! We haven't done any public coming-out thing, but with our family it's kind of like trying to hide an elephant. You don't put it in the side show. It just is.

Apart from the boost of social admiration and a shared reality, our children have a rich and varied set of devoted adult friends. Our family is far less insular than most we know. We and our kids enjoy a large "extended family." We visit, people drop by, we are socially active with family, lesbian friends, gay male friends, straight single moms, straight couples with kids — all people who connect with us and have a special relationship with our kids. We feel it's very important to spend time with people in all types of families. We get together monthly with a lesbian moms-and-kids group — a group of diverse people in unique situations. It is a relief and a joy to connect with and learn about others doing the same thing in different ways. It helps us show our boys that they are special but not weird.

I am proud of my family. Maureen and I are so very lucky to have our Adrian, our Jeremy, and our Paul. And so, I believe, are they to have us.

Challenging Complacency with my Sons

HEIDI RANKIN

AT THE TENDER AGE OF SEVEN, SILAS, MY OLDEST SON, LEFT HIS NOVA Scotian home for an adventure at his aunt Rachel's summer camp in Vermont. The camp had a non-competitive environment, full of sun, water, crafts and kids. Silas attended day camp for four years, living for three weeks of each summer with Rachel and his four cousins. His younger brother, Noel, began going to the camp when he was five, and attended for four summers as well, with cousins of like age (it's a big family!). The trail eventually continued to include my third and last child, my daughter, Madison. The summer weekends in Vermont were spent camping with Rachel and friends — swimming, singing, playing instruments, and games.

The missing piece of this story is that Aunt Rachel, my ex-husband's sister, is a dyke. My children were immersed for many summers in a lesbian environment. Rachel lovingly included them in her expansive community, and my children created an extended family, gaining inner knowledge of lesbian culture.

Little did I know at the time that my young boys were in training for future life with mom. I couldn't have planned it better myself. After ending my seventeen-year marriage, I came out to my three children. At the time, they ranged in age from seven to fourteen. My coming out was a dream come true: no one lost their cool or rejected me. Because I came out with my partner, Lee, a woman with whom I had had a long-distance relationship for two years, I was not accused of being a "fake lesbian" (a term used by a friend's children because she didn't have a lover when she came out to them!).

I was feeling secure enough in myself — with support from others — to step back and allow the kids to move through their feelings. I tested my communication skill training, and "active listened" with my children. We have never looked back. This is not to say it has always been rosy or easy. But we are busily moving through the challenges as they arise.

The big challenge for my children was to welcome someone "else" into my life. Fortunately, they did not feel that their dad was displaced by my partner, the way they felt when he became involved with a new woman. They were more willing to include Lee in their lives because they had the opportunity to welcome her as an individual — to create new relationships without the "traditional step-parent constraints."

The boys still presented predictable challenges, however. Their lives with me and Lee certainly included many more lesbians than usual, and fewer men and traditional nuclear families. I sometimes feel sad about the lack of families like ours in this small province (Prince Edward Island). It is not a simple thing to find other lesbians with kids, particularly older boys. But the inspiring thing is to watch the boys give full body hugs to other lesbians — to remain open in their hearts to loving women.

Let's have a reality check here: Lots of lesbians do not choose to have men or older boys in their lives. I don't have many judgements about these women. It can be a loving stretch to spend time in the company of boys. Silas is now sixteen and six feet tall, and Noel is thirteen. We have dealt with puberty, testosterone, anger, physical aggression and power-over behaviour. I have kept talking, used all my coping strategies to remain open and loving, and encouraged my lover to remain open as well. There *is* a difference when the children in your life are biologically your own. I don't have choices when it comes to staying connected to them. I need to — and I want to. I have a personal commitment to sending them out into their daily lives as responsible, caring, tolerant, compassionate individuals.

How idealistic, you might say. Sometimes, I feel that I have fooled myself. It is a *long-term* commitment to see this through with boys ... to hold the intention that they will be healthy, participating boys/men in their relationships with family, friends and women.

There are small payoffs — little shiny nuggets that help me remain hopeful: their revulsion to homophobic movie audiences;

their understanding of sexist commentary in the media; their complicit laughter in lesbian humour, which often originates with them. These are subtle events and behaviours, but I celebrate them all the same.

Silas approached me last year with a broad smile on his face, and proudly announced that now he and I had something in common — we both liked girls! I laughed and suggested we could have a great time together appreciating women. He concurred, but then, after a thoughtful pause, added, "I don't think we have the same taste, Mom — no offense, but I'm not at all attracted to Lee!"

We keep telling Silas how lucky he is to be living with two dykes. A quick test for any young woman he becomes involved with is to tell her that we are lesbians. If she's homophobic, she was the wrong choice!

All three kids share their lesbian family with the wider world in different ways. They casually bring their friends to the house, casually introduce them to Lee, and casually, if asked, call her "Mom's roommate." Silas' justification in not elaborating on this is that "if they don't get the 'mom's roommate' part, then they're not quite ready." On the other hand, if asked, Silas will never withhold information. Noel invites his friends home and does not censor his language or behaviour, but does not offer any *extra* information. Madison, who basks in the attention of two loving, attentive women, tests her friendships by sharing the fact that her mom is a lesbian. The girl she chooses to spend the most time with has a lesbian mom as well, and this offers her comfort.

The last few years have been full of changes and challenges for all of us. Many of them are changes we could not have forseen. Perhaps one of the gifts I have brought my kids, particularly my boys, is a constant challenge to complacency in life — a conviction that living on the edge can be healthy.

Girls Like Me (Or Not)

J.A. HAMILTON

I WAS TRYING TO TALK TO MY TWELVE-YEAR-OLD DAUGHTER ABOUT MASTUR-bation. I fiddled and twiddled my fingers. I tapped my knees. At last I sighed and said, "You know, honey. You do know it's perfectly ... uh ... natural. To ... er ... masturbate."

Meg had sandy blond hair falling over her shoulders. It obscured her face. She gave no hint of having heard me. She was intensely focussed on the book — *Earth to Matthew* by Paula Danziger — closed on her lap. "Read this," she finally said. "Here, Mom, *read* this cover."

She shoved the book at me without turning to me or exposing her face. Automatically, to myself, I read, "Danziger's usual fast pacing ... will grab readers."

Then I shook myself. "Meg," I said, realizing I'd been sucked in again by the girl who wanted to be excused from Family Ed class because "I know that junk already." "Meg, honey, Meg. Do you know what masturbation is?"

A nod of the head so fast and stiff I almost missed it.

"It's when you touch yourself," I continued. "Touch your genitals. Er ... to give yourself pleasure. I want you to know it's perfectly ..." Words escaped me. "Perfectly? Natural. Yes. It's natural."

Meg jerked to face me. Her expression was vehement. Very intense. Alight with wicked glee, she said, "Oh, Mom, you would think that."

"Think what?" I asked.

"Think it was natural."

I was confused, so I waited.

"Because that's what you do."

"I do?" Wait just a minute here, I thought. Discussing masturbation in general is fine, but we are not about to discuss my sex life. Uh-uh. No damned way. In another life maybe. My cheeks heated with embarrassment. But hadn't I just said masturbation was natural? "Everyone does it," I said, settling on "everyone" with relief.

A smell of almonds rose from Meg's body. She barkingly laughed and adjusted her position so the leather of the couch cushions squeaked under her. "You would think that," she repeated, her eyes fired up with mischief, "because that's what you and Joy do!"

Joy was my girlfriend, lover, partner, mate. I blinked rapidly. "Excuse me?"

"You and Joy," Meg crowed. "Because you're lesbians!"

I nodded. "Oh," I said weakly, "oh. Well, that's very ... pithy? Witty of you."

Meg laughed uproariously and punched me in the knee.

Lesbian. The "L" word. What I am. A lesbian. A big "L" lesbian. When Joy and I first travelled to Ontario together, her ex-husband told people his wife was in Toronto with her "lesbian lover."

Lesbian Lover. Big "L" stuff. Hundred-feet-tall lesbian stuff.

I'm a hundred-foot-tall lesbian mom, muddling through motherhood.

I got my kids the commonplace way, through men I was involved with and in love with. I "came out" gradually between the first and second babies, then all the way out after Meg was born. I didn't stop to ask whether it was fair to raise kids when I was a dyke, because I believed there was nothing wrong with being a dyke, but I did spend time fretting about how the homophobia of others would affect them.

The first time I can recall my sexuality being an issue for either of my girls was when Meg was in kindergarten. She befriended a brown-haired spark of a girl named Mary, daughter of Robert and Wanda, a fundamentalist Christian couple.

The family lived in a woebegone, pale-yellow, two bedroom house on the other side of town. Although Robert had writerly aspirations, he was disabled in some invisible way and seemed mostly to hang around the house. Robert didn't have any bad habits that I could see — he didn't beat Wanda or carouse or drink their welfare cheque away — but he was a chauvinist of the worst order. He expected Wanda to do the family's laundry in an old wringer washer. He expected Wanda to bake the family's bread. He expected Wanda to stay barefoot and pregnant. During the time Meg was Mary's best friend, Wanda gave birth to three more children. Poor Wanda, I thought, poor Wanda. She didn't even drive. Robert tooled around town in his blue VW van, but I never saw Wanda anywhere but at her house when I was dropping off or picking up Meg.

My lover at the time was a woman named Shiela. Shiela and I speculated about whether Robert and Wanda would be good, neutral or bad influences on Meg. Their house, though small and dark, seemed full of affection. Wanda, though browbeaten, seemed sweet. And Robert, though mysogynist, seemed to genuinely like kids — without overdoing it in a creepy way.

We voted to send Meg when she was invited and wanted to go.

Fair play. Mary had spent long hours at our house.

Yet when we picked Meg up after a first lunch at Mary's, she climbed in the car and gripped my arm. She said, "Oh, Mommy. Mommy!" Her face was blanched. "Robert and Wanda do God!"

God? Oh, God, I'd been worried about homophobia, not God.

I knew Robert hoped Shiela and I — the nature of our relationship apparently escaped him — were of his religious persuasion. I knew this because he often stood outside his van in our turnaround when he came to pick up Mary, and proseletized, and because he'd noted a Bible that Shiela, a writer, kept in her studio for research purposes. I'd told Robert we were agnostic, leaning heavily on the "haven't-decided-yet" emphasis for fear of losing Meg her best friend.

"God, honey," I said to Meg. "Let me try to explain God to you." I did my best to tell her about religion, to say the religion Mary's family had wasn't anything Meg needed to feel persuaded by. When she was older — a teenager — she could explore different beliefs and decide for herself.

Our couch was a wood-framed thing. It was the next thing to a piece of trash we could have without sitting in the dump. It was very uncomfortable. I was sitting on it, one wood bar crushing into the backs of my knees, when my lover's voice penetrated my *Books in Canada* fog.

Shiela, across from me in an old, wine-red chair, quietly and urgently repeated my name. I looked at her. She gestured to Meg. I looked at Meg. Five years old and no bigger than a button, Meg was skipping around our red dining room table. She wore a denim skirt which bounced to expose her legs. Her hair sparked in a shaft of sunlight when she rounded the corner closest to us.

She was singing. In a sing-song voice, oblivious to us, she was singing, "I'm gay with Mary! I'm gay with Mary! I'm gay with Mary!"

She sounded enchanted.

She sounded completely, head-over heels in love.

Shiela and I watched, then raised our eyebrows at each other. Then at Meg. Then at each other.

I cleared my throat. Right away I imagined the implications of being "gay" with a fundamentalist's daughter. Right away I thought: Shut Meg down. "What should we do?" I whispered.

"Don't ask me," she said, "but if Robert ever hears her ..."

I nodded reluctantly. "Meg," I called cheerfully. "Meg, honey, come here a sec, will you?"

Her bubble popped. Into her Mary-world arrived this mother thing. She plopped down beside me.

I slung an arm around her shoulder. "Do you know what 'gay' is?"

"Happy," Meg said confidently.

Shiela smiled. I rubbed my face, frustrated by how hard parenting could be.

"I'm glad you're happy with Mary," I said. Shiela nodded encouragingly. Meg blinked up at me, entirely innocent. "It's good to be happy with your friends. Very good. But the word you used, 'gay,' that also has another meaning, honey. It means two women who love each other."

"I love you, Mommy," Meg said earnestly.

"Two grown-up women who love each other, Meg, like Shiela and I do. Or two grown-up men. That's 'gay.'" I took a deep breath. The hard part was upon me. "Some people don't like gay people. It's not because gay people are bad, honey, it's just because ..." How to explain prejudice? "The thing is, Robert and Wanda might get upset if they hear you say you're gay with Mary. It's okay to be gay with Mary," I said quickly, backtracking, "but just don't tell Robert and Wanda."

"Huh?" said Meg.

The first concrete evidence I received that my homosexuality had affected Sarah, my older daughter, was when she came home from grade seven and told me kids had been badmouthing gays at recess. "I set them straight," Sarah said proudly.

"Did you, dear?" I asked.

"Yes, I did. They were saying queer, homo, faggot and I got really mad. I told them what lesbianism really is."

"Un-huh?" I said.

"I told them it wasn't about boys and stuff like they said. I told them it was about sex."

Out of the lethal mouths of babes.

She added, "I was almost going to tell them about you, but then I decided not to."

One of my acquaintances was a homosexual woman named Winnifred. Her daughter, Grace, and Sarah were best friends, died-in-the-wool-can't-live-without-you-chums. Grace was forever overnight at our place and Sarah was forever overnight at Winnifred's.

After about three years of this, after Winnifred and I became somewhat closer, Sarah confided that she and Grace had had a "meaningful long talk. One of the things we talked about," Sarah told me, "was you and Winnifred."

"Me and Winnifred?" I asked. I was dicing onions so my eyes were smarting. I turned to look at my daughter.

Sarah pulled her long hair into a messy bun. "About you guys being lesbians."

I was taken aback. "You didn't know Winnifred was gay?"

"No," Sarah said, "I knew."

"Then I don't get it. Grace knows Shiela and I are gay ..."

"Yeah," said Sarah, "she does. But we'd never said so to each other."

"Said so?"

"Yeah, you know. Said our moms were gay." Sarah tore at a leaf of lettuce and ate it. "Are we having hamburgers again?"

"Is that true?" I asked. "I thought you both having lesbian moms was a bit of a refuge. A safe place where you didn't have to hide."

"It's not the easiest thing in the world, you know, to have a queer mother. I never talk about it. Not ever."

Having a lesbian mom was hard on my girls. Absolutely. No question about it. The worst time was when a couple Shiela knew decided their daughter Cindy couldn't hang out with Sarah. The way Shiela heard it, and the way Sarah confirmed it after hearing it from Cindy, was that Cindy couldn't be friends with Sarah any more because "Sarah's mother lives with a lesbian."

I ached for Sarah and for Cindy.

"They want to call you and warn you," Shiela confided.

"Warn me?" I said. "Who? Cindy's folks?"

"Yeah, to tell you that you're living with a lesbian."

"You're kidding, right? You're kidding?"

Shiela grinned.

"You're not kidding," I said, my voice rising. "Those morons never figured out that I'm not only living with a lesbian, I'm living with my lover?"

Shiela let go a full-bodied laugh.

This thought was fun for us (maybe, sort of, sometimes in a warped way), but the experience was painful for the youngsters. Cindy and Sarah were reduced to talking at school. They couldn't phone each other. They had to call friends in common who could phone to relay messages.

After Shiela and I split up, and I moved with the girls back to Vancouver, Meg, by then in grade six, befriended a girl named Linda. I adored Linda. She pretty well lived at my house, there forty-eight out of forty-eight weekend hours and many week-night overnights. I wasn't coupled, nor seriously dating, so my lesbianism didn't come up. The few times I was out with someone in a sexual way, contact happened elsewhere.

One day I was on my knees scrubbing the bathtub when Meg screeched to a halt by the door. Linda, screeching behind her, slammed — *thump* — into her. Meg girded herself on the doorframe. Hyper, she yelled, "Tell her. Tell her. You are, aren't you? You're gay, Mom, aren't you? Tell her!"

I got up slowly, my sodden cloth dripping onto the tiles. "Well," I said slowly, "yes. Yes, I am. I am gay."

"See?" Meg cried happily. "I told you so!"

Meg and Linda bolted off.

"Wait!" I threw the dripping rag in the tub and followed them.

"What?"

"Wait up," I said, puffing into the kitchen. "Listen, Linda. I want you to know … some people think lesbians … hurt kids. I want you to know that's just stupid. Lesbians don't."

Meg said, "Hah!" and giggled. She elbowed Linda. "Didn't I tell you she was gay?"

Why did this stuff make me so tongue tied? "You should be aware that not everyone thinks lesbianism is normal. It is, but some people are very silly about it. So you might want to consider that when you decide who to tell."

I was thinking here about every straight woman I'd ever told and how right away, even if I had asked her to keep it confiden-tial, she'd tell her husband and a couple of friends. She'd never even stop to think how bringing me out, with its hundreds of serious and sometimes life-threatening ramifications, might be dangerous for me. It could hurt my kids, my employment and my housing.

I was out. I was way out. But that didn't mean I wanted Linda to tell Meg's friends at school. Or her own mother, in case her mother wigged out and ended the girls' friendship. This wasn't idle speculation. I'd stood in my hallway one day telling Linda's mom I wanted to move from the East End to Kitsilano and she'd wrinkled her nose. "Oh, no!" she'd said, taking my elbow confidentially. "Too many homosexuals over there." She'd shivered in distaste.

When I was dating Joy and cogitating about a commitment — should I?; shouldn't I? — Meg and Sarah had a hard time. Sarah didn't see why we weren't a good enough family as we were, just the three of us, or how she'd get any attention if I was all goo-goo eyes over some "babe." The kids had only seen me coupled the five years Shiela and I had been together. Since then, date-wise, I'd been very discreet — I'd never had girlfriends who spent the night. But Joy was serious.

Joy was coming out. She talked about how troubling a process that was for her one afternoon at the water park at Granville Island.

Meg piped up with, "Me too! It takes me forever to come out to my friends."

We both turned to look at her. She was shivering under a towel.

"Come out?" I said. I had scratched "J and J" into the picnic table and I ran my fingers over the scars.

"About you, Mom." Meg bit a nail.

"Oh," I said. "About me. Right." I smiled sheepishly over at Joy.

Meg didn't know who was the girl and who was the boy. Who was the man and who was the woman. But she kept deciding for us, though, and announcing it to us: "Joy's the man because she has smaller breasts."

"Mom's the man because she's taller."

"Joy's the man because she has a mustache."

"Mom's the man because she wears cowboy boots."

We counteract this a bit — pointing out that we were lesbians because we were women and that we didn't have to have one of us be the man, but it didn't seem to make much difference to Meg. Meg was absorbing homophobia through her pores. And no wonder. It was endemic.

There was the doctor I saw when I returned to the city, who knew I was a mom before she knew I was a lesbian, and when she found out the latter, burst out, "And you have custody of your children?"

Or there was the acquaintance who, visiting me, discovered Jane Rule novels on my shelves and stopped calling. Stopped chatting when we bumped into each other in the neighbourhood, too, physically backing until she had put five or so feet between us — the distance at which I could not lean over and "just kiss her." (As lesbians are wont to do to straight gals, I guess.)

Or in a lighter vein, Madame Helga. I stopped in at Madame Helga's storefront advertising "Palm and Crystal Ball Readings" just after a woman I'd been briefly involved with (pre-Joy) left for the east coast. Madame Helga's prophecy was to be my entertainment, my consolation prize.

I sat across from Madame H. at a heavy mahogany desk and declined the crystal ball reading for forty dollars.

Helga reached for my hand. She wore a ton of gold jewelry that tinkled when she moved. She turned my hand palm up. "You will live to ninety-six in perfect health," she intoned.

Ms. Thick as a Stick. Ms. Lame Brain. This was impossible and preposterous. But I didn't interrupt. I didn't raise my eyebrows. I wanted her to go on.

Her voice quavering with sincerity, she said, "You aren't married, am I right?"

"No, I'm not," I said. Very mystical, indeed. No wedding band. No tan from where a band had been removed.

She said, "You have kids?"

"Two, uh-huh," I said.

She peered at me shrewdly. "Why did your marriage break up?" She traced the lines on my palm softly, as if they were braille.

I thought about possible answers, but finally ventured, "Because I'm a lesbian?"

She didn't drop my hand, but I felt it involuntarily jerk. Slowly she said, "I see. Uh. Well. Yes. Well." She dropped her eyes and appeared to be riveted by something in my life line. "Sometimes this can be all right."

"Oh! Oh yes, I *know*."

Madame Helga made a noise in her throat. The blue velvet drapes at her window were open a crack and the sun floated dust in the air. "Well. Yes. But there can be problems. Do you find yourself nurtured?"

I added a leer to my voice. I said, "*Wonderfully* nurtured."

She said, "Yes. Uh-huh. But do you receive any, uh … " She frowned. "… *spiritual* fulfilment?"

I knew how pathetically prejudiced such a question was, but I could not stop myself from enjoying it. I had sudden, spiritual visions of breasts. I groaned and said, "Yes, oh yes, yes!"

Madame Helga narrowed her eyes. "Which one of you is the man?"

"Excuse me?"

"In lesbian couples one of you is the man."

I frowned and said, "We're women. That's why we're called lesbians."

Madame Helga shook her head so firmly her earrings hit her face. She shouted, "No!" She stopped and modulated her voice. "They *say* there's a man."

I wiggled my eyebrows suggestively. "We're both *all woman*," I said, leaning in towards her.

Madame H. said, "No! Because *you'd* be the woman." She grabbed for my hand again. "Because it says in your palm you need someone to look up to." Helga dropped my hand, reached for a cigarette, lit it with a gold lighter, trembling, and said, "Twenty-five dollars, please, Mrs. Lesbian."

A month ago Sarah came out. Not *about* me, but *to* me. "Mom," she said, "I *think* I might be bisexual."

"Um," I said. I wanted to be carefully noncommital, but thoughts plundered my brain: Bisexual? My little hetero girl? Sarah, are you *sexually active*? Huh? Huh? And — oh my God, does that mean living with lesbians makes lesbian daughters? Did I turn Sarah into a dyke? Despite all my careful "it's-fine-if-you're-straight" mini-lectures?

Then, God, just *God*. I said, "Um?"

"Or a *lesbian*. I think I might be a lesbian."

I cleared my throat. "Uh ... do you ... have you ... er?"

"Been sexual? No. This is just speculation." She grinned at my discomfiture.

I breathed in relief.

"Everyone says liking girls is just crushes. Puppy love. A stage."

"Well," I said, "it might be."

"Or maybe I *am* a lesbian."

"Do you need to figure that out right now?" I asked.

"Yes!" Sarah said, "yes! It's my identity!"

Meg came zooming into the living room towing her friend DD. "I told DD you're gay, Mom," she said.

Meg was in grade seven. Linda had moved away. DD was the new girl in Meg's life.

I was sewing gathered slipcovers for footstools and looked up from the machine.

DD said ponderously, confidingly, leaning in toward me, "I don't mind."

"Good of you," I muttered. Out loud, I said, "Do you have any questions?"

Meg interrupted. "She wanted to know am I?"

"Uh-huh?" I said said and bit a thread.

"I said nope."

"Good," I said. I nodded. "Both *my* parents were heterosexual. Being raised by them didn't make me straight. A parent's sexual orientation doesn't influence kids' sexual orientation."

"Oh, that's a *good* point," said Meg appreciatively, nodding.

I went back to my sewing.

"There's one other question DD has, though, Mom."

I let up on the pedal and looked again. "What's that?"

"What you and Joy do in bed." Meg cracked up. She bent over and held her stomach she was laughing so hard.

I rolled my eyes. I declined to answer.

"What I want," I said at the writers' meeting, "is a book for kids where lesbianism isn't the issue. Not *Heather Has Two Mommies*. Heather knows she has two mommies. A book where Heather has an adventure and her mommies are just background, as normal as sun."

The famous writer leaned across the table. "I've written a book like that," he said. "It's coming out in '96."

"Really?" I said. "That's heartening to hear."

"I'll tell it to you," he said.

A woman whispered, "He charges thousands of dollars to tell stories at elementary schools."

The famous writer told me a story that was just as he'd promised, a story where a little girl has two mothers, yet the story is about the little girl's adventurousness.

When he finished I thanked him. "That was it, all right. Too bad my little girls will be all grown up by the time it comes out."

"I'll send it to you," the famous writer said. He shoved a slip of paper across the table. "Write your address for me."

When I got home from my business trip, the famous writer's manuscript was in my stack of mail. I scanned it quickly, smiling, then passed it along to Meg. "This is about a girl like you," I explained.

"Like me?" Sounding long-suffering and bored, she read it out loud to her friend DD. "It needs pictures, Mom," she said, interrupting herself.

"It's just a manuscript. Pretend there's pictures. Pretend you're much younger."

Meg read on. She finally cottoned on to the fact that the protagonist had lesbian parents. She thrust her face forward in disbelief. "Mom! Mom! This is a book about a girl like me!"

"A girl like me," I thought.

Meg wrote a little note to her friend Lisa and left it where I couldn't help but see it. "Do you have a crush on Lisa?" I asked her.

"No way!" Meg said.

Sarah, at the dining room table, observed, "If you don't have a crush on a girl, you'll be the only person in this family who doesn't."

I frowned. "Really, Sarah. If Meg is heterosexual, that's just fine. That's a fine thing to be."

Sarah laughed out loud.

Meg said, "Mom, make her shut up!"

"Sarah," I said warningly. I turned to Meg. "Meg, honey, don't listen to her. You can be straight. Sexuality doesn't matter, Meg. Other stuff matters, like love, like kindness. Like truth."

"Like girls like me?" Meg asked.

"Oh yes," I said. "Girls like you and your sister, exactly."

"Out" in the Community

TANYA GULLIVER

SOMETIMES BEING A MOTHER REALLY TERRIFIES ME. THE WORD "MOTHER" presumes such awesome responsibility. A mother has to be a doctor, a teacher, a judge, a therapist, a chef, a cleaner and so much more. Most of all, a mother offers guidance and love to her children to steer them through their life on the smoothest possible course. I wonder if I'm really able to do all of this, at a time when I'm still trying to figure out who I am and what direction my own life should take.

When I was younger, I decided that I didn't want to go through nine months of morning sickness and hours of labour. I figured that, when I wanted a child, I would adopt. Having grown up in a home with an adopted brother and sister, as well as thirty-four foster children, adoption and fostering were natural ways of parenting to me.

When I realized that I was a lesbian, I decided that I wanted to have a child with my partner, whoever she was. My first girlfriend and I talked about this a lot. She really wanted to have a baby, and we thought about asking my brother to donate sperm so that it would be the next best thing to me impregnating her. We never reached the point of carrying through this plan before our relationship ended.

I had never thought about becoming part of a "ready-made" family, but that's what has happened in my life. My partner, Louise, and I have been together for two years. She is the mother of three boys (Tim, seventeen; Jay, twelve; and Jesse, eleven) from two previous relationships.

Tim lives on his own in a nearby town, and was previously living with his grandmother. Shortly after we met, he and I discussed our ages (I'm almost nine years older than he). When he told me that he was dating people my age, I knew that it wouldn't be reasonable to even attempt to have a mothering role in his life.

Jesse and Jay live with Louise and me, and this ready-made family has provided me with some real ups and downs over the past two years. When Louise and I met, she was in the process of leaving a physically and emotionally abusive four-year relationship with another woman. Our relationship provided her with the strength she needed to make the final break. The end of that relationship was painful for Louise and the boys. The boys witnessed a great deal of abuse at the end, and Jesse even had to call 911 to get the police to break up a fight. As well, shortly after I began living with Louise and the boys, the Children's Aid Society threatened to remove the children if they continued to live in the apartment because Louise's ex-partner still had access to it. As a result, Louise and the boys moved into my house with me. The grieving process that they were going through meant that I had to take on most of the responsibility for our lives, as well as providing emotional support to help them through this time. This was not an auspicious beginning to a relationship, and was perhaps too much of an introduction to motherhood.

I joke sometimes that what I really needed at the beginning was a nine-month adjustment period, similar to pregnancy. This is probably something that all of us could have used. The boys began calling me their "co-mom," which, while flattering, was perhaps too much too soon. I was put in the position of having to be responsible for them and their lives, and yet they barely knew me. It was a rather quick change in all of our lives.

I had been married before becoming involved with Louise, and I had also had lesbian relationships before that. Most people in my life, especially in my professional life, did not know that I had ever had lesbian relationships or that I defined myself as bisexual. I was involved with the gay and lesbian community in Durham Region where I live, but this was not known in the general community.

When Louise and the boys moved in, I was halfway through a three-year term as a trustee with the Durham Board of

Education. Although I was not known to be a lesbian, I had recently faced rampant criticism and homophobia because of my attitudes towards AIDS education. Our board had been targeted by a group of "concerned citizens" who felt that one of our video resources promoted masturbation, premarital sex and, worst of all, was neutral (or even positive) towards homosexuality. The group also claimed that the local AIDS Committee (of which I was a board member) was trying to infiltrate the schools, to spread a message that premarital or homosexual sex was good. The group used the video to gain an audience at the board level and within the community. They used fear tactics to raise the concern with the public, and even staged demonstrations at the board office.

The AIDS Committee, members of the gay and lesbian community, concerned students and community members organized a group called "Concerned Citizens for Progressive Sexual Education" (CCPSE). CCPSE, which I joined, advocated for sexual education that discussed both abstinence and safer sex. My views were considered to be an affront to certain community members, who began lobbying to have me removed as a trustee. Some of the letters to the board calling for my resignation referred to me as "that gay trustee," even though at the time I was still married and in a heterosexual relationship.

When Louise and I first became a couple, I was wary of revealing the nature of our relationship in case the campaign against me got any stronger. I stopped hiding my sexual orientation, but did not do anything to reveal it. I did play a parental role with the boys at their school, but didn't define it as such. The boys referred to me as their mom when they were with their friends, or just called me by my first name.

Finally, in the fall of 1993, I decided that it was becoming impossible to hide my lesbianism — and, anyway, I wasn't comfortable hiding it. I wrote a "coming out" article for *Quota*, a now defunct Toronto lesbian newspaper. In advance of the article's publication, I distributed copies to my fellow trustees. Their reactions were fairly positive, although some of them said they would have preferred not to know.

During this time, Louise and I registered the boys in a new school, as my house was in a different district from their former apartment. I was listed, without any problems, as a parent on the registration forms. The school had a new principal that year, so in addition to introducing myself as a trustee I told him that I was coming out publicly as a lesbian and had enrolled my kids in his school. Within two days, both the area superintendent and the director had been informed and had contacted me about my "coming out."

The news media picked up on the story but the coverage was all positive. Two editorials praised my honesty in revealing this part of my life. One of the articles was written as a "lifestyle" piece and included a photo of the four of us and comments from the boys. Although we were a little worried about the reaction the boys would get at school, our fears were unfounded. Teachers were impressed with our "courage" while the boys' fellow students thought it was "cool" that their picture was in the paper.

Predictably, though, there was significant outrage from "concerned parents." The board issued a statement acknowledging that sexual orientation was protected grounds under the Ontario Human Rights Code and refused to discuss the matter any further. A movement to defeat me in the next election was successful, however, and a slate of Christian candidates ran and won several seats on the board. As a result, sexual education is once again being attacked.

One of the ironies of my coming out, as one of the local papers noted, is that when I was first elected I was childless, but now I have children and should be able to understand the needs of parents to a greater degree.

Too often, I hear concerns that gay and lesbian parents will raise gay and lesbian children. So far, it seems that all three of our boys are happily heterosexual. We are very supportive of this, and encourage them to be their own people. Occasionally, when we tease one of them a little after he has spent an hour on the phone with a girl, he will toss it right back at us — if we say, "Jay has a girlfriend," Jay usually replies, "So do you!"

We do have to deal with our own internalized homophobia and sexism when raising children, especially boys. On one occasion, Jesse put on a bra, stuffed it with balloons and paraded around the house. He then wanted me to put makeup on him. I obliged, but Louise was very upset when she saw him. I think, though, that allowing him to do this once got it out of his system, and he's never shown an interest in doing it again. On another occasion, Jesse shaved his legs because "the hair was too long." We really didn't want to discourage him from doing this, but we also didn't want to encourage it. We felt we were walking a fine line, as neither of us usually shaves our legs and we didn't want to perpetuate male/female gender stereotypes. In the end, we told him that it was his choice, that most men don't shave their legs, and that he would have to use his own razors if he were to continue to do this.

One of the things that has really surprised me is how accepting the boys' friends, and other students in general, have been about their having lesbian mothers. For both Jay and Jesse, having a lesbian mother is all they have ever known. They don't make a big deal out of it, but they never try to hide it either. At the beginning of school this year, Jesse had to write a description of himself and he included the fact that he had two mothers in his piece. He also wears to school his shirt that reads, "My Ontario includes gay and lesbian families," and is very proud of it. The boys' friends treat both Louise and me as parents, without even thinking about it. They say things like "Which one of your moms is home?" or "Ask a mother if you can ..." The boys have never had any type of unpleasantness at school or in the neighbourhood because of our sexual orientation.

At a recent birthday party one of the guests began calling people "fag" and "queer." I took him aside and explained that it wasn't appropriate to call people such names, and that we definitely didn't tolerate it in our house. A look of great understanding came onto his face, and he immediately stopped.

Within our community, we have encountered very few problems except for a little confusion. Either of us can take the boys to the doctor without any questions being asked. At school, I sign notes and tests, although all letters home are still addressed to Louise only. The boys' teachers were initially uncomfortable with our situation, but gradually this has changed. One of Jesse's teachers refers to us as "these people" — in an effort, I think, to avoid saying "mothers" or "parents." On the other hand, the vice-principal says "your mothers" in reference to us when talking to the boys.

Most of my friends knew that I was a lesbian, and were quick to consider the boys to be my children. Acceptance from my family has been much slower. It is often difficult for gays and lesbians to gain the acceptance they want and deserve from their families. I know that, in my case, it has been a long struggle for my parents to finally realize that this is not a phase. One of the common reactions of parents who learn that their child is gay or lesbian is to sadly declare that "now we won't have any grandchildren." Ironically, many parents, including my own, do not consider the children of their child's partner to be grandchildren in any way. In heterosexual relationships, acceptance of such children often occurs less quickly than the acceptance of biological children, but it usually happens eventually. My parents are gradually making progress in this area, but it is very slow. At least my mother has stopped referring to Jesse and Jay as "your roomate's kids." My sister has been very accepting of the boys, and they are considered cousins to her daughter. As well, Louise and I are both considered to be aunts, rather than just me.

I have always been a very political person. When Bill 167 was before the Ontario legislature, we all got involved in the lobbying effort. Louise and I took the boys to the Campaign for Equal Families office in Toronto, and they helped work on the campaign. A few times the boys missed school to help out, but the education they got at the campaign office was better than anything they could have learned in school. The boys looked up postal codes to learn the ridings of MPPs, made rally signs and faxed letters. As a family — particularly one from outside of Toronto — we were also asked to participate in a number of media interviews for newspaper, radio and TV. These ranged in kind from local papers in our community, to BBC radio and

CBC *Prime Time News*. On the day of the vote on the second reading of the bill, we did a total of eight different interviews.

We also all wrote letters to our MPP. Jesse's letter was particularly touching, and became an important part of the Campaign for Equal Families. His letter was blown up into a small poster, and distributed throughout the gay and lesbian community. One MPP even used Jesse's letter during the debate, and Jesse was asked to read his letter at a rally at Jarvis Collegiate in Toronto. Eight hundred gays and lesbians gave him a rousing standing ovation before he even started speaking.

His letter read:

> To all MPPs,
> My name is Jesse Giroux and I am ten years old. I live with two mothers. I am asking you please with all my heart to vote yes on the same sex rights bill. Please don't split this family up by voting no.
>   Sincerely yours,
>   Jesse Giroux

The boys were both heartbroken when the bill was defeated, but are prepared to continue working for change. The next step will be for all of us to work on lobbying at a federal level to get sexual orientation added to the Charter of Rights and Freedoms. We will also be considering a legal challenge to the adoption laws.

It was very important to me that the kids were involved in the lobbying effort. As a political person myself, I know that politics will always be a big part of their lives. And, since they have both expressed interest in having me adopt them, lobbying for change was a good introduction to the political process.

I love Jesse and Jay very much and consider them to be my children. They do, however, require an incredible amount of time and energy. I had not anticipated being the mother of almost-adolescent boys at my age (I am fourteen years older than Jay, and fifteen years older than Jesse). Jay and Jesse find it amusing that I am relatively young, but they also appreciate that, for example, I share with them a similar taste in music. I had also assumed that, when I became a mother, I would start with babies and not half-grown young men. Entering the life of children halfway through their childhood is very difficult. They are very set in their ways, and so am I.

I have come to believe that being a step-parent is a difficult proposition, regardless of one's sexual orientation. Being a lesbian step-parent just presents different challenges in the larger world.

Homophobia in Schools

HANNAH MCLAUGHLIN

~~❦~~

Introduction

IT IS HARD TO PINPOINT WHEN I DECIDED TO RESEARCH THE TOPIC OF homophobia in schools. In years past, I was a student in several classrooms in which families were talked about in class units. Never was a family like mine discussed. I was raised by a good mother who did her best raising her two "girl-women," as she called us. I grew up having to watch what I said around my friends and my mother's co-workers. She is an Episcopal Priest and a professor of medieval church history. She could have lost her job teaching as well as the ability to work as a priest, something she values almost as much as being a mother. My mother is not alone in her endeavours as a mother. "Approximately 10-11 million American women are lesbians. 20-30 percent of these lesbians are also mothers. Thus the approximate number of lesbian mothers is about 2 million in the United States alone" (Lyons, 1980, p. 232, citing Martin and Lyons, 1972).

The voices of children of lesbians are too often not heard. These children are taken from their homes by the courts and harassed in schools because of homophobia and misconceptions about these hard-working mothers who also happen to be lesbians. "If she (the lesbian mother) chooses to express her lesbianism, she runs the risk of becoming involved in a custody battle over the right to raise her children. At present, the likelihood of her winning such a battle is no greater than 50 percent" (Rand, Grahm, Rawlings, 1982, p. 27). I hope to shed some light on how the children of these often unacknowledged women feel about their lives at school and home.

The first section of this article is a brief overview of the limited research on how the children of lesbian mothers (like myself) are affected by a largely homophobic society. The main thing about my mother's lifestyle that affected me while growing up was having to keep secrets about my mom from my friends and from my mother's co-workers. I hope that through this paper, this book, and other writings that will follow in the future, more teachers, parents and administrators will see that the children of lesbians need to be acknowledged and made to feel welcome and wanted in their schools and neighborhoods.

The second part of this article is a description of the sample of fourteen children and their seventeen parents, all of whom I interviewed. They told me about their experiences with schools and school teachers in their mostly open and accepting communities. I will discuss if and how these children are affected by their communities, and what that means to their relationships with their friends and their families.

Overview of the Current Research

One can find a large amount of research on the topic of whether a lesbian mom should raise her children and whether she will influence her children to become homosexuals. Given that the term "lesbian mother" indicates something unnatural to most of society, there is an unfortunate need for lesbians to prove themselves to a homophobic society. One woman put it rather nicely: "Everyone always said I'd make a great mom. I love children. It doesn't make sense to give up my plan for having a child just because I am a lesbian" (Pies, 1990, p.138).

My main concern here is with the children of lesbians and how they are affected by influences outside the home. It seems that there is a general consensus in the research that it is *not* the influence of the mothers on the children that's a problem. Greene and Bozett give a good synopsis of this issue: "It is evident that homosexuality is compatible with effective parenting … children do not seem in any way to be at risk or harmed because of parental homosexuality. Moreover, the parent-child bond may be closer than is found in more traditional families" (Green and Bozett, 1991, p. 213).

My second concern is one specific influence outside the home: how the schools are reacting to the children of lesbians in their classrooms. Elaine Wickens and her fellow researchers have found two prevailing opinions regarding the matter of gay families in the schools. One opinion is that the children of homosexual persons should be acknowledged in the classroom, to assure them that their family is not bad and unmentionable. The other opinion is that homosexuality should stay out of the classroom — that there is no place for it in society. What about the children of homosexuals in this latter case? These children will grow up with the idea that they are bad, that they have no place in society just because they have parents who happen to be gay. Says Wickens: "There are 8-10 million children in 3 million gay families in this country" (Wickens, 1993, p. 25, citing American Bar Association, 1991). That's a whole lot of children to alienate from society.

Researchers found that some teachers don't know how to handle having the children of lesbians in their classrooms. A teacher interviewed by Wickens et al. chose not to conduct a "family" unit because she didn't know how to change her pre-existing unit to include the lesbian family of one of her children. Many teachers are afraid that they will lose their jobs if they speak out and tell children that it is okay to have two moms or two dads.

The final important topic I wish to address is how children feel about being raised by mothers who fit somewhere outside the "norms" of society. The voices of these children will change the opinions of society in the future. There was a consensus amongst my interview subjects that children both young and old have a hard time coping with having a family that is "different" than that of most of their friends and classmates. However, they love their mothers. They also seem to have grown emotionally from their experiences. And there is some hope in the wider world. Schools and teachers are trying to incorporate lesbian and gay families into their classroom curricula despite limitations from school boards and the general population. "One goal in a country that prides itself on being a democracy is to teach all people to include all people" (Wickens, 1993, p. 28). As the children I interviewed grow up to become adults themselves, they may be able to make more changes toward a more inclusive society.

The Interview Method

Before starting my interview process, I put together a set of three questionnaires. The first was a background information questionnaire filled out by the parent(s) in order to make the parent interview shorter. It consisted of questions about family background, including names and ages of family members and the parent's relationship status, etc. The second questionnaire was the parent interview, which asked in-depth questions about the parents' experiences with homophobia in the schools, their impressions about their children's experiences, and concluded with an open-ended question: Was there anything unique to their family that I should know about? The final questionnaire was the children's interview. It consisted of questions about school and family, and what the children liked and disliked about both. Again, I asked an open-ended question: Was there anything important they wanted to tell me about their life and their family?

I began the process of finding families to be interviewed by asking my mother for lesbian mothers that she knew. Through her contacts, I was able to find one family with four children; this family had two children and one mother who were willing to be interviewed. I then talked to my co-workers and friends at the school I attended, Antioch College. Here, I had much greater success. Through the lesbian network in Yellow Springs, Ohio, I was put in touch with five families, with a total of six children, who were willing to be interviewed. All five of these families were interviewed face-to-face in their homes. I tape-recorded all the interviews and transcribed them for the study. I also asked the parents to sign a release form to allow me to interview children under eighteen years of age. As I exhausted my contacts in Yellow Springs, I began to think about other options for attaining my goal of ten interviews with children. It was at this point that I decided to use my knowledge of computers and the Internet. I looked at the questionnaires and restructured them slightly to allow for the inability to ask follow-up questions on the Internet. The changes made were minimal, but insured that there could be fluidity in answering the questions that I asked and no misinterpretation of what I wanted. They consisted of extra questions that were added to the initial questionnaires to make up for the lack of verbal responses. I also wrote an introduction to the questionnaires explaining my intentions and thanking the participants for their help as well as asking for their ethnicity. As I received responses from the mothers, I uploaded the questionnaires to my mail account from my computer and sent them individually (as a set of three) to the women who responded. I received four sets back. These comprised the rest of my interviews.

All the mothers in this study are self-described lesbians. The children are seven boys and seven girls, ranging in age from eight to nineteen.

Family Background Information & Parent Interview

In all, there were fourteen children and seventeen parents who voluntarily participated in this study. They made up a total of ten families, four of whom were interviewed over the Internet. Six children and eight parents were in the Internet group. The rest of the children and parents were interviewed in the subjects' homes. In the interviews attained over the Internet, only one parent answered each of the questionnaires. In face-to-face interviews, both parents were present except in one instance and one or both of the parents answered each question.

The questions I asked of the parents were:

What are your names and ages?

What are your family origins?

Are you currently in a relationship?

Do you have equal guardianship of your children?

Do you share parenting equally?

Did the current relationship begin after the children were born/came into the family?

How do you feel you have been treated by your children's teachers?

The answers to these questions yielded this information:

The parents I interviewed ranged in age from twenty-five to forty-nine. The average age was 36.2 years. The children in this study ranged in age from eight to nineteen, with an average age of twelve. Some of the children had older or younger siblings who were not included in the study.

Six families were European American. One family considered themselves to be Black Jews. One family was bi-racial (African American/European American), and one family was African American.

Eight of the mothers were currently in a relationship and two were not. Only one co-parent was not interviewed due to separation. Seven co-parents did not have equal guardianship. For some co-parents this was because the law did not permit it. In these cases the biological mother had guardianship. One couple did have equal guardianship of their children.

Five couples shared parenting equally, and three did not. The biological mother took more or all responsibility in the latter case. For two mothers, this question was not applicable since they were not in a relationship. Nine relationships had started after the children were born, involving thirteen children. In one instance a son was adopted as an infant into the current relationship.

Twelve parents indicated that they had been treated respectfully by their children's teachers. There was one parent (in a relationship) who had encountered some possible homophobia over assumptions made by her child's counsellors regarding her fitness as a (single?) mother. One parent remembered her daughter being hassled on several occasions.

Most of the parents in this study expressed the belief that their overall good treatment was due to their constant, equal involvement in school matters and reinforcement of their status as co-parents when they met with teachers and went to school events. When asked about this, one mother commented, "I would say, respectfully, most interactions I've had with the teachers have been on typical academic stuff and haven't dealt with issues of having a different ... 'that different type of family.' Everyone has been very receptive and respectful. I would like to qualify that Yellow Springs is different than most places."

Another stated, "Although it wasn't talked about, people knew that my partner and I were together. We were invited to potlucks where there were heterosexual couples as well. It was kind of accepted that we were a family unit." Many parents have had some problems with teachers misunderstanding them or assuming that the mother was a single mother because she was not married. These assumptions and problems were considered to be nothing more than minor annoyances and easily handled. One mother's final statement might just describe how many gay and lesbian parents in the US feel today: "raising kids is difficult under the best circumstances and takes real dedication. It takes even more serious dedication to help kids overcome the strong social stigmatization that accompanies homosexuality."

The Children's Voices

Interviewing the children was a lot easier than I had thought it would be. Most of the children were very open and sharing, although some found it hard to talk about school and being teased. Five of these children were girls and four were boys. The age range was from eight to nineteen years, with an average age of 12.9.

The questions I asked of the children were as follows:

Do you ever get teased by kids at school because of your mom?

Do you know people around your age who have two moms or a single lesbian mom?

Do you have friends who know about your mom(s)?

Do you like school?

Is there anything that this questionnaire hasn't covered that you think is important for me to know about you (something that might be special to your family or is important to my understanding of you and your life)?

These questions yielded the following responses:

Nine children had not been teased by other children because of their mom(s). Of the children who answered "no," one child was not "out" about his mom's sexual orientation to any of his friends, and one child had not been "out" about his mom's sexual orientation until late high school, but was out at the time of the interview. This child said: "… it was only recently that I've been able to call her (the co-parent) my other mom. To say I have two moms and let people figure out what that means. I'd say that was maybe the last two or three years that I've been able to do that. It's difficult because it's not just my confidentiality when I do that, it's her's (my mom's) as well and her lover's as well, so it's not always an easy thing to do."

Five children answered "yes," indicating that they have been teased by other children because of their mother's sexual orientation. Two of these children were girls and three were boys. There were no significant differences found in the sex of the children for this question. Out of the children who said "yes," one child had been teased by his friends: "We're just joking around," they said. (Since the interview, it has come to my attention through close friends of the family and my own that this child has been through a rough time with these same friends. He has been harassed by them because of his mother's sexual preference.) Two have been harassed on many occasions and are really upset about it. When asked what kinds of things she got teased about one girl said, "About my mom and since they know about my mom then they start to tease about the clothes I wear and I get mad. I just want to hit them."

One child's parents referred to a couple of homophobic incidents in the school where the child had been cornered and harassed, and therefore, although the child did not mention the harassment, she was included as a "yes." The parents recalled: "I remember one real bad episode where kids cornered her in sixth grade. It wasn't directly on the basis her having a gay family, it was just childhood meanness but in that situation one of the students slapped her across the face and made some very outrageous … using strong curse words about 'your lesbian mother: Go home and cuddle up to your lesbian mother; your lesbian dyke mother.'"

All of the children who were teased were between eight and thirteen years of age, with an average age of 10.6. This is an age range during which children typically tease each other a lot; this tendency could be of some interest to those doing research in this area.

Nine children answered "yes" to knowing other children with gay or lesbian parents. Two of the children who answered "yes," have not told anyone at school about their mothers (one told his friends after finishing high school). Five children are open and up front about their moms. One child has been open but has been harassed at least once and is bothered by this. "I used to be afraid that some of my friends would find out, or anybody at school, but now I don't. It's hard to know what to do when I hear people queer-bashing. Sometimes I speak up, but sometimes I don't feel safe doing that."

One child was very out about her mom and has been so for most of her life.

Five children answered "no" to having peers with gay or lesbian parents. Two of these children are very open about their moms, have friends who know about their moms and have had little or no trouble with harassment in school. Three children have been harassed one or more times, and two of these children have had a very hard time with continuous incidents in school.

All fourteen children have some friends/playmates who know about their mom(s). One child wasn't out to his friends in school until he left high school (and his mother stopped teaching in the area). One child felt that she didn't have many friends because of her mom's identity. One child felt that he couldn't tell his friends at school about his moms, but has friends from other areas that do know about his moms.

Six children said, "yes," they do like school. Six children said, "no," they do not like school. One child does not like school because of the harassment she has to deal with there. Two children said that they liked school sometimes, but that there are academic aspects that they don't like.

Five children (three girls and two boys) said they had nothing to add about their life or their family at the end of the interview. Nine children answered with a desire to tell me about how they love their moms and how they have been raised well despite the social pressures they feel exist against their families.

One child of the nine who answered the question was afraid his friends would find out before he "came out" to them. One child had to keep his mother's identity a secret for fear of her losing her job as a high school teacher. Three children wanted people to know that having a gay parent is okay — they aren't weird. As one child said: "I really think that the myths that single families are detrimental, that if your parents are gay you are wrong and that if you don't have a man around that you won't learn how to be a man. I try to go against these myths and say, hey, look — I'm a normal person. I think it's different having opposite sex parents be gay. I think that's an interesting issue and I think it needs to be considered. It's not necessarily bad but it definitely changed who I am. I really liked having two moms. Just cause I think it's cool." This child also wants us to know that the myths about the "horrors" of lesbian mothers are wrong. He feels lucky and privileged to have grown up in this way. All of the children who answered the final question seem to have excellent and open relationships with both of their moms. These children feel that they can be open about everything in their lives, and they also talk about their own lives with their moms on a regular basis. Said one: "I love both of my mothers. I think of them as my mothers not as my mom and Cindy. They are my family. And if my mom and Cindy break up, Cindy will still be a part of my family. I like having her around."

No sex differences were found in the responses to this question. The children who answered this question were all above the age of ten, and therefore had more experiences to draw upon.

Conclusion

It has been a truly eye-opening experience to read about and research the lives of so many people who, like myself, have lesbian mothers. Most of the children that I talked to and read about are extremely proud of their mothers. Some would even shout it from the roof tops if they could do so without repercussions from the outside world, including schools (administrators, teachers and peers), mothers' places of employment, extended family, and the state. Some even come out about their moms despite the outside influences. Eighty-five percent of the children in my study were out about their moms in the school that they attended. These children ranged in age from eight to nineteen. One child whom I interviewed felt strong enough about himself to say something when he was angered by the disregard of his family type by his teacher. He wrote her a letter explaining his love for his mother. He felt he had to say *something*, but could not get past the repercussions that might come with signing his name. These words could very well depict what the other children feel, whether or not they feel that they can express it to others outside their family:

> Dear Ms. Tripp,
> As a student in one of your classes just beginning the family unit, I was offended by the exclusion of gay and lesbian families in the introductory packet to our unit. If the packet is an attempt to include all types of families then please don't leave out the kind of family I live in and have lived in for most of my life. I would appreciate it if you would include gay and lesbian families as a type of family that really does exist.
> As the son of a lesbian mother, when I looked on the list for a description of my family and it wasn't there, I felt like my type of family wasn't considered "real." For me, *Kate and Allie* just does not cut it!!!
> Sincerely,
> *Someone who is proud of his mom!*

For many families, this kind of "speaking out" could mean the break-up of a solid and stable home. As I have shown here, children are being raised by their lesbian mothers as well as (if not better than) they would be raised by a heterosexual mother of the same socio-economic level. Still, many courts refuse to accept the research which demonstrates that children raised by lesbian mothers are *not* negatively affected by their mother's lesbianism. Statistics support the conclusion that they *are not* any more likely than the children raised by heterosexual parents to turn out to be lesbian or gay (Gottman, 1990). In fact, the opposite seems to be true: the vast majority of lesbians and gay men in the United States today come from families headed by heterosexual parents. The research also shows that many children have grown up in their lesbian mothers' homes without detriment (Gottman, 1990; Lewis, 1980; Green, 1978). These same children have had some added hardships because of hostile *outside* influences, *not* because of their mothers' supposed pathology.

The older children in my study (thirty-five percent of the subjects were over twelve years of age) have not suffered excessively from their mothers' lesbianism. The research shows that the older children seem to have grown to be more mature and capable adults through coping with instances of hostility and homophobia, and seem to be more able (than the children of heterosexual parents) to cope with the natural hardships of life as adults in this society (Gottman, 1989; Lewis, 1980).

It is possible that homophobia in the courts as well as the unfamiliarity with lesbian-headed households in the schools cause these children to have problems. With nearly eleven million children growing up in lesbian or gay families in the U.S. alone, how can we make the decision that they don't have a right to be considered a family? Many of the children in my study had to keep secrets about their lives from their friends, neighbours and school teachers, and even, sometimes, from their own extended families as well. How safe can the life of a child be if that child is constantly having to watch what he or she says when talking about his or her family? Children sometimes feel that they can't invite friends over after school because friends and peers might find out about mom's lovers or lesbianism, and then mom could lose her job, or they could lose their moms. It is my contention, based upon my personal experience as well as my research that if homophobia in the courts and schools could be reduced, or at the very least, laws put in place to protect lesbian mothers and their children, these issues for children would at last begin to disappear.

Acknowledgments

I dedicate this paper first to Ellie, my mother, and to Betsy, my second mother (for, without Betsy's influence, I wouldn't have been a psychology major). This paper is also for all the lesbian mothers out there who are raising wonderful and aware children, despite the hardships and injustices of this society. Lastly, I dedicate this paper to the children of lesbian mothers who will grow up to make a difference in the world and show society that we are not strange and have not been negatively affected by our mothers' lesbianism.

A special thanks should also go to my academic advisor, Dr. Patricia Linn; without her help and support, I would have never gotten through my last quarter of college and the research on which this paper is based.

References

Casper, V., S. Schultz and E. Wickens, "Breaking the silences: lesbian and gay parents and the schools," *Teachers College Record*, 94, 1 (1992), pp. 110-37.

Gelder, L. V., "A lesbian family revisited," *Ms.*, 1, 5 (1991), pp. 44-7.

Gottman, J.S., "Children of Gay and Lesbian Parents," *Marriage and Family Review*, 14, 3-4 (1989), pp. 177-96.

Green, D.G. and F.W. Bozett, "Lesbian Mothers and Gay Fathers," in *Homosexuality: Research Implications for Public Policy*, J.C. Gosiorek and J.D. Weinrich (eds.), (Newbury Park: Sage Publications, 1991), pp. 197-214.

Lewis, K.G., "Children of lesbians: their point of view," *Social Work*, (May 1980), pp. 198-203.

Lyons, T.A., "Lesbian mothers' custody fears," *Women and Therapy*, 2 (1980), pp. 231-40.

Pies, Cheri A., "Lesbians and the Choice to Parent," *Marriage and Family Review*, 3-4 (1990), pp. 137-54.

Price, J. H., "High school students' attitudes toward homosexuality," *The Journal of School Health*, 52, 8 (1982), pp. 469-74.

Rand, C. D. Graham and E. Rawlings, "Psychological health and factors the court seeks to control in lesbian mother custody trials," *Journal of Homosexuality*, 8, 1 (1982), pp. 27-39.

Wickens, E., "Penny's Question: 'I will have a child in my class with two moms — what do you know about this?'" *Young Children*, 48, 3 (1993), pp. 25-8.

*Parents &
Children:
Reflections
on Identity*

Another View of Lesbians Choosing Children

ANGELA BOWEN

IN 1976, ADRIENNE RICH SAID, "WE NEED TO IMAGINE A WORLD IN WHICH every woman is the presiding genius of her own body. In such a world women will truly create new life, bringing forth not only children, if and as we choose, but the visions and the thinking necessary to sustain, console and alter human existence, a new relationship to the universe. Sexuality, politics, intelligence, power, motherhood, work, community and intimacy will develop new meanings. Thinking itself will be transformed. This is where we have to begin."[1] Well, lesbians, we have begun. At least, the bringing forth of children as we choose has begun. It's the visions and thinking, the politics, the community — all that other business — that I want to discuss here.

I remember how resentful I felt when the true deal about marriage hit me and I realized that all the people who had been urging me along that path knew the truth about it but no one had told me. I'd asked all the women I could talk to what marriage was really like. And everyone — including those who professed to care about me — were under societal pressure to uphold the myth so they wouldn't disillusion young women. Didn't want people to accuse them of being bitter. Then when I made the discovery that I'd been rooked, and wanted to know was this all, what I heard was, "Oh, girl, of course that's what marriage is, you should know that, what did you expect? Don't be so naive." Accompanied by all those sly winks, the wise nods and the beginnings of the talk about men as those little boys whom you could coddle and make think that they're big and strong, etc. Well, I made up my mind that if anyone asked me, I'd sure as hell tell them all of it — including the few good things that I could somehow scrounge up for them — the truth as I saw it.

Lately, while I've been doing some serious thinking about trying to get at my truths, what struck me was that motherhood has been such a constant factor in my life for the past twenty-five years that I never even considered that I'm not heading out of motherhood, even though my children will be grown. It will be with me for as long as I live. It's a forever fact that never ceases to be. My firstborn died one month short of his fourth birthday in 1966. And I remember the first Mother's Day after he died, wondering if I was still a mother. Well, as it happened at that time, I had a foster daughter and a stepdaughter. So clearly I was still a mother even though my muddled grief didn't allow me to think so. But I believe now that even if I didn't have those older girls to mother, I still would have been a mother, because you don't cease being one even though you outlive your child. You're never again not a mother, just as you're never again a virgin once you have sex. Just as you're never again not conscious once you become a feminist. So you are never again not a mother once you have a child. It's the only really forever relationship. Even if you decide to no longer mother someone you've mothered in the past, it's still an ongoing relationship, if only one of refusal. You're only done with it when you die. Now, just think about that. I came to that realization only two weeks ago.

One week ago I was in Washington, D.C., at a lesbian conference on aging called Passages and the panel was asked, "What was it like being a lesbian of your age? — which is fifty-two — and we were told to define our answers in terms of being an activist, a feminist, disabled, whatever — and I chose to speak in terms of feminism, because it so totally transformed my life. Three times in my life I've felt transformed. Once when as a teenager I discovered dance, again when I was in my late thirties and discovered feminism and then at forty when I became a lesbian. Now, I've heard women say that being a mother transformed their lives, but I can't say the same. I was a mother at twenty-six, long before I felt the consciousness of feminism. But I felt reborn because of feminism and it is that feminism which has allowed me to even begin to question the whys of motherhood.

In my youth, women didn't much question the desire to be mothers, even when they didn't want husbands. I remember as a little girl saying, "I want to have children but I don't want a husband." And people would kind of think that was cute and laugh and I didn't know why they were laughing. Then when I was a teenager, they would try to make me explain how I would go about this. I'd say, "Well, when I'm about twenty-eight (to me that was pretty old) and I finish travelling all over the world dancing (which I did manage to do), I'll pick out a healthy, intelligent man, have two children by him, he'll go his way and I'll take the children and go my way." And they would say, "Oh yeah, you think you're going to pull that one off?" But if I were a young woman today, that wouldn't be a farfetched plan — they're doing it all the time. Lesbians and non-lesbians. We're all doing it. We keep reading the papers about broken, single-parent families. But what the statistics don't tell us is that those families aren't necessarily broken — a great many are quite deliberately planned that way.

But why do we plot and plan to have these children? What do they offer? What does motherhood offer to lesbians? Is it really worth it? Why do we do it? Is it maternal instinct? What is maternal instinct, really? Is it a response to societal conditioning? Are we exhibiting rebellious defiance, showing that as lesbians we can have children without your participation or approval, you men, so up yours? Is it the wish to create that perfect childhood we never had for ourselves? Is it the ego of perpetuating ourselves? Is it simple curiosity? Or the yearning to have the experience every woman feels she has the right to? But if so, where did that yearning come from? If it's instinctual, why doesn't every woman have it? And if these aren't enough questions for you, what are yours? And after all those questions, as lesbians, we still have to go out of our way to acquire children. But today's technology assures us that we don't have to go as far as we used to. These days we can make the choice to have babies if we want to.

In the excellent anthology on lesbian parenting, *Politics of the Heart*, Jan Clausen says, "We don't move by rules, we move toward what we love. We don't have or not have them for political reasons. Having kids, being with kids, looking toward a new generation is part of being human. And in one sense I think the current public and publicized interest in having babies is another way the lesbian feminist community is stretching into a newfound sense of its rights to the full range of human and female experience."[2] Now, what about that full range of human and female experience?

Well, being pregnant is a unique experience and after three births, I can tell you that in each of my completed pregnancies, the first trimester, the last trimester, the birth and postpartum experience didn't exactly thrill me. There is something to be said for the second trimester, though. There's a private little feeling between you and one other little being that no one else can feel and the movement of the baby inside is quite sensuous once you get used to it. Now I may be strange, but out of this whole sacred, mystical feeling that I've seen written about in such glowing terms for so many years, that's about what I've got to say. Let's hear it for the second trimester.

After the obvious anxiety of the pregnancy, waiting to see if what came out of you is a complete, viable, healthy human person, then begin the years of seeing that they eat enough, burp enough, poop enough, sleep enough, air enough, bathe enough, exercise enough, walk, talk, smile, play, recognize, stimulate, or separate from you enough. You've got to see that they have playmates, develop manual dexterity, don't kill that playmate, are polite enough, get inoculated, know their numbers, colors, ABCs, read, dress themselves, pick up their toys, don't run into the street, get good marks, listen to the right music, go to a decent school, impress the teachers, don't eat sand — or doo-doo, etc. Then, when they get older, it's school, cultural development, the right companions, dating, talking about relationships, drink, dope, sex, condoms, AIDS, college, marriage, grandchildren, etc. And all the while you're trying to have a life. And you're trying to affect the future of this world to insure that life goes on for yourself and for them and for theirs. And all the while you live with that constant, lurking anxiety about your children that you who are not parents can't even begin to understand.

Now here's another in that range of human and female experience. Most of us who had borne children would never consider giving them away, even though in some cases we know someone who would do a better job than we could. And of course we love them, so that counts for everything. Well, sometimes we do — and sometimes we don't. I don't mean that in the trivial sense of exasperation that overcomes us periodically when we say, "Sometimes I really hate that kid." I mean sometimes parents have children that they really don't, simply can't, love. But who admits it? Just last week a woman spoke a cliché to me I've heard over and over. She said of her seventeen-year-old son, "I love him but I just don't like him very much." I smiled. What could I say? I've used those same words myself, as so many of us do. But lately I've been wondering what they mean.

The myth abounds that we love our children. Well, we are bound to them, we're responsible to and for them, but it's not always possible to feel that automatic love for a child that we are assured comes naturally to every mother. We're all born with inherent differences, our personalities don't necessarily mesh, no matter how hard we try, and you may happen to get a kid you just don't like or love and who doesn't love you. And don't be so sure it's that unusual either. This may just be one of the best kept dirty little secrets the world over. As Marilyn Murphy says in *Politics of the Heart*, "As a love relationship, motherhood bears some resemblance to that of an arranged marriage, wherein a woman chooses, or is forced, to enter a relationship with a person she does not know, but whom she is expected to love and take care of until one of them dies."[3] So if you seek motherhood to experience the full range of human and female experience posed by Jan Clausen, you'd be only fair to yourself if you included the realities I've just mentioned. We, of all people, don't need to romanticize motherhood.

Motherhood was named an institution and examined by Adrienne Rich in her comprehensive *Of Woman Born*. It is at one and the same time the most revered and most reviled of institutions. Lesbians notoriously have refused to live in institutions. That's why we're right out here being our sweet lesbian selves. Yet many of us who read Rich's classic work, along with other books on motherhood from the '70s, such as

The Baby Trap, lesbians who've analyzed and agonized, still have found themselves craving the experience of motherhood. So they've plunged right in, many others follow and it's growing. Still, if we're going to do motherhood, it's good to be able to talk about how, in our honest lesbian ways.

It's quite clear that you newer mothers will have far more support for your choices than we old-timers had. You have the groups you've formed while talking about choosing children. Lesbian choice groups lead to lesbian birthing classes, lead to lesbian children's play groups and on to lesbian mother and children communities. But who is part of those communities? How do you form your household? Some of those questions are being dealt with all over the lesbian feminist communities here and abroad. What model of childraising will you initiate or imitate? Nuclear, extended, interfamilial, multicultural, mothers, partners, other mothers, child-free friends? The possibilities are bounded only by our imaginations. But we're lesbians, so of course we can break the mind boundaries set up around childraising, right? Do you expect that you'll bring together groups of mothers and children who live in the same neighbourhood, houses, apartment buildings, apartments? Will you share parenting with other mothers and some child-oriented single women? Will only your lovers have access to your children? Will your ex-lovers have access to the children you have nurtured jointly? Will grandparents, aunts and uncles be included as we are more out to our own families? Will you create networks of diversity for them, people with different ethnic and class backgrounds, who are trying to overcome the variety of internalized "isms" we're all infected with? Children raised this way would be choice children indeed.

But you know, I have to say that there is something about the notion of choice children that's a bit off-putting. Does the title "Lesbians Choosing Children" mean that other women did not choose to have them? Does it mean that by definition the children of the new lesbians are somehow better than the children who came here in the time before all these new choices were available? As a Black woman, I feel a gut rejection of the notion of choice children. And here's another question I have

— being a Black woman who had children the old-fashioned way. For those of you who took up the banner of true feminism, how will the babymaking and childbearing choices you are making now affect the work you've already put into coalition building, into self-examination, into throwing off the shackles of your own racism, classism, homophobia, ableism, ageism? What do you do with the children you bring here in defiance of the patriarchy, which says, "You don't deserve to have children, since you've chosen this life style?" What will you teach them? Whose allies will you raise them to become? To whom will you be trying to prove yourselves worthy? Your families, neighbours, teachers, social workers, employers, the corner grocer, the postman? And who or what will you sacrifice to prove yourselves worthy? Me, my children, your integrity, feminism, your own soul? Yes, we have some ethical child rearing choices ahead as more children of lesbians enter our community of women.

Were you around during the last ten to twenty years making women who had children the old-fashioned way feel as if we should hide our children away, not mention them, leave them at home while we attended women-only events? I somehow don't expect that will happen in this new environment of lesbian choice. Were you among the brave new women of the '70s who set up those cruel "only girl children acceptable" parameters, making us choose between leaving our boys at home (if we would find sitters), or staying at home with them, rather than joining our sisters in shaping our movement? I hope we've come too far for that, even if so many lesbians today weren't choosing to have children. Did you ever support a sister with children by offering to babysit, by including her children in invitations, or even by simply inquiring after them, giving her an opportunity to acknowledge that they just might be as important to her as the demonstration, the mailing, the rap session? It's still not too late. And for those of you just beginning to raise children, do women of colour, poor women, disabled women now have the support of you and your children in our struggles? Or do you have more important concerns now that you have your child's welfare at stake? In

Politics of the Heart a woman is asked how having a child affected her being out as a lesbian and her reply was, "If anything, I went back into the closet a little more. Before, I didn't compromise my freedom ... but after ... it wasn't just me at stake. I didn't really go back in the closet, but I'm not willing to get in trouble or ... make her life harder. There is something I love more than my own freedom and that's her." But Pat Parker, in the same anthology, says, "We had had to do some serious consciousness-raising among family and friends. We simply made it clear that anyone wishing to participate in this child's life had to accept the premise that she had two mothers. The school got it that she would be picked up by whichever of us was available, that the permission slip was signed by whoever remembered to do it, that potluck food was prepared by whoever had time. And I still had to go to the school after her first Mother's Day there and make it clear that she should come home with two Mother's Day gifts or none at all."[5] What will you teach your children? To align themselves with heterosexuals, becoming yet another source of oppression against us? Or will you teach them to assume that our fight is also their fight? Will you be trying to raise people who can be your own friend and ally later in life, radical little warriors in the battle? Or yet another bunch of greedy yuppies mixed and matched and blended with the offspring of heterosexuals so that they won't have to suffer any slight discomfort by being considered different? Do my children, my grandchildren have future allies in your children? Or when they've all grown up will mine need to start from scratch to teach your children and grandchildren the ground rules about racism, ableism, classism because you have been so busy blending and hiding for the sake of your choice children that my children can't even find allies anymore?

Among the women who joined the second wave of feminism in the late '60s and early '70s, there was a commitment to address racism and classism as well as sexism. That commitment drew many women of colour into feminism. Now, once consciousness dawns, you don't choose or not choose to be a feminist; there's no choice about it. Still, it was difficult for many of us who were born into communities of colour because it meant rebelling against our root communities, which insisted that feminists were white, middle-class women looking to advance themselves into the existing structures of a racist and classist society. That argument still abounds today, although it recedes gradually — very gradually — as the skeptical communities of colour see where principled feminists come down on most of the issues. But the struggle, begun two decades ago, to hammer out our difficulties so that we can identify and acknowledge our differences, assuage the hurts, hear one another's oppression and work together to confront our common enemies, has only just begun, really. We can't expect in these very few short years to overcome hundreds of years of separation, divide-and-conquer tactics by intransigent men and unenlightened women, as well as our own internalized terror and self-protection. So for those of us who've already stuck our faces out the door, rather than retreating into the closet to protect our children, we need to work to develop surroundings conducive to cushioning our children from the hostility of heterosexism by finding competent, loving allies among lesbians, gay men and progressive heterosexuals who will know and honor who we are. By hiding, we're not helping our children. And putting our lesbianism on hold until they're grown is no solution. We can come up with more creative solutions to mothering than retreating into a closet.

Just recently, I figured out one way to provide more support for my daughter, my life partner and myself. Tomorrow, four loving women, one who has a child and three who do not, will participate with us in a bonding ceremony between them and my daughter. These are women we've come to know and respect, who have talents, love and warmth to share with her; she's an absolute gem and can give something back to each of them in turn. No one person can or should try to be the be-all to another. We have so many resources in the community that mothers don't need to end up feeling the full burden of trying to do it all themselves. In fact, the more of us who share our children within the community, the better for all of us, single women with much to give and receive, and the children as well.

As Sweet Honey in the Rock tell us, "Your children are not your children: they are the sons and daughters of life yearning for itself."

My mother, an immigrant from the West Indies, was aware of her need for assistance when my father died in 1938 and left her a widow with seven children. She sought out allies. We each had at least two godparents, some of us three. But as we grew up and began to identify the grown-ups we might bond with more naturally, she allowed each of us that connection after carefully checking out the people we had chosen. If she didn't like them, she let us know, but that didn't happen too often — we had pretty good judgment. So each of us had special adults and we're all the richer for it. Surround your children with the kind of people whose influence on them will please you.

I'd like now to get back to those lesbians who hide once they are parents. It's hard to answer people who think that their children are such delicate flowers that they can't undergo the trauma of having to face the reality of their parents being different from other parents. My daughter's fine about most of it, except that she can't stand for me to be on TV talking about being a lesbian. I tell her that I understand how she feels, but she needs to think about the children in South Africa or in the Palestinian camps in Israel if she thinks she's suffering because she sees my face on TV! That tends to put things in perspective a bit. And, although she may not like it, she does respect that this is my life and she'll have to choose later how to live her own. Children are strong, resilient and brave when they're given reason to be.

They also get grown and gone eventually and you're left with yourself to live with always. And they're left with the lifelong remembrance of you and what you told and showed them about how to live. Giving up your principles in the name of motherhood can be a pretty self-defeating choice. For one thing, you don't like yourself as much as you used to. For the children's sake you have become a bit less of a proud dyke than you used to be before you had them to worry about, so you resent them. Then, by hiding, you're telling them that if the larger society tells them to shut their mouths about anything that doesn't sit well with the powers that be, you think they should go along with that.

And let's not forget too that kids watch and absorb our brand of integrity even if it doesn't seem to sink in at the time. I've heard my nineteen-year-old son saying something about me in pride to other people that I never hear him address directly to me. And I can't even count the number of times children, not just mine but others, have come back and told me that they appreciated my having stood firm in some piece of conflict we'd had where they had yelled, screamed and cried because they were being made to take a difficult path. But, quiet as it's kept, they also remember the times you took the other, not so noble path. Those aren't the times they tell you about, but they sure as hell remember them. Well, you watched your parents and you sure as hell remember what they did, don't you? I know I do. Still, when all is said and done, there are no guarantees. You can spend all those good years you've got and still not end up in concert with your own children. They might decide to become the epitome of everything you can't stand.

I'm going to close by answering the question so many of us mothers hedge about when we're asked. We don't feel we can answer, for whatever reason. It goes, "If you had to do it again, would you have children, knowing what you know now?" My answer is no. Right now, I feel the weight of all the years of mothering that I'll never shake off. The trips I haven't taken, the books I haven't read, the solitude I haven't enjoyed, the books I haven't written, the women I haven't loved. Maybe if you asked me again in ten years I might feel differently, but somehow I doubt it. If I had to do it all over again, I'd mother children, as I've done; but I wouldn't have them myself. I'd take some off their mothers' hands for a couple of months at a time, or even a few years. One of my most positive mothering experiences in addition to my birth daughter, was with my teenage foster daughter for a period of three and a half years. That was over twenty years ago and between then and now, many children have thought of me as their mother — whether I wanted them to or not.

I'm only one voice among many, speaking my own truth to the best of my ability. The most helpful thing I can say is, if you have children, for your own sake and for theirs, don't hoard them to yourselves. Share them. And for those of you who choose not to have children, share in the nurturing of some other women's children. Our children, of course, are our future. But everyone else's children are our future too. So whatever else we decide, let's share the children in whatever ways we can: physically, spiritually, financially, mentally; let's take care of one another's children as well as one another. Because we've got a long way to go and we'll only make it by expanding our consciousness enough to create better ways of doing it together.

(Excerpted from a speech delivered at University of Massachusetts, Boston, in January, 1988. The complete version is published in pamphlet form by Kitchen Table: Women of Color Press, as part of the "Freedom Organizing" Series.)

Notes

1. Rich, Adrienne, *Of Woman Born*, (New York: Bantam Books, 1977), from the afterword, p. 292.
2. Pollack, Sandra, and Jeanne Vaughn (eds.), *Politics of the Heart: A Lesbian Parenting Anthology*, (Ithaca, NY: Firebrand Books, 1987), p. 339.
3. Ibid., p. 126.
4. Ibid., p. 118.
5. Ibid., p. 99.

Coming Out x Three

SHIRLEY LIMBERT

FINALLY, THE CAR WAS LOADED. THE LAST BOOK HAD BEEN PACKED, THE LAST picture stacked behind the front seats. I looked around the house I had lived in during my children's growing up years — the house I had shared with them and their father. I looked out of the kitchen window and down the path past the pear trees to the horse barn and paddocks.

I remembered the time my middle son, Simon, tried to ride the new strawberry-coloured pony, Pink Pumpkin, and how she had dragged him around the field, determined that he wouldn't ride her — although, eventually, he did. I remembered Paul, my oldest, bringing his girl friends to pet the horses and watching them lose their hearts to Tara or Jane or ID.

Today, mixed in with the excitement of moving to my new life and my new community, I felt a lot of sadness. Standing in the middle of the family room, doing a quick check, my eye fell on the ribbons and trophies from countless horse shows. I thought of my youngest son, Andrew, and the times I had stood in freezing cold arenas to watch him jump horses, smelling the sweet horsey smells, hearing the creak of leather saddles and the thumping of hooves on sawdust. Jayne and I would stand together, as close as we dared in such a public place, and proudly watch him collect his ribbons.

Jayne — was she the push I had needed to move on? I'd never meant to stay this long in this marriage — had told my husband-to-be that I was a lesbian way back when we were young in the fifties and I'd wanted children and a father for them. The fifties were when being a single mom was definitely not okay, as I found out. In fact, it was only one step better than being a lesbian. I was both of those fear-fraught things when I married; when I tried to go straight; when I was harassed by my family for my sexuality; when I was nineteen. Now my sons were teenagers.

I closed the family room door and checked my bedroom one last time, and my attention was caught by an old, red, woolly hat — the last thing left in my room. I stuffed it in my pocket and thought back a couple of weeks, to my "coming out" time with my sons.

Simon, my middle son, lived in a small apartment in an old house in Chinatown, Toronto, near the Ontario College of Art where he was a student. His apartment was all angles and shadows and stained glass, and on this particular day it was full of hats. Apparently, Simon's friend James worked at a theatrical outfitters and had dropped off a huge cardboard box full of fancy Victorian hats that were to be picked up the next day. Simon had opened the box, and the hats, with a life of their own, had spilled out over the couch and floor. I'd called ahead to tell Simon I had something important I wanted to talk with him about, and as he ushered me in, motioning me to sit on the couch with him and the hats, he kept glancing at me then quickly looking away, trying to gauge what might be coming. Or did he know?

As I sat, he got up and went into the bedroom. He returned in a moment with a full-length mirror, which he propped on the opposite wall. Our eyes met through the mirror as he sat down, and my stomach fell out. I felt as if I stood alone on the brink of the rest of my life. I felt as I imagine people feel just before they faint or die.

Simon threw a couple of lacy beribboned hats at me and put a natty straw boater on his own head. With the boater tilted at a rakish angle over one eye, he looked like the quintessential Victorian bourgeois. "What's up Mum? Take a deep breath," he said, echoing the times I'd asked him in the past to tell me something he found difficult to say. I took a deep breath.

"Simon, do you know I'm a lesbian?"

The words beat against the walls, hit the ceiling and re-bounded back at me: *lesbian, lesbian, your mother's a lesbian, my son.* I'd finally said the words aloud to him.

He was staring at me as the words beat their path around the room. "I guessed, Mum. It's good to hear you actually tell me, though." A silence.

We looked at each other reflected in the glass. Hats, Simon and me. We have always shared confidences, he and I, more so than I have with my other sons. And now this — the biggest, most important confidence of my life — I had finally shared with him. The straw hat slid slowly over one eye and he gave me a lopsided grin, feeling the importance of my words. Then he voiced his concerns about his father: Did he know? I assured him that his father had always known this about me, that I had told him I was a lesbian before we were married. I did not tell Simon that his father thought he could change me, and that, for a long time now, I had felt myself physically and emotionally removed from him. I tried to explain to Simon my need to have my own place, my own community and freedom of movement. I could never have these things if I stayed in the family home.

We had come to the end of the hats, the end of our conversation and the start of another way of being mother and son.

"How did you know about me, Simon?" I asked as I left. He smiled and, picking up a baseball cap, put it on back-to-front. I was reminded of him as a little boy and my heart lurched. Could we keep our special connection? Would it all be okay?

"You're the only Mom I know who took her kids to gay marches," he said. Then he gathered his things and we hugged.

"I love you, Mom."

As I left, Simon was tidying the hats before leaving for class. I realised that I had been laying the groundwork for these coming out conversations with my sons for many years.

I sighed as I locked the door of what was no longer my house, and got in the car. Coming out. The many ways of doing it. I will spend the rest of my life coming out in different ways to different people, I thought. I'll never hide myself again. It's a promise I made to myself.

My eyes swept the familiar landscape, paddocks, fields, barn — and I remembered coming out to Andrew, my youngest son.

After talking with Simon, I thought it would be easy to catch up with Andrew. He was usually to be found in the barn with the horses, either grooming or riding them or cleaning up. I had reckoned without his antennae for problems. For a couple of days after I'd spoken to Simon, Andrew had seemed to be avoiding me. I'd go into the barn and he would have an excuse to leave it. It was as if he sensed something was afoot and didn't want it to happen. Eventually, it was Simon who told him I was thinking of moving out and that I needed to talk to him. Very reluctantly, he met me in the barn. I perched on the feed bin, where I'd sat so many times before to chat. Andrew stood in the aisle with the curry comb, brushing his horse. My mind went back to the first time he had groomed his own pony, when he could barely reach the top of her back and had to stand on a box to pull her mane.

He looked across at me quickly and then away.

"You're leaving us?" My son is nothing if not direct, when he has a mind to it.

"I'm moving out, not leaving you." I felt desperate, wanting so much for him to understand. "I love you, Andrew. I'll always be your mother, but I need to live my own life now." A pause. "Andrew, I'm a lesbian." Why did I feel that I wasn't telling him anything he didn't already know? I continued, "This is not a new thing for me, and just because I'm telling you doesn't mean anything will change in how I feel about you. I love you and your brothers. It's a sad time for your father and me. We've shared so much over the years — your growing up, for example — but this isn't something sudden in my life. I've always been a lesbian. For various reasons that we can talk about later, one of which was having children and a father for them as well as a mother, I've lived a life that I feel I need to move on from."

Andrew nodded, not looking at me but staring with huge tears in his eyes at the shiny chestnut coat of the horse. She snuffled and moved around, wanting his attention.

"But why do you have to leave Dad and us? Why can't you still live here with us and live your own life?" An aching question from my big son — a question containing all the anguish of the abandoned child. I jumped off the feed bin and moved towards him, but he dodged around to the other side of the horse.

"Darling, I've lived that way for too long. I need to live away for now, to sort things out."

He turned to me fiercely, the tears spilling down his cheeks, "What about Dad, then?"

He turned and ran out of the barn. Abandonment was the issue for him, not my being a lesbian. I was abandoning him, his father and his brothers. His life was being disrupted. I lost sight of him as he rounded the barnyard, still running, heading for the woods. My heart was sore.

It was nearly three months before he would speak to me again.

I started the car. I was on my way to the rest of my life. My oldest son, Paul, was waiting in Toronto at the sparkling new apartment in the women's co-op. A couple of my women friends were there too, unloading the U-Haul. I let in the clutch, started down the long drive and thought again of Paul and the day I had come out to him.

Paul and I were to meet in High Park. I got there early and wandered about, wondering where I was going with all this coming out talk. Why did I feel I had to do it now? Why not wait a bit longer, until the boys were gone? Of course, I knew the answer: I couldn't go on denying who I was and am.

When I had first come out as a lesbian to myself and my lover, it was back in the fifties. I was fifteen and proud and not very discreet. I smile to myself as I think of this. I'm still proud to be a lesbian and I'm working on being discreet. Eventually, my mother found out about my lover and me, and she was horrified. At that time, in the late fifties, psychiatric care was recommended as the "cure" for lesbians. I don't think my mother would have gone as far as shock treatments for her only child — they were also considered a part of that "cure" — but the threat was there. I was harassed until, at age eighteen, I met a man I could care for and had a son, Paul. Again my mother was furious. She continued to harass me until eventually I married and spent the following years living with my husband, raising my sons and longing for women.

The park was bright with sunshine and I sat on a bench idly scuffing stones with my toes. Suddenly, my six-foot son was beside me.

"Practising for soccer?" he smiled.

Here I go again, I thought. Butterflies, like elephants in boots, were stomping in my stomach. "Do you want to sit or shall we walk?"

"Let's walk, Mum. You sounded so serious on the phone. It's easier to walk don't you think?"

I got up from the bench and kissed him. What would his reaction be? He couldn't remember the time when there had been just he and I in the world. Maybe coming out wouldn't be so difficult this time. Paul, I knew, had a longtime friend who had been raised by her lesbian mom and her mom's lover. He knew the family, had spent time with them. Would he be okay with his own mother being a lesbian?

We walked and talked, Paul's long shadow beside my shorter one. As it turned out, he was fine with the news. He was another son not surprised that I was a lesbian; and his reaction to my leaving was calm. Yes, he understood that I must live my own life. Of course I should move out if I wanted to. Dad would be fine. Paul became efficient: When, where, how could he help? If I felt I must go, he would encourage and support me. Of course he did not want our home to break up, but I must do what I needed to do. Hadn't I always encouraged him and his brothers to do that? Paul sank his energies into action.

As I continued my journey to my new life, I realised that it wasn't coming out to my children as a lesbian that was hard for them. I had, in one way or another, prepared them all their lives for this moment. The hard part was their feeling that, by leaving, I was breaking up their home base, their port in the storm.

It has taken time for my sons to work through their emotions around my leaving, but my actual coming out to them was a reinforcement of something that they had always sensed. In the end, the act of saying the words directly to them was a measure of my perception of their maturity.

"Guranma"

K.S.M.

I AM ABOUT TO SAY THE WORD "LESBIAN" TO MY ADULT SON FOR THE FIRST TIME. I will not say it face-to-face, or via technology, but with my fingers brushing a piece of paper, with my pen in hand. For twelve years I have never felt the urge to do this — why do I feel it now? And how does a woman and mother grant the truth of her own substance from so far away? I am not only far in miles, but in the distance which age and maturity bring.

These questions haunt me when I am touched by the whirling magnetism of the lives of my sons. We meet at the centrifugal edge of experience, the beginning or ending of crises and tensions. Now I want to find a zone of comfort in which to share, beyond the barrier of privacy I've maintained.

My dream of a country sojourn had easily taken shape. I was glad that my younger son had agreed to move East with me for a year's trial. We had reached this major decision while sitting in a crowded, suburban McDonald's. This was our version of mother-son heart-to-hearts: hamburgers, french fries, and intense conversation on his turf.

Once we were settled in, thirteen-year-old Max easily became a social butterfly. I scheduled myself in as taxi service. Somehow we managed to slow down enough to hear the total silence of rural life. Together, we saw for the first time a clear rural sky, with stars so brilliant they startled each of us to reach beyond the limits of our smogged-up perceptual fields.

The following summer, Max decided to go back to the city with his dad. I spent a week crying. My vision of mothering had included me side-by-side with my kids until they were eighteen — then letting go. This particular letting go was a little premature.

Max left on a hazy summer day, one amongst a host of others

that made up a string of toneless weather reports. As we walked into the airport terminal, I saw beside me a competent teenager, fully prepared for the next phase of his life. I was proud that I had nurtured his keen ability to carry himself forward. Outside, I leaned against the fence, waving and seeing a movement in the plane's window that I knew was him, smiling at me. Then the plane lifted off and my son was airborne.

With my eyes, I followed the airbus as it purposefully shrank until it was only a dot, a speck. The sky gave nothing back to me as I scanned the monochromatic dust. Then, suddenly, it transformed into particles of light, and I knew my son would create himself beyond the reign of my consciousness. I let him go. I met him in my mind, and I felt trust, I felt strength, I felt joy.

My career as a long-distance parent had begun. I found myself in the middle of multi-level motherhood, characterized by the continuous flux of hellos and goodbyes. Our hellos became more appreciative, our goodbyes deeper.

On the first day of the year, my partner and I walked deep into the woods. We were two women, followed by our two dogs and three cats, accompanied by the singing of winter birds. We walked to the site of the freshwater spring, which trickled over red earth and powdery snow. We built a small fire to boil water for tea. We broke our fast with Christmas cookies, and sprinkled wheat berries to nourish the wildlife around us. And we spoke the words in our hearts, of commitment and love.

That morning, Kim and I had deliberately gathered many special things into our pack — such as my mother's embroidered hanky — to symbolize the gathering of loved ones to join in our marriage ceremony. We exchanged rings in the clear light of midday. It seemed as if these rings pulled in the energy of all creation. We knew that we'd never remove them, wanting as we did to keep each other near at all times. We talked of our hopes of sharing this love and commitment with our families and community.

Hand in hand, we turned homeward to the distractions of our daily lives.

The sudden roar of the stovepipe demanded our attention. A red heat glow verified our fears: a flue fire. Kim rushed to the rooftop and poured baking soda down the chimney. I ran to the cellar for soft dirt.

As I tossed the dirt into the stove, our phone rang again and again. It was my older son, Jerry, calling to say that he and Bonnie had a new baby boy! Filled with relief, I called up the now cool stovepipe to Kim to announce the birth of my first grandson, Tyler! Back on the phone, my relief turned to anxiety as Jerry explained that Tyler was in intensive care, with a patched-up, collapsed lung.

Across the room, our woodstove had calmed down; the only residue of the fire was a hot metallic odour. In a short while, Jerry called again. The euphoria of childbirth had nearly been suffocated when Bonnie's heart had failed within hours of her giving birth. She had been in extreme danger, and had revived as doctors were about to transport her onto major life supports.

My kitchen shrank until it became a cubicle barely large enough to contain Jerry, the phone, and me. My son's mellow voice softened, and turned inwards to the source of his tears. And there was only silence between us, which neither of us knew how to fill.

I felt dwarfed by a myopic intensity, yet I managed somehow to make travel arrangements. Though I heard little and my feet seemed numb, I entered unfamiliar ground: I inhaled the hot metallic air of the subway as we neared City General; and held tightly to Bonnie's hospital-bed rails while the robot monitors dictated the frailties of her soft inner tissues' "numbers."

Bonnie has survived the long struggle to recover from the strobe-like pace of birth and collapse. Her eyes, vibrant with life, have inspired my search for the skills to re-energize my own life.

He sings out my name, and I recognize myself: "Guranma." This name touches at once my own infantile, pure joy in existing, and my elder self, individual and slowly pacing into the universe.

This name-giving between me and my first grandson is like a mantra for creation. He sings out my name, "Guranma!" And I answer, "Yes, Tyler!" And we each of us link our destinies.

Last spring, we had a full week together in which to sing names to each other. We spent two days on the floor with trains, blocks, balls and diapers. One afternoon, Tyler and I went to the backyard to sort through a mass of tangled branches. Tyler sang, "Guranma! Boughs for you!" and talked of squirrels, flowers and boughs. How poetic, I thought, this two-and-a-half year old seriously stacking boughs.

Later, when I told Jerry and Bonnie how touched I'd been by Tyler's language usage, they grinned and let me into their own family language game. Instead of "bough," Tyler had been saying "baum" — the German word for "tree," which he had been taught by his German-speaking Opa.

Now I remember Tyler and trees, branches, boughs, baum — all balm for my spirit. And I realize that a word, a name, can be a personal, harmonious sound, vocalized in a moment of freedom. How sensible are women today who rename themselves! With names like these, my spirit soars, and I can touch my loved ones — the joy in my life.

Dear Max,
I'm wanting to say "hello!" and to bring you cheer and love and hugs, and to be part of your busy days.

Thank you for the beautiful Georgia O'Keefe book. She's one of my heroes. Others are Joan Baez and Leonard Cohen, just for starters. A friend once asked me who I would choose for a mythological mother, and I immediately said Joan Baez. Her face, her voice, her poetry.

I've been writing and I want to tell you about it. I am writing a piece about being a lesbian parent. I want to send it to you when I've finished. Can you stand this? I don't believe I've ever used the name "lesbian" with you.

Have the best of winters! Wishing you lots of happiness and depth of feeling.
Love,
Mom.

There is a point in intimacy when I feel that I *am* those tiny, soft, practically invisible hairs which cover my loved-one's body. And there is a moment wherein I anticipate emotions before my loved one names them. There is a blending within a relationship when I imagine my loved one's face in my breath.

Because I have also felt these things for my sons and grandson, and because I value our relationships, it is important to let them know now that I name these feelings particularly with the woman I love.

And so I tell my son of the fullness of my life, and that it is full specifically because I embrace the name of lesbian. My greatest joy, my greatest desire, my deepest anger or sadness will only be equal to the intensity with which I nurture my lesbian life. I test all of myself against the sureness of this identity.

Non-existent & Struggling for Identity

VICKY D'AOUST

WE DO NOT EXIST.

We aren't in the news. We aren't on TV. We certainly are not mentioned at school or in the community. Mainstream/malestream media do not acknowledge us, and very few alternative publications include articles about us.

Why? Because we do not exist.

Who are we? We are women who have disabilities and are lesbian mothers.

Our multiple minority status is difficult to understand unless one looks at the various contributing factors: women exist as persons only by the legal statute of the Persons Act; lesbians have primary status as women, and secondary status as women who love women. This latter affiliation has a negative stigma which sometimes overrules any positive status acquired by virtue of being female: Lesbians are not seen to be "real" women. We are told that "real" women have children (and, usually, husbands). We are told that lesbians do not have children. So lesbian mothers form another category of women who are relegated to a marginal position that is not enviable in the least.

Lesbians who have children (either by becoming pregnant through various means or by adoption/co-parenting) are not discussed in public. We do not exist in the public consciousness. We raise our children in our homes, our children go to school, we take our children to the playground, we even shop with and for our children! But we do not exist. In the literature of gay and lesbian parenting there is a consistent theme of struggling to hide — to hide parental status from the gay and lesbian community, and to hide gay and lesbian status from other parents and the rest of society.

Describing lesbian mothers, Ellen Lewin writes:

They understand that homosexuality is generally disap-
proved of, and want to protect their children from being
stigmatized in the way they feel themselves to be. Some
of them also understand that motherhood tends to be
perceived as contradictory to lesbianism, so that the
mere fact of being mothers can protect them from being
identified as gay. As Valerie Thompson, the mother of a
twelve-year-old daughter, said: "Of course I have the
mask. I have a child. I'm accepted (as heterosexual)
because I have a child and that's a kind of protection.[1]

Finally, add to this mixture the status of women with disabilities. We form another group that is marginalized because, as
everyone knows, disabilities are "bad," even if it is politically
correct to support charities by sending (guilt) money. Disability
is feared like death and taxes because it is just as inevitable. The
roles assigned to disabled people — the roles of the sick, the
passive and the grateful — are not in the least desirable:

The models of disability which most commonly inform
the role of people with disabilities are the 'personal
tragedy' and medical models of disability. Those who
subscribe, consciously or unconsciously, to these models
view disabled people as individuals whose experience is
determined by their medical or physical condition.[2]

Some people even think women with disabilities would be
better off dead, or perhaps just having never been born. Yet,
some of us women with disabilites were born without disabilities and acquired them through accidents or violence, while still
others became disabled through illness or are becoming progressively disabled as we continue to live.

And, yes, some of us happen to be lesbians. But lesbians with
disabilities do not exist: "The general public, disabled people
and even non-disabled lesbians assume that disabled lesbians
do not exist, rendering us effectively invisible. The invisibility
protects us and, at the same time, isolates us."[3] We are usually
not visible in community events or public relations campaigns. We
may not be visibly "out" in the disability community and may not

even participate in the organizations or activities of people with disabilities.

Some of us lesbians with disabilities (who may or may not have partners) have children. Some lesbians with disabilities are mothers, by choice or chance. But, wait: Lesbian mothers with disabilities do not exist. We are not part of the community of mothers or the community of lesbians or the community of people with disabilities. Once again, we do not exist.

Even a very brief review of support material available to gay and lesbian parents will show that information on disabled lesbian parents is not available, although information on adopting disabled children is sometimes presented. Similarly, a list of resources for disabled parents — both mothers and fathers — yields information on technical assistance, support groups and literature, but nothing about parents with disabilities who are gay or lesbian.

So, women with disabilities who are mothers and lesbians are effectively and actually invisible. We go about our lives trying to avoid as many barriers as possible and, in the meantime, we recreate our invisibilities. I know, because I do it. My life as a woman with disabilities who is a lesbian mother is full of identity management. It is a part of my everyday life to determine how best to present my "selves" to the world, to my daughter and to my inner self. This practicality of living is not exclusive to lesbian mothers with disabilities, but it is particularly problematic for us.

Now that I have described the interlocking puzzle of my status, I will attempt to describe some of these problems. In the paragraphs that follow, I will alternate between describing myself and others as lesbians with disabilities who are mothers, mothers with disabilities who are lesbians, and lesbians who are mothers and women with disabilities, to demonstrate our identity dilemma.

Multiple Minority Status[4]

A multiple minority group, then, is any group of people who are singled out from others in the society in which they live for differential and unequal treatment because they are defined as members of more than one minority group and who therefore regard themselves as objects of this combination of collective discrimination.[5]

Women with disabilities who are lesbian mothers are faced with multiple barriers and levels of discrimination, which are not merely the sum of our oppressions. In an article exploring the experiences of disabled lesbians, Joanne Doucette quoted one woman as saying: "It is commonly assumed that disabled women are asexual, and hence cannot be mothers or lovers. Some people think there's no such thing as disabled lesbian mothers. It's not true. I'm the proof of that."[6] There may only be a small number of us, but we do exist, despite stereotypes about sexuality, disability and motherhood. As a small minority in terms of numbers, we have less access to support, less solidarity within our group and, because of barriers in the existing minority communities, less opportunity for participation outside the group than other minorities. Mothers who are lesbians with disabilities must find common ground and support among a diversity of groups: other mothers, other lesbians and other people with disabilities.

Women as a group continue to struggle for equality in society, in the workplace and at home. We struggle to be free from violence and stereotyping. Lesbians, as a sub-group of women, also have to fight against stereotypes and violence in a more particular way. Lesbians must fight against society's expectations of heterosexuality as much as they fight against sexism and inequality in general. For most women, gender is difficult to hide, but lesbians often have a choice (if it can even be called that) to be "out" or identified as a lesbian. It could be said that every day when a lesbian goes out into the world, she must choose whether or not to come out all over again. She must make this choice for each new face, because identity is so elusive. It is not an easy choice because, in some circumstances, the stigma attached to lesbianism can be permanent and damaging.

"Coming out" is also an issue for those of us who have visible (and invisible) disabilities. But being disabled does not preclude being homophobic and being a lesbian does not guarantee awareness and being female certainly does not a feminist make. The lesbian mother with disabilities has to face multiple levels of oppression based on different levels of identity. One lesbian mother I talked to found that "most mothers were more open to my disability than to my lesbianism, but most lesbians had more trouble with me being disabled than me being a mother." The mix of oppressions might not always be the same, but lesbian mothers with disabilities always risk facing more than one barrier. Joanne Doucette quotes a lesbian with disabilities making this astute observation:

> I do not think that lesbian feminists have quite the fixed stereotypes that the general public has, perhaps because there is a higher level of awareness of us within this segment of the population. I do find, however, that like the general public, they often do not see accessibility as a human right but as a privilege and so they can get affronted when we are not grateful for something they have done. Then they see us as demanding ... Most lesbians are just as uneducated and prejudiced as the rest of the population.[7]

Women with disabilities are considered to be "deviant" and "defective." Our "coming out" is to ask for help. Every time we ask for a door to be opened, a call to be made on our behalf or for physical assistance, we are seen again as disabled. The preconception of us as helpless, sick, inferior or even evil, makes our needs, our dependence, even more difficult. Regardless of our physical disabilities or lack thereof, regardless of our mental health or mental illness, our identities are managed by how much of ourselves we need to show, reveal and expose in order to cope.

Women with disabilities try as much as possible to minimize the "handicapping effects" of having a disability. The social construction theory of disability demonstrates that our physical or mental disabilities are not in and of themselves problematic. Instead, environmental inaccessibility, structural inequality and systemic attitudinal discrimination create handicaps. Theoretically, this is a very good way to explain how disabilities can become handicaps. But, on a daily basis, women who have disabilities do have to "cope" with the physical and/or mental limitations imposed on them by the disability itself, in addition to those imposed by society. This means making your disability less distracting in daily life. Some researchers have considered this a form of denial or "passing," which implies that women with disabilities who do this are not acknowledging reality. For me, this is similar to being closeted or passing for straight when, in reality, one is a lesbian. However, I do not agree that this is denial or even that it is a false reality. It is part of *our* lives that we live as lesbians, as disabled women and mothers, regardless of how we are perceived by others. Our management of our identities is essential to our survival — whether that identity is about our sexual orientation or our disabilities.

Some women with physical disabilities just get used to not doing some things, because places are inaccessible. Women who are deaf know that most TV shows aren't captioned and that most public services have no TTY device that can be called directly. Women using wheelchairs know which buses won't take them and which restaurants are not accessible. So we avoid the barriers and make our lives as little trouble to others (and ourselves) as possible.

Doucette suggests that, while coming out as lesbians can be a form of resistance for disabled lesbians, "coming out is a two-edged sword. It can result in more isolation, public violence, rejection by friends and families, loss of jobs, ejection from nursing homes and other institutions and denial of services."[8]Furthermore, lesbians with disabilities find that even some parts of the lesbian community are inaccessible, including women's clubs, bars, camps and festivals[9], lesbian community centres, lesbian phone lines, lesbian newsletters and books, erotic bookstores and even language itself. The community of lesbians is often constructed on a minimal budget and the needs of disabled women are costed out and weighed against other needs. Most lesbians who have disabilities are significantly restricted in how they can participate in the lesbian community.

Mothers with disabilities, too, are restricted in their activities with their children. They are not able to fully take advantage of the same range of options available to other mothers. Instead, most mothers with disabilities are far more isolated and restricted in their choices. The problem is further compounded by the fact that most services in the community are categorized by type of disability and age, and often only children with disabilities are eligible for assistance in home care or education. Parents with disabilities are not considered for these services, and often find the system far more willing to remove children to state care than provide financial support to assist in parenting at home.[10] The result of inadequate support *may* be that children of mothers with disabilities grow up too fast and become more responsible earlier than other children, or they may have disabilities or learning problems too. In some cases, the problems of children of mothers with disabilities are blamed on poor parenting skills and the disabilities of the mother. In reality, the disabilities or difficulties of the child are indeed a social construction — a direct result of inadequate resources and inaccessibility to resources.

Despite the argument that disabilities are central in the lives of women with disabilities, those of us who are mothers also have to live as mothers, not just as disabled women. Like other women with disabilities, mothers with disabilities spend as much time as possible preventing our disabilities from being a problem. We also try to minimize the negative impact of having children. Mothers with disabilities need to have an income, either from state or work sources, which does not create additional barriers to participating as a mother in society. Ensuring adequate child care and homemaking assistance is a priority for most mothers with disabilities. A great deal of effort is put into ensuring that the children are not restricted by the disability of the mother, and that the mother can parent to her best ability "in the best interests of the child."

Lesbians with children may also make attempts to ensure that motherhood doesn't prevent them from participating in community activities. Some lesbians seek out other lesbians with children for support, some try to find any women who are mothers for support.[11] Lesbian mothers struggle to find a level of safety in bringing their children to events or in talking about their needs as mothers within a community where children are not often present. Although some women choose to "postpone lesbian life" or hide their lesbianism from their children and other parents, others are able to live both as lesbians and mothers in public. These women help create visibility for lesbian mothers. A lesbian of colour, Angela Bowen, made an interesting observation about the difficult decision of being out as a lesbian mother:

> So, for those of us out who've already stuck our faces out the door, rather than retreating into the closet to protect our children, we need to work to develop surroundings conducive to cushioning our children from the hostility of heterosexism by finding competent, loving allies among lesbians, gay men and progressive heterosexuals who will know and honour who we are. By hiding, we are not helping our children. And putting our lesbianism on hold until they're grown is no solution. We can come up with more creative solutions to mothering than retreating into a closet.[12]

Still, whether we are in a closet, in a house, in school, in care or in a wheelchair, we are often invisible as lesbian mothers with disabilities. We may be invisible because we choose to be, or we may be invisible because it is safer, it hurts less, it is easier and less complicated. We may be invisible because society does not want to see us. But, in truth, we are everywhere. Literally. Anywhere you see women, there are lesbians. Anywhere you see women, there are women with disabilities of all kinds. Anywhere you see women, there are mothers. Lesbian mothers with disabilities are everywhere — yet we do not exist. What do we do if we do not exist? We struggle for a sense of self.

Finding a Sense of Sel(f)ves

Identity politics are very important to lesbian activists, and feminists in general. People with disabilities, too, hold entire conferences on the issue of "self-identification" of disability. The practical issues faced by mothers with disabilities may not be significantly different for either straight or lesbian women, but sexual orientation is a critical *identity* issue. I recognize that there are other categories besides straight and lesbian — some women identify as either bisexual or transgendered. Because being a mother, in itself, requires an extensive network of people, sexual orientation is important in that it has a dramatic effect on the make-up and strength of an individual's network. Being a bisexual woman, or a woman who had children in a heterosexual marriage, or a woman who enjoys sexual contact with men but identifies as a lesbian, can have a significant impact on how a mother with disabilities finds support in her community or communities.

Imagine applying for a job and having to answer a list of questions about sexual activities. Would we identify ourselves sexually? What if we were offered employment equity measures as a reward for reporting our membership in "categories"? Would we identify ourselves if there was something in it for us? This is one dilemma that lesbians, women with disabilities and mothers face. Most of the benefits of identifying as a lesbian, as disabled, or even as a mother, are outweighed by the possible negative effects of public disclosure. Disclosing gender and race offers different conundrums: if we refuse to identify as female or as women of colour, if that is what we are, who are we fooling? Who are we hurting?

We — lesbian mothers with disabilities — need to first know who we are, before we can find our own answers to these questions. Who are we? How do we define and identify ourselves? I can only really speak from my own experiences, but other lesbian mothers with disabilities have offered their assistance and I will speak for "us," basing my comments on a plurality of experience.

One woman spoke to me about having no problem with her disability, because it was self-evident and non-intrusive. She was able to parent and work and continue on her own path without her physical disability creating barriers. (Her physical disability affects her spine, although she can walk unaided.) However, she felt, as a *mother*, that raising her daughter in the women's community was difficult. She was not always able to find safe and welcoming places for her child. Her membership in a community and identification with lesbians, she felt, was in conflict with her motherhood. Women with disabilities who are lesbians and mothers need the support of other lesbians. We shouldn't have to choose between being mothers and being lesbians. A common lesbian refrain is quoted by Dian Day in her article "Lesbian/Mother": "Real lesbians don't have children. This is proclaimed with equal loudness by both straight women (and men) and 'real' lesbians ... Real lesbians are not interested in children — especially male children."[13]

A lesbian couple, who both have disabilities and are mothers of their own birth children and co-mothers of each other's children, talked to me about being more able to relate to other mothers than to single women with disabilities. This echoed comments made by lesbian mothers, who found they had more in common with single, straight mothers than with childless single or lesbian women. This couple, each of whom had different physical disabilities, also mentioned that their ability to deal with their own disabilities assisted them in understanding each other's limitations. This brings up a big issue for women with disabilities in general, whether they are straight or lesbian: should their partner be someone with a disability (and if so, should it be a similar disability) or someone without a disability? This debate may be akin to the controversies in inter-racial or inter-religious marriages, where there is also concern about compatibility and equality.

Women who have disabilities and are lesbians may find they have a much smaller "pool" of potential partners due to the fact that the lesbian community is indeed much smaller than the heterosexual community, and the community of lesbians with disabilities is smaller still. Some lesbians with disabilities are very comfortable having relationships with any other lesbian, regardless of whether she has a disability. This may cause problems, however. In at least one case that I am aware of, there is a power imbalance. An acquaintance of mine, who has cerebral palsy, has a lover who is not disabled and who does most of the driving and chores. Although the woman with cerebral palsy is the mother of a child, her lesbian lover, who is not disabled, does more of the physical work and in some ways resents this obligation. This situation, however, is also one of dependancy: the woman who is more "able" can withold favours and support whenever she wants to. There can be healthy ways to deal with this kind of situation, but some lesbians with disabilities have chosen to avoid the imbalance by seeking out partners who share similar disabilities, or at least share experiences with disability.

One mother I spoke to, who is deaf and a lesbian and is co-parenting her child with a hearing woman, also said that being lesbian is less problematic for her than being deaf. Although she said that being deaf, a mother and a lesbian were all important to her in different ways, she identified first as being deaf, then as a lesbian. She does not feel the same sense of identity in the lesbian community as she does in the deaf community because "most of the lesbian community are hearing, they do not understand deaf[ness], no matter if I am a lesbian." In her family of origin and with her child, being deaf was more of a problem than being a lesbian or being a mother. Her most central role, however, was that of mother, because she is always a mother. Still, every day a different part of her identity emerges, depending on context. At work her central identity is that of being deaf; around her partner, it is being a lesbian. "I feel that I am riding a merry-go-round," she says.

This woman felt that other mothers were both homophobic and supportive. If they were deaf, she could come out to them as a lesbian, but she felt that she could not do so with hearing mothers. The commonality among deaf mothers made her feel safe. As a mother, however, she found the lesbian community to be often "child phobic." Some lesbians even told her they did not like children. "Among the lesbian community, where most of them do not accept children and disability, it is quite tough for me to attend [events] and try to mingle with them. I have to teach them about deafness first, before trying about children."

The most positive thing in this woman's life was meeting and being in a relationship with a woman who understands her deafness. "Being with a wonderful partner who is not disabled and has no child is most rewarding to me. I feel very valuable to be with her and she is working hard to understand my deafness and try better about my mixed-race son. It is very rare to have that experience when not many lesbians with [hearing] disabilities who have children have a hearing partner."

Many lesbian mothers with disabilities express a sense of isolation. Without the support of their birth family, and with alienation from some of their past lovers or even husbands, many lesbian mothers felt alone in the world. One of the most satisfying experiences for them was meeting others in the same boat. If women can benefit from the support of other women, and mothers benefit from meeting with other mothers, so lesbian mothers profit from contact with other lesbian mothers. It makes sense, then, that women with disabilities who are lesbian mothers need this contact and peer support even more. It helps us identify ourselves.

It is difficult to avoid comparing ourselves to the "selves" that are portrayed as desirable and normal to the "rest of the world." Being a lesbian is different than being straight, being disabled is different than being non-disabled, being a woman of colour is different than being a white woman. But the liberating part of being a lesbian with disabilities who is also a mother is the impossibility of ever achieving any semblance of the "norm" — and not wanting to. One of the most oppressive assumptions about women (and men) with disabilities is that we want to be other than what we are — that we want to be "normal." Friends, family, educators, rehabilitators, and many of those who offer services are all attempting to make something resembling normal out of the "disabled" person. Many disabled people "pass" as normal and have internalized the idea that normal is better, thus emulating the norm that provides status and success. However, disabled woman Pam Evans clearly has a different view:

> The real liberation is essentially our own. For we are all accomplices to the prejudice in exact proportion to the values and norms of our society that we are prepared to endorse. We are *not* normal, in the stunted terms the

world chooses to define. But we are not obliged to adopt those definitions as standards to which we must aspire — or, indeed, as something worth having in the first place.[14]

Out & About (not)

As I have indicated, one of the significant issues for me in my experience as a mother is that of identity management. I have always wanted to be private about my sexual contact with individual women, but not about my politics. Being a feminist was never something I felt the need to hide, but being a lesbian was more of a risk for me. I am afraid that children are still not immune to the homophobia expressed to (and about) their parents. Most women with disabilities have a difficult time hiding their disabilities from the public. Even women with invisible disabilities are often labelled by the system that provides services to them. However, being a lesbian can (perhaps sadly) be hidden from the "authorities." As a mother, then, I must make the choice whether or not to be identified as both disabled and a lesbian.

I have experienced clinical depression and hospitalization, and I am very aware of the dangers of having my child removed from my home. I sometimes need support from the child welfare system simply because I am more isolated than some other women, but it is frightening to think that it is possible I might be discriminated against on the basis of disability, mental health or lesbianism. I try to reduce the risk as much as possible, for my sake and for my child. The fact that I have needed assistance in dealing with an identified but invisible disability has made me more vulnerable to being examined for other "weaknesses."

An American disabled woman is quoted by Jenny Morris as saying:

> I pretend to forget how deeply disabled people are hated. I pretend to forget how this is true even within my chosen home, the lesbian and feminist communities. My survival at every level depends on maintaining good relationships with able-bodied people.[15]

It is this dependance on others that makes our identities particularly important to manage. Most women with disabilities have contact at some point with the social services system for rehabilitation, income assistance, medical services or child care. Managing identity — or focusing on disability rather than sexuality — is sometimes a requisite for getting and keeping services (although it shouldn't be). Women with disabilities are consumers of many more systems than most women. We use the medical, social and service systems more regularly. This includes using specialized transportation, interpreters, personal care attendants and caregivers in and outside of the home. The requirement for heavy use of support people often makes it difficult to have a choice of just who those people will be, and this, in turn, makes it difficult to be honest and out with all people. If you are dependant on a transit driver to pick you up, yet afraid of harassment or persecution if the driver knew you were a lesbian, concern for your own safety might outweigh the need to be out. Yet if you are in the company of another lesbian, or people with whom you are out, it can be difficult to maintain privacy during the third party intervention of personal care attendants or interpreters. Here are a couple examples of such difficulties: discussing, through an interpreter, a plan to attend a lesbian festival presumes that the interpreter will not use that information against you; using an attendant to lift you into bed with your lesbian lover also presumes that the attendant will not withdraw other services or tell people about your personal life. It is very difficult to be free and feel safe about lesbianism when disabilities make us already vulnerable to abuse.

Dependency on others goes hand in hand with lack of privacy, which also leads to shame and invisibility for lesbian mothers with disabilities. Hiding any evidence of lesbian interests from my homemakers became a weekly ritual for me until I came out to the home support co-ordinator. I was afraid that I might lose services or that specific workers would stop coming if they knew I was a lesbian. Having your home open to professional people makes it less safe to be who you are in your own home. One autobiography by a lesbian with disabilities, Connie Panzarino, makes a strong statement about the feeling of needing independence and privacy as a lesbian. At the Michigan Womyn's Music Festival, Connie met a lesbian named Judy. "I wished I was able-bodied, just so I could get up quietly, without waking my attendant, get dressed, and figure out some excuse for needing to go over to the cabin to check on the refrigerators or something in case Judy might be up having another meal."[16]

One deaf lesbian friend told me she couldn't count the number of times she wished she could pick up a phone and call a woman without using an operator as a third party. Our disabilities often necessitate the involvement of others, and we thereby lose privacy. Women with disabilities are often heavy consumers of professional and para-professional support. For this reason, lesbians with disabilities and mothers with disabilities have a great deal in common. Non-mothers and lesbians without disabilities have less contact with intrusive agencies and can be relatively sure that their homes are safe places. Having children or having disabilities makes you subject to protection agencies, social workers, homemakers, and doctors.

Indeed, one of the reasons that women who are mothers and also lesbians with disabilities do not exist (publicly) is because so much of our lives is public and so little of our lives is private. Without a private life and without a safe place to be out, we must be invisible in public. This is not always a choice — not all women with disabilities can hide their disabilities and some lesbians cannot hide their orientation and generally motherhood is something that can be disclosed or not depending on the situation. However, for women with children, disclosure of one's identity is dictated by the fact that the children often take priority. Family, social workers and so-called friends are famous for offering advice to women with disabilities, and lesbians, about how to better meet the needs of the child. They offer advice "for the child's sake." In most cases, this advice is based on the assumption that the status quo is *not* meeting the needs of the child. Therefore, suggestions are made to assist the mother — for example, advice to be not so obvious about the lesbian "thing" — in serving the child better. In extreme cases this can mean removing the child from the home. Lesbians have often lost custody to family members, ex-spouses and protection agencies due to a perceived inability to provide for the child:

> The overwhelming strategy of the courts (although this is
> slowly changing) has been to deny lesbians custody of their
> children, as punishment for lesbianism. The "learned
> judges" use three main arguments to support this violation
> of basic human rights. They argue that the child will 1) grow
> up sexually abused (if a girl) or rejected (if a boy); 2) grow up
> stigmatized by her/his peers because of the mother's sexual-
> ity; and 3) be more likely to grow up gay.[17]

These are similar arguments to those used to take children
away from disabled mothers: the child will be neglected because of the disability of the parent, or be forced to serve as a
caregiver inappropriately, or the stigma of having a disabled
parent will harm the child, or there will be environmental and
institutionalized phobia around disability.

A disabled lesbian mother has a significantly increased risk
of losing custody to the state or an ex-partner, or as the Sharon
Bottoms case in Virginia has shown, a grandparent:

> Lesbian relationships involving children are also subject
> to legal interference by nonlesbians who are not parents
> to the child. These third parties can include interested
> relatives, foster parents, or the state. In these cases, the
> third party must generally prove the mother unfit.[18]

Women with disabilities face similar discrimination. In
many cases, they are not given the opportunity to parent. It is
difficult, if not impossible, for most disabled parents to adopt
or successfully get access to new reproductive technology. In
some situations, being single is enough to prevent women with
disabilities access to motherhood, but being a lesbian with
disabilities makes it significantly harder to access the traditional
and not-so-traditional ways to have and keep children. In one
of the most widely read texts on lesbian and gay parenting,
April Martin asks the reader to consider his or her own health
before deciding to have or adopt children:

> Especially if you are planning to make babies biologically,
> but also if you are just committing yourself to the role of

parent, it behooves you to get a thorough medical evaluation. It is worth knowing ahead of time if you have a health condition which might interfere with your ability to parent ... Your decision will be your own, but it should be an informed decision, made in the best interests of your child.[19]

Perhaps without intent, the implication of this passage is that having health limitations would do damage to the child and that it would not be in the best interest of a child to be raised by a "sick" parent. However, on just the next page, Martin distinguishes between sickness and disability by suggesting that, "if you have physical limitations or disabilities, you may wonder whether you will be able to provide the physical care a baby or toddler needs, or to continue to work and provide for the family's financial needs."[20] The only other discussion in the book about disability is in reference to adopting or raising disabled children or "special needs" children. The author does not make it clear that disabled lesbians and gay men are equally competent parents as those without disabilities.

It may be that these oversights can be explained by the fact that the author was well informed about the limitations of social and economic programs to support women with disabilities. In Canada, for example, there are very few support resources for disabled parents raising children. In her autobiography, Connie Panzarino, who is not a mother, wrote about wanting to be a parent. As a lesbian with disabilities, she was aware of the limitations imposed by lack of support services:

> I knew I had had no choice. I remember reading about several women with disabilities losing their children to foster care or adoption because Medicaid wouldn't pay for personal assistance to help them take care of their children. If I had taken Dawn with me from California, Social Services could have done the same to me and taken her away. After all, she wasn't legally my child, and even if she had been they wouldn't have provided me with attendant services to help me care for her. But I knew

that I would have been a better mother for Dawn than her own mother.[21]

As an adoptive mother myself, I do not like to compare myself to my child's birth mother or even compare myself to other mothers that I know. As a lesbian mother, I am very sensitive to criticisms which I feel are unfairly hurled by straight mothers or by lesbians who are not mothers. As a woman with disabilities, I am very aware of my differences and, perhaps, proud of how deviant from the supposed norm I am. However, it is as a mother — especially a mother of a girl who is becoming a young woman — that I am also keenly aware of the difficulties facing young women in achieving a sense of self-confidence and self-love in a world which promotes an unachievable norm.

Because of these difficulties, coming out to a child at any age is always an issue. In the literature I have read about parenting and lesbians, the advice is usually *tell tell tell*. I have rarely read that it is wise to hide the sexuality of a parent. But these advice books are decontextualized and, sometimes, psychologized. Common sense tells us that honesty is better than deceit. However, context is very important. A single lesbian mother with a five-year-old may not have as much need to discuss her sexuality as do a lesbian couple with teenage children.

As well, we are not always in relationships. It is much harder to conceal one's lesbianism when one has a woman lover in the house. How can you be a lesbian if you are single? My daughter once told me she preferred me when I was straight. I asked her what she meant by "straight," and she replied "without a woman friend (lover)." I asked again if she meant without anyone, just alone, and she said, "yes." She wanted me to be single, not straight. Straight, to her, was the way I was when I had no partner and had much more time with her — she saw it as single parenting.

My daughter had to get used to many things: new disabilities which I acquired after adopting her; my sexuality; and, because of a racial difference, we dealt with an ethnicity issue. I think that children are more able to deal with difference if they experience it early on. My daughter had many more problems adjusting to my "new" disabilities than she did to the ones she knew about when we met. When I had adopted her, as a five-year-old, she had not been aware of my sexuality and I did not have the disabilities I now have. Her adjustments to my new disabilities and my lesbianism were significant and similar, and occurred over time.

Race, sexuality, disability, ethnicity, class and numerous other "categories" are part of our lives as lesbian mothers with disabilities. But the categories that define our realities are not the same as our realities. In fact, quite the opposite. Our lives exceed and overlap all categories, and we cannot be constrained by other people's perceptions. As women, we already fight against male-defined values, goals and standards, but as women with disabilities who are lesbian mothers, we must find our own place to be. Our identities cannot be homogeneous because we are not homogeneous, and our relationships to our communities will be different.

There are some similarities among all women, however, that can help us understand each other. Women may not identify as being disabled but might actually have experiences that are similar to those of women who do identify as disabled. Lesbian mothers, for example, might be adult survivors of sexual abuse, recovering addicts or alcoholics, students (this should be at least a temporary disability), consumers of mental health services or many other less obvious "handicaps." All of these contribute to commonalities among lesbians that transcend the limits of disability. Straight mothers with disabilities claim that their biggest problems have to do with finances and accessibility. This includes not being able to afford specialized help or technical aids and not being able to access traditional services. All of these problems exist for lesbians with disabilities as well, yet seem to be less a priority than issues of sexuality, identity and parenting.

Becoming Visible: Lesbian Mothers with Disabilities

For some of us, choosing to identify with one or more of our "roles" may not be difficult; in my experience, however, the opposite is true: lesbian mothers with disabilities are constantly challenging the assumptions about their motherhood, disability and sexuality, and have to swing between roles to keep up. I think this movement from being "mother" to "lesbian" to "woman with disabilities" has some advantages because it reduces our rigidity. However, on a personal level, it is just plain tiring. How useful it would be if we had one word to describe "us" and our experience.

First, we must recognize that we do experience multiple minority status and that our lives are complicated by the exponential nature of this status.Our plurality is not only significant in our individual lives; among women with various disabilities there is incredible diversity. Blind women who are lesbian mothers may (or may not) have much in common with lesbian mothers who are deaf and lesbian mothers who use wheelchairs. Women with psychiatric disabilities who are lesbian mothers; lesbian mothers with learning disabilities or invisible disabilities — all are struggling for a sense of self. Our lives are filled with challenges — challenges from the outside about our right to mother, to love and to live; and challenges from the inside about giving ourselves and our children as much as we possibly can. We need as much support as we can get in order to survive and emerge as visible in our communities.

This support will come first from within, from our own connections with other lesbian mothers with disabilities. Support will also come from our allies: lesbian mothers without disabilities, or straight mothers with disabilities. We will also require the support of all lesbians, all mothers, all people with disabilities, because we are all part of larger communities, not just the lesbian or disability communities. Our children, whether or not they are themselves disabled, are part of the larger community and need access to the entire range of opportunities as much as we do.

We must de-categorize service and deconstruct disability, so that all women, all mothers, all people with disabilities have access to services, regardless of sexuality, disability or maternal status. We must ensure that our visibility is not only seen, but really noticed by those who have the power and ability to make a difference.

We do exist. We are everywhere.

Notes

1. Lewin, Ellen, *Lesbian Mothers: Accounts of Gender in American Culture*, (Ithaca: Cornell University Press, 1993), p. 110.

2. Morris, Jenny, *Pride Against Prejudice: Transforming Attitudes to Disability*, (London: The Women's Press, 1991), p. 180.

3. Doucette, Joanne, "Redefining Difference: Disabled Lesbians Resist," in *Lesbians in Canada*, Sharon Dale Stone (ed.), (Toronto: Between the Lines, 1990), p. 61.

4. Maria Barile's 1986 sociology paper, "Dis-Abled Women as Deviant," (written as part of a Masters in Social Work at McGill University) was of particular help to me in understanding the issues of intersection/action.

5. Deegan, M.J., *Multiple Minority Groups: A Case of Physically Disabled Women*, (University of Nebraska, 1982).

6. Doucette, p. 62.

7. Ibid., p. 68.

8. Ibid., p. 69.

9. It appears that Michigan deserves special mention for its efforts to make the camp and festival accessible and accommodating for women with disabilities of all kinds.

10. For a good description of how exclusion from policy of women with disabilities has an adverse impact, see: Blackford, Karen, "Erasing Mothers with Disabilities Through Canadian Family-Related Policy," *Disability, Handicap and Society*, 8, 3 (1990).

11. Lewin, p. 120.

12. Bowen, Angela, "Another View of Lesbians Choosing Children," see pp. 253-64 in this book.

13. Day, Dian, "Lesbian/Mother," in Stone, p. 36.

14. Quoted in Morris, p. 38.

15. Lambert, Sandra, "Disability and Violence," *Sinister Wisdom*, 39 (1989), p. 72.

16. Panzarino, Connie, *The Me in the Mirror*, (Seattle: Seal Press, 1994), p. 246.

17. Day in Stone, p. 42.

18. Robson, Ruthann, *Lesbian (OUT) Law: Survival Under the Rule of Law*, (Ithaca, NY: Firebrand Books, 1992), p. 131.

19. Martin, April, *The Lesbian and Gay Parenting Handbook*, (New York: Harper Perennial, 1993), p. 29.

20. Martin, p. 30.

21. Panzarino, p. 252.

On Being a Single Lesbian Mother in South Africa

VANESSA-LYNN NEOPHYTOU

I AM A THIRTY-YEAR-OLD, SINGLE, WHITE, LESBIAN MOTHER LIVING IN NATAL, South Africa. My daughter, who lives with me, is four-and-a-half years old. I am presently a lecturer in Sociology at the University of Natal. I am also undertaking a Masters thesis on lesbian mothers in South Africa.

It has taken me many years to become who I am — a lesbian activist in my own country. I have experienced fulfilling lesbian relationships; I also entered a heterosexual marriage while knowing I was a lesbian. I have avoided the issue of self-identity; been embraced by caring lesbian friends; and argued for gay and lesbian rights, while still avoiding marches on the street with my gay and lesbian comrades. I have raged silently within myself, allowing only my poetry to express my frustrations and contradictions. I have journeyed and it has been long.

I have struggled with being a lesbian mother from the moment I became pregnant — particularly because, at that moment, I was married to a man. I know it is very difficult for many lesbians to accept that some lesbians enter marriage or are married. I have often had to work through and think about how I became — or allowed myself to become — involved with a man, knowing that I was a lesbian. When I began a relationship with a man, I received severe condemnation from the lesbian community, particularly the small community in Durban, where I lived. The condemnation became worse when I discovered that I was pregnant and, bowing to family pressure and my own guilt, entered into marriage.

I left my husband when my daughter was eighteen months old. Those eighteen months before I made the decision to leave were the loneliest of my life. I had lost my old friends and could not be comfortable in "married life." I found it difficult to befriend heterosexual couples, newlyweds with babies on the way, my husband's boss — all the people with whom I was supposed to "fit in." I continually felt like a misfit. My self-esteem was low and although my husband was kind and loving towards me, I could not accept my situation. I poured all my love and affection onto my daughter, and this process of nurturing her was my only positive experience at that time. Once I made the decision to leave my husband — not an easy one to make — I went to the legal aid clinic on campus. On their advice, I was very careful not to disclose that I was a lesbian. Apparently, because of my lesbianism, the state could remove my daughter from me even if my husband agreed that I was to have custody.

Starting life afresh at the age of twenty-six, and with an eighteen-month-old baby, is not easy for anyone. It was particularly difficult for me in that I "came out" as a lesbian — which meant joining organizations and socializing with lesbians and gay men — but I also had to be discreet about my sexuality because of the divorce action. I also had to come out to my mother (for the second time) and deal with her shock. I received a very different response from the one she had given me when I was twenty. This time, I was twenty-six, I had a child, and I had far more politicized ideas about being a lesbian. I will never forget what she said to me: "When you were married, I thought I would have a photo album to fill for the rest of my life with pictures of family Christmasses, Easters, birthdays. Now there won't be a photo album." No photo album! I felt as if I had ceased to exist.

I sought help. I immediately joined "Sunday's Woman," a lesbian support group in Durban. Because the divorce took a year to go through, though, I was often treated with suspicion by other lesbians and my identity was often questioned. In fact, I was often treated this way simply because I had a child. Even those lesbians who did not know that I was separated from my husband felt that I could not be a "real" lesbian because I had a child. This is an attitude I too often encounter — that having a child somehow renders your sexual identity questionable; that women cannot have children and be lesbians. When I met the woman with whom I became involved, it was a lot easier to fit into and be accepted by the community. This also made me realize how difficult it is to maintain a lesbian identity when one is single — much less, single with a child. My new relationship was an invaluable experience for me. My lover was highly politicized and would not tolerate nonsense from my ex-husband. I became stronger as a mother, a lesbian and a woman through knowing her. She taught me to be proud of my lesbianism, and she opened up a world of politics hitherto unknown to me.

Around this time, I remember my anxiety about my daughter's nursery school teachers knowing I was a lesbian. I went into crisis each time my lover took my daughter to school or brought her home. I kept saying that we should wait until my daughter was older before being so open about our relationship. I felt that when my daughter was older she would be able to tell me if she was being picked on by a teacher. My lover and I argued late into many nights about the struggles I was experiencing within myself: not wanting to collude or sanction homophobia in our society, yet wanting to protect my daughter; wondering when the time would be right to be completely open about my sexuality, yet continually contradicting myself in my words and actions. I remember that once all three of us when to Mitchell Park, a spot in Durban that is inundated with heterosexual families on weekends. We were walking around, the three of us, holding hands and looking at the animals and flowers, when we suddenly encountered a barrage of verbal abuse from another family. I could tolerate their words of hatred, but I feared the danger in which they placed my daughter.

One of the positive ways in which I chose to deal with all that was happening in my life was to organize a workshop on lesbian parenting for the members of Sunday's Woman. In 1992, my lover, a friend and I hosted the workshop. We probed issues concerning lesbian motherhood. The one thing that repeatedly came up was that most lesbians in the workshop felt that they could not be mothers — they had never, in fact, conceived that they could be mothers. They felt that, by choosing to be lesbians, they had closed the door on motherhood. I learned that I was resented because I had already had my child, before coming out as a lesbian. Artificial insemination and adoption were illegal, and therefore were not seen as options. No one I knew considered being "subversive" and doing their own artificial insemination; no one considered lobbying the government for adoption and artificial insemination rights. I was pleased to have conducted the workshop and to have gained insight into other lesbians' thoughts about being mothers. The workshop was a turning point in my life. It prompted me to change my Master's thesis into my current one — that is, an examination of the experiences of lesbian mothers in South Africa.

Towards the end of 1992, I realized that I could no longer sustain myself and my daughter on my tutor's income, so I began to look for work. Through a friend I received a position at a non-governmental organization in Durban. I was lucky that I didn't have to worry about coming out at work (I was introduced by my friend as a lesbian), or about facing discrimination because of my sexual orientation. The person who employed me knew I was a single lesbian mother, and it was never an issue. This experience was unlike those of many of my friends, who had to continually maintain separate work and private lives. Soon, I was caught up in my new job, as well as tutoring in sociology and trying to make some headway with my thesis.

The next year was not easy for me, financially or emotionally. I had to deal with the break-up of my relationship, which resulted in me losing confidence in myself and even doubting my sexuality. The year passed eventually, and events took a turn for the better the following year. I was offered a teaching post in the Sociology Department in Pietermaritzburg, a small town about seventy-five kilometres from Durban. Full of enthusiasm, I moved there with my daughter and we settled into my new life. I had no idea that 1994 would turn out quite the way it did.

In 1994, something deep down inside me snapped, and I did not, could not, step out delicately. After all, I was not exactly in the closet, so there would be nothing new in merely stating that I was a lesbian. What to do, I asked myself. I decided to stride out tall and strong, angry and decisive. I stepped straight into a Johannesburg Newspaper interview that took up most of the women's page of the *Sunday Times*.[1] My photograph was included with my words. Although I was misquoted, as I had expected, I did get the message across: I am a lesbian; I am a lesbian mother and a lesbian activist; I will no longer keep quiet. The spin off: more interviews, nationally and, later, internationally;[2] a television interview; the decision to become involved in lesbian politics at both a local and national level; and an exciting conference in Germany, where I presented my findings to date on lesbian mothers in South Africa.

Having reached this point, I began to search for other avenues of expression, and other like-minded lesbians and activist groups. This search was not difficult — my public exposure had had an impact on the lesbian community and I received dozens of phone calls each day. I began to network, and the result was the formation of Lesbians in Natal Kwazulu (LINK), with me as the public representative to the media. Our aim was to develop links with national and international groups, and to affiliate our group with the National Coalition that has just recently formed in South Africa to lobby the government to entrench gay and lesbian rights.

At the same time, I encountered tremendous apathy and resistance from lesbians. I found myself engaged in the old debates, and arguing that everything we do is political, so being a lesbian is not a personal, private "keep it to yourself" affair. I tried to understand that each lesbian is different and that I could not expect everyone to come out as I had done. After all, I had to remind myself, look how long my own journey to activism had taken. On the other hand, I was struggling with my increased awareness of what was at stake in my country and with the conviction that there was no excuse not to come out — there was no time to waste hiding in the closet.

At work I was very lucky to receive the full support of my colleagues, particularly the head of my department, who said he would not accept any derogatory comments made to or about me by any staff member or student on campus. I was still concerned about my daughter's safety and the reaction of her teachers — although, so far, nothing has occurred at the school to cause me concern. I did begin to receive anonymous phone calls, and still do, and I sometimes worry that my public profile will cause me to be hurt. But I feel too strongly about being a lesbian and a lesbian mother to back down now. I do not like the society in which I live, and will endeavour, whenever possible, to challenge the value system that informs it.

Let me tell you how I view South Africa. It is a heterosexist, patriarchal, racist, classist, misogynous and homophobic society. It is a society in which homophobic attitudes, underpinned by narrow stereotypes and ignorance, continue to marginalize and oppress lesbians. It is also a society in which people, bruised and battered from apartheid, are willing to forgive and want to move forward, fighting for change. I am one of those people, and I am fighting so that, one day, when I describe my country, I can omit at least half of the above adjectives. I am realistic enough to know that many things cannot be altered in a patriarchal society — but that will never stop me from trying to alter them.

What is this activism? What must be changed? To address these questions, I need to describe the political situation for gay men and lesbians in South Africa today. And, in order to do this, I must briefly describe the change from apartheid to the new dispensation, and the impact of this on the gay and lesbian community as a whole. It is therefore important to consider the conditions that existed in South Africa under the apartheid regime prior to the April 1994 elections. The conditions were those of an oppressive society. Structures and laws racially divided the country, enforced an orthodox Christian system, and curtailed freedom of speech and association. Apartheid artificially protected the minority white middle class; hence, the majority came to see themselves as apolitical. I would argue that this tendency still largely predominates today.[3] Apartheid was a system declared to be a crime against humanity by the international community: 16.5 million people were criminalized by apartheid laws; 4 million people were forcibly removed from their homes and land. The horrifying statistics continue to be revealed[4]. South Africa has been, and still is, one of the most violent societies in the world.

The apartheid government sought to make homosexuality illegal. But, as a result of campaigns fought by white middle-class men against anti-homosexual laws in the late 1960s, the government chose to minimize the effect of homosexuality rather than criminalize it totally (M. Gevisser and E. Cameron, 1994). The result was that sodomy and other so-called "unnatural acts" remained illegal; artificial insemination remained illegal for single women; up until 1987, single people could not adopt children; and there was no recognition of gay and lesbian partnerships. Furthermore, in 1989, South Africa became one of the few countries to legislate the age of consent for homosexuals to nineteen, whereas it is sixteen for heterosexuals. Lesbians were not recognized by the law. While on the one hand this might seem like a positive thing, it actually served to render us invisible as a community.

Under the new dispensation, there is a move in our society towards democratization — a move embodied in our Bill of Rights and Interim Constitution. South Africa is the first country in the world to have a (interim) constitution with a clause offering specific protection to gay and lesbian people. This clause outlaws unfair discrimination based on a person's sexual orientation. However, a final constitution is due to be drawn up by a Constituent Assemby in 1995, and there is no guarantee that this clause will be retained. In addition, I think it is extremely important to note that, out of twelve appointees in our Constitutional Court, only two are women.

As a consequence of all this, in 1994 the Equality Foundation was formed by gay and human rights lawyers, to address gay and lesbian issues. Their aim was to ensure that sexual orientation was not removed from the final constitution. "Lawyers for Gay and Lesbian Equality" was formed in August 1994 to monitor new legislation and make sure that it conforms to the Bill of Rights, and to prepare challenges to the Constitutional Court. Furthermore, a December 1994 conference was held by the Centre of Applied Legal Studies at the University of Witwatersrand, Johannesburg, for the purpose of uniting the vast spectrum of groups involved in human rights and gay and lesbian issues, and providing a lobbying body to challenge the Constituent Assembly. As a result of the conference, the National Coalition for Lesbian and Gay Equality was formed. The coalition consists of activist and lawyer's groups, who together are planning a careful legal strategy to ensure that Gay and Lesbian rights are upheld in the final constitution.

We need to strategize carefully. Otherwise, a conservative coalition of both Black and Afrikaner nationalists could lobby to have the non-discrimination clause excluded from the final constitution. It is very interesting to note that even while gay and lesbian activists have been uniting on issues, so have a broad spectrum of religious groups. These groups have banded together and raised funds for goals that are in direct opposition to ours. Their influence in society is not to be taken lightly, as they have the power to whip up national hysteria over issues that directly affect our private lives. As a lesbian, I am used to having gay and lesbian marches, plays and film festivals picketed by groups like Christians for Truth; but the formation of these religious groups into an organized body with an anti-gay, pro-nuclear-family stance is quite another thing.

The transition from apartheid to an African National Congress (ANC) government occured through a negotiated settlement. South Africa did not experience a revolution, which brings about direct change. The significance of this fact is that most of the old laws of the apartheid government are still on the statute books today. Furthermore, while the new Bill of Rights is progressive, it is merely a framework of principles through which existing laws still need to be tested in the Constitutional Court.

The majority of people in South Africa do not know about the existence of a national Lesbian, Gay and Bisexual Rights Charter. It was drawn up in 1993 by gay and lesbian organizations, in the hope that it would act as a judicially recognized guideline for the interpretation of future non-discrimination provisions protecting the rights of gay and lesbian people. This has not occured. The reality is that all the existing laws on the statute remain — laws that discriminate against gay men, lesbians and lesbian mothers. Consequently, there is a conflict between the existing laws and the Interim Constitution. We fear that many of the present discriminatory laws might not be changed. When the final constitution is drawn up in 1995, these are the issues we need to address: the decriminalization of sodomy; the testing of adoption laws — in theory, gays and lesbians can adopt, but in practice this is not the case; the amendment of the Human Tissues Act, which states that it is illegal for unmarried women to be artificially inseminated; taxation laws which discriminate against all women; the lack of partnership benefits for lesbians and gays — particularly medical aid, pension and provident fund benefits; discriminatory immigration and naturalization laws; and the lack of recognition for same-sex unions.

From a socio-political perspective, it is important to note that lesbians remain largely invisible in South Africa, even within the gay community. Until recently, the gay movement has been dominated by white, middle-class men. This left very little space for lesbians, particularly those who are not white or middle class, to find and establish support networks. An organization in the Witwatersrand, called Gays and Lesbians of the Witwatersrand (GLOW), has been doing considerable outreach work into the townships. But being black and lesbian is an experience completely different from mine. Conditions in the townships are still appalling and most black lesbians live at home. This means sharing a room with possibly four other family members. Black lesbians simply do not have the privacy and space which white people take so much for granted. Furthermore, it seems that the level of homophobia in the black community is even higher than that in the white community. Black lesbians who come out are most often rejected, not only by their friends and family but by their entire community. They risk being totally isolated.

In South Africa, each time we say that we are lesbians we challenge the status quo. Our struggle is to work towards a society where heterosexuality and homosexuality are equal options. Given that I have grown up in the stranglehold of apartheid, and am an activist, I am highly politicized. I want change.

As for the question I am most often asked about my personal situation — "Does your daughter know you are a lesbian?" — the answer is yes. For a long as that answer remains a problem in our society, my struggle for change will continue.

Notes

1. Interview in the *Sunday Times*, Johannesburg, September 1994.

2. Second interview in the *Sunday Tribune* in Durban, Natal, November 1994; two radio interviews in Germany, December 1994, conducted while I attended an international conference on lesbian politics, "Just A Lifestyle."

3. My research for my dissertation has validated this.

4. Watson, W., "Lesbians in South Africa: A brief overview of the political and social situation," (December 1994), to be published as conference proceedings.

Lover & Mother

DORSIE HATHAWAY

IT IS IRONIC THAT THE ACT THAT MAKES MOST OF US MOTHERS TO BEGIN WITH is least associated with the permanent condition called mother-hood. I sometimes ask myself why I try to have a full life — after all, I have three children. According to society's paradigm for mothering, I have no right to an independent existence.

As for sex, I "should have" retired from this after the birth of the last child. Performance artist Holly Hughes once said, "There is no word for a woman who is a mother and a lover." This statement has particular resonance in my life, because I am both mother and lover. It's very strange to me that the very act that produces most children is, after the fact, the one most estranged from images and icons of mothering. I am that taboo come to flesh: a mother; a lover; and, worse, unapologetic.

Over the past twenty years, I have managed to challenge or destroy almost every social convention I assimilated during childhood. As a child, I never fit in, never identified with anyone else as a role model. There was no one in my life to show me who, or what, I was becoming. Like many young women in the United States, I became pregnant early on in my life. I also married the wrong person; divorced; met another wrong person a year later; got married almost three years later; had two more children; left the second husband under scary circumstances; moved in with my mother; got a divorce and a restraining order; and spent most of a year in a profound depression.

When I got some ambition, I undertook a four-year course in health sciences. This led to greatly increased self-esteem, as I discovered that I was, first, a good student; and later, an excellent student. I also had motivation — three young children and no child support.

Four years after leaving my marriage, when my children were four, six and eleven, I came out as a lesbian. That journey was one of the most difficult of my life. I was sailing off the edge of the map, certain there was no return, so strong were the calls of my own heart and mind. I was stepping out into the Unknown.

In the months after coming out, I began to dream. Nightly, women from my past appeared, and talked to me: women I hadn't seen in fifteen or twenty years; women I had never really seen before. I dreamed back into my life all the lesbians whose paths I had crossed, women from whom I could have learned much if my vision had not been altered by cultural blinders. These women told me that they had been there all along — as had my lesbian Self.

I acknowledged my complete affection for, and interest in, women; but I still could not envision how I would meet anyone, much less have a relationship. Cut to Women's Studies 101, at Portland State University, the summer of 1986. I was there to learn, but I was also on a quest to find Other Lesbians. Girlfriend Number One appeared in two of my classes. We clicked. We were together for almost three years.

Making time together was not easy. She had never had a lover with children before, and I had no road map for being a lesbian and a mother. My mother, with whom I lived in those early years, was still having a lot of trouble accepting the new and improved me. So I packed up the kids nearly every weekend and, from Friday night to Sunday afternoon, moved in with Girlfriend Number One. We tried for domestic bliss every weekend. We even hired a sitter to keep the kids on long weekends so that we could go to the coast. My mother was cross about this, and felt that I was being irresponsible. She felt that I had no right to leave my kids and have fun with another adult for three days. In her time, it would have been unthinkable.

My girlfriend and I made mistakes with each other — we adapted too much, and not enough. Love itself was not sufficient, and eventually we outgrew our early bonds. When we finally broke off our relationship, it was by mutual agreement. I was sure I'd never meet another girlfriend, another partner, someone who would want to be my lover and a co-mom.

I was wrong. In the intervening years, I've been involved in several significant relationships. And I'm getting better at this business of negotiating a life. Do I make this sound easy? It wasn't. It isn't. It's hard. I've had to try and figure out how to be a lesbian, and how to be a girlfriend, and how to be true to myself and my relationships — all the while being a full-time mommy. I've made mistakes in choosing partners, rushed into things too fast, screwed it up. At times, I became involved with lovers who wanted me to take care of them, too — and the last thing I needed or wanted was another child.

Trying to develop and maintain a relationship, while simultaneously managing children, a home, a career, and the sprains and strains of daily life, is tough! You have to be adept at handling changing priorities, and you have to be clear in your communication. It's critical to set time aside to talk with your lover, to be adults together. You can lose sight of each other, become overwhelmed by the details of managing your lives.

Outside of large cities, there's little social support for lesbian family-building (or, as some people say, "family-blending"). When women with children take up residence together, there is usually no ceremony. There are no cards one can purchase to announce the new family, to invite recognition. Your mutual families of origin don't usually show up bearing gifts.

And it is difficult to manage to have what's called "a sex life." What does that mean, anyway? I don't have a "cooking life" or a "television-watching life" or a "grocery-shopping or kid-chauffeuring life." I have a life. All those things are part of my life. And my life is not like a jigsaw puzzle, because no matter how I try, the pieces will never fit together neatly. Most of them don't even overlap. Whenever I manage to pay attention to, or combine, two major areas at once, I feel it's a victory.

So how do we make time to be lovers? We steal. We steal minutes and moments: when the kids are out of the room; under the table during dinner, her foot on mine; we speak in code, with raised brows and downcast eyes, with smiles and whispers. In the garage, as she's leaving for work, the door to the house is shut and I kiss her hard against the car, touching her soft spots, telling her exactly what I will do with her tonight when the house is quiet.

My partner needs me as her confidante, friend and lover. My children need me as their mommy, cook, chauffeur and referee. I want to be her goddess of love, her Aphrodite; and I need to be their mother-earth, their Demeter. It always comes down to choices between major life needs: do we stay up late to be lovers, or do we go to bed at a decent time so we can be good daytime workers and mommies? Often, we do both — becoming short on sleep, making time for love and responsibility. We go to bed late, and settle for less sleep and more sex, because it's what we need and want right now. I admit here that sometimes we have almost fallen asleep in the middle of love-making.

I'm always conflicted, torn between love and parenting. I want to have it all: career, family and romance. Popular magazines say I should set aside "quality time" for the kids, for my lover, for my job. I have every intention of working on quality time, but first I have to pay the bills, let the dog out, pick the kids up from school, return my girlfriend's phone call, and plan tonight's dinner.

On a recent business trip, my partner was seated with a co-worker she knows to be conservative, and deeply religious. He asked, "So, are you two going to have more kids?" It seems that we are legitimized in the straight world by having children; that somehow we are seen as parents first, and lesbians second. And it's true that we're getting as much relationship support from straight couples with kids these days as we are from other lesbians. The folks with children "get it." They understand that you need time to be adults, friends, and lovers with each other, completely apart from your full-time parental commitments. They're the ones who volunteer to take the kids overnight so that we can have time alone.

I wish there was a term that could embrace and embody Demeter and Aphrodite in one woman. At this point in my life, with a teen and a preteen in the house, I can only imagine taking my lover's hand and disappearing into the bedroom. I can't disown Demeter — I'm a mother. And I won't disown Aphrodite — I am a lover. This is my life.

Confronting the "I" in the Eye:
Black Mother, Black Daughters

MAKEDA SILVERA

1995

I AM SORTING THROUGH AN OLD TRUNK IN MY CLOSET, WHERE OVER THE YEARS
I've tossed journals, letters, notes and some half-finished short
stories. In this old brown trunk I come across a journal covering
four weeks in 1981. I'm a little surprised to realize how much
of it is about parenting, taking care of ... and very little about
me, the "I," and the other parts of my identity. At the time I was
a young, single, heterosexual Black mother of two girls aged
four and six.

Leafing through the pages, I am immediately struck by the
repetition of parenting. I am taken by the persistent routine.
The mundane. The details ... waking the children, washing and
dressing them, preparing the breakfast, preparing lunch, taking
them to school, cooking, washing, cleaning. The emotional
swings from high to low. Yet I am drawn into the simplicity of
that stage of motherhood: the wiping of a runny nose, the
cuddling after a bad dream, the gratitude that comes after a fairy
tale and a good night kiss.

At the end of the diary there is a quote from Adrienne Rich.
That quote encompassed my most private feelings and
thoughts about motherhood and child care, but I didn't know
it would stay with me. I "met" Adrienne Rich in 1980 through
her book *Of Woman Born: Motherhood as experience and
institution*. It was a remarkable read. I was in awe of her
candour, her bravery. I had never, up to that time, read anything that spoke so honestly, so loudly about motherhood as
an institution, and the ways in which we as women are oppressed in that institution.

There were vast differences in our lives, sharp contrasts. She was a white, married, middle-class feminist, with sons; I was Black, single, working class, the mother of daughters. I emphasize here "Black" and "working class," because these words carry in their meaning the impact that race (as we know it), colour and class hold in an unequal society, a society that devalues personhood when it is not white, middle-class. Yet the book struck many different notes and mirrored much of my own experience, as mother, as woman.

The familiar shifts in emotions are the only things that have remained the same. Gone are the runny noses, the routine, the dependent children with simple needs.

1983

> I have met a wonderful and exciting woman — each day she grows more beautiful. We are in love and have committed ourselves in what seems like a flash of the eyelid to share our lives together with my two daughters.

It was wondrous, rapt, surprising. For me, a heady giddy ride on a motorbike, blindfolded. Magic. A world open with possibilities.

I was whole, not object. My daughters — six and eight years old — my lover and I embraced our new-found family with wild innocence. We basked in the newness of it, went on picnics, overnight camping trips, went to children's movies, romped in wading pools, jumped skipping ropes.

But we had to come out of the magical cloud and back to the dirt. Our community and its moralistic banner of "keep our values alive" was hard on us. The shame in the eyes of family members when they looked at me, the friends who stopped visiting, stopped talking, stopped calling. It was a cold goodbye. It was then that I understood the full weight of my decision and how it could affect my daughters. My identity had changed, and with it, theirs. I was now Black, mother, lesbian; they were now Black girls living with their Black lesbian mother and her mixed-race woman lover.

It was a strange and scary place to be, Toronto in 1983. I didn't have to try to fit into some other personality, I was finally me. And I was also very scared. In the Jamaican language, "I" means I. When we say "I-and-I," we are saying "we" — that we are alike, part of the same community. Now I was alone, no other "I" would look me in the eye. There was no other "I" that I could find to talk with, to get support from. Cut off from I-and-I, from family and community, I understood the meaning of "silenced," but I also understood what it means to be silent, as in silent time, time alone. From that, I went on to find myself as a Black lesbian mother.

Often, when the cards are turned on their faces, it is the Queen, the woman, the mother, the girl, that comes up "bad." Worse than bad, evil, is the Black lesbian mother, for she is even more dangerous than a Black lesbian; she is dangerous for she is the lifeline.

I had time to think about all the Black sisters I had known before: how we sang, how we laughed, how we cried, how we made plans and had hopes. The Black sisters, mothers, I knew before: how our children played together, how they laughed, how they cried too, how they told stories. Being a Black lesbian mother changed all that. Now I was contaminated, had lost my mind, gone psycho, become a sodomite. Now they must not only try to protect themselves from me, but protect me and my poor Black daughters from me.

Black sisters who knew me on every single demonstration in the Black community in the 1970s and 1980s now looked the other way, calling, "shame, shame." Perhaps I should be hard on the brothers, the Black men, the ones I typed letter after letter for, the ones who were past lovers; perhaps I am too hard on those sisters, who were trying so hard in a white world to be the best for the Black brothers, the Black men.

But some things that happened in my early days as a young lesbian Black mother are hard to forget, hard to forgive: being shut out by both my Black sisters and my Black brothers, being denied and watching my children being denied our culture. The silence and whispers, the homophobic remarks, the sucking of the teeth when we passed by, the sudden breaks into a degrading song about my sexuality.

Culture is important. Home is important. History is important. As a Black mother, I had to instill courage and hope in my daughters. We live in a racist, sexist, class-conscious society, a woman-hating one. For Black people, it is our families, our culture, our home, our language, our food, our music, our laughter, our history that lets us ground ourselves, find a place, have confidence.

To refuse this, refuse to let our children take part in the community, to be of the community, to learn from the community, to eat the community's food, drink its drinks and dance its songs, to make them pay for a mother's "sins" — that is the abomination.

As a Black lesbian mother, I have had to struggle to secure a place for "I" in the "I-and-I." I had to make sure I held on to the culture so I could pass it on, with my own questions and criticisms, so my daughters and the daughters of other "I"s could have a history to talk about, a culture to share.

For a time, the only solace was at home, in the community I had created in my own home, the culture housed there. The music, the food, the language, I brought to the house. It seemed like a long, long time before there were other "I"s to talk to, laugh with, share with.

It was around that time that I discovered Black woman, lesbian, mother, poet Audre Lorde. Her book *Sister Outsider* was company and consolation when I needed to hear, see in print, a Black lesbian, speaking about being lesbian, being a mother, speaking about Black community, speaking about heterosexual Black women and the rift between us, speaking about internalized racism, internalized homophobia, and speaking in a language I spoke, too.

Being a Black lesbian parent is hard: this society holds that to be Black is to be undesirable, to be woman is to be object, to be lesbian is to be sick, to be a Black lesbian mother is to be an undesirable object, one that is sick. Our children are not unaware of this, nor do they escape it. When you place gender-colour-sexuality in a sexist-racist-homophobic society — then parenting is not only bringing up children, it is political.

Still, I feel tremendous freedom and joy in being a lesbian parent, in being a Black lesbian mother and in having a partner to raise my children with. It's often not tangible enough to explain — it is like having best friend, lover, sister, and more, all wrapped up in one package.

But part of what I want to talk about in this essay, or rather to begin to explore, is Black lesbian mothers and Black daughters as sexual beings. In other words, confronting the "I" in the eye — Black mother: Black daughters.

1995

I am Black. I am lesbian. I am mother. I am sexual. I am the mother of daughters in their late teens. They are hetero/sexually active, I am lesbian/sexually active.

Still, there is something very different when one is writing as a single parent of children under nine years, than when is writing about teenagers or young women — all the more so when the mother is a lesbian. Black mother lesbian. Black daughter. Both sexual beings, in a society where homosexuality is still largely perceived as deviant.

(I want to say here that I am fully aware of the problems parents on the whole experience with adolescents, no matter what the sexuality of the parent or parents. In general, parents with teenagers sometimes think they are raising strangers. It is a struggle to know the strangers they have become, and we wish they were more like how they were at six or eight years of age. But the child wants autonomy, and she will do what she must to get it.)

When "I" confront the eye, or the eye looks into the eye it mirrors, the eye looking into the "I" will often flinch away, because the mirror is showing an "I" that the other "I" does not want to see. The mirror is showing an "I" to the eye, an "I" that isn't normal in a white, male world. And the eye wants to see the normal.

Homophobia has challenged my daughters' response to having a lesbian mother. Many teenagers, young adults themselves, deny that there is such a thing as a parent's sexuality; they do not want to acknowledge it. Sex is something they don't often talk to you about, because often the assumption is that you wouldn't understand hetero/sexuality, that you don't understand or even like men or you would be with them, therefore you cannot give advice. My daughters speak/confide in my heterosexual friends about difficulties they might be having with their boyfriends. This might have everything to do with the fact that I am their "mother," or it might be because I am their *lesbian* mother and therefore not "qualified" to give advice. They also have grown up with one of my closest friends, a heterosexual man, as a constant in their lives. Men, who have always been part of our circle of friends, have always been welcome in our home.

Over the years, I haven't seen many workshops for lesbians who are raising teenagers or pre-teens. It is an area that should be looked at and discussed with other mothers — there must be a better way of dealing with the sexuality than through silence.

I think it is the sexual mother that frightens the community, that forces the family to close their eyes. After all, in these communities, lesbians do not exist, so don't bother to talk about a lesbian mother — how can she exist? I recall one of the biggest criticisms I got from family, from friends and from my community was the way I "flaunted" my sexuality like a red rag, a flag on a pole. They could tolerate me as a lesbian, as a mother, but not as a lesbian sexual mother, living with a woman lover. This was counter-culture, counter-Black, counter-mother.

"Why should the children have to know? Why should they be involved? Why should they get hurt?" They accuse, but they do not ask themselves, "Why are we hurting the kids? Why are we using our power this way, as community? Why are we using our power this way, as a family? Why are we using our power this way, as friends?"

That we never hid that we were lesbians from our children, that we never hid, from the beginning of the relationship, that we were sexual, has had its high and low points, but for me the highs far outweigh the lows. Since they were seven and nine, my daughters have asked questions freely about women loving women, they've jumped in and out of our bed. Bed was the place where we sometimes watched TV as a family, played board-games, read to each other; it was a place they came for comfort, to talk about the day at school.

It was the place where my oldest, at eight years, asked what "lesbian" meant. We answered and she was satisfied.

We continued our lives as a family, and for a number of years, painfully stayed away from the Black community, the place that had loved me, the place where I was once sister, daughter, friend. Determined to create a place for ourselves, an extended family, a Black, of colour, lesbian and gay community, we moved from our apartment to a house, armed with a vision of organizing black and lesbians of colour who wanted, needed, an extended family. Our house was a bright array of colours: Black, Caribbean, Asian, Native lesbian mothers with children, living together, creating for ourselves what we were being denied.

That "house" became a refuge for women of colour coming out, and the launching pad for a joyous and militant lesbian sexuality. We supported, comforted, laughed and teased each other, strengthened by our new, if tiny, community.

We had strong role models for our daughters and for many of the other children in the household. Our house was organized and full of love and hope.

Through those years, the parenting felt easy, because there was support all around; we confronted the "I" in the eye and loved the "I." We all moved on, as families must do, but that bond, and that sense of family, of home, still holds us together.

Enter adolescence, and it seems that all the bonding, all the warm comfort, love, security, never was. Enter the real teacher, the dominant culture, the world outside, the street. The real teacher has come to receive her favourite pupil, adolescence. The adolescent does not want to be seen as different by the dominant culture; it tells her that this is the correct thinking. The teacher feeds the adolescent's fears.

The adolescent looks in the mirror and sees the "I" she doesn't want to become. Her sexuality is awakening, her relationship is ripe, she needs to wear the right clothes, have the right body, the right mother. The newspapers, the TV, the radio, the movies, the schools, the world at large, assert that she doesn't want to be like her lesbian mother. It is a difficult period for any lesbian mother. Now, looking back at how I started this essay, I think: how easy life seemed then, even with the ironing, the cleaning up after; in return, there was a love, innocent and unflawed.

Dealing with the culture's hatred towards lesbianism and lesbian parenting is frustrating, tiring, but dealing with one's children's unspoken homophobia is painful. Much of it is not about them, it is not about them hating the Black lesbian mother who raised them, not about them hating the mixed-race woman who also raised them; it is about the dominant culture teaching them, often quietly, that women loving women is wrong.

That quiet homophobia has manifested itself in different ways over the years. Some are common in lesbian households, familiar: the friends not coming over; the children always going to their friends' houses; the friends not sleeping over but having them sleep over; the dinners at friends' houses; the look that passes from face to face when a lesbian dance is mentioned (which means sex, which means women rubbing on women); the unspoken "please, don't come to the school and tell the teacher"; the unspoken "why are you so out, everybody knows you, knows you are lesbian and we are your daughters." It is making sure one has a boyfriend or many boyfriends, because one doesn't want to be like Mother. It is staying away from feminist events, not reading any feminist literature thrown all around the house, hiding any books and posters of lesbian sexuality, if and when an occasional friend happens to come by. Yet, despite themselves and their sometimes internalized homophobia, they still love sitting around and listening to the chatter of women friends, lesbian and heterosexual. They still seek the closeness and the warmth of the women's voices, pay attention to their stories.

As a lesbian mother, I make it a point to let my daughters know that I have choices, and that I take those choices, no matter how unpopular. This is where the unspoken resentment and homophobia has manifested itself more clearly — in my daughter's response to "I" as a public figure and as a mother who is non-monogamous. They are afraid to look the "I" in the eye because the "I" they see as their mother bears no resemblance to a "good mother." Good mothers go about their business quietly, good mothers are discreet. The mother who writes and travels across the country speaking on controversial topics — including that of her lesbian sexuality — and the mother who has a strong and militant lesbian presence, is an embarrassment. Why doesn't she write "quietly" about lesbian identity?

And a lesbian mother who chooses to be non-monogamous is often perceived as "unfaithful," "bad"; she becomes a lesbian jezebel. This is what our culture teaches. This is what my daughters have observed and learned from the culture and from other adults who believe monogamy is the "right" way. And a lesbian mother who does not follow these rules runs the risk of being an "outsider" not only in the larger culture, but also in the "lesbian community."

In saying all this, I want to acknowledge the pride and admiration my children also feel in knowing that "I" as mother. I hear it at times in their voices, when they speak about a particular book of mine being used in a class, when their friends speak about me in admiration, whenever I travel to new places. But that pride, that admiration, is a mixed bag filled also with resentment and homophobia. It speaks not only to their resentment of the "I" as Black lesbian, but to the "I" as an unconventional lesbian mother and to the "I" who has not spent "enough" time with them. But, though their lives have certainly been unconventional and conflicted, despite themselves they have an interest in the unconventional. For some months now, I keep running into my youngest daughter with her girlfriends at rallies, women's dances and other women's events; places that, years ago, she would have had to be dragged to. My eldest daughter is strong-willed and obviously has a clear sense of herself as woman, and I envision the day when we will sit together, sharing stories as women and laughing.

Awareness is slowly coming, although sometimes I feel that it comes too slowly. Just as boys act out sexism against their mothers because that is what the culture teaches, so do the daughters and sons of lesbians act out homophobia. My daughters have helped me to understand, to look closely at, how the "isms" creep into family, how these dictate the terms for mothers and daughters, how these "isms" filter unnamed resentments. They have helped me to better understand my own mother — the feelings of resentment I held, both justified and unjustified — and they have ironically brought us closer over the years as I, Black Lesbian Mother, ask my Black heterosexual mother for advice and solace.

Although the terrain has been rough at times, I don't believe my daughters have ever doubted my love for them. I believe that loyalty, love, and courage are the most valuable gifts that I, Black Lesbian Mother, could ever impart to my daughters. As they become young adults, I can see changes in their views on sexuality; they are more vocal on the right to choose and less afraid of unpopular choices and difference. They are more at ease with a Black Lesbian Mother who is a writer. They are growing into women, less afraid to Eye the "I" in the eye.

A Mother-Daughter Conversation:
Alix Dobkin & Adrian Hood

AS TOLD TO TONI ARMSTRONG JR.

Alix Dobkin was born in Manhattan on August 16, 1940. Her long-time involvement in music includes working steadily on the folk circuit since the '60s. Her women's music credits include performing, recording and touring since 1973.

Adrian Leighton Hood was born on October 21, 1970. She lived with her parents until her mother and her mother's lover Liza moved to the Catskill Mountains in 1974. She lived with her father from ages five to eight, when he remarried and relocated to Woodstock.

Alix: My life is so different from the life of your "conventional mom." It has a lot of built-in stresses for both of us. Ever since you've known me, I have been a lesbian; even though I came out when you were a year and a half old, as far as your conscious life, you've never known me to be anything else. I have always felt so positive and wonderful — and still do — about my choice, that I've never felt any shame or embarrassment about it, and I've never felt like I had to apologize or hide it from you. So you were always exposed to a very positive attitude about, first of all, my being a lesbian, and, second of all, I think that my direct relationship with women's culture — the fact that I've been so active in it for the last fifteen years — has been a great plus for us in many ways. I'd like to talk about that, I think it gives us a lot that we share. Like Toni Senior and Toni Junior (the Armstrongs — see "Mothers & Daughters," March 1988 *Hot Wire*), the festivals — Michigan — is our major focus of women's music together, although you do come to concerts ...

Adrian: Not any more ...

Alix: ... not so much any more, but ... the older you get, the less interested you are.

Adrian: No, the less time I have.

Alix: Right, the busier you are. But I think we ought to back up a little bit, because it hasn't always been this easy for you to be at concerts with me — as you recall. Your father, years ago, got very upset, first of all, about my being a lesbian, second of all, about my being a public lesbian, and, third, about you travelling with me and being visible as my daughter. He felt for a couple of years that I was exploiting you for my own political purposes.

Adrian: He didn't want me in women-only space because he did not want me anywhere that he was not allowed to go, where men were not allowed to go. He didn't feel it was good or healthy for me. And then I started dating. And then he wished I was there all the time.

Alix: I'll never forget four or five years ago when you were just budding into your beautiful, gorgeous self and started seeing boys — your father told me on the phone, "I wish Michigan lasted all summer." I could hardly believe it, because he had been so opposed to your going anywhere with me — you weren't allowed to travel with me, you weren't allowed to appear in concerts with me.

It has been a very positive experience for us, because you always had a very privileged position at women's events, especially concerts or festivals where I was performing. Both of us have a very privileged position in these spaces and situations, we get a lot of extra special perks and attention, so it's not a normal lesbian mother and daughter experience for us. It's been a wonderful thing, and that's been both of our experience in women's culture, we have visibility and recognition.

It's been one of the great pleasures of my life, seriously, that I have been able to participate in building a culture that was accessible to you, and that gave you particularly, and girls your age in general, the choice that we have, this institution of women's culture that you can choose to be in. You've experienced it and you're much richer for it, so I'm pleased that I had something to do with helping create that. That's been a great source of pleasure for me, and it gives me just indescribable pleasure to be at the festival with you and see how you relate to women whom I know and love and think so highly of; to see your independent relationship with them has been a wonderful plus for me.

Adrian: This is only recent, though. For so long I would go to these events and I was "Alix's daughter" — that was my title. But throughout the years I have gotten to know many women, especially at Michigan, and have established wonderful relationships, wonderful friends. I work in the workers' area with women, though some of my best friends don't have anything to do with where I work. I've met most of the women through you, but I've established my own independent relationships with them. We correspond and are in touch throughout the year, and then we see each other at Michigan. And the festival really is probably the most significant thing in our life that ties me into women's music.

Alix: One thing that is such a thrill to me at Michigan is to not only walk around with you and talk to women and to hang out with women, but to go to concerts with you now that you really appreciate the quality of the music. Mom used to say that it's the highest form of art, and I agree because nothing unites people in the moment like music does. When we're responding in the same way in the same moment together, it's a very exciting kind of communication.

Adrian: Liza [Cowen] and I were talking the other day about when I was younger — I guess around five — and all I used to want was for you and my dad to get back together. I think it's in the back of every child's head whose parents have been divorced. And in a way I still would love it if my dad and my mom were married. But then when I lay awake thinking about that, I think, yeah, it's a great fantasy, but then Liza wouldn't be in my life, Denny [Brown] wouldn't be in my life, I wouldn't have this perspective on life that I have and this whole other culture that I would never have been exposed to. And I've gained so much from it.

Alix: Yes, Adrian, I remember you telling me about how you'd learned so much ahead of other kids in relationships when Liza and I were together for six years and you lived with us, and we were a family.

Adrian: And we still are.

Alix: When Liza and I broke up, though, it was in some ways maybe even more devastating to you than it was to me, and yet you got through it. You still have a very close and strong relationship with Liza, even through all that separation and difficulty and trauma. It was a catastrophic event for both of us, and you've survived that and come through it, and with my getting together with Denslow and breaking up with her, and having these big changes in your life that you had no control over that you had to react to, and you did. You've learned an awful lot about relationships and an awful lot about life.

Adrian: I definitely agree with that. And I really respect it. I respect our living situation right now so much, living with you and Liza with our poor old dog that is older than all of us, and our cats. I'm closest to you and Liza, definitely, out of all twenty of my parents, and to watch the way you react to each other and the way you live together and work together is very special.

Alix: That's an important point, about growing up in a lesbian subculture.

Adrian: Oh, it's different. I've had both.

Alix: You still have both; you've had them for a number of years. I find that it's a wonderful gift that I'm able to give you, to have this situation where you can see how women can relate to each other, how it's possible. You have a growthful, positive relationship, and also you can compare, because you've got examples of both. I remember when you went to live with your father, you would tell me, "My father never yells at me." Remember that? "My daddy would never yell at me." And I would say, and Liza would say, "Oh, yeah? Just wait." So it was a great education for you to live with him and then to live with his wife and your stepbrother — that's a wonderful family, and you're lucky to have them as well.

Adrian: Right. I remember thinking, "All I want in life is a normal family; I want a mother and I want a father, and I want a sibling and a dog and a white picket fence, and I want us all to live together"- and now that I have it … Oh God! It's so conventional.

Alix: There were certainly stresses when you were little and lived with Liza and me. People have to understand, this was in a rural, backwoods area — nobody there is even separated let alone divorced — let alone a lesbian.

Adrian: They didn't even know what lesbian meant, or Jewish. And from New York City — three Jews …

Alix: … radicals …

Adrian: … two of whom had their heads shaved, combat boots, overalls that came up to their knees …

Alix: Our overalls?

Adrian: They were floods, Mom. Your pants were always too short for you. And the "I hate men" bumper-stickers and "I'm a lesbian" bumper-stickers ...

Alix: No, no, no! See, that's to the eyes of the young! That's what it seemed like!

Adrian: Well, it seemed like that to them, I mean, you were not ashamed, you were not hiding ...

Alix: ... *au contraire*!

Adrian: My kindergarten teacher hated me, she hated me and it had to have been because of you. I remember one time I got sick on the school bus on the way to school and my bus driver — I had two bus drivers, one in the morning and one in the afternoon, and they were the only people at that whole school who liked me ...

Alix: ... and they were really the only ones who ever saw us!

Adrian: ... my bus driver brings me into the classroom, and he tells my teacher, I don't remember what her name was ...

Alix: ... Miss Horrible ...

Adrian: ... Mrs. Horrible — no that wasn't her name — anyway, I got sick, and all she said was "So?" Meanwhile, here I am this five-year-old kid who just threw up all over the school bus, who's deathly ill, and I remember you and Liza coming to pick me up at school, and was I embarrassed — you had on the work boots and the shaved heads, and Liza probably had her broken nose and the black eye — I remember walking through the hall and it was just very, very hard. All I wanted was a normal family.

Alix: And all I wanted was not to have to be involved in a straight community, and having a kid means you have to be involved in that community. I had to be a parent, I had to interact with other parents, I had to interact with all kinds of different people I would no more pick out than the man in the moon. It was a great stress for both of us, because it brought elements into our lives that were very difficult. And we did not have a good time with each other. It was a very hard, isolated time. You had hardly any friends and any kids lived far away, I had to drive you, it was a big production for you to get to play with friends, so you didn't really have all that many social resources at all. That left you dependent on us. And you know, we were lesbian separatists — this is not your ideal. I mean, we were as nice as could be to you, I certainly did as much as I could, but we were at each other's throats all the time. I don't know if you remember this, but it was a constant battle between us. You were a very willful child and I'm a very willful individual too. The situation didn't suit us, and that's why you went to live with your father. We were at the end of our rope. Sam offered to take you in New York, and you went to live with him.

That was a very painful, nightmarish experience for me in many ways. You can speak for yourself. But for me, I was ridden with guilt, wondering had I done something wrong, and was this the right thing to do. But I knew we couldn't continue it the way it had been going — it was just too hard. And so I tried to reconcile it, and we saw each other every two weeks — and that was a nightmare. It took us a number of years to get to the point where we could see each other every week. When I think back to how bad it was, it blows me away ... the contrast is stunning. I remember in 1978 when you were eight years old, Adrian, we were only seeing each other every couple of weeks, and our parting scenes were tragic, heart-rending drama-ramas. I remember saying, "I can't imagine how it will ever be good with us; I can't imagine how we could ever have a good life together, how this could ever work out." Yet it has, more than I could ever have dreamed. Which isn't to say we don't have our conflicts, of course, but I'm very proud of you, and very pleased with how you've turned out, and I know that you're a wonderful feminist and you love women and you are loyal and devoted and you have really good values and you stick up for yourself.

Adrian: I'm proud of you, too. I am, I have my wishes — wish you weren't as out as you are; I wish that being a lesbian, which is something I respect, wasn't such a major part of your life — that it wasn't your career, your lifestyle, your everything. That is often hard. And I wish that there were more ... I'm not even sure exactly what I wish that there was, but ... you being on the road a lot is hard, though it was much harder when I was younger. Before I went to boarding school we used to have the hardest times when you'd go away. When I first lived with my dad I remember our phone conversations, which just left me crying and crying. When we're separated it's very hard for me. And even now, when you go on the road I get so sad. It's a very difficult life. Yeah, there's a lot of wonderful aspects of it, but it's very, very hard. It's hard when someone says, "What does your mother do?" If it's someone that I can't tell you're a lesbian, well, "She's a folksinger ..." "Oh really? Does she perform ever?" It's hard. You are a lesbian and there's no way of hiding it.

Alix: That's right, you're stuck with it. And you're straight. I remember a letter that you wrote to me a couple of years ago — do you remember that letter? When you said that you had been worried that I wouldn't love you as much if you were heterosexual? You wrote me a beautiful letter, and you said that you realized that I would love you no matter who you were or what choices you made for your life, that you really believed it.

Adrian: Do you still have it?

Alix: Yes, of course — it's a very beautiful letter. You realized that I would love you even if you weren't a lesbian. You know without a doubt that's true.

Adrian: Within the past few years, I always felt a little uncomfortable being straight at Michigan. There was this time period when I was a kid, when I was identified as a child, when I was "Alix's daughter," and that's who I was at the festival. But then, when I got to be around fifteen, sixteen — maybe even fourteen — I was looking older, so people started with, "Oh, maybe she's a lesbian." I was thinking, "Oh-my-god, I'm going to be identified as a lesbian, what am I doing here?" and it would make me nervous a little bit. But now I feel so comfortable — so welcome and so accepted as being straight. It's just wonderful. I've gained so much from my lesbian friends.

Alix: All my life revolves around lesbian culture — my identity as a professional lesbian, my commitment to lesbian culture and international lesbian culture — and I can't even imagine what my life would be like any more without it. Although I do sometimes wish I could be more in the mainstream just to experience how normal people live, I remember when I did that years ago and I hated it. I couldn't stand it. So I don't know how I'd do in any other profession. All I know is, women's culture has given me a great many gifts, and I feel very privileged and pleased that I can offer them to you and your generation, for you to choose or not to choose, but at least to know that it exists, that you can love women ...

Adrian: If you weren't involved in the culture, I think it would be much easier and so boring. Even though it's been hard, it's been worth it. It's been worth the struggles that we've gone through. Like I said before, my fantasy used to be to have my mommy and daddy married and living together — but if I'd gotten it, I would have missed out on so much.

Living as a Lesbian Mom

COLLEEN GLASS

IN THE FALL OF THE YEAR WHEN MY CONSCIOUSNESS WAS TURNED WITH MY body, I found myself choosing to leave a marriage. I left with nothing but my eleven-year-old daughter and our suitcases. I could no longer honour the vows my husband, Paul, and I had made. As I chose to change our lives, my aspiration was that there could continue to be understanding and compassion in our hearts.

My daughter, Oona, and I moved into familiar Ottawa South, where Oona was enrolled in an enriched French Immersion programme in the neighbourhood public school. The woman who shared the apartment with us for four months was briefly my lover. She was good to my daughter, and at first we cared for each other.

Oona did not know about the lesbian life-choice I had made — not yet. My parents, who live in southern Ontario, were not told of the extent of my changed life-choices either. One brother, who lived in town, stayed at an arm's distance; and my oldest brother, who was in England at that time with his family, was the last to know.

Oona and I had left a home and community in the Gatineau hills which I had helped to build. Now, my old friends from the country days were gone. No one dropped by with a casserole. I suspect Paul may have thought I was coming back, until the New Year's Eve when he fell in love again.

I spent the next four and a half years learning the hands-on operation and maintenance of research laboratory buildings systems. Ironically, now that I had to "support" us, I was on crutches all that first, bright autumn. I tore an Achilles tendon while playing Sunday afternoon dyke basketball, and that put me on sticks for the first three months of a four-year apprenticeship programme (the government department I was working for had assigned me — an enthusiastic "Woman In The Trades" graduate — to an all-male maintenance crew). It was a real eye-opener for me, experiencing for a brief time what disabled people live and work with *all* the time. Navigating through doorways, climbing icy concrete steps, carrying a lunchtray — all these required daily stress-filled strategies. Long after the winter on crutches was over, I would remember how privileged I was to be physically able.

Our lives, it seemed, had exploded and imploded at the same time. All the choices I made then — ten years ago — formed the context within which I found myself a Lesbian Mom. I was trying to transplant, to survive, to "come out" and, at the same time, remain a good mom, a good role model, for my girl. In reading my journal from that time, it is obvious to me that I was feeling the need to justify what I had done: "… I'm doing the best I know. I am who I am. I am weak and allowed to make mistakes. I have the right to be brave."

My daughter spent every other weekend with her dad at the farm and stayed connected to her roots in the country throughout her teens. Her paternal grandmother has always been a strong, caring force in Oona's life. Thankfully, this continued, as I was in too much pain that first year in town to see even Oona's needs clearly.

Telling my daughter, my biological family and friends about my new awareness and choices was easier once I was able to reach out and into the lesbian community. My tried-and-true woman friend, LeeLee, came by our apartment often. She understood my common "baby-dyke" fear of being new in the community and the isolation I was feeling as a single mom. In reaching out and caring about what happened to Oona and me, she and her magnificently large heart helped to build a larger lesbian community. In her efforts to involve me, she continued to talk to me about a woman, Jan, who had a small boy and had started a lesbian mom's support group! The concept of such a group was liberating in and of itself. Lee encouraged me to call Jan — and eventually I did. By reaching out to Jan for help, by looking at how homophobia could affect Oona, by feeling my deep fears and by saying "dyke" a lot, the tide started to turn.

When I was ready and my feet were back on the ground, I summoned the courage to tell Oona where my heart had led me. I told her that I felt I could love again — and that this time I was in love with a woman. I still remember her thoughtful expression and the connection she made that I was a lesbian, like our friend Lee. On the way home in the car she chatted away about lots of things, not too concerned with my choice, and perhaps relieved that what she must have already suspected and not known how to ask was out in the open. If I had honoured feelings then as I do now, I would have spent more time exploring her feelings with her. I would have asked her how it felt to have left her home in the country, her kitten, Drac, and her father. Maybe I would have made more time to bake muffins together, casually, listening for Oona's cues and being there more often to share her struggle for understanding.

The Lesbian Moms' Group met once a month at each other's houses. Our numbers would vary from two or three moms to three times as many. The kids were always wildly wonderful. We organized active pool excursions, skating and hot chocolate on the canal, bowling on the weekends, hikes, sleepovers and babysitting exchanges. When one of the moms was very sick in hospital, we took shifts at her apartment with her toddler. Most of all, we had pot-luck dinners and talked about everything. Our get-togethers provided an occasion for our kids to play and to talk with other kids about whatever they wanted. (Oona was the oldest child — a great older sister to the many little boys.) We made an impression of "normal" on ourselves and on our kids — we rolled with the punches together, laughed a lot, and some of us remain good friends to this day. Today, I see notices in the local gay, lesbian and bisexual newspaper about a similiar lesbian moms' group — still meeting in the wave pools, I betcha'!

I admire the courage of lesbians who have decided, with their children and supportive families, to come out into the larger straight community — to neighbourhood families and friends, and at parent-teacher meetings, for example. My process was tentative. I was protective of Oona and encouraged her not to tell her school friends, just in case she would be hurt. In my chosen line of work I learned that, in the old boy's network that prevails in the trades, men had refused to work with women who were "different." It is the woman who becomes isolated and ends up suffering and fighting the system to survive. To this day I remain in the closet at work, yet assertive in establishing and maintaining female faces in a predominantly male workforce.

In retrospect, I think the way this played out for me was perhaps not the best way for Oona. Now, I would do more work on exploring what she needed, not what I assumed she needed. I do remember one very positive thing that we did together. About a year and a half into our new life, I went to the art supply store and bought a utility sketchbook. On it I wrote: "OUR BOOK by Colleen Glass & Oona Hayes. August '87." On the cover I drew a picture of Oona and me with our arms around each others' shoulders. Oona looks thirteen, with an orange tee-shirt and freckles and shoulder-length hair. I'm a smiling, spike-haired and green-tank-topped woman. The words inside read:

> We agreed that if we shared a book — like this one — we could mark down how we felt and thought about issues that concerned us — individually and together. If I want to express myself, I can try to write out my feelings or draw them or make a collage or point to them in this book. Then Oona can see my work — I'd leave it someplace where I know she'd read it — and can better understand where I am and what I am feeling. She can do the same thing for me, and I will know her better as well. We're NOT SURE what will happen, but let's see ...

What a great gift we proceeded to give each other! Space to reflect and then articulate our feelings, our needs. Time to absorb what was happening in each others' lives. A way to plan for the big trips, the responsibilities, the allowances. At the back, we wrote and enclosed our agreements. In them, we said what we expected and needed from each other: "... allowances

... chores ... patience and understanding ... TV limits ... phone times ... nail polish (either tidy or off) ... fairness ... freedom!" We also agreed that if something was bothering either one of us, we'd mention it within three days, to start to unravel the conflict that inevitably builds. This book was a great invention, and later on I started one with Dan, my partner Jan's son, as well.

My daughter is now in her second year of university studies in southern Ontario. Jan and I have sold our house in Ottawa South and bought a small "ranch" where we are raising lesbian horses and two co-dependent dogs! And that *small* boy, Dan — he's six-foot-one, in grade eleven, and plays "an all-over centre" for a Junior B hockey team. Three and a half years ago he chose to live with his dad, and comes home to visit every other weekend.

I believe sharing the details of our lives is important. If they are shared honestly and openly, they support understanding. And when you *understand* something, you experience a "link-up," a sameness at a gut level — a sharing with others. At the best of times, the result is goose bumps! This interdependence is a felt reality, not some concept or theory or pie in the sky.

The Tibetans express this ecology in a prayer of thanksgiving. They address their gratitude to "... all beings, our Mothers." Opening, knowing, giving of ourselves is what we do best as moms. As lesbians, maybe we just groove a little bit more on that *sameness* thing.

Growing up with a Lesbian Mom

OONA HAYES

I STILL REMEMBER THE CRISP AUTUMN AFTERNOON WHEN MY MOM CAME OUT
to me. I still remember how nervous she was, and how serious
our conversation was. She said she had something to tell me,
and did I remember Jan? My response: "You're gay!" She was
so surprised that I knew, and I was happy that I had anticipated
what she needed to tell me.

Mom was justifiably nervous about telling me of her new
life-choice, but I had grown up in a gay-positive environment
and I wasn't concerned so much about what she was telling me,
but rather that she had trusted me, a thirteen year old, with such
adult-like information. At that point, I didn't see how her
life-choice would affect both our lives; she told me she was gay,
I nodded and listened, and then we went on to talk about other
things. In retrospect, I would not have had it any other way.
However, my innocence that day about how our lives were to
change was not to last long.

As the child of a divorced family, I'm the first to say that
divorce is difficult on the children. When my parents first
separated, I was relieved that there were no more fights, accusations and bad feelings. I was happy that they were happier, so
to speak. Living with the reality of separation is quite a different
matter. I did not see my father as much as I used to. I lived with
only one parent, my mom, and while we became pals and
continued to have a good relationship after the separation,
aspects of our life together were difficult. I was entering junior
high school, and my mom was entering college, and suddenly I
felt much more adult-like than I had before the separation. I
was expected to be more independent and to help around the
house more often. It took a while for my personality to adjust!

Many of my friends and classmates had traditional families,

with siblings and biological parents all under one roof. I felt somewhat bashful that I did not live in this reality anymore, although I understood that it was for the best. I also felt badly for my parents, who I knew were lonely. Then my father found a new partner, and so did my mom. I gleefully told my friends about my dad's new partner, but carefully deflected questions about my mom's "single" status.

Even though I grew up with a gay godmother and older gay friends, I was not comfortable "coming out of the closet" with my mom's life-choice. Her choice came at a time in my life when I was desperately trying to fit in, as were all the other junior high students. Needless to say, I did not want to stick my neck out about anything that would make me different. Junior high school is not exactly the hotbed of gay activism — in fact, it's a time when most kids are trying desperately not to be associated publicly with their budding hormones, let alone with those of their parents! So I remained silent about my mom's newfound happiness and our "blended" family (to use a term from grade seven family studies class).

I've recently come to recognize that this silence, this pretence regarding my family life, was the most harmful part of living in a lesbian-parented family. Mom and Jan were always supportive and intensely sensitive about our privacy and my feelings. They wanted me to have friends over, to be able to "act normal" when entertaining friends. Nevertheless, I worried about how my friends would react to the news that my mom and Jan were partners, and always hesitated before inviting anyone to stay over. In an incident in grade eight, the class bully was giving me grief and ended up shouting across the empty library, "Well, at least my mom isn't gay." Devastated, I went to a friend's house and recounted the whole incident, including the taunt. Her response was an antagonistic, slightly distressed, "Well, she *isn't* gay, *is* she?" My suspicions were confirmed — it was better to be silent than not. It isn't fun living a double life, especially when it isn't your choice in the first place. I wasn't gay, it wasn't my choice — why did I have to hide my home life from my friends? I'm sorry to say that I initially blamed my mom and Jan for this predicament.

At that time, our family was involved in a lesbian parenting group. For some time, I was the only teenager and the only girl in the group. While the mothers chatted, the little boys played, and I would stand around, unsure of my place. I really needed a supportive peer group at that time, and unfortunately I didn't have one. This absence succeeded in alienating me more from the idea of our gay family. For some time, our family was more of a "living arrangement" for me. That's not to say that I did not care for my mom, Jan, or Jan's son. It's just that I did not feel supported in the way that society told me I should be supported.

I now know that this peer support is essential for the children of gays. There are many adjustments for these children, whether they are born to gay parents or are parented by "straights" who later become gay. It's essential for children to have friends who understand and support their family life. This support reflects on the family as a whole, as well. How are children to grow to respect their families if they don't feel respected by others?

This last question has bothered me for the last few years. By the latter part of high school — about five years into my mom's partnership with Jan — I started coming out to friends. By this time, I had settled my priorities and decided that I needed support from my friends — either they would accept and support me and my family or I would find new friends. I wasn't worried that they wouldn't accept my mom's homosexuality (I'd long since dropped the insensitive "friend" of junior high), but that our friendship would somehow become more strained. My friends were all very supportive, curious and thankful that I'd finally "come out" to them with the news of my lesbian family! Just like I'd known about my mom's important news before she told me, they knew about my family before I told them.

Now that I'm in university, I live away from home. All the friends I've made here are supportive and caring about my family life. This support has led me to question those homophobic hold outs I encounter in my daily life — from overt homophobia that refuses to recognize gay families in provincial legislation to the more subtle homophobia that hisses in a darkened movie theatre when two women share an on-screen kiss.

Together, my mom and Jan and their gay and straight friends make up one of the most caring, warm, friendly and progressive communities I know. I am disgusted by, and frustrated with, this homophobia that whispers "perversion" at the mention of gay families and would deny us our rights. I sometimes feel that homophobic people are the "perverted," as they insist on hating something that can be, and most often is, very caring and beautiful — the "blended" gay family. However, as much as it's satisfying to think this, portraying homophobes as perverted, hateful people does nothing to change our mutual predicament. I know that the root of their homophobia comes from misunderstanding, and I've made a commitment to take on this misunderstanding by telling people of my experience in a warm, caring lesbian family (of eight years!) and in the lesbian community. Society as a whole must come to recognize gay families, not as perversions but as valid forms of an institution that has existed beyond the scope of our collective memory. It seems ridiculous to me now that in an age of many global problems and readjustments, our supposedly enlightened society should fight against gay family rights.

I'm a semi-independent adult now, and I no longer deal with issues of secrecy and confusion over my family life. However, I'm aware of many lesbian and gay families that are just forming, and for them we must challenge the stereotype of the traditional, nuclear family. We must listen and support the children of gays and lesbians, and hear their perspectives. Their moms and dads are doing the best they can, and it's high time that we all recognize and respect their efforts.

Lesbian Parents & the Law

Bill 167 & Full Human Rights

SUSAN URSEL

BILL 167 WAS A PIECE OF LEGISLATION INTRODUCED IN 1994 BY THE
government of Ontario, Canada, to eliminate discrimination
against lesbian and gay relationships and families. The bill eventually went down to defeat, but not without a battle, reminders of
which will continue to resonate in all the battles yet to be fought.

The events leading up to the introduction and defeat of Bill
167, and the public attention given these events, strike me as
truly significant developments in the history of our struggle —
the struggle of lesbians and gay men — for full human rights.
We shaped, rather than simply responded to, the depiction and
discussion of ourselves and our lives in the public sphere. For
many of us, the bill itself was a galvanizing force, politicizing us
and giving us a reason to organize and work for our own rights
and to speak proudly about our lives — sometimes, for the first
time ever. Working on the campaign was exhilarating, frightening, maddening and enlightening. It brought together our communities in ways that are constructive and creative; at the same
time, as I will describe later in this article, Bill 167 runs the risk
of dividing us as thoroughly as any other debate about rights.

My interest in this began about four years ago when I became
involved with the Coalition for Lesbian and Gay Rights in
Ontario (CLGRO). In 1989, in an ambitious project, CLGRO
had sought out and sifted through the variety of opinions in our
communities on the subject of spousal recognition. Responding
to a growing awareness within our communities that recognition of our partners was an issue that concerned many of us,
CLGRO achieved a remarkable consensus among its members,
given the wide range of opinions available, and produced a
document entitled "Happy Families." The irony of the title still
sometimes irks me, but I think it is a fair comment on the state

of our family lives in the late twentieth century. At one level, we have created "happy" families for ourselves, despite oppression, discrimination, violence and prejudice. At another level, the sardonic twist I hear in the words satisfies my need to acknowledge the fragility of our happiness, the ambiguity of our conceptualization of "family" and "self," and the reception we get from the more accepted heterosexual "happy families" in our culture.

In the months which followed the release of the CLGRO document, the CLGRO Working Group on Spousal Recognition began to generate public and governmental acknowledgement and partial understanding of the issues. This was necessary in order to make change conceivable. The Working Group used media releases, press conferences, public speaking engagements and all the strings we could pull with the New Democratic Party (NDP) government in Ontario to advance the goal of the CLGRO paper: uniform and complete recognition of same-sex spouses in all provincial statutes, including those conferring benefits and those imposing obligations.

The Working Group, and other groups such as the NDP Lesbian, Gay and Bisexual Caucus (LGBC), representatives from other centres in Ontario and individuals interested in the issue, met with representatives of the Ontario NDP government time and again between 1990 and 1994. We believed that change could and would be brought about by this government because they had campaigned on the basis of support for lesbians and gays. The issue was discussed with the attorney general of the day. In June 1992, he publicly promised to act on legislative recognition of our partners, only to retreat from this promise. We sought the support of other ministers for a broad legislative initiative. In meeting after meeting, movement forward on the part of the government was imperceptible. "Intractable" problems were cited as reasons for the government's failure to act. We were told that changing the conflict of interest guidelines to include disclosure of a same-sex partner's interests would expose closeted politicians to outing. The alternative, that actual conflicts of interest could occur with impunity, seemed not to be a problem for those raising the issue.

Then, in September 1992, the human rights board in Ontario determined that the province could not deny its gay and lesbian employees pension benefits, such as surviving spouse benefits, which are accorded to opposite-sex spouses of employees. The government publicly announced its intention not to appeal this decision, effectively stating its agreement in principle with the concept of recognition of our partners. Yet the decision and the inactivity of the legislators left the offensive laws on the books and no action seemed to be imminent to deal with it.

Tensions escalated between those pressing for change and those capable of bringing about change. Confrontations began to occur. In the winter of 1992/93, Ian Scott, MPP for the province's riding of St. George-St. David, stepped down. St. George-St. David is the home of Toronto's gay and lesbian communities. In a contentious series of riding meetings, the NDP riding association there refused to nominate a candidate until the government announced its timetable for legislation on relationship recognition. This "rebellion" resulted in the appointment of a candidate by the Ontario office of the party, who suffered a humiliating defeat to the Liberal candidate, Tim Murphy. Murphy rode into office on the promise that he would do what the NDP government had failed to do: introduce legislation that would amend the provincial statutes which discriminated against gay and lesbian partners. He backed up this promise with a concurrent promise by his party leader, Lyn McLeod — thus setting in motion the series of events which lead to the introduction of Bill 167.

In June 1993, Murphy introduced his eagerly awaited private member's bill, which was promptly and aptly referred to as "Murphy's Law." The bill merely repeated what lesbian and gay partners had already gained as a result of the human rights decision, and did nothing to begin the task of amending all the pieces of legislation which gave benefits, rights and responsibilities to opposite-sex partners but not same-sex partners. Throughout the summer and fall of 1993, lobbying efforts continued, in an attempt to persuade the government to act. The government responded by stating that it would conduct public consultations, through hearings, on the Murphy bill. It then cancelled those consultations in December of 1993.

Through the winter of 1993/94, lobbying efforts, publicity, picket lines in front of the attorney general's office and at government caucus retreats expressed the mounting frustration and fear of the community and its supporters that this government would do nothing on the issue until it was too late. At about the same time, the Law Reform Commission of Ontario released its studies on the discrimination inherent in Ontario laws which fail to recognize gay and lesbian citizens, their partners and their families.

Then, in a series of "eleventh hour" meetings with those who had been lobbying on the issue, the government indicated it would do something, although it vacillated between various models of what it would legislate. In the end, it introduced Bill 167, opting to correct most of the discriminatory laws in Ontario by incorporating both an opposite- and same-sex spouse definition into them. Premier Bob Rae, who until then had been largely absent from any discussion of the issue and had declined to meet with community representatives despite repeated requests, appeared on the scene briefly to announce that there would be a "free vote" on the bill. A "free vote" meant that all MPPs would be permitted to "vote their consciences" on whether laws which discriminated against gay and lesbian citizens should be changed or not.

On May 19, 1994, Bill 167 barely scraped through its first reading. On May 24, at an enthusiastic and energetic community meeting in Toronto, the Campaign for Equal Families was born. Thus began the most intensive and well publicized lobbying and media effort that Queen's Park (home of the Ontario government) had ever seen. The campaign garnered attention and respect on an international scale. Ultimately, though, it was unable to overcome the entrenched prejudice, cowardice and political cynicism that was legitimized by Premier Rae's "free vote," and hypocritically exploited by Liberal Leader Lyn McLeod, who voted against the bill in one of the most publicized "flip-flops" of recent political history. On June 9, 1994, the bill went down to defeat.

That night, our community, in the tens of thousands, marched in the streets. The campaign to rebuild the momentum for positive change began. Hundreds of volunteers from across the province refused to allow the campaign to die with the bill. At a strategy meeting in August 1994, members gathered to discuss what the campaign could or should do next. A new stage in the process was begun, with a view to creating a viable, long term organization. Simultaneously, a working group came together to establish a litigation fund, based on the understanding that while the legislative road might be temporarily blocked, the need to challenge discriminatory laws in court continued.

As we ride this next wave of activity, we must bear several things in mind: the lessons we can learn from the experience of long- and short-term lobby efforts to enact legislative change; the acknowledgement we must make that public debate about our rights has been centred not on *human* rights, per se, but on a concept of contractual rights; and the realization that success in even getting our issues onto a legislative agenda is an incremental, long-term process.

The question of our contractual rights to enjoy the same employment benefits as heterosexuals has, up to now, described most of the limits of the debate. And in the intensely contractual world we have created for ourselves, this is probably appropriate ground on which to begin the discussion. It is not that difficult for most people to understand the analogy between opposite- and same-sex spouses when it comes to benefits which are contracted for in the workplace and form part of the package of compensation for all employees. It is not hard to understand the idea that gay and lesbian employees contribute into pension plans at the same rate as their heterosexual counterparts, and yet partake of the benefits at a reduced rate because they are statutorily prevented from providing their partners with survivor benefits. We intuitively understand the unfairness of paying for something which we do not get; the exchange of money for goods and benefits through contracts is fundamental to our society.

Most people can understand this basic economic argument, and its unhappy corollary — that if heterosexual employees continue to enjoy this unbalanced privilege because of their sexual orientation, they in fact are making money from the deal at the expense of their homosexual colleagues. Throughout the campaign, and in opinion polls afterwards, this is the area in which we consistently were able to achieve an unprecedented degree of acceptance from the heterosexual community.

People also seem more and more willing to accept the existence of lesbian and gay relationships in some other spheres. The idea of a man being consulted about his gay partner's health care in critical situations is no longer foreign to many — indeed, the alternative seems barbaric and unnecessarily cruel. The legal changes necessary in order to ensure this simple humanitarian practice are not that controversial, and have begun to be made in Ontario through the Substitute Decisions Act.

As we move further away from issues of money and limited recognition of our relationships, the arguments become more divorced from the reality of gay and lesbian people and more grounded in the unresolved fears and tensions that many heterosexual people have about gay men and lesbians. We must consider how those fears were exploited in the Bill 167 debate, and decide how to address them.

Nowhere is the unresolved nature of the recognition of lesbian and gay humanity clearer than in the current controversies over marriage and children. At its most benign, there is a profound ambivalence among many heterosexuals about according gay and lesbian relationships the same degree of respect, honour and privilege that they now accord their own relationships, both married and common law. The language used to describe the ambivalence is circuitous, agonized and uncomfortable, just as the feelings informing the language are painful, embarrassed and embarrassing. While the issue of marriage was not part of Bill 167 — it is a federal, not a provincial, matter — it was invoked again and again in the legislative and public debates. It seemed impossible for some people to understand that respect could be given our relationships without diminishing heterosexual marriages — in fact, without addressing the issue of heterosexual relationships at all.

Frequently during the debate around Bill 167, the feelings and language around marriage and relationships erupted into debased and accusatory polemic and actions against gay men and lesbians. Gays and lesbians, the discussion goes, should not be accorded the holy sanction of marriage because (in no special order): God doesn't want us to be married; the Church doesn't want us to be married; we don't *really* want to get married; we don't really understand the "true" and deep significance of marriage; letting gays and lesbians get married would detract from the institution's importance and would somehow diminish the status of those who now participate in marriage; only people who intend to procreate with each other should get married (this would be news to many diverse types of people who are now married); only people like the heterosexual majority should be able to get married; and finally, as a proxy for all of the above, only people of the opposite sex should be allowed to get married.

Now this language, or language like it, has been used throughout history to deny the rights of other groups to marry and to enjoy other full rights of citizenship in civil society. Students of the American institution of slavery and its abolition certainly understand the proscription of full rights as being a fundamental method of enforcing perceptions of a less than human status. As well, persons with disabilities, particularly psychiatric disabilities, have had their right to marry curtailed throughout history. Heterosexual couples who chose not to use the institution of marriage, but instead wanted their common law relationships recognized, also lived for years in our society in a kind of demi-monde of barely recognized intimacy, or told outright lies about the nature of their relationships. These particular attempts at enforcing a lesser status because of perceived difference are no longer accepted as right, good or proper. But the exercise in constructing negative difference through exclusion from general social institutions goes on with gay men and lesbians.

In the case of gay men and lesbians, as with the other examples, the language used is that of a majority trying to ascribe differences and a less than human status to a minority in order to justify oppression. This does not mean we should fall into the trap of arguing that all people are the same and all relationships just "versions" of one true heterosexual relationship. But the effort in society at large to harmfully differentiate gay and lesbian experience goes on — in spite of the basic human understanding that many, many people of all sexual orientations seek to relate to an "other," to build a life with that person, to create family or kinship networks with that person. While this message began to be expressed throughout the campaign, it did not have a chance to gain a sufficient profile in order to demystify our lives and to make them understandable and, yes, even accessible to the mainstream heterosexual society.

Instead, resistance was expressed not through blatant attacks on lesbian and gay relationships, but in the language of uncertainty and hesitation, with appeals to the lesbian and gay communities to understand and react sympathetically to the deep seated and firmly held fears that allegedly still held sway in this province — fears which would justify discrimination against gay men and lesbians, not because we were undeserving of human compassion, but because we were just *too different* to receive full human rights just yet. Time and again, lobbying meetings with ministers, MPPs, political staff, and the media elicited this response: Why didn't we just understand that we were just asking for too much, at this time?

In the end, this was an extremely clever approach to what the politicians, at least, viewed as an intractable, no-win political dilemma. They could vote for the bill, and be branded as apologists for the lesbian and gay community; or they could vote against the bill and be branded as a retrogrades of the worst sort, the kind who were against human rights for a vulnerable minority. But appeal to fear — the entrenched and often admittedly irrational fear of gay and lesbian people — and the politicians could appease the opponents of the bill by acknowledging their "concerns" and, at the same time, demand that the gay and lesbian communities be patient and understanding, all in the name of the same humanitarian impulse that led us to demand our rights in the first place. After all, what kind of cavalier and callous community would choose to ride roughshod over one of the most basic and indeed childlike emotions we know — simple, mindless, unknowing fear? Surely it would be better and more useful to the cause of the gay and lesbian community, the politicians argued, to gently lead the fearful ones than to bludgeon them with the hard edge of the law? The fact that it is this very fear that leads to further intangible harm to gay men and lesbians did not figure in their analysis.

If the marriage issue began to uncover the real parameters of the discussion about gay and lesbian rights, adoption ripped the lid off. From full-fledged, hateful accusations about the fitness of gay and lesbian parents to raise children, to the questionable assumption that somehow lesbians and gay men will raise their children *not* to be heterosexual, to the amusing appeal of "some" feminists that allowing gays and lesbians to adopt will somehow further alienate women from their biological capacity to bear children, the discussion of adoption was identified variously as the point beyond which the heterosexual majority will not go, or the point at which we lesbians and gay men have just gone too far.

We need to make some room on this tortured terrain for a review of the merits of these arguments.

Number one, there is *no* evidence that gay fathers or lesbian mothers have a particular propensity to abuse their children in any greater numbers than their heterosexual counterparts. Turning the question on its head, we could equally say there is no evidence that shows heterosexual parents make less abusive parents.

Number two, there is no evidence (and heterosexual parents of homosexual children who *tried* their damnedest to raise their kids straight can testify to this one) that children of gay and lesbian parents grow up in any greater numbers to be gay and lesbian than their peers raised by heterosexual parents do. But even if the sexual orientation of the parents was significant, we would have to ask "so what?"; either we are according equality of respect to gays and lesbians or we are not. If we are, this "issue" should not matter. If it *does* matter, then society is not truly according equality to gays and lesbians.

Number three, there is no evidence of psychological harm being visited upon the children of gay and lesbian parents by their parents *because* their parents are gay or lesbian. Now, this is not to say that there is no harm in this regard visited upon these children by others *outside* the immediate family nexus. But again, this is not a question of the behaviour or orientation of the parents so much as a question of the current incapacity of some in this society to behave according to the Golden Rule, which is, in this case: don't treat other people's children in nasty underhanded ways designed to undermine their faith in their parents, lest others do it to you.

If the myths do not stand up to scrutiny, what is the truth of the situation?

The truth of the situation is that gay men and lesbians do have children, whether they are conceived with their current partners or come from previous relationships.

The truth of the situation is that some lesbian and gay couples, like childless couples everywhere, long to raise a child, even one not biologically their own, because they believe that it is right to provide a child with a loving family, period.

The truth is that there are gay and lesbian children and teenagers who are unwelcome in their birth families because they are different, and who are desperately seeking loving parents who will understand them.

The truth of the situation is that lesbians, in particular, are choosing to bear and raise their own children in ever increasing numbers. The other truth of this situation is that the non-birth parent is not legally recognized as having parental rights and responsibilities. She cannot give parental consent, even to emergency medical treatment; she cannot travel with her child lest she be considered a "kidnapper"; and she cannot be required to support or care for the child in the event of relationship breakdown. And — the greatest fear of all for these families — she cannot be assured of custody of her own children, no matter how many years she spent raising them, loving them, caring for them, and living with them.

Perhaps the greatest success and the greatest failure of the campaign for Bill 167 revolved around this issue. We were able to begin to articulate our realities about adoption, and therein lay some success. But we were not able to articulate them fast enough, or in sufficient detail, or with the necessary acceptance to open the door to the further discussion. The highest level the discussion on this issue reached was to accept that a biological parent might have *acceptable* reasons for wanting his or her same-sex partner to adopt the biological parent's child or children. But this understanding came too little and too late to afford a basis on which to address the *real* and underlying issue — that gay and lesbian people might adopt the children of heterosexual people. At its most brutal, the issue might be expressed as: "It's all right for gays and lesbians to mess up their own children, but they are not getting their hands on ours."

We must examine this development in the campaign around Bill 167 closely, because this is where many of the future battles for our rights will be fought. We would do well to ask our society, often and loudly, several tough questions if we are to push this discussion beyond the stalemate it reached in the campaign: Is the reaction to our demand for rights, ranging from ambivalence to unease to hatred, really so much about gays and lesbians? Are these unexamined feelings really the correct basis for determining rights of full human participation in society? Is society doing the just and fair thing when it says that lesbians and gay men can have *this* many rights and no more? Would society accept these limitations if placed on any other groups in our communities? What is the legacy of intolerance being taught to the next generation when the rights of one group are circumscribed because of attributed difference?

In the answers to these questions lies the beginning of the answer to a great conundrum of our time: how to honour difference among ourselves but treat each other with equality.

We cannot afford to forget about the events leading up to Bill 167, any more than we can afford to forget about the events centred around the bill's introduction and defeat. If we are going to learn anything about ourselves, about our issues and about how to win rights, we must examine how these events arose, and how the bill itself failed. And we must recognize how, despite all this, we can say that we achieved something of momentous proportions simply by bringing ourselves into the possibility of everyday discourse.

Money Money Money

LEVI & ET ALIA

The following is an excerpt of an electronic mail correspondence
via computer between Et Alia, a researcher, and her partner,
Levi, a freelance writer.

From: Levi@Dykewords.ca Wed July 6 10:31:41 1994
To: Et_Alia@Dykewords.ca
Subject: Money

Hi Sweetie
We have a problem ...
Glasses & a cavity.
What are we going to do?

From: Et_Alia@Dykewords.ca Wed July 6 10:55:53 1994
To: Levi@Dykewords.ca
Subject: Re: Money

Oh, Honey,
Whose glasses? Whose cavity?

From: Levi@Dykewords.ca Wed July 6 10:58:24 1994
To: Et_Alia@Dykewords.ca
Subject: Re: Re: Money

Glasses for me, and Sami has a cavity — but I don't have the
money to pay for either ... do you?

From: Et_Alia@Dykewords.ca Wed July 6 11:04:18 1994
To: Levi@Dykewords.ca
Subject: Re: Re: Re: Money

Money's really tight right now — I'm scraping together everything I have so that we can buy that house. I wish my benefits

covered you two! This is the sort of thing I pay into health insurance for!!

From: Levi@Dykewords.ca Wed July 6 11:15:51 1994
To: Et_Alia@Dykewords.ca
Subject: Re: Re: Re: Re: Money

I know your benefits don't cover me (the heterosexist bastards) but why not Sami — you can prove he is financially dependent on you, can't you?

From: Et_Alia@Dykewords.ca Wed July 6 11:24:11 1994
To: Levi@Dykewords.ca
Subject: Re: Re: Re: Re: Re: Money

Remember when I applied to Revenue Canada to make Sami my dependent for tax purposes? They said that it didn't matter that he was living with me, and it didn't matter that I was supporting him. The only thing that mattered was whether he was related to me by marriage, blood or adoption. And, it's the same with my benefits. If Sami was my son, he at least would be covered — but the way things stand now, neither of you can use my benefits. It would be so much easier if we were a heterosexual couple!

From: Levi@Dykewords.ca Wed July 6 12:26:48 1994
To: Et_Alia@Dykewords.ca
Subject: Money cont'd

Heterosexuals? I don't think so!!!

From: Et_Alia@Dykewords.ca Wed July 6 12:28:36 1994
To: Levi@Dykewords.ca
Subject: Re: Money cont'd

If you could be recognized as my "spouse" and Sami as my son — even though he is your biological child — you could be covered by my benefits. I could claim you as "equivalent to spouse" on my taxes, deduct your tuition fees (when I pay them). But because we're the same sex — we get no benefits! You know, if I could even claim either or both you and Sami as dependents for tax purposes, the attendant tax breaks would relieve some of the financial pressure that we experience.

From: Levi@Dykewords.ca Wed July 6 12:35:28 1994
To: Et_Alia@Dykewords.ca
Subject: Re: Re: Money cont'd

It's such a bitch! I make no money writing — but can claim Sami for tax purposes. You support us all and can't claim anything! So we can hardly afford to live off your salary! It really pisses me off. If Ontario had put through that bill (167) you could have at least adopted Sami so we could both be his legal parents & you could claim him as a dependent for taxes and benefits.

From: Et_Alia@Dykewords.ca Wed July 6 13:09:25 1994
To: Levi@Dykewords.ca
Subject: Re: Re: Re: Money cont'd

I don't want to annoy you here — but I'm not sure I want to adopt Sami. The decision to become his "mother" is a really serious one — and one I'm not sure I'm ready to make. What I want is to have my benefits and taxes acknowledge the financial contribution I'm making to this family. I want spousal benefits for the financial support I give you and I want to be able to deduct Sami's dentist bills from my benefit plan.

From: Levi@Dykewords.ca Wed July 6 13:18:23 1994
To: Et_Alia@Dykewords.ca
Subject: Re: Re: Re: Re: Money cont'd

You'd think after almost three years living together you'd know whether or not you want to be Sami's mother!

From: Et_Alia@Dykewords.ca Wed July 6 13:26:12 1994
To: Levi@Dykewords.ca
Subject: Re: Re: Re: Re: Re: Money cont'd

Levi, you know we've talked about this a lot — I have never wanted children. Now I do know I want you — but I'm just not sure yet what role I want to play in his life. I'm sorry.

From: Levi@Dykewords.ca Wed July 6 14:02:47 1994
To: Et_Alia@Dykewords.ca
Subject: Money & the house

Well, speaking of Sami & money & your relationship with him
... The lawyer called. She wants to know how we want to have
the title of the house. I hope I've got this right — I think she
said we can be either "joint tenants" or "tenants in common."
If we are "joint tenants" then if anything happens to one of us,
that person's share in the house goes to their heirs. If we are
"tenants in common" then if anything happens to one of us —
their share of the house goes to the other owner of the house.
The latter method is supposedly good in situations where the
family would contest a will that said that you wanted your
dyke partner to inherit your millions.

For me — I think the house should be yours if something
happens to me ... but if something happens to me, then to
you, I don't want your heirs to inherit both of our shares in
the house (unless of course your heir was Sami). I want at
least my share of the house to go to Sami since that is all the
money that I have in the world!! So for me the question of
how we do title is closely linked to whether Sami is your heir
or not.

From: Et_Alia@Dykewords.ca Wed July 6 14:13:03 1994
To: Levi@Dykewords.ca
Subject: Re: Money & the house

Since (as I said earlier) I am not sure what I want my relationship to Sami to be, I can't say whether I would want him to be
my beneficiary. Like you, I would want you to have the house
if I died. But if we both did — I don't know. I think we should
have the title so that we each own half of the house and then
sort out who gets those halves in our wills.

From: Levi@Dykewords.ca Wed July 6 14:22:39 1994
To: Et_Alia@Dykewords.ca
Subject: Re: Re: Money & the house

Okay by me — I'll tell the lawyer ...

Why the hell does money & being dykes have to be so HARD?

Maybe it's easy for those rich corporate dyke types (but even they don't have the spousal/kid tax breaks of the rich corporate heteros), but for us struggling on the edge it's the shits. It still sits ill with me that the government fucked up on that same-sex benefits bill (watering it down especially irks me).

From: Et_Alia@Dykewords.ca Wed July 6 14:35:16 1994
To: Levi@Dykewords.ca
Subject: SEX Benefits

At least the government tried.

You know, I was listening to the CBC's *Cross Country Check-Up* and callers were being asked about the proposed same-sex benefits bill. One caller said that originally, spousal benefits were meant to support wives who chose to stay home and support children rather than work outside the home. He said the government was getting too far from the original intention of spousal benefits, which was to make it financially easier for families. That makes me MAD! This criticism of same-sex benefits assumes that somehow two working partners in a (childless) same-sex relationship would be somehow able to unfairly take advantage of such a benefit plan. First off, I have never heard any criticism of childfree heterosexual couples taking advantage of spousal benefit plans, regardless of the employment status of both partners. Second, if both partners in a relationship are fortunate enough to have employers offering spousal benefits, it is not possible to "double-up" on those benefits.

However, given the proliferation of non-permanent, contract and part-time work, there is likely to be more of a demand on (heterosexual) spousal benefits from employers who do offer them. I doubt straight, dual-income childfree couples would gladly give-up their spousal benefits so that they would only be available to those couples who have children.

Similarly, it is not possible to gain any tax advantages if both partners are bringing in substantial incomes. In fact, it has been pointed out in those circumstances, unmarried couples have the tax advantage. Any dual income gay couple seeking legal recognition of their union would be adding to the tax base, not subtracting from it.

From: Levi@Dykewords.ca Wed July 6 15:03:42 1994
To: Et_Alia@Dykewords.ca
Subject: Re: SEX Benefits

Yes — Gay DINKs aren't going to benefit financially from adoption/spousal benefits (since presumably they already have their own benefits), but people like us will. One income ... two people & a child ... no benefits ... it's tough.

From: Et_Alia@Dykewords.ca Wed July 6 15:16:32 1994
To: Levi@Dykewords.ca
Subject: Re: Re: SEX Benefits

You know, honey — I'm going to get in trouble if I don't do some work! Can we finish this discussion at home tonight?
    ILU

From: Levi@Dykewords.ca Wed July 6 15:18:54 1994
To: Et_Alia@Dykewords.ca
Subject: Re: Re: Re: SEX Benefits

Sure — I've gotta run & pick up Sami anyway ...
    Talk to you later.
    Oh & ILU2

Ancient Affections:
Gays, Lesbians & Family Status[1]

KAREN ANDREWS

~∽⋙~

Introduction

I TAKE MY TITLE FROM THE INTRODUCTION TO *DE PROFUNDUS*, OSCAR
Wilde's long and poignant apology to his lover, Lord Alfred
Douglas.[2] It was written during Wilde's incarceration almost a
hundred years ago, when he was ordered by an English court
to serve the maximum sentence for homosexual acts. Today,
lesbians and gay men are still embroiled in the court process,
both in Canada and elsewhere. However, in the last twenty
years, the courts have seen openly lesbian and gay people
challenge society — society that professes to value equality
above all else — into offering equality to them. Defiant, proud,
angry and politicized gay men and lesbians have used the
courts to try to win equality, as part of a larger struggle for the
liberation of us all.

Under the fundraising slogan of "We Are Family," I litigated
for same-sex health benefits from 1985 to 1991.[3] I learned
valuable lessons about politics, governance, media, bureaucracies,
law, courts and lawyers. The most important lessons I learned,
however, were about myself. For me, the phrase "transformative
power of law" has a deep and personal resonance. Unlike most
practitioners and academics writing in the area, I was a community activist who personally litigated this controversial and
complex issue. Unlike most community activists and litigants,
I have since had legal training.

When I began my struggle I had concrete objectives, and, as
I pursued my goals, I was the object of both praise and criticism.
More recently, in law school, I have had the opportunity to
reflect about the goals I pursued through litigation. Using my

case and cases like mine, this paper explores some of the paradoxes and problems of the legal process. I conclude that, with respect to "ancient affections and family status," cases like mine represent both reform and rebellion, subversion and compromise.

Strategy: We Are Family, Or Are We?

Since the beginning of my action for same-sex health benefits in 1985, many gay and lesbian people across the country have used legal arguments similar to mine to better the circumstances of their own lives. In short, the argument goes something like this: we are not that much different from you, so, at the very least, give us what you get, too.

The tangible benefits of this argument can be hard to calculate, but they most assuredly exist. The Canadian military, for example, has rethought its policies of exclusion and persecution with respect to lesbians and gay men and the armed forces.[4] Several large insurance companies in North America offer same-sex benefit coverage to an increasing number of employers who are requesting it.[5] New advocacy statutes in Ontario, Canada, have defined "partner" in gender neutral ways.[6] A gay man was granted refugee status in Canada on the basis of his persecution as a homosexual in his native Argentina.[7] Most important, however, is the mainstream and commonplace attention that our lives are now attracting: on Oscar night, a lesbian can thank her partner; in landlord and tenant court, a landlord can be held to account when gay tenants are harassed;[8] travel guides now highlight sections for the gay and lesbian vacationer. Some progress addresses gays and lesbians as individuals, while some progress addresses gays and lesbians as partners in relationships.

When it comes to "family status," however, many commentators point to serious and thoughtful concerns about legalizing and legitimizing same-sex relationships — concerns that go to the heart of the argument about "sameness."[9] Why exactly would gay men or lesbians wish to involve themselves in a statutory regime that has so clearly failed their heterosexual

counterparts? Why involve gays and lesbians in the legally im-
precise exercise of line drawing? Why seek that which is not
sought by so many people who can marry? Are gay and lesbian
relationships not so inherently different that the "add homosexual
and stir" approach will create more problems than it solves? Will
legalizing these relationships create an unhealthy hierarchy of its
own within the gay and lesbian community? Is it really not a new
society — instead of new families — that we need?[10]

In Carol Smart's view:

> ... a primary goal must be to jettison the privileged
> status of the heterosexual married couple but not in
> order to create a different hierarchy of unmarried house-
> holds. The aim is not to extend the legal and social
> definition of marriage to cover cohabitees or even ho-
> mosexual couples, it is to abandon the status of marriage
> altogether and to devise a system of rights, duties or
> obligations which are not dependant on any form of
> coupledom or marriage or quasi marriage.[11]

That observation becomes troubling, however, when one
considers how many people get married and, in fact, do so with
little or no coercion.[12] The problem is that most people spend
most of their lives in what they would call a family. Most people
marry and most divorced people remarry. Needs and depend-
encies flow from those relationships, and those needs are recognized, albeit in an often inadequate and haphazard way, in
everything from life insurance policies to collective agreements,
statutory regimes that divide property to credit card applications. Alas, even in the progressive and generous future painted
for us in *Star Trek*, where the need for money has been eliminated, women who marry usually change their names.

I think that the law will be slow to respond to the challenge
of Carol Smart because most people see themselves as part of a
family before they see themselves as individuals, and therefore
most people could not begin to think of reordering legal relationships in any way other than in a familial way. To most of us,
"family" is just good and normal.

"Family" may be "good and normal" to most people, but litigating family status is complicated business because, as it turns out, "family" is also complicated. The law itself uses different definitions, depending upon the legal issue at hand. In Canada, a "spouse for the purposes of child support[13] is different from a "spouse" for the purposes of the Coroners Act.[14] "Dependants" in the context of a dental plan are different from "dependants" for the purposes of immigration[15] or "dependants" on the income tax form,[16] all of whom are different again from "spouses" in the context of welfare or family benefits.[17] Even within statutes, confusion abounds. In Ontario's *Succession Law Reform Act*, for example, "spouse" is defined in one way for cases of intestacy and in another way for cases where support as a dependant is being claimed.[18] As Diana Majury has written:

> … although there may be legitimate reasons for determining that who constitutes a family should be different in different circumstances and for different purposes, there is no apparent rationale underlying the differences currently contained in Ontario's legislation.[19]

She writes further:

> The definitions of "spouse," "family" and "dependant" vary from statute to statute; in most situations, there are no obvious reasons for the variations.[20]

Cases that attempt to define or broaden the meaning of "family" embarrass the courts and the legislatures because they unearth a confused and uneven mess of family-based legislation that is often premised upon notions of how people once lived, although they live that way no longer. Courts often go to great lengths to both deny and disguise these misplaced assumptions. This is evident in both the *Mossop*[21] and *Layland*[22] judgements. In my case, the woman with whom I lived could have been denied welfare *because* of my financial support of her, but, on the other hand, be unable to access my provincial health coverage *despite* my financial support of her.[23] Generally, "spouse" and "dependant" seem to be broadly defined if the government is seeking to avoid the economic support of an individual, whereas, when a benefit is being conferred, the opposite is more likely to be true.[24] As Mary O'Brien has observed: the ways in which productive and reproductive social formations relate to each other must be opened up to a more rigorous and refined critique.[25]

In both the *Mossop* case for bereavement leave and my case for health benefits, Dr. Margrit Eichler provided evidence opposing the government's intransigent position. Despite the government's attempts to obfuscate Dr. Eichler's position, she emphatically held that if "family" was to be these cases' deciding factor, then no single indicator was always present in every familial relationship. She further argued in *Mossop* that what is at stake is not a comparison with other kinds of families, but that in both *Mossop* and *Andrews* familial relationships existed in and of themselves. She gave evidence in *Mossop* that there were significant segments of the population which accepted homosexual relationships as familial ones, and in her affidavit in the *Andrews* submissions, she chastised the government, saying that sexual orientation *per se* was not a useful basis for determining eligibility for social benefits.[26]

Perhaps in that brief moment in time where the "norm" was defined by men who worked full-time and who supported wives and children at home, policies which reflected family benefit schemes and women's economic dependence made sense. If they made sense then, however, they obviously do not make sense now.[27]

Litigating in the Family Way

What is really at the heart of the gay and lesbian challenges around "family status" is the contested terrain around social programmes — who should pay for them and who should benefit from them. As Freilen and Kitchen point out, the family has become an "ideological battleground" with both ends of the political spectrum purporting to be "pro-family." Central to the debate [is] how the responsibility for children should be shared among parents, the community and the government.[28]

Case after case singles out the fact that gay sex is not procreating sex. In *Mossop, Andrews, Anderson v. Luoma*,[29] *Singer v. Hara*,[30] and *North v. Matheson*,[31] the fact that children will not come of the relationship, despite the fact that children may be *part of* the relationship, distinguish somehow these couples from infertile couples, old couples, adopting couples, and couples who have chosen childlessness.[32] It would seem that the state and the judiciary have convinced themselves that generalized social benefits can be denied to gays and lesbians on the basis of this fact of biology. What the gay and lesbian community should say — with more vigour, in my view — is that social benefit programmes ought to benefit everyone and not just those with biological children of their own. Further, the health care system, the education system and the daycare system, for example, are, in part, underwritten by those who have no children. It is simply unconscionable, then, to deny the childless, or those who are non-biological parents, their share of the benefit pie.

A point that is frequently misunderstood, too, in the debate for same-sex benefits, is that we want nothing more than that for which we are already paying. We contribute to the Canada Pension Plan — why can we not have access to the survivor pension scheme? We contribute to the Canadian Unemployment Insurance scheme — why can we not qualify under the same terms as heterosexual workers?[33] Some of us are alumni members to a university facility — why should our partners not have the same access to it as any other married partner? The ultimate question becomes the same one that feminists debated during the pay equity struggle — how can society avoid equality for lesbian and gay people when we have been carrying more than our fair share of the load for generations?

It is of great significance to note that the most important and ground breaking campaigns undertaken by lesbian and gay activists in Canada have had their genesis at the workplace. For many of us, work is central to who we are. For many, it is understood that it is career and not family that is the only source, or the only dependable source, of economic security. For many activists, our private lives became embroiled with our working lives. In my view, the equality arguments are easier to make there — we do the same work, so give us the same working conditions.[34] What John Damien fought for in Ontario in 1975 — the right to do his job and not be harassed or fired because of his sexual orientation — became my struggle ten years later, to do my job and make the same pay despite my sexual orientation.

Within unions, the support for these arguments has been strong. Unionists understand the old credo that "an injury to one is an injury to all." They understand that you cannot negotiate a *collective agreement* and leave out a significant percentage of your bargaining unit. Before anyone else, both the national office of the Canadian Union of Public Employees and my Local 1996 provided me with invaluable financial and moral support. Working people know that the so-called "fringe benefits" are no longer "fringe." In fact, they represent an increasing percentage of the shrinking wage.[35] It was my experience that, with only a little bit of coaxing, unionized people understood that denying the lesbian and gay worker family or spousal benefits represented a different job rate for equivalent jobs, and undermined solidarity. In short, it threatened everyone.[36]

Clearly, *Mossop*, *Egan*, *Andrews*, and *Anderson v. Luoma* raise complicated issues about how society is economically and socially organized and about how the state is deeply "implicated in both the constitution and regulation of the family."[37] However, "there is no simple relationship between law and the economic structure of society."[38] For many people, then, the place to begin to understand these relationships is in the statutes themselves.

For me, the statutes can be divided into three groups. Some statutes confer benefits to "spouses" that are germane to having a spouse and are not relevant to those who do not have one.[39] Other statutes confer benefits to "spouses" that are arguably inappropriate.[40] Still other statutes confer benefits that should be broadened to include others in their schemes.[41]

In my case, I litigated to get my partner included on my provincial health plan, which was paid for by my employer. The government resolved the dispute by redesigning the administration of the plan in a way that did not offend non-traditional households: where, formerly, families had received the same "family number," the new scheme gave each individual card holder his or her own number and my fight became moot. I would be loathe to suggest that the solution was not appropriate or just. In fact, we had argued for precisely the government's remedy, only to be told that "family numbers" were necessary support for the institution of the family! The irony is that the pill was a hard one to swallow. Governments and bureaucracies will go to great lengths to avoid acknowledging the existence of gay and lesbian households. In Ontario, they chose to eliminate heterosexual privilege rather than give homosexuals the same privilege. As a feminist, I applauded the change. As a lesbian, it broke my heart.[42]

How many times have we, as students of the law, been told that the law is about line drawing? We fight about where to draw it or about erasing it all together. As gay and lesbian activists, we come to the game after it has already begun. Avoiding participation in elite institutions does not afford escape from the versions of reality propogated by such institutions.[43] It can be argued that cases like *Mossop, Anderson v. Luoma, Egan* and *Andrews* perpetuate the privatization of costs that should be borne by society as a whole. You will get no disagreement from me. To solve the problems that gay and lesbian households present, however, it seems to me that existing categories of "family" can either be expanded to include us or dismantled and refitted to fix wider social problems. The question is, does it really matter which tactic we choose? At the end of the day, doesn't everyone benefit from the restructuring of categories and policies that most often date from a time when personal relationships were organized differently and when a person's relationship to a wage and an employer was also different?

For me, the gay and lesbian challenge to family benefits is at the forefront of a much larger movement — a movement demanding societal change. Families headed by single mothers, reconstituted families and the unmarried and childless, for example, now comprise significant numbers of the population. If the category of "family" is litigated in such a way that it becomes too big to hold any meaning, we can try to rebuild it in more appropriate or different ways. If the category is dismantled because, for reasons of homophobia and bigotry, lesbians and gays cannot be included into it, again the larger society benefits, because we have to rebuild, refit or reorder.

Similarly, I would ask: are gays and lesbians the same as other members of society or are we different? And does it really matter, anyway? With respect to tooth decay and braces, I argued that we were the same. It was easier. In my opinion, it was demanded of me by the world in which I lived and by the legal system in which I operated. Ironically, when I argued sameness, I became invisible. (The government responded by taking away everybody's family number and replacing them with individual numbers.) Ironically, when I argued sameness, my experience indicated to me that society will move to more equitable and socialized schemes in order to win my silence again.

It was simply too much for a court or government to acknowledge my life in any kind of bureaucratic or legislative way so they redesigned the whole thing such that we all got a better result: gay and lesbian households disappeared, but so did everybody else's. For me, *Andrews* meant that lesbian and gay families got a little publicity and everybody got an improved system for health care administration. I would argue sameness again, and again risk becoming a token. I would argue sameness again and risk my meanings and identity being defined by those who have let me in. The risks are worth taking: first, we can change the complement, culture and environment of the "clubs" that let us in; second, the lessons of the Trojan Horse are valuable ones for the political strategist to remember.

The law grows to accommodate new problems and to address new dilemmas, though it rarely does this with much elegance. In her article, "Redefining Families: Who's in and Who's Out,"[44] Martha Minow ruminates about her fears and worries about bringing family status litigation to court in the first place. She worries that the flexible definitions chosen by their users can be abused. She worries about expanded families that are chosen by their participants, and the definition of expanded family that is used by government to achieve its own ends and evade its responsibilities. We all must be vigilant to the dangers, but, in the end, Minow participated in this kind of litigation in New York when one lesbian was denied access to the child she had had with another lesbian. According to Minow, it was a case where people should be "able to choose to enter family relationships but not free to rewrite the terms of those relationships."[45]

In Canadian litigation of a similar kind, *Anderson v. Luoma* stands for the unhappy proposition that a lesbian can behave as despicably as any man who evades his parenting and child support obligations and because she is outside the statutes, she can get away with it. While Professor Minow correctly observes that "people have demanded and created legal solutions to their mounting distrust within social relationships,"[46] many segments of the lesbian and gay community still want to define their lives outside of statutes. Neither Brian Mossop, Jim Egan or I embrace any conventional models of matrimony, nor do we seek to replicate the rituals of heterosexuality into our own lives.

It should be noted that the above attitudes and beliefs are not held by all gays and lesbians, nor, to confuse matters further, are they unknown among many heterosexuals. The law must, however, intervene when there is disputed custody of children who have arrived through artificial insemination or adoption by same-sex parents. The law must intervene when one same-sex partner is pillaged economically by the other. The law must intervene when someone is evicted from a rent controlled apartment because a longtime companion has died of AIDS.[47] The words embroidered on Aaron Miller's panel of "The Quilt," for me, represent the most satisfactory definition of "family" around: "the bond that links your true family is not one of blood but of respect and joy in each other's life."[48] Bureaucrats, politicians and lawyers may not appreciate such a standard, but I would hope that most people, gay or straight, would be hard-pressed to argue with it.

Generally speaking, lesbians and gay men do not exist. When movies are adapted from gay books, gay themes disappear. When biographies are written about homosexuals, the homosexuality is often only discovered between the lines, if at all. We are denied our place in sports, politics, science and art. When gays and lesbians choose to bring their stories and their grievances to court, they are doing a profoundly radical thing. Where once we were dragged there on the basis of a criminal charge or a custody dispute, lesbians and gays are now appearing of their own accord. We have every reason to believe that the judiciary will not listen but they are nevertheless forced to hear. During those many years of shaking hands and raising money for legal bills, I was confronted by many who had concerns about the "middle class" nature of the case. I met Separatists, Anarchists and Marxists, among others. What never failed to amaze me was the reluctance of these women to label themselves and, especially, to label themselves to their families.[49] "What difference would it make" many would say, "that they treat her as they do my brother's wife?" "It makes a huge difference," I would think, "or else those words would not be so difficult to say." The importance of "voice" is well documented in the liturgy of feminism. We are diminished when we cannot speak the words that define our lives. Few lesbians and gay men live lives free of hiding. I respect the fear that so many live with for so much of their lives but the courage of those who speak our words in union halls, churches, courthouses, schools and banks must also be acknowledged.[50] Many question the activities that "leave untouched the idea that law should occupy a special place in ordering everyday life."[51] Arguably, "in accepting law's terms in order to challenge law" the gay liberationist concedes too much.[52] From my experience, there is no doubt that "... the legal process translates everyday experience into legal relevances, it excludes a great deal that might be relevant to the parties and it makes its judgements on the scripted or tailored account."[53]

But there is also no doubt that court cases put pieces of the lesbian and gay agenda on the six o'clock news. Further, by employing the imagery of idealized family life, "[it] permeates the fabric of social existence and provides a highly significant, dominant and unifying complex of social meaning."[54]

In other words, court cases about family status, spousal benefits and relationship recognition have given us a kind and volume of publicity that we have never had before. It has upset many of our enemies. It has given many others pause to think. Added to the shrinking categories of sexual outlaw, criminal, manhater and paederast, we have become parents, employees, taxpayers and senior citizens. It has been nothing short of a public relations boon.

The bulk of the academic commentary on same-sex benefit litigation, and indeed, academic commentary on other controversial, equality-based or political litigation seem to me to miss a crucial point: people litigate usually because they are desperate; they litigate because they have exhausted all other avenues of possible remedy; they litigate because they have nowhere else to turn in order to solve the serious dilemmas of their lives. It may be a profitable game or challenge for the lawyer and it may make an interesting and publishable paper for an academic, but it is none of these things for the participant. Rather, it is the participant's life that is at issue, it is his or her life that is being judged. The areas that these cases have touched upon include old age security payments, hospital and prison visitation, eviction, bereavement leave, entitlement to Unemployment Insurance benefits, child support, disinheritance and health coverage. These are not trivial things. The significance to the litigants involved must be a given. What lawyers do with great skill and what legal academics can do even better,[55] is sever the issues at stake from the persons involved. For me, it has always been profoundly ironic that cases that we as lawyers study are always named for the participants yet the participants never meaningfully factor in to what the case was really about. Case preparation and academic writing done this way is disrespectful, pedantic, pompous and judgemental. Legal scholarship, like the law itself, often posits itself "... outside the social order, as if through the application of legal method and rigour, it becomes a thing apart which can in turn reflect upon the world from which it is divorced."[56]

Boyd and Sheehy write of the dangers inherent in "tackling concrete issues without reference to a wider theoretical framework."[57] Thankfully, however, they acknowledge that it is "perilous" to concentrate exclusively on theory but I would go further. It is perilous to ignore, as some do, the experience and reality of regular people trying to be lesbian or gay in a straight world. It is perilous to posit utopian or theoretical goals, as some do, and then argue that the successes of the gay and lesbian movement are illusionary, misguided or wrongheaded. I agree with Boyd and Sheehy when they argue that "... more attention to theory might also illuminate significant differences between short and long term goals and might influence strategy choices for specific legal issues."[58]

I agree with Didi Herman when she suggests that the lesbian and gay movement may find "illuminating" the lessons of feminist legal struggle and that some activists may indeed decide to "... de-centre engagement with law reform and to develop alternative political strategies that spring from feminist theory and practice."[59]

This is not terribly contentious, though many would make it so. The issue here seems to be praxis, the place where theory reconciles itself with practice, the place that measures how people ought to live with how people really do live. My litigation for family status, and other litigation like mine, earnestly tried to achieve it. I heed Carol Smart when she writes that praxis ensures that "... the insights of theory are reflected in the politics of action and that the insights of practice are reflected in theory construction."[60]

Maybe someday, somebody will get this right. In the meantime, we can only do our best, and sometimes our best has been enough. Things have changed and they have changed for the better.

If we date the modern movement for lesbian and gay rights beginning with the Stonewall riots in New York City in June of 1969, then our successes have been remarkable. Further, and more importantly, they have been the successes of ordinary people living on the frontlines who have simply stood up and said "enough." I for one will participate more theoretically in the debate for same-sex family status and more fully in the general movement for social justice when my fears have been conquered, when my rights have been secured, when the battle for my equality has been won. Until then, I am with the drag queen throwing a rock on a Greenwich Village street, I am making submissions in order to convince a tribunal that a gay or lesbian taxpayer should get the same Canada Pension Plan survivors' entitlements as their heterosexual counterparts, I am wearing my old fundraising button with conviction and with pride.

Notes

1. For Mary Trenholm, Erin Trenholm and Kirsten Trenholm who taught me everything I know and have come to cherish about lesbian families. My thanks to Kathy Arnup for her encouragement and editorial support and to Brenda Brooks for setting me straight. My indebtedness to Professors Shelley Gavigan, Mary Jane Mossman, Toni Williams and Brenda Cossman for their comments and assistance while this paper was being written, and more importantly, for their presence at the Osgoode Hall Law School.

2. Oscar Wilde, *The Soul of Man and Prison Writings*, (Oxford: Oxford University Press, 1990), p. 38.

3. *Andrews v. Ontario* (Ministry of Health) (1988), 64 O.R. (2d) 258 (Ont. H. Ct.) [hereinafter *Andrews*]. My thanks to Curt Lush of Toronto for coining the slogan.

4. See *Douglas v. Canada* (1992), 58 F.T.R. 147, where Michelle Douglas brought an action for damages and declaratory relief against the Canadian Armed Forces for the career limiting restrictions that were placed upon her when her lesbianism was discovered. In its decision, the court held that Douglas' Section 15 rights under the *Canadian Charter of Rights and Freedoms* [hereinafter *Charter*] were denied to her and that the force's policies were in contravention of Section 15 as well.

5. When my case started as a grievance to my employer about their failure to provide me with family health benefits, their private insurance carrier, CUMBA, quickly moved to provide me with them in November 1985. Since then, Confederation Life, London Life, Great West Life and Standard Life among others have offered this type of coverage to both unionized and non-unionized employers who request and pay for it on behalf of their employees. In the most recent Public Service Alliance of Canada arbitration proceeding with respect

to this issue on March 24, 1994, Canada Post has been ordered to pay the benefits claim filed by an employee to cover the cost of glasses for his same-sex spouse.

6. See *Consent to Treatment Act*, S.O. 1992, c.31., s. 1(2), and the *Substitute Decisions Act*, S.O. 1992, c.30., s. 1(2), where "two persons are partners for the purpose of the Act if they have lived together for at least one year and have a close personal relationship that is of primary importance in both persons' lives." I would add further that, in my view, this would never have happened if there had not been a climate or environment created because of the same-sex benefits cases coupled with the urgent needs presented by the AIDS crisis.

7. Peter Hawkins, "Gay Refugee Deported," *Xtra*, (May 1992), p. 9.

8. *Mercedes Homes Inc. v. Grace*, O.C.J. (Gen. Div.), Sutherland, J., (November 3, 1993).

9. For a current list, see Ontario Law Reform Commission, *Report on The Rights and Responsibilities of Cohabitants Under the Family Law Act*, (November 17, 1993), at footnotes 71 and 72.

10. Barrett and McIntosh, *The Anti-Social Family*, (London: Verso, 1982), pp. 158-9.

11. Carol Smart, *The Ties That Bind: Law, Marriage and the Reproduction of Patriarchal Relations*, (London: Routledge & Kegan Paul, 1984), p. 146.

12. Rights and privileges based solely on status are, indeed, problematic. It is important to recognize, however, that perhaps only those who have rights can imagine not having them. Many who argue for a dismantling of a "rights based" society are often the same people who have the power and privilege not to claim them when it suits them not to claim them. When a heterosexual woman, for example, chooses not to marry, it costs her little and after all, she can always go through with it if she is presented with a tax, pension or immigration problem that matrimony can often solve. When a lesbian argues for the right to marry, it can seem insensitive, patronizing and unfair to tell her that this is a misguided and inappropriate thing for her to want to do. Many within the gay and lesbian community seek the social and religious support of the ceremony. Many others see it as the most expedient way to the tax break.

13. *Family Law Act*, R.S.O. 1990, c.F.3, s.29.

14. *Coroners Act*, R.S.O. 1990, c.C.37, s.1.

15. *Immigration Act*, R.S.C. 1985, c. 52, s.2(1).

16. *Income Tax Act*, S.C. 1991, c.49, s. 118(6)(*b*).

17. In section 1(1)(*p*) of the Regulations to the *General Welfare Act*, R.S.O. 1990, c. G.6, a "spouse" is a person of the opposite sex to an applicant who has declared to a welfare administrator that they are a spouse, one who is required to support an applicant under the provisions of a court order or domestic contract, a person with an obligation to support an applicant under the *Family Law Act* or a person of the opposite sex who has resided continuously with an applicant for a period of not less than three years.

18. *Succession Law Reform Act*, R.S.O. 1990, c.26, s. 1 and s. 57.

19. D. Majury, "The Meaning of Family for Lesbians and for Women Generally: The Implications of Family Based Policies in Ontario and Alternatives for Future Policy Directions" (unpublished), p. i.

20. Ibid., p. 1.

21. In 1985, Brian Mossop, an employee with the federal government, applied to take a day of bereavement leave to attend the funeral of his lover's father. The litigation [hereinafter *Mossop*] stretched over eight years, from a Board of Inquiry of the Canadian Human Rights Commission, (1989) 10 C.H.R.R. D/6054, to the Federal Court of Appeal, (1990), 71 D.L.R. (4th) 661, to the Supreme Court of Canada, (1993) 1 S.C.R. 554. Mr. Mossop never did get his day. In a highly technical decision, *Mossop* failed. But the court clearly left open the possibility for other challenges to be made, by imploring counsel to make *Charter* arguments to them next time. With the decision given in *Haig v. Canada (Minister of Justice*, (1992) 94 D.L.R. (4th) 1, by the Ontario Court of Appeal, it is now widely accepted that "sexual orientation" is to be considered an analogous ground of discrimination under Section 15 of the *Charter.*

22. In *Layland v. Ontario (*Ministry of Consumer and Commercial Relations), (1993) O.J. No. 575, two men argued that the failure to issue them with a marriage licence was discriminatory. The majority conceded that there existed no statutory provision excluding the union of persons of the same sex and, also, that many classes of married persons did not procreate and therefore fall within the traditional purpose of marriage. Despite this, however, the majority held that there existed a common law limitation on marriage to persons of the opposite sex and that it did not constitute discrimination contrary to s. 15 of the *Charter* [hereinafter *Layland*].

23. This point was highlighted in the Ontario Ombudsman's Opinion File Number 47699 dated February 20, 1987, at page 6, as part of Dr. Hill's report that investigated my allegations of discrimination with respect to the administration of the Ontario Health Insurance Plan.

24. This is the great danger of recent things like the Ontario Law Reform Commission looking at gays and lesbians in the context of family law, property and pensions. (See Ontario Law Reform

Commission, supra, note 9.) The report recommends extending some statutory rights and obligations to lesbian and gay cohabiters. The problem is that the federal government controls such areas as tax and immigration, so that gays and lesbians can face increased obligations provincially while getting none of the corollary benefits federally. In July 1993, for example, a Victoria gay couple faced such a Catch-22 situation. Josh Gravel had his enhanced medical insurance benefits cancelled because the provincial government maintained that he was in a common-law relationship with another man. The couple maintain, however, that until such laws as the *Income Tax Act* are changed, the government is trying to have things both ways. See "Couple Caught in Catch-22," *Xtra*, (September 17, 1993), p. 23.

25. M. O'Brien, "Feminism and Revolution" in *Politics of Diversity*, (Montreal: Book Centre Inc., 1987), p. 425.

26. In *Mossop*, the Ontario Human Rights Tribunal found that when the matter of the *Ontario Human Rights Code* and "family status" was discussed by Parliament, Mark MacGuigan was reluctant to define what it meant and said that he trusted the Commission to do it. Counsel for the government strenuously argued that the tribunal should confine itself to "the plain meaning of family." This is odd and confusing given that in the next paragraph, counsel went on to say that the tribunal should not give "family" its "narrowest" or "broadest" meaning which seems to suggest that the meaning of "family" is not so "plain" after all. The Federal Court of Appeal, however, did not accept that "family" was a fluid term. J.A. Marceau wrote that he did not understand exactly what was meant by taking a functional or sociological approach to defining family and that the tribunal had no authority to reject the generally understood meaning of the term. "Family," for the Federal Court of Appeal, had a meaning not so "uncertain," not so "unclear" and not so "equivocal" that it needed to be interpreted by the courts in every instance.

27. See Freilen and Kitchen, "Family Portrait," in *Perception*, 14, 2 (1990), p. 46, where they report that only sixteen percent of Canadian families have a full-time, stay-at-home mother and an income-earning father.

28. Ibid.

29. (1986), R.F.L. (2d) 127 (B.C.S.C.), [hereinafter *Anderson v. Luoma*].

30. 11 Wash. App. 247, 522 P. 2d 1187 (1974).

31. (1976), 20 R.F.L. (Man. Co. Ct.).

32. See Mary Mendola, *The Mendola Report: A New Look at Gay Couples*, (1980), p. 254, where she finds that twenty-five percent of lesbians and seventeen percent of men surveyed who considered themselves part of a "gay marriage relationship" reported that either they or their partner had children.

33. In November, 1993, an Unemployment Insurance Board of Referees ruled that Lisa Jeffs could qualify for UI because she had moved to a new location in order to look for work and reside with her same-sex partner. A similar inquiry is not held, however, if an opposite-sex partner does the same thing. Unhappily, the government is appealing.

34. This is a contentious point but I would argue that it has been problematic to begin or concentrate the struggle for lesbian and gay rights with demands rooted in sexual practices. What the litigation for same-sex benefits has done is focus attention on our lives as workers, employees, partners and parents and I would leave it up to the reader to weigh what has been the more effective approach in winning the battle over bigotry, hatred and fear.

35. This was another point also accepted by the Ombudsman's investigation with respect to my case, see note 23, where on page 6, Dr. Hill cited the *Monthly Labour Review* in the United States that found in white collar occupations, benefits constituted nearly forty percent of an employer's average outlay for labour expenses.

36. For a discussion of gays and lesbians in the union movement, see Sue Genge's article "Lesbians and Gays in the Union Movement" in Linda Briskin and Lynda Yanz, *Union Sisters*, (Toronto: Womens Press, 1983).

37. J. Fudge, "The Public/Private Distinction: The Possibilities of the Limits to the Use of Charter Litigation to Further Feminist Struggles," (1987) 25 O.H.L.J. 483, p. 511.

38. C. Smart, "Feminism and Law: Some Problems of Analysis and Strategy," *International Journal of the Sociology of Law*, (1986), p. 111.

39. Perhaps the *Evidence Act*, R.S.O. 1990, c. E.23, is such an example. Section 11 exempts a husband or wife from disclosing any communications made to them by an accused spouse during the marriage. The section does, in my view, attempt to recognize the unique and intimate characteristics of a relationship like marriage. I would also argue, however, that the *Act* should similarly exempt same-sex partners from such disclosure as well.

40. Under Regulation 628 of Ontario's *Highway Traffic Act*, R.S.O. 1990, c.H.8, transferring the ownership of a car to another requires that you must have that car certified unless, of course, you are transferring it to a spouse. If the issue is one of road-worthiness and public safety, I would argue that all such transfers of ownership should require certification and not just the ones between the unmarried.

41. In the case of a spouse's transfer to a new employment location, there exists the assumption that the remaining spouse will want to re-locate as well. This, however, does not always happen. Likewise, if two sisters resided together and one wanted to move in order to continue to live with the other on her employment re-location, why should she not qualify for Unemployment Insurance on her move as well?

42. A social worker from Winnipeg told me of a situation where the welfare department was approached by two men receiving individual payments requesting a lesser family rate because they were living together as a gay couple. Anyone who knows a little about welfare administration will notice how remarkable the department's decision was to refuse the request. In my own case, the government emphatically wanted the woman that I lived with to be on premium assistance for which she was periodically eligible rather than have my employer, who indicated to them that they were willing, pay it.

43. I.M. Young, "Social Movements, Differences and Social Policy," *University of Cincinnati Law Review*, 56, p. 535.

44. M. Minow, "Redefining Family: Who's In and Who's Out," *University of Colorado Law Review*, (1991), p. 269.

45. Ibid., p. 282.

46. M. Minow, "Beyond State Intervention in the Family: For Baby Jane Doe," *University of Michigan Law Review*, 18 (1985), p. 948.

47. *Braschi v. Stahl*, (1989), 74 N.Y.S. (2d) 784 (Ct. App.).

48. Cindy Ruskin, *The Quilt*, (Pocket Books, 1988), p. 121.

49. In an informal poll taken by *Xtra* (a Toronto periodical for the gay and lesbian *downtown* community) in June 1991, half of three hundred respondents claimed to have told both of their parents of their orientation. Nine percent said that they had told only their mother and five percent said that they had told only their father. Thirty-seven percent of the respondents claimed that they had told neither parent.

50. In my own case, I managed a partial victory but it represents my greatest litigation regret. The word "lesbian" did not appear in any of the documents, nor was it used in argument. On the advice of my lawyers, we decided that "same-sex relationship of some permanence" would be less offensive to the judicial ear. As it turned out, he was offended, anyway.

51. Carol Smart, *Feminism and the Power of Law*, (London: Routledge, 1989), p. 5.

52. Ibid., p. 5.

53. Ibid., p. 11.

54. Barrett and McIntosh, p. 29.

54. Barrett and McIntosh, p. 29.

55. As Carol Smart has recognized in her discussion of the quest for a feminist jurisprudence, the feminist legal practitioner must operate where the scope of feminist practice is severely limited. Further, she faces the very real problem of acting as a feminist while maybe jeopardizing a client's case by doing so. See Smart, *Feminism and the Power of Law*, p. 67. From my law school experience, this tension and dilemma was never appropriately considered. Many legal academics have never even met a client let alone tried to help one, which exacerbates, in my view, the chasm that exists between legal education and legal practice and does little to assist a progressive law student with ambitions to practice and remain progressive.

56. Ibid., p. 11.

57. S. Boyd and E. Sheehy, "Canadian Feminist Perspectives on Law," *Journal Of Law and Society*, 13 (1986), p. 321.

58. Ibid., p. 384.

59. Didi Herman, "Are We family?: Lesbian Rights and Women's Liberation," *Osgoode Hall Law Journal*, 28 (1990), p. 815.

60. Smart, *Feminism and the Power of Law*, p. 69.

Living in the Margins:
Lesbian Families & the Law

KATHERINE ARNUP

LIKE ALL WOMEN, LESBIAN MOTHERS ARE PROFOUNDLY AFFECTED BY THE political and legal climate within which they live and raise their children. In many jurisdictions, lesbianism is still considered a "crime against nature," and a revelation of lesbianism can lead to criminal charges and imprisonment. As the American poet and essayist Minnie Bruce Pratt reminds us, "how I love is outside the law."[1] While the sexual activities in which lesbians engage are no longer criminalized in Canada, provided they take place within the privacy of their own homes, nonetheless lesbians' relationships with each other and with their non-biological children remain largely "outside the law." Furthermore, in a number of American states, even "private acts" between same-sex partners remain criminalized.[2] The recent flurry of anti-gay initiatives in the United States coupled with the huge opposition to the inclusion of any further sexual orientation protection in Canada indicate that the battles we have fought for the past twenty-five years are far from over. In this article, I will discuss the issues of child custody, alternative insemination, adoption, and the legal position of sperm donors and non-biological lesbian mothers, in order to explore the ways in which state institutions and legal structures impact upon our lives.

An examination of the history of lesbian mothers' efforts to secure custody of their children conceived within heterosexual relationships reveals that, in this respect at least, lesbians are still, if not outside, then barely on the margins of the law. Prior to the 1970s, few lesbian mothers contested custody in court. Fearing the implications of open court battles and recognizing that they were almost assured of defeat at the hands of a decidedly homophobic legal system, many women "voluntarily" relinquished custody, in exchange for "liberal" access to their children. On occasion, lesbian mothers were able to make private arrangements with former husbands, often lying about their sexual identity in order to retain custody of the children. Such arrangements are still common today, although the numbers are impossible to determine, given the necessarily private nature of the agreements.

During the 1970s and '80s, with the support of the gay and lesbian movements and of feminist lawyers and friends, lesbians began to contest and, in a limited number of cases, win the custody of their children conceived within heterosexual marriages. In contrast to many American jurisdictions, in which lesbianism per se has been deemed a bar to custody,[3] judges in Canada have adopted what might appear to be a more "reasonable" approach. Examining closely aspects of each applicant's lifestyle, judges have sought to determine what effect, if any, the mother's lesbianism will have on the well-being of the child.[4] In making this assessment, judges have followed a pattern established by the first two reported[5] lesbian custody cases in Canada. Since these cases exemplify the treatment of lesbian custody cases by the courts, I will discuss them in some detail.

Case v. Case was the first Canadian case to deal specifically with the issue of lesbian custody. In July 1974, Mr. Justice MacPherson of the Saskatchewan Queen's Bench granted custody of the two children to their father. In considering the significance of the mother's lesbianism, the judge noted that "it seems to me that homosexuality on the part of a parent is a factor to be considered along with all the other evidence in the case. It should not be considered a bar in itself to a parent's right to custody."[6] That statement is contradicted by the judge's discussion of the mother's "life-style." Describing the father as a "stable and secure and responsible person," the judge added that, "I hesitate to put adjectives on the personality of the mother but the evidence shows, I think, that her way of life is irregular." In considering her role as vice-president of the local gay club, he added, "I greatly fear that if these children are raised by the mother they will be too much in contact with people of abnormal tastes and proclivities."[7] Thus, while Mrs. Case's lesbianism was not in itself a bar to custody, her "lifestyle" was.

K. v. K., a 1975 Alberta custody dispute, provides an interesting contrast. Comparing the two cases, the judge stated:

> The situation before this court is, in my view, different. Mrs. K. is not a missionary about to convert heterosexuals to her present way of life. She does not regard herself as gay in the sense that heterosexuals are "morose ..." Mrs. K. is a good mother and a warm, loving, concerned parent.[8]

The judge stated further that "Mrs. K's homosexuality is ... no more of a bar to her obtaining custody than is the fact of Mr. K's drug use." Having had the opportunity to examine both Mrs. K. and her lover, the judge concluded that "their relationship will be discreet and will not be flaunted to the children or to the community at large." Mrs. K. was awarded custody of her child.

Discretion on the part of the homosexual parent has continued to be cited as a justification for awarding custody to that parent. In a 1991 Saskatchewan case, the judge awarded custody of two children to their aunt, a woman who had been involved in a lesbian relationship for twelve years. In discussing the relationship between the two women the judge noted:

> I found these two women to be rather straightforward. Their relationship does not meet with the approval of all members of society in general. They were neither apologetic nor aggressive about their relationship. They are very discreet. They make no effort to recruit others to their way of living. They make no special effort to associate with others who pursue that lifestyle. In short, D. and H. mind their own business and go their own way in a discreet and dignified way.[9]

A 1980 Canadian case followed the pattern set by *Case v. Case*. Gayle Bezaire had originally been granted custody of her two children, but as a result of "changed circumstances" the original order was reversed, giving custody to the father. The second custody order was upheld on appeal. The details of this case, as in many custody battles, are complex. It *is* apparent that the mother violated a number of the provisions of the original order. At least one of these, however, represented a "catch-22" situation. In his original order, the judge had ordered the mother to live alone. He explained: "I am attempting to improve the situation, and this includes negativing any open, declared, and avowed lesbian, or homosexual relationship." In this order, Judge MacMahon sought to inhibit the lesbian "life-style" of Mrs. Bezaire while declaring that her lesbianism was not in itself a bar to custody.

Imposing conditions like these is a common practice in cases involving a lesbian or gay parent. The practice is based on the assumption that a parent's homosexuality may negatively affect the child, but that those effects can be overcome if the parent meets certain conditions, such as not co-habiting with a lover, not sharing a bedroom with a lover, and not showing affection of any kind in front of the child. Paula Brantner has recently commented on the unfairness of these conditions: "Heterosexual parents are not routinely asked to forgo sexual relationships with other adults to obtain custody of their children — lesbian and gay parents are." The impact of these conditions on the lives of lesbian and gay parents is severe. Brantner notes: "… gay parents are forced to make impossible and intolerable decisions. Parents who fail to comply with the court's restrictions may lose their children. If they do comply, they may lose their partners or the ability to be openly gay and to maintain contact with other gay persons, which takes its own psychological toll."[10]

The contradiction between the liberal acceptance of homosexuality and the setting of conditions is evident in dozens of cases involving lesbian and gay parents. As early as 1974, an Australian judge noted that "[t]he days are done when courts will disqualify a woman from the role of parent merely because she has engaged or is engaging in some form of extra-marital sex, be it heterosexual or homosexual." Despite this statement,

Judge Bright ordered the mother not to sleep in her lover's bedroom overnight or to let her lover sleep in her bedroom overnight. As well, the children were required to visit a psychiatrist at least once a year.[11]

In hearing the *Bezaire* case at the Ontario Court of Appeal, the appellate judges were critical of the conditions imposed by the trial judge, which, they felt, reflected a condemnation of lesbian parenting. Mr. Justice Arnup stated:

> In my view homosexuality, either as a tendency, a proclivity, or a practiced way of life is not in itself alone a ground for refusing custody to the parent with respect to whom such evidence is given. The question is and must always be what effect upon the welfare of the children that aspect of the parent's makeup and lifestyle has.[12]

The appellate judges argued, then, that each case must be judged on the basis of its evidence. This standard, known as the nexus test, means that it must be demonstrated that the parent's homosexuality will have a negative effect upon the child. Even such a fair-minded approach, however, contains within it a pit-fall for a lesbian mother. Because of the "rampant heterosexism" of our society, the child of a lesbian might well be the object of abuse and ridicule by neighbourhood children if the mother's lesbianism were discovered or even suspected. Such an experience would, of course, be an unpleasant one for the child. Anticipating such derision, the courts in Canada, as in the United States, Britain and elsewhere, have opted primarily for paternal custody rights, thereby reflecting and reinforcing the prevailing attitudes towards lesbianism.

These cases illustrate the distinction which judges have drawn between what they determine to be "good" and "bad" lesbian mothers. Good lesbian mothers, women who live quiet, discreet lives, who promise that they will raise their children to be heterosexual, who appear to the outside world to be heterosexual single parents, have in recent years increasingly succeeded in winning custody of their children. "Bad" lesbian mothers, women who are open about their sexual orientation, who attend gay and lesbian demonstrations and other public events, and who view their lesbianism positively or as one aspect of an entire challenge to society, are almost certain to lose custody of their children to their ex-husbands.

Nancy Polikoff, mother, writer, lawyer, and long-time activist in the struggle for lesbian custody rights, notes:

> While no formula will guarantee victory in courtroom custody disputes involving lesbian mothers or gay fathers, one thing is clear: the more we appear to be part of the mainstream, with middle class values, middle-of-the-road political beliefs, repressed sexuality, and sex-role stereotyped behavior, the more likely we are to keep custody of our children. On the other hand, communal child-rearing arrangements, radical feminist activism, sexual experimentation — these choices are all predictably fatal to any custody action. The courtroom is no place in which to affirm our pride in our lesbian sexuality, or to advocate alternative child-rearing designed to produce strong, independent women.[13]

An examination of the reasoning provided by judges to explain their determinations in custody disputes reveals that such an analysis is not merely the result of paranoia on the part of lesbian researchers. Under current family law provisions in Canada and in most jurisdictions in the United States, the paramount standard applied in disputes to determine who should be granted custody is "the best interests of the child."[14] No precise rule or formula exists, however, for determining *which* household or family arrangement operates in the child's best interests. Until recently in Canada, and still in many jurisdictions in the United States and elsewhere, parental fitness represented a key element of the "best interests" criteria. Judges relied on a variety of factors for determining the "fitness" of each parent, including past and present sexual conduct, the grounds for the termination of the marriage, the guilt or innocence of each party, and the "quality" of the home to assist them in determining the best custody arrangements for the children.

These tests were used to brand virtually every lesbian who attempted to gain custody as an "unfit" mother.

With the passage of family law reform legislation in Canada in the 1980s, criteria for determining custody were amended and, as a result, parental behaviour *in and of itself* could no longer be considered a bar to custody. In Ontario, for example, the *Children's Law Reform Act* specifies that the "best interests of the child" shall be the determining factor. The legislation directs the judge to consider "all the needs and circumstances of the child," including the relationship between the child and those persons claiming custody, the preferences of the child, the current living situation of the child, the plans put forward for the child, the "permanence and stability of the family unit with which it is proposed that the child will live," and the blood or adoptive links between the child and the applicant.[15] The section explicitly states that "the past conduct of a person is not relevant to a determination of an application ... unless the conduct is relevant to the ability of the person to act as a parent of a child."[16]

While the revised legislation might appear to improve a lesbian mother's chances for success, there are a number of ways these provisions can be interpreted by a homophobic judge to rule against her application for custody. First, a judge may refuse to recognize a "homosexual" family as a permanent and stable family unit. Homosexuals, after all, are not permitted to marry and therefore do not meet this standard heterosexual measure of "stability." The "closeted" nature of many gay and lesbian relationships, and the absence of any census category to "capture" same-sex partnerships, also render it virtually impossible to offer statistical evidence of the longevity of same-sex relationships. Given these obstacles, a lesbian mother might find herself unable to demonstrate the "permanence and stability" of her "family unit."

A "lesbian life-style" may also be used to find that a lesbian mother is unlikely to provide a "suitable" home for her child. As *Case v. Case* demonstrates, judges have deemed activities like attending lesbian rallies and dances, exposing the child to other lesbians and gay men, and discussing lesbian issues openly in the home negative factors in considering the application of lesbian mothers for custody of their children.[17] Thus, despite the apparently fair-minded language of family law reform, judges can and do find ways within the law to deny lesbian mothers custody of their children.

This reality presents a lesbian mother seeking court-ordered custody with a number of difficult choices. If she presents herself in court as an "avowed lesbian," if she admits to coming out at work or at school, she stands less chance of winning custody of her children, especially if she meets a determined challenge from her ex-husband. Within this legal context, most lesbians "choose" to act as "straight" as possible to win custody of their children. Such strategies tell us far less about the belief systems of lesbian mothers than about the attitudes and prejudices of the courts. As Julia Brophy has noted: "A custody dispute is not the forum in which to mount a feminist critique of the family."[18]

As we engage in our political theorizing, we must not forget the incredible toll of pain and grief faced by lesbian mothers who continue to lose custody of their children. We must remember as well that contested custody cases take an enormous financial toll on women, often costing thousands and thousands of dollars in legal fees, with no assurance of victory. Even if a lesbian mother wins in court, she lives with the ever-present danger of the case being re-opened because of allegations of "changed circumstances."[19] Most lesbian mothers still face these battles virtually alone.[20]

A recent custody case in Richmond, Virginia, serves as a startling reminder of the fact that the issue of child custody for lesbian mothers is far from resolved. In September 1993, Henrico County Juvenile and Domestic Relations Court Judge Buford M. Parsons Jr. awarded custody of Tyler Bottoms to his maternal grandmother, removing the two-year-old child from the care of his biological mother and her lesbian partner. The judge's ruling was based solely on the fact that the mother is a lesbian. Parsons relied on *Roe v. Roe*, a 1985 Virginia Supreme Court case that found homosexual parents to be unfit parents with no custodial rights to their children.[21] In that case, the court found that living with a lesbian or gay parent placed "an intolerable burden" on a child. While Sharon was successful in her initial appeal of the decision, Tyler remains with his grand-mother, pending yet another appeal.[22]

While initially most lesbian mothers who came to public attention were women who had conceived and given birth to children within heterosexual partnerships or marriages, in the past fifteen years, increasing numbers of lesbians have chosen to conceive and bear children, either on their own, or within a lesbian relationship. Since the late 1970s, an undetermined number of lesbians have requested artificial insemination ser-vices at infertility clinics and sperm banks across North Amer-ica. Many of these requests were denied once the applicant's sexual orientation was revealed. In some instances women were informed that the clinic had decided not to inseminate *any* single woman, claiming that they feared single mothers would launch child support suits against the medical facility should the insemination be successful.[23]

To date, no legal decisions have been issued concerning infertility clinics which discriminate against single women or lesbians. In the only documented American case, a woman launched a legal action against Wayne State University when its medical centre rejected her application for artificial insemina-tion. Fearing the repercussions of a protracted legal battle, the clinic abandoned its restrictive policy, granting her application before the case could be heard by the courts.[24] In Canada, a complaint is currently before the British Columbia Council of Human Rights. The complaint, alleging discrimination on the basis of sexual orientation and family status, was filed against Dr. Gerald Korn, who refused to provide artificial insemination services to two women on the grounds that they are lesbians. The women initially complained to the British Columbia Col-lege of Physicians and Surgeons, who denied their claim. The Human Rights Council has agreed to proceed with the case.[25]

Perhaps anticipating requests for donor insemination from single heterosexual women and lesbians, legislative initiatives in a number of jurisdictions in the United States have re-stricted access to insemination services to married women.[26]

No Canadian legislation yet exists, although recommendations to this effect have been made by a number of commissions.[27] Most recently, the Royal Commission on New Reproductive Technologies supported the right to assisted insemination for single women, and explicitly for lesbians. The report recommends that "[c]riteria for determining access to assisted insemination services should not discriminate on the basis of social factors such as sexual orientation, marital status, or economic status."[28] This recommendation took many feminists by surprise, particularly since it contravened a public opinion poll which indicated that a majority of Canadians surveyed (seventy-one percent) opposed lesbians' access to reproductive technologies.[29]

In light of access barriers to clinical services, it is not surprising that many (if not most) lesbians prefer to make private insemination arrangements. Here, however, legal measures designed to medicalize the practice of alternative insemination present yet another roadblock. In recent years, a number of jurisdictions in the United States and elsewhere have passed legislation declaring artificial insemination to be a practice of medicine, thereby legally restricting its use to licensed practitioners. The Ontario Law Reform Commission in 1985 recommended the passage of similar legislation.[30] Should such a measure be implemented, it would force women engaging in private insemination arrangements to remain "clandestine" about their activities in order to avoid legal sanctions. Surprisingly, perhaps, the Royal Commission report condones the practice of private insemination, recommending that "[s]perm should be provided to individual women for self-insemination without discrimination on the basis of factors such as sexual orientation, marital status, or economic status."[31] Whether any of the recommendations of the report will be enacted, however, remains to be seen, especially in light of the fact that the commission was established by the Conservative government of Brian Mulroney, now no longer in power.

Another legal issue faced by lesbians is the legal status of the sperm donor. While artificial insemination was initially treated by the courts as the legal equivalent to adultery against the woman's husband, gradually the courts have moved to a position that recognized the child as the legitimate offspring of the recipient's husband, provided he had consented to the insemination procedure. The husband was thereby legally obligated to support the child. Most legislation now specifies that the parental rights and obligations of the donor are replaced by the paternal rights of the husband.

The issues are considerably more complex in the case of a lesbian or unmarried heterosexual woman and a known donor. In such instances, women who arrange a private insemination — most of whom are lesbians — face the risk of paternity claims by sperm donors. To date, no Canadian cases have been reported, but in six of the seven reported American cases, sperm donors seeking paternity rights have had their claims upheld by the courts. The decisions have ranged from placing the sperm donor's name on the child's birth certificate to granting access rights.[32] Such decisions have been made *even* in cases where the insemination was performed by a licensed practitioner, thereby ignoring relevant legislation which extinguished the rights and obligations of donors. In one 1989 case, the Oregon Appeal Court concluded that, despite the statute, the donor had shown himself interested in performing the duties of a father and was therefore entitled to paternity rights similar to those of an unwed father.[33] In a similar Colorado case, the Colorado Supreme Court ruled in favour of the donor, crediting the donor's claims of having bought toys, clothing, and books for the child, as well as establishing a trust fund in the child's name, as evidence of his desire to parent.[34]

A lower court ruling in the sixth American case promised to reverse this trend. In an April 1993 proceeding before the Family Court of the City of New York, a sperm donor (Thomas S.) sought a declaration of paternity over the objections of the child's biological mother and her partner, the child's co-mother. The donor, a gay man, had agreed initially that he would have no rights or obligations to the child and that he would recognize the women as the child's co-mothers. He had no contact with the child for the first three and a half years of the child's life and began seeing her only after contact was initiated by the women, in response to requests from their other daughter regarding her biological origins. Five years later the donor decided that he wished to see the child without her co-mothers and to introduce the child to his biological family. For reasons he did not specify, he did not feel "comfortable" introducing the child's mothers to his parents. When the women refused to comply with his request, the donor commenced an action for paternity and visitation.

At the lower court level, the judge denied the donor both paternity and visitation rights. Judge Kaufmann ruled that a declaration of paternity "at this late time in [the child's life] would not be in her best interests." In a stunning recognition of lesbian families, Judge Kaufmann declared that "in her family, there has been no father." Because the donor had agreed to respect that family and had not made any effort to "father" the child in her early years, the judge denied his claim. That ruling was overturned on November 17, 1994, on appeal. At the Appellate Division of the Supreme Court of New York, in a three to two decision, the court ruled that Thomas S. was entitled to an order of filiation. The issue of visitation was remanded for a further hearing, the results of which are not yet known.[35]

In the final American decision, the Oregon Court of Appeal upheld a lower court decision which denied the sperm donor any paternal rights. In that case, the donor had signed an agreement waiving his paternal rights. When a dispute arose over visitation, the parties entered into mediation. After several sessions, they reaffirmed and re-signed their original agreement.[36] It was on that basis that the appeal court upheld the original decision.

While all of the cases to date have involved only the issues of access and a declaration of paternity, the implications extend far beyond those claims. A declaration of paternity can accord any or all of the following: sole or joint physical or legal custody, visitation, decision-making in such areas as education, religion, and health care, custody in the event of the mother's death, denial of permission to change residence or to adopt, obligation to provide child support, and inclusion of the donor's name as father on the child's birth certificate.[37] As the National Center for Lesbian Rights in the United States has noted: "in our system of law there are only two options. Either the donor is merely a donor, with no parental rights or relationship with the child whatsoever, or he is a father, with all of his parental rights intact. There are no gray areas in the law here, and, when in doubt, the courts tend to grant donors full parental rights in cases involving single mothers."[38] Clearly, these cases have far-reaching implications for the lives of lesbian mothers and their children.

In marked contrast to sperm donors, the legal status of non-biological lesbian mothers has for the most part been denied by the courts in both the United States and Canada.[39] While these women have helped to care for and financially support the children of lesbian families, courts have repeatedly *refused* to grant their claims for visitation rights upon dissolution of the lesbian relationship or custody rights upon the death of the biological mother. In the only reported Canadian case dealing with this issue, the judge rejected a lesbian mother's application for support for herself and her children born during the course of her relationship with her former lesbian partner. The court sided with the non-biological mother who maintained that she had no legal obligation to support either the biological mother or the children.[40] As Karen Andrews notes elsewhere in this volume, *Anderson v. Luoma* stands for the unhappy proposition that a lesbian can behave as despicably as any man who evades his child support obligations and because she is outside the statutes, she can get away with it."[41]

As more lesbian couples choose to become parents, courts will increasingly be faced with the issue of the rights and responsibilities of non-biological lesbian mothers. Many areas of children's (and parents') lives are affected, including medical authorization, visitation, support, and custody upon dissolution of the parental relationship, and guardianship in the event of the death of the biological mother. To date, in an effort to secure legal rights for the non-biological parent, lesbian parents have sought a variety of legal mechanisms including second-parent adoption and joint custody. Second-parent adoption is the option used by step-parents in heterosexual relationships when they create a new parenting arrangement following the dissolution of the original marriage. Such an option is not widely available to lesbian parents. A 1993 American article noted that only in California, New York State, Washington D.C., Minnesota, and Vermont can the partner of the birth mother legally adopt the child, thereby sharing parental rights with the birth mother.[42] According to a 1994 newsletter of the Gay and Lesbian Parents Coalition International (GLPCI), the following jurisdictions have granted at least one second-parent adoption: Alaska, California, District of Columbia, Illinois, Massachusetts, Michigan, Minnesota, New Jersey, New York, Ohio, Oregon, Pennsylvania, Rhode Island, Texas, Vermont, and Washington. England also recently granted a second-parent adoption.[43] In all other jurisdictions in the United States, and throughout Canada, only one parent of each sex can have legal rights to a child. Thus, the birth mother must relinquish her rights to enable the non-biological mother to adopt the child. In granting a second-parent adoption, a New York State judge recently commented that requiring the biological mother to relinquish her rights "would be an absurd outcome which would nullify the advantage sought by the proposed adoption: the creation of a legal family unit identical to the actual family setup."[44] An alternative to adoption is joint custody, a legal arrangement available to heterosexual parents upon dissolution of their relationship. This option is also being quietly pursued by lesbian parents as a means to gain parental rights for non-biological mothers. This option, however, grants only a temporary status for the co-mother and is still subject to challenges by biological relatives of the child.[45]

While both second-parent adoption and joint custody hold some promise as ways of gaining legal rights for non-biological mothers, the effort to secure them may also pose a danger for lesbian families. As Nancy Polikoff has noted: "The stress of entering the legal system and potentially submitting the family to evaluation according to standards rooted in homophobia and heterosexism is as much a deterrent as the uncertainty of asserting untested legal theories."[46] Lesbian families pursuing such options must weigh carefully the financial and emotional costs of state intervention against the benefits of the legal recognition of their family constellation, should their application be successful.

In the absence of effective, risk-free legal mechanisms, the following documents can be drawn up in an attempt to insure that the non-biological mother's parental rights are recognized by the courts: co-parenting agreement, statement of guardianship in a will, and a medical authorization form. While none of these mechanisms is a guarantee, they serve, at least, to indicate the intention and wishes of both parents.[47]

The final area which I wish to consider is adoption and foster parenting. For untold years, lesbians have become mothers through foster parenting and adoption. Here, legal measures designed to limit homosexuals' access to children have forced prospective adoptive or foster parents to present themselves to social service agencies as single women, regardless of their relationship status. In this realm, even more so perhaps than in the areas of child custody and insemination, secrecy and concern for privacy prevail. Even those women who are willing to talk about their adoptive experiences ask that confidentiality be guaranteed, since they are rightfully afraid that their children may be removed from their home, should the mother's sexual orientation be revealed.

The question of adoption reveals in a dramatic fashion that many segments of society still harbour irrational and unfounded fears and prejudices about the dangers posed by relationships between lesbians or gay men and children. Those fears persist despite the almost complete lack of evidence of child abuse perpetrated by lesbians or gay men. Thus, lesbians wishing to adopt or foster children still face enormous barriers. Lesbians, for example, cannot adopt a child as a couple. Instead, one of the members of the couple must apply for adoption. If that application is successful, then the partner may, in some jurisdictions, apply for a second-parent adoption.

Adoption can take many forms, including public adoption (through an agency such as the Children's Aid Society), private adoption through an agency, independent adoption, and international adoption. With the exception of public adoption, all of these forms are costly, and any type of adoption is fraught with uncertainty and long periods of waiting. For lesbians wishing to adopt, however, these problems are compounded by legal barriers. In only two states in the United States, New York and California, are lesbians and gays legally protected against discrimination in the adoption process. Even that protection does not mean, of course, that individuals will not face discrimination; it offers some limited guarantee that an individual will not be turned down solely on the basis of sexual orientation. In two other states, Florida and New Hampshire, openly lesbian and gay prospective parents are prohibited by law from adoption. In Ohio, the Supreme Court interpreted the state adoption law in such a way as to allow a gay man to adopt. In all other states, no specific legislation related to sexual orientation and adoption exists.[48] It must be noted, however, that in thirty-eight American states, the Department of Social Services is administered by the county, as opposed to being state regulated. That means that there can be huge variations across the state on how decisions on adoption and fostering for same-sex couples are determined.

In Canada, adoption falls under provincial jurisdiction, and as a result, policies vary across the country. In a number of jurisdictions, including Ontario and British Columbia, lesbians and gay men are eligible to adopt as single people. In those provinces, the best interests of the child, rather than the applicant's sexual orientation, govern the decision. Nowhere in Canada, however, can same-sex couples apply to be adoptive parents. Recently, officials at the Children's Aid Society (CAS) in Metro Toronto announced that they favoured allowing same-sex couples to foster-parent and adopt children. Despite this support, however, CAS Executive Director Bruce Rivers noted that until the law governing adoption changes, the CAS is unable to amend its policy.

In her book, *The Lesbian and Gay Parenting Handbook*, April Martin offers the following advice to lesbians and gays considering adoption. First, they should obtain the services of a lawyer, one well versed in issues related to sexual orientation and the law. Second, they should seek out other lesbians and gays who have already been through the adoption process in their state. Finally, Martin warns prospective parents not to lie at any time during the adoption process. While they may be safe in remaining silent about their sexual orientation, "lying about your sexual orientation constitutes fraud and is grounds for taking your adopted child away when the fraud is discovered."[49] Given the enormous variations in legal practices on the adoption front, and the fact that new developments are occurring almost daily, lesbians considering this parenting route would do well to follow this advice.

The legal position of lesbian mothers has improved considerably since the first custody cases began to appear before the courts in Canada, the United States and elsewhere, some twenty years ago. Lesbian mothers and their children are gaining acceptance in schools, daycare centres, and communities across North America. Lesbians are contesting homophobic laws and practices in the areas of adoption, foster parenting, and child custody. No longer is it a judicial certainty that a lesbian mother will lose custody of her children. Despite these gains, lesbian mothers still risk losing their children and many are fighting these battles ever day. In the realm of family law, there is no one strategy, no right way to proceed. Lesbians facing these issues should seek legal counsel, since laws vary tremendously from province to province, state to state and country to country.[50] Equally importantly, they need the support and help of other lesbian parents who understand the anguish that these struggles bring.

Notes

1. Minnie Bruce Pratt, "Poetry in Time of War," in *Rebellion: Essays 1980-1991*, (Ithaca, NY: Firebrand Books, 1991), p. 228.
2. In *Bowers v. Hardwick*, the U.S. Supreme Court upheld the constitutionality of a Georgia statute which criminalized homosexual acts. That 1986 decision represented a major setback for efforts to improve the custodial position of lesbian and gay parents, and has been used to support the view that lesbian and gay parents cannot be fit parents. See *Bowers v. Hardwick*, 106 S.Ct. 2841 (1986).
3. For a discussion of the *per se* approach, see Robert A. Beargie, "Custody Determinations Involving the Homosexual Parent," *Family Law Quarterly*, 22, 1 (Spring 1988), pp. 71-86.

4. For a discussion of these cases, see Wendy Gross, "Judging the Best Interests of the Child: Child Custody and the Homosexual Parent," *Canadian Journal of Women and the Law*, 1 (1986), pp. 505-31; Katherine Arnup, "'Mothers Just Like Others': Lesbians, Divorce, and Child Custody in Canada," *Canadian Journal of Women and the Law*, 3 (1989), pp. 18-32.

5. Not all cases which appear before the courts are reported in legal journals. It is a common occurrence in cases in which homosexuality or lesbianism is a factor to seal the records, ostensibly to protect the privacy of the individuals involved. This practice presents a problem for both lawyers and researchers in the field of lesbian custody. Those cases which are reported become accessible to judges and lawyers for their use in future cases, and thereby assume an importance beyond their individual significance.

6. *Case v. Case*, (1974), 18 R.F.L. 138 (Sask. Queen's Bench).

7. Ibid.

8. *K. v. K.*, (1975), 23 R.F.L. 63 (Alta. Prov. Ct.), 64.

9. *D.M. v. M.D.*, 94 Sask. R. 315, [1991] S.J. No. 672;

10. Paula A. Brantner, "When Mommy or Daddy is Gay: Developing Constitutional Standards for Custody Decisions," *Hastings Women's Law Journal*, 3, 1 (Winter 1991), pp. 105, 107.

11. *Campbell v. Campbell*, (1974), 9 SASR, 25 at 28, cited in Margaret Bateman, "Lesbians, Gays and Child Custody: An Australian Legal History," *Australian Gay and Lesbian Law Journal*, 1 (1992), p. 49.

12. *Bezaire v. Bezaire*, (1980), 20 R.F.L. (2d) 365 (Ont. C.A.).

13. Nancy Polikoff, "Lesbian Mothers, Lesbian Families: Legal Obstacles, Legal Challenges," *Review of Law and Social Change*, 14 (1986), p. 907.

14. This test replaced the "tender years" presumption, which dictated that maternal custody was always in the best interests of the child, particularly in the case of young children.

15. *Children's Law Reform Act*, R.S.O. 1980, c. 68, section 24.

16. Ibid.

17. *Case v. Case*, (1974), 18 R.F.L. 138 (Sask. Queen's Bench). Although this case was decided prior to the family law reforms referred to above, the judicial reasoning applied by Mr. Justice MacPherson would still be allowed under current family law.

18. Julia Brophy, "New Families, Judicial Decision-Making, and Children's Welfare," *Canadian Journal of Women and the Law*, 5 (1992), p. 496.

19. Custody cases can be brought back to the courts for reconsideration at any time on the basis of "changed circumstances." These can range from the marriage of one of the parties to the "discovery" of a lesbian mother's sexual orientation.

20. From its formation in 1978 until its demise in 1987, the Lesbian Mothers' Defence Fund (LMDF) provided lesbian mothers in Canada with invaluable legal, financial, and emotional support. The LMDF produced the *Grapevine*, a newsletter reporting on custody cases across North America, assisted in fund raising, and organized monthly potluck suppers for lesbian mothers and their children. For a discussion of LMDF, see Sharon Dale Stone, "Lesbian Mothers Organizing," in *Lesbians in Canada*, Sharon Dale Stone (ed.), (Toronto: Between the Lines, 1990), pp. 198-208. For American organizations, see the resource section of this book.

21. *Roe v. Roe*, 228 Va. 722, 324 S.E.2d 691 (1985). The Virginia Supreme Court found that living conditions would "impose an intolerable burden upon her [the child] by reason of the social condemnation attached to them." The court noted as well that "the father's unfitness is manifested by his willingness to impose this burden upon [his daughter] in exchange for his own gratification."

22. For an initial report on the case, see Nancy Wartik, "Virginia Is No Place For Lesbian Mothers," *Ms.*, (November/December 1993), p. 89. The appeals court decision overturning Judge Parsons' original order was unanimous. Judge Sam W. Coleman III wrote that "a child's natural and legal right to the care and support of a parent and the parent's right to the custody and companionship of the child should only be disrupted if there are compelling reasons to do so." (AP wire service, June 21, 1994).

23. For a discussion of such arguments, see Katherine Arnup "Finding Fathers: Artificial Insemination, Lesbians, and the Law," *Canadian Journal of Women and the Law*, 7, 1 (1994), pp. 97-115.

24. *Smedes v. Wayne State University*, No. 80-725-83, (E.D. Mich., filed July 15, 1980). The case was widely reported in the American press: e.g. "Woman Sues to Be Mother," *Bulletin* (Philadelphia), (July 17, 1980), and "A Single Sues for Artificial Insemination," *Seattle Times*, (July 17, 1980), p. A5.

25. See "Lesbian Couple Charge Doctor and College with Discrimination," *Gazebo Connection*, 14, 8 (September 1993), p. 2.

26. On this issue, Robert H. Blank notes: "the question of allowing single or lesbian women access to AID has been approached explicitly in few jurisdictions and rejected in virtually all." Blank, *Regulating Reproduction*, (New York: Columbia University Press, 1990), p. 151.

27. See, for example, Saskatchewan, Law Reform Commission of Saskatchewan, *Proposals for a Human Artificial Insemination Act*, (March 1987).

28. Recommendation 99 (d), *Proceed With Care: Final Report of the Royal Commission on New Reproductive Technologies*, p. 485.

29. The report noted: "Although most Canadians surveyed did not support lesbians having access to DI, [Donor Insemination] to provide a service in a discriminatory way by denying access, without evidence that a resultant child would be harmed, is contrary to the Charter and also contravenes our ethics of care." *Proceed with Care*, p. 456.

30. Ontario, Ministry of the Attorney General, Ontario Law Reform Commission, *Report on Artificial Reproduction and Related Matters*, (1985).

31. Recommendation 94 (f), *Proceed With Care: Final Report of the Royal Commission on New Reproductive Technologies*, p. 480.

32. See "Sperm donor wins fight with lesbians," *Toronto Star*, (26 July 1991), p. F1. For a discussion of these cases, see Katherine Arnup, "Finding Fathers: Artificial Insemination, Lesbians, and the Law," *Canadian Journal of Women and the Law*, 7, 1 (1994), pp. 97-115. See also Katherine Arnup and Susan Boyd, "Familial Disputes? Sperm Donors, Lesbian Mothers, and Legal Parenthood," in *Legal Inversions*, Didi Herman and Carl Stychin (eds.), (Temple University Press, in press).

33. In *Kevin N. McIntyre v. Linden Crouch*, the insemination was performed by a licensed practitioner, and Oregon legislation specified that under such circumstances, the donor has "no right, obligation or interest with respect to a child born as a result of artificial insemination" and the child has "no right, obligation or interest with respect" to the donor. ORS 109.239 section 5, 1 and 2. *McIntyre v. Crouch*, 780 P. 2d 239 (Or. App. 1989). The seventh case, under the same legislation, was decided in the mother's favour, presumably because the parties had a written agreement extinguishing the donor's rights.

34. Interest of R.C., (1989, Colo.) 775 P2d 27.

35. *Thomas S. v. Robin Y.*, 1994 N.Y. App. Div., Lexis 11385. I am grateful to Julie Shapiro for furnishing me with the results of this appeal.

36. *Leckie v. Voorhies*, Case No. 60-92-06326 (Ore. Circuit Court, April 5, 1993), (unreported); and *Leckie v. Voorhies*, No. A79785, May 25, 1994, 128 Ore.App. 289.

37. For a discussion of the implications of donor rights, see National Center for Lesbian Rights, "Lesbians Choosing Motherhood: Legal Implications of Donor Insemination and Co-parenting," reprinted in *Lesbians, Gay Men, and the Law*, William B. Rubenstein (ed.), (New York: New Press, 1993), p. 543.

38. Ibid., p. 546.

39. For an in-depth discussion of the parental rights of non-biological mothers, see Nancy D. Polikoff, "This Child Does Have Two Mothers: Redefining Parenthood to Meet the Needs of Children in Lesbian-Mother and Other Nontraditional Families," *Georgetown Law Journal*, 78 (1990-91), pp. 459-575.

40. *Anderson v. Luoma*, (1986), 50 R.F.L. (2d) 127 (B.C.S.C.). The biological mother did succeed in winning a property settlement.

41. Karen Andrews, "Ancient Affections: Gays, Lesbians and Family Status," see pp. 358-77 in this book.

42. For a recent successful case of second-parent adoption, see re: the adoption of Evan, 583 N.Y.S. 2d 997 (N.Y. Sur. 1992). The judge determined that the second-parent adoption was in the child's best interests. He noted that the adoption "would bring no change or trauma to his daily life; it would serve only to provide him with important legal rights which he does not presently possess."

43. *GLPCI Network*, (Summer 1994), p. 6.

44. Ibid., p. 534.

45. In the past three years, at least two lesbian couples in the Ottawa area have successfully applied for joint custody orders. See Nicole LaViolette, "Family Affair: Providing joint custody for same-sex parents," *Capital Xtra*, 17 (January 27, 1995), p. 13.

46. Polikoff, "This Child Does Have Two Mothers," p. 526.

47. For a discussion of these efforts, see Karen Spallina: "Lesbians Choosing Parenthood," *Guild Practitioner*, 50, 1 (Winter 1993), pp. 21-4.

48. For a discussion of a legal challenge to Boston's foster parenting regulations, see Neil Miller, "A Time for Change," reprinted in *Lesbians, Gay Men and the Law*, William B. Rubenstein (ed.), (New York: New Press, 1993), p. 541.

49. April Martin, *The Lesbian and Gay Parenting Handbook*, (New York: HarperCollins, 1993), p. 541.

50. For assistance in finding a knowledgeable and supportive lawyer, contact your local lesbian/gay rights organization. If no such organization exists, try a women's centre or other support centre. It is extremely important to find a lesbian positive lawyer. For other organizations, see the resource section in this volume.

Bibliography

Canadian Sources:

Achilles, Rona, "Donor Insemination: The Future of a Public Secret," in *The Future of Human Reproduction*, Christine Overall (ed.), (Toronto: Women's Press, 1989), pp. 105-19.

Agger, Ellen, "Lesbian Mothers and Custody Rights," *Fireweed*, 1 (Autumn 1978), pp. 64-7.

Agger, E. and F. Wyland, "Wages Due Lesbians," *Quest* 5, 1 (1979), pp. 57-62.

Arnup, Katherine, "Lesbian Mothers and Child Custody," in *Gender and Society: Creating a Canadian Women's Sociology*, Arlene Tigar McLaren (ed.), (Toronto: Copp Clark Pitman, 1988).

Arnup, Katherine, "'Mothers Just Like Others': Lesbians, Divorce and Child Custody in Canada," *Canadian Journal of Women and the Law*, 3, 1 (1989), pp. 18-32.

Arnup, Katherine, "'We are Family!': Lesbian Mothers in Canada," *Resources for Feminist Research*, 20, 3/4 (Fall/Winter 1991), pp. 101-7.

Arnup, Katherine, "Finding Fathers: Artificial Insemination, Lesbians, and the Law," *Canadian Journal of Women and the Law*, 7, 1 (1994), pp. 97-115.

Bell, Laurie, *On Our Own Terms: A Practical Guide for Lesbian and Gay Relationships*, (Toronto: Coalition for Lesbian and Gay Rights in Ontario, 1991).

Boyd, Susan B., "Child Custody Law and the Invisibility of Women's Work," *Queen's Quarterly*, 96, 4 (Winter 1989), pp. 831-58.

Boyd, Susan B., "What is a 'Normal' Family? *C v. C* (A Minor) Custody Appeal," *Modern Law Review*, 55 (March 1992), pp. 269-78.

Brophy, Julia, "New Families, Judicial Decision-Making, and Children's Welfare," *Canadian Journal of Women and the Law*, 5 (1992), pp. 484-97.

Brownstone, Harvey, "The Homosexual Parent in Custody Disputes," *Queen's Law Journal*, 5 (1980), pp. 186-240.

Day, Dian, "Lesbian/Mother," in *Lesbians in Canada*, Sharon Dale Stone (ed.), (Toronto: Between the Lines, 1990), pp. 35-47.

Dineen, Claire and Jackie Crawford, "Lesbian Mothering," *Fireweed*, 28 (Spring 1989), pp. 24-35.

Eaton, Mary, "Lesbians and the Law," in *Lesbians in Canada*, Sharon Dale Stone (ed.), (Toronto: Between the Lines, 1990), pp. 109-32.

Edwards, Bob, "Just Be Quiet About It: Lesbians Still Face Custody Obstacles," *This Magazine*, 26, 5 (1992), p. 10.

Epstein, Rachel, "Breaking with Tradition," *Healthsharing*, (Summer/Fall 1993), pp. 18-22.

Ferris, Kathryn, "Child custody and the lesbian mother: an annotated bibliography," *Resources for Feminist Research*, 12, 1 (March 1983), pp. 106-9.

Gavigan, Shelley A.M., "A Parent(ly) Knot: Can Heather Have Two Mommies?"

in *Legal Inversions*, Didi Herman and Carl Stychin (eds.), (Temple University Press, in press).

Gross, Wendy, "Judging the Best Interests of the Child: Child Custody and the Homosexual Parent," *Canadian Journal of Women and the Law*, 1, 2 (1986), pp. 505-31.

Herman, Didi, "Are We Family?: Lesbian Rights and Women's Liberation," *Osgoode Hall Law Journal*, 24, 4 (Winter 1990), pp. 789-815.

Leopold, Margaret and Wendy King, "Compulsory Heterosexuality, Lesbians and the Law: the Case for Constitutional Protection," *Canadian Journal of Women and the Law*, 1 (1985).

Lesbians Making History, "People Think This Didn't Happen in Canada — But It Did," *Fireweed*, 28 (Spring 1989), pp. 81-6.

O'Brien, Carol-Anne and Lorna Weir, "Lesbians and Gay Men Inside and Outside Families," in *Canadian Families: Diversity, Conflict and Change*, Nancy Mandell and Ann Duffy (eds.), (Toronto: Harcourt Brace, 1994), pp. 111-40.

Ryder, Bruce, "Equality Rights and Sexual Orientation: Confronting Heterosexual Family Privilege," *Canadian Journal of Family Law*, (1990), pp. 39-97.

Stewart, Susan, "A Lesbian Mom Re-Invents the Extended Family," in *Mothers Talk Back*, Margaret Dragu, Sarah Sheard and Susan Swan (eds.), (Toronto: Coach House Press, 1991), pp. 191-205.

Stone, Sharon Dale, "Lesbian Mothers Organizing," in *Lesbians in Canada*, Sharon Dale Stone (ed.), (Toronto: Between the Lines, 1990), pp. 198-208.

Ullyott, Kathy, "My folks are gay," *Chatelaine*, (November 1990), pp. 103-7.

Wyland, Francie, *Motherhood, Lesbianism, and Child Custody*, (Bristol: Falling Wall Press, 1977).

Wyland, Francie, "Lesbian Mothers," *Resources for Feminist Research/Documentation sur la recherche féministe*, 12, 1 (The Lesbian Issue — Etre Lesbienne, March 1983), pp. 41-3.

American and British Sources

Abbitt, Diane and Bobbie Bennett, "Being a Lesbian Mother," in *Positively Gay*, Betty Berzon and Robert Leighton (eds.), (Millbrae, CA: Celestial Arts, 1979), pp. 123-9.

Achtenberg, Roberta (ed.), *Sexual Orientation and the Law*, (New York: Boardman, 1985).

Ainslie, Julie and Kathryn M. Feltey, "Definitions and Dynamics of Motherhood and Family in Lesbian Communities," *Marriage & Family Review*, 17, 1/2 (1991), pp. 63-85.

Alice, Gordon, Debbie and Mary, "Lesbian Mothers," in *For Lesbians Only: A Lesbian Separatist Anthology*, Sarah Lucia Hoagland and Julia Penelope (eds.), (London: Onlywomen Press, 1988), pp. 304-6.

Alpert, Harriet (ed.), *We Are Everywhere: Writings by and about Lesbian Parents*, (Freedom, CA: Crossing Press, 1988).

American Psychological Association, Committee on Women in Psychology and Committee on Lesbian and Gay Concerns, "Lesbian Parents and Their Children: A Resource Paper for Psychologists," (Available from American Psychological Association, Public Interest Directorate, 750 First Street N.E., Washington, DC 20002-424.)

Armanno, Benna F., "The Lesbian Mother: Her Right to Child Custody," *Golden Gate Law Review*, 4 (Fall 1973), pp. 1-18.

Baggett, Courtney R., "Sexual Orientation: Should It Affect Child Custody Rulings?" *Law and Psychology Review*, 16 (Spring 1992), pp. 189-200.

Baptiste, D., "Psychotherapy with Gay/Lesbian Couples and Their Children in Stepfamilies: A Challenge for Marriage and Family Therapists," *Journal of Homosexuality*, 14 (1987), pp. 223-38.

Basile, R.A., "Lesbian Mothers I," *Women's Rights Law Reporter*, 2 (December 1974), pp. 3-18.

Bateman, Margaret, "Lesbians, Gays and Child Custody: An Australian Legal History," *Australian Gay and Lesbian Law Journal*, 1 (1992), pp. 47-71.

Beargie, Robert A., "Custody Determinations Involving the Homosexual Parent," *Family Law Quarterly*, 22, 1 (Spring 1988), pp. 71-86.

Beck, Evelyn Torton, "The Motherhood That Dare Not Speak Its Name," *Women's Studies Quarterly*, II, 4 (Winter 1983).

Benkov, Laura, *Reinventing the Family: The Emerging Story of Lesbian and Gay Parents*, (New York: Crown Publishers, 1994).

Berzon, Betty, "Sharing Your Lesbian Identity with Your Children: A Case for Openness," in *Our Right to Love: A Lesbian Resource Book*, Ginny Vida (ed.), (Englewood Cliffs, NJ: Prentice-Hall, 1978), pp. 69-74.

"*Bezio v. Patenaude*: The Coming Out Custody Controversy of Lesbian Mothers in Court," *New England Law Review*, 16 (1981), p. 331.

Bozett, Frederick W. (ed.), *Gay and Lesbian Parents*, (New York: Praeger, 1987).

Bradley, David, "Homosexuality and Child Custody in English Law," *International Journal of Law and the Family*, 1 (1987), pp. 155-205.

Brantner, Paula A., "When Mommy or Daddy is Gay: Developing Constitutional Standards for Custody Decisions," *Hastings Women's Law Journal*, 3, 1 (Winter 1992), pp. 97-121.

Brown, Katie, "Family Values," *Deneuve*, 2, 6 (December 1992), pp. 24-9 and 55-7.

Budd, Sharon, "Proud Lesbian Motherhood," in *The Lesbian Path*, Margaret Cruikshank (ed.), (Monterey, CA: Angel Press, 1980), pp. 163-70.

Burdens on Gay Litigants and Bias in the Court System: Homosexual Panic, Child Custody, and Anonymous Parties," *Harvard Civil Rights and Civil Liberties Law Review*, 19 (1984), pp. 497-559.

Burke, Phyllis, *Family Values: A Lesbian Mother's Fight for Her Son*, (New York: Vintage, 1994).

Cade, Cathy, "A Lesbian Birth Story," in *Birth Stories: The Experience Remembered*, Janet Isaacs Ashford (ed.), (Freedom, CA: Crossing Press, 1984).

Campbell, R.W, "Child Custody When One Parent is a Homosexual," *The*

Judges' Journal, 7 (1978), pp. 38-41 and 51-2.

Casper, Virginia, Steven Schultz and Elaine Wickens, "Breaking the Silences: Lesbian and Gay Parents and the Schools," *Teacher's College Record,* 94 (Fall 1992), pp. 109-37.

"Children in Gay Families: An Investigation of Services," *The Homosexual Counselling Journal,* 3, 2 (April 1976).

Clark, "Lesbian Mothers Lose Custody," *Gay Community News,* (May 16, 1981).

Clemens, M.A., "In the Best Interests of the Child and the Lesbian Mother: A Proposal for Legislative Change," *Albany Law Review,* 48 (1984), pp. 1021-44.

Corbett, Susan, "A Complicated Bias," *Young Children,* (March 1993), pp. 29-31.

Corley, Rip, *The Final Closet: The Gay Parents' Guide for Coming Out to Their Children,* (Miami: Editech Press, 1990).

Cramer, D., "Gay Parents and Their Children: A Review of Research and Practical Implications," *Journal of Counseling and Development,* 64 (1986), pp. 504-7.

Crawford, S, "Lesbian Families: Psychosocial Stress and the Family-building Process," in *Lesbian Psychologies: Explorations and Challenges,* The Boston Lesbian Psychologies Collective (ed.), (Chicago: University of Chicago Press, 1987), pp. 195-214.

"Custody and Homosexual Parents," *Women's Rights Law Reporter,* 2 (December 1974).

"Custody Denials to Parents in Same-Sex Relationships: An Equal Protection Analysis," *Harvard Law Review,* 102 (1989).

"Custody: Lesbian Mothers in the Courts," *Gonzaga Law Review,* 16 (1980).

DiLapi, Elena Marie, "Lesbian Mothers and the Motherhood Hierarchy," *Journal of Homosexuality,* 18, 1/2 (1989), pp. 101-21.

Dooley, David S., "Immoral Because They're Bad, Bad Because They're Wrong: Sexual Orientation and Presumptions of Parental Unfitness in Custody Disputes," *California Western Law Review,* 26 (1990), pp. 395-424.

Editors of the Harvard Law Review, *Sexual Orientation and the Law,* (Cambridge, MA: Harvard University Press, 1989).

Erlichman, Karen Lee, "Lesbian Mothers: Ethical Issues in Social Work Practice," *Women & Therapy: A Feminist Quarterly,* 8, 1/2 (1988), pp. 207-24.

Evans, Beverly K., "Mothering as a Lesbian Issue," in *Lesbians and Child Custody: A Casebook,* (New York: Garland Publishing, 1992), pp. 131-40.

Evall, Joseph, "Sexual Orientation and Adoptive Matching," *Family Law Quarterly,* XXV, 33 (Fall 1991).

Falk, Patricia, "Lesbian Mothers: Psychosocial Assumptions in Family Law," *American Psychologist,* 44, 6 (June 1989), pp. 941-7 [and in *Lesbians and Child Custody: A Casebook,* Dolores J. Maggiore (ed.), (New York: Garland Publishing, 1992), pp. 55-72].

Fishel, A.H., "Gay Parents," *Issues in Health Care of Women,* 4 (1983), pp. 139-64.

Gantz, Joe, *Whose Child Cries: Children of Gay Parents Talk About Their Lives*, (Rolling Hills Estates, CA: Jalmar Press, 1983).

"The Gay Family," in *The Rights of Gay People*, E. Carrington Boggan et al (eds.), (New York: Avon, 1981), pp. 103-15.

"The Gay Parent: A Special Custody Case," *Oregon State Bar Bulletin Forum*, 1 (1979).

Gibbs, Elizabeth D., "Psychosocial Development of Children Raised by Lesbian Mothers: A Review of Research," *Women & Therapy: A Feminist Quarterly*, 8, 1/2 (1988), pp. 65-75.

Gibson, Clifford Gay (with cooperation from Mary Jo Risher), *By Her Own Admission: A Lesbian Mother's Fight to Keep Her Son*, (New York: Double-day, 1977).

Gil de Lamadrid, Maria (ed.), *Lesbians Choosing Motherhood: Legal Implications of Donor Insemination and Co-Parenting*, (San Francisco: National Center for Lesbian Rights, 1991).

Gil de Lamadrid, Maria, "Lesbians Choosing Motherhood: Legal Implications of Co-Parenting," in *Lesbians and Child Custody: A Casebook*, Dolores J. Maggiore (ed.), (New York: Garland Publishing, 1992), pp. 195-218.

Goldyn, L., "Gratuitous Language in Appellate Cases Involving Gay People: 'Queer Baiting' from the Bench," *Political Behavior*, 3 (1981), pp. 31-48.

Golombok, Susan, Ann Spencer and Michael Rutter, "Children in Lesbian and Single Parent Households: Psychosexual and Psychiatric Appraisal," *Journal of Child Psychology and Psychiatry*, 24, 4 (1983), pp. 551-72.

Goodman, Bernice, "The Lesbian Mother," *American Journal of Orthopsychiatry*, 43 (1973), pp. 283-4.

Goodman, Bernice, *The Lesbian: A Celebration of Difference*, (Brooklyn: Out and Out Books, 1977).

Goodman, Bernice, "Some Mothers are Lesbians," in *Women's Issues and Social Work Practice*, Elaine Norman and Arlene Mancuso (eds.), (Itasca, IL: F.E. Peacock Publishers, 1980), pp. 153-81.

Goodman, Ellen, "Homosexuality of a Parent: A New Issue in Custody Disputes," *Monash University Law Review*, 5 (1979), pp. 305-15.

Gottman, J., "Children of Gay and Lesbian Parents," in *Homosexuality and Family Relations*, F.W. Bozett and M.B. Sussman (eds.), (New York: Harrington Park, 1990), pp. 177-96.

Gould, M., "Lesbians and the Law: Where Sexism and Heterosexism Meet," in *Woman-identified Women*, T. Darty and S. Potter (eds.), (Palo Alto, CA: Mayfield, 1984), pp. 149-62.

Green, Richard, "Sexual Identity of 37 Children Raised by Homosexual or Transsexual Parents," *American Journal of Psychiatry*, 135 (1978), pp. 692-7.

Green, Richard, "The Best Interests of the Child with a Lesbian Mother," *Bulletin of the American Academy of Psychiatry and the Law*, 10, 1 (1982), pp. 7-15 [and in *Lesbians and Child Custody: A Casebook*, Dolores J. Maggiore (ed.), (New York: Garland Publishing, 1992), pp. 73-84].

Green, R., J.B. Mandel, M.E. Hotvedt, J. Gray and L. Smith, "Lesbian Mothers and Their Children: A Comparison with Solo Parent Heterosexual Mothers and Their Children," *Archives of Sexual Behavior*, 15, 2 (1986), pp. 692-7.

Hall, Marny, "Lesbian Families: Cultural and Clinical Issues," *Social Work*, 23, 5 (September 1978), pp. 380-5.

Hanscombe, Gillian E. and Jackie Forster, *Rocking the Cradle: Lesbian Mothers, A Challenge in Family Living*, (Boston: Alyson Publications, 1981).

Hanscombe, G.E. and J. Forster, "The Right to Lesbian Parenthood," *Journal of Medical Ethics*, 9 (1983), pp. 133-5.

Hare, Jan and Leslie Richards, "Children Raised by Lesbian Couples: Does Context of Birth Affect Father and Partner Involvement?" *Family Relations: Journal of Applied Family and Child Studies*, 42, 3 (July 1993), pp. 249-55.

Hare, Jan, "Concerns and Issues Faced by Families Headed by a Lesbian Couple," *Families in Society: The Journal of Contemporary Human Services* 75, 1 (1994), pp. 27-35.

Harris, Barbara S., "Lesbian Mother Child Custody: Legal and Psychiatric Aspects," *Bulletin of the American Academy of Psychology and the Law*, 5 (1977), p. 75.

Harris, Mary B. and Pauline H. Turner, "Gay and Lesbian Parents," *Journal of Homosexuality*, 12 (1985), pp. 101-13.

Herrington, "Children of Lesbians, Developmentally Typical," *Psychiatric News*, (October 19, 1979).

Hitchens, Donna J. and Barbara Price, "Trial Strategy in Lesbian Mother Custody Cases: The Use of Expert Testimony," *Golden Gate Law Review*, 9 (1978/79).

Hitchens, Donna J., D. Martin and M. Morgan, "An Alternative View to Child Custody: When One Parent is a Homosexual," *Conciliation Courts Review*, 17 (1979), p. 27.

Hitchens, Donna J., "Social Attitudes, Legal Standards, and Personal Trauma in Child Custody Cases," *Journal of Homosexuality*, 5, 1-2 (1979), pp. 89-96.

Hitchens, Donna J., D. Martin and M. Morgan, "Child Custody and the Homosexual Parent," *The Judges' Journal*, 18 (1979), p. 33.

Hoeffer, Beverly, "Children's Acquisition of Sex Role Behaviour in LesbianMother Families," *American Journal of Orthopsychiatry*, 51, 3 (1981), pp. 536-44.

Hornstein, Francis, "Children by Donor Insemination: A New Choice for Lesbians," in *Test-Tube Women: What Future for Motherhood*, Rita Arditti, Renate Duelli Klein and Shelley Minden (eds.), (London: Pandora Press, 1985), pp. 373-81.

Hotvedt, Mary and Jane Mandel, "Children of Lesbian Mothers," in *Homosexuality: Social, Psychological, and Biological Issues*, W. Paul, J. Weinrich, J. Gonsiorek and M. Hotvedt (eds.), (Beverly Hills, CA: Sage Publications, 1982), pp. 275-85.

Huggins, Sharon L., "A Comparative Study of Self-Esteem of Adolescent Children of Divorced Lesbian Mothers and Divorced Heterosexual Mothers," *Journal of Homosexuality*, 18, 1/2 (1989), pp. 123-35.

Hunter, Nan D. and Nancy D. Polikoff, "Custody Rights of Lesbian Mothers: Legal Theory and Litigation Strategy," *Buffalo Law Review*, 25 (1976), pp. 691-733.

Hunter, Nan and Nancy Polikoff, "Lesbian Mothers Fight Back: Political and Legal Strategies," *Quest*, 5, 1 (Spring 1979), pp. 55-7.

Jullion, Jeanne, *Long Way Home: The Odyssey of a Lesbian Mother and her Children*, (San Francisco: Cleis Press, 1985).

Kahn, Y.H., "Hannah, Must You Have a Child?" *Out/Look*, 3, 3 (1991), pp. 39-43.

Kirkpatrick, Martha, Ron Roy and Catherine Smith, "A New Look at Lesbian Mothers," *Human Behavior*, 5, 8 (August 1976).

Kirkpatrick, Martha, Catherine Smith and Ron Roy, "Lesbian Mothers and their Children: A Comparative Survey," *American Journal of Orthopsychiatry*, 51, 3 (1981), pp. 545-51.

Kirkpatrick, M., "Clinical Implications of Lesbian Mother Studies," *Journal of Homosexuality*, 14 (1987), pp. 201-11 [and in *Lesbians and Child Custody: A Casebook*, Dolores J. Maggiore (ed.), (New York: Garland Publishing, 1992), pp. 101-12].

Kleber, David J., Robert J. Howell and Alta Lura Tibbits-Kleber, "The Impact of Parental Homosexuality in Child Custody Cases: A Review of the Literature," *Bulletin of the American Academy of Psychiatry and Law*, 14, 1 (1986).

Klein, Renate Duelli, "Doing It Ourselves: Self-Insemination," in *Test-Tube Women: What Future for Motherhood*, Rita Arditti, Renate Duelli Klein and Shelley Minden (eds.), (London: Pandora Press, 1985), pp. 382-90.

Koepke, L., J. Hare and M. Moran, "Relationship Quality in a Sample of Lesbian Couples with Children and Child-free Lesbian Couples," *Family Relations*, 41 (1992), pp. 224-9.

Kraft, P., "Recent Developments: Lesbian Child Custody," *Harvard Women's Law Journal*, 6 (1983), pp. 183-92.

Kweskin, S.L. and A.S. Cook, "Heterosexual and Homosexual Mothers' Self-Described Sex-Role Behavior and Ideal Sex Role Behavior in Children," *Sex Roles*, 8 (1982), pp. 967-75.

"Lesbian Mothers Fight Back," *Quest*, 5, 1 (Summer 1979), pp. 54-74.

Levy, Eileen, "Lesbian Motherhood: Identity and Social Support." *Affilia*, 4, 4 (Winter 1989), pp. 40-53.

Levy, E., "Strengthening the Coping Resources of Lesbian Families," *Families in Society*, 73 (1992), pp. 23-31.

Lewin, Ellen, "Lesbianism and Motherhood: Implications for Child Custody," *Human Organization*, 40, 1 (1981), pp. 6-14.

Lewin, Ellen and Terrie Lyons, "Everything in Its Place: The Co-existence of Lesbianism and Motherhood," in *Homosexuality: Social, Psychological, and Biological Issues*, W. Paul et al (eds.), (Beverly Hills, CA: Sage Publications, 1982), pp. 249-73.

Lewin, Ellen, *Lesbian Mothers: Accounts of Gender in American Culture*, (Ithaca, NY: Cornell University Press, 1993).

Lewis, Karen Gail, "Children of Lesbians: Their Point of View," *Social Work*, 25, 3 (May 1980), pp. 198-203, [and in *Lesbians and Child Custody: A Casebook*, Dolores J. Maggiore (ed.), (New York: Garland Publishing, 1992), pp. 85-100].

Liljesfraund, Petra, "Children Without Fathers," *Out/Look*, (Fall 1988), pp. 24-9.

Loulan, J., "Psychotherapy with Lesbian Mothers," in *Contemporary Perspectives on Psychotherapy with Lesbians and Gay Men*, T.S. Stein and C.J. Cohen (eds.), (New York: Plenum, 1986).

Lyons, Terrie, "Lesbian Mothers' Custody Fears," in *Women Changing Therapy*, Joan H. Robbins and Rachel J. Siegel (eds.), (New York: Haworth Press, 1983), pp. 231-40.

Maddox, Brenda, "Homosexual Parents," *Psychology Today*, (February 1982), pp. 66-9.

Maddox, Brenda, "In Front of the Children," in *Married and Gay: An Intimate Look at a Different Relationship*, Brenda Maddox (ed.), (New York: Harcourt, Brace, Jovanovich, 1982), pp. 133-51.

Maggiore, Dolores J. (ed.), *Lesbians and Child Custody: A Casebook*, (New York: Garland Publishing, 1992).

Martin, April, *The Lesbian and Gay Parenting Handbook: Creating and Raising Our Families*, (New York: HarperCollins, 1993).

Martin, Del and Phyllis Lyon, *Lesbian/Woman*, (New York: Bantam Books, 1972).

Matteson, David R., "The Heterosexually Married Gay and Lesbian Parent," in *Gay and Lesbian Parents*, F.W. Bozett (ed.), (New York: Praeger, 1987), pp. 138-64.

Mayadas, L. and W. Duehn, "Children in Gay Families: An Investigation of Services," *Homosexual Counseling Journal*, 3, 2 (1976).

Melton, Rebecca L., "Legal Rights of Unmarried Heterosexual and Homosexual Couples and Evolving Definitions of 'Family,'" *Journal of Family Law*, 29 (1990/91).

Millbank, Jenni, "Lesbian Mothers, Gay Fathers: Sameness and Difference," *Australian Gay and Lesbian Law Journal*, 2 (Spring 1992), pp. 21-40.

Miller, J., R. Jacobsen and J. Bigner, "The Child's Home Environment for Lesbian Versus Heterosexual Mothers," *Journal of Homosexuality*, 7, 1 (1981), pp. 49-56.

Morin, S. and S. Schultz, "The Gay Movement and the Rights of Children," *Journal of Social Issues*, 34, 2 (1978).

Moses, A. Elfin and Robert O. Hawkins, Jr., "Gay Parents," in *Counseling Lesbian Women and Gay Men: A Life-Issues Approach*, (St. Louis, IL: C.V. Mosby, 1982).

Mucklow, B. and K. Phelan, "Lesbian and Traditional Mothers' Responses to Adult Response to Child Behavior and Self-Concept," *Psychological Reports*, 44 (1979).

National Center for Lesbian Rights and National Lawyers Guild, *A Lesbian and Gay Parents' Legal Guide to Child Custody*, (San Francisco: National Centre for Lesbian Rights, 1989).

Newman, Leslea, *Heather Has Two Mommies*, (Boston: Alyson Publications, 1989).

Noble, Elizabeth, *Having Your Baby by Donor Insemination*, (Boston: Houghton Mifflin, 1987).

Nungesser, Lonnie, "Lifestyle of Lesbian Mothers," *Journal of Homosexuality*, 5, 3 (Spring 1980).

Nungesser, Lonnie, "Theoretical Bases for Research on the Acquisition of Social Sex Roles by Children of Lesbian Mothers," *Journal of Homosexuality*, 5 (1980), pp. 177-87.

Oddone, Maureen, "Going Public with a Private Hell: One Lesbian Mother's Custody Battle," *Advocate*, 224 (1977), pp. 34-5.

Pagelow, Mildred, "Heterosexual and Lesbian Single Mothers: A Comparison of Problems, Coping, and Solutions," *Journal of Homosexuality*, 5, 3 (1980), pp. 189-204.

"Parent and Child: *M.J.P v. J.G.P.*: An Analysis of the Relevance of Parental Homosexuality in Child Custody Determinations," *Oklahoma Law Review*, 35 (1982).

Patterson, Charlotte, "Children of Lesbian and Gay Parents," *Child Development*, 63, 5 (October 1992), pp. 1025-42.

Patterson, Charlotte, "Children of the Lesbian Baby Boom: Behavioral Adjustment, Self-Concepts, and Sex-Role Identity," in *Contemporary Perspectives on Gay and Lesbian Psychology: Theory, Research, and Applications*, Beverly Greene and Gregory Herek (eds.), (Beverly Hills, CA: Sage Publications, in press).

Pegesser, L., "Theoretical Bases for Research on the Acquisition of Social Roles by Children of Lesbian Mothers," *Journal of Homosexuality*, 5, 3 (1980), pp. 177-88.

Pennington, S., "Children of Lesbian Mothers," in *Gay and Lesbian Parents*, F. Bozett (ed.), (New York: Praeger, 1987), pp. 58-74.

Pies, Cheri, *Considering Parenthood: A Workbook for Lesbians*, (San Francisco: Spinsters Ink, 1985).

Polikoff, Nancy D., "Gender and Child Custody Determinations: Exploding the Myths," in *Families, Politics, and Public Policy: A Feminist Dialogue on Women and the State*, Irene Diamond (ed.), (New York: Longman, 1983), pp. 183-202.

Polikoff, Nancy, "Lesbian Mothers, Lesbian Families: Legal Obstacles, Legal Challenges," *Review of Law and Social Change*, XIV (1986), pp. 907-13 [and in *Lesbians and Child Custody: A Casebook*, Dolores J. Maggiore (ed.), (New York: Garland Publishing, 1992), pp. 229-38].

Polikoff, Nancy, "This Child Does Have Two Mothers: Redefining Parenthood to Meet the Needs of Children in Lesbian-Mother and Other Nontraditional Families," *The Georgetown Law Journal*, 78 (1990), pp. 459-575.

Polikoff, Nancy D., "Lesbians Choosing Children: The Personal is Political Revisited," in *Lesbians and Child Custody: A Casebook*, Dolores J. Maggiore (ed.), (New York: Garland Publishing, 1992), pp. 3-10.

Pollack, Sandra and Jeanne Vaughn (eds.), *Politics of the Heart: A Lesbian Parenting Anthology*, (Ithaca, NY: Firebrand Books, 1987).

Rafkin, Louise (ed.), *Different Daughters: A Book by Mothers of Lesbians*, (San Francisco: Cleis Press, 1987).

Rafkin, Louise (ed.), *Different Mothers: Sons and Daughters of Lesbians Talk About Their Lives*, (San Francisco: Cleis Press, 1990).

Rand, C., D.L.R. Graham and E.I. Rawlings, "Psychological Health and Factors the Court Seeks to Control in Lesbian Mother Custody Trials," *Journal of Homosexuality*, 8, 1 (1982), pp. 27-39.

Reese, Susan Elizabeth, "The Forgotten Sex: Lesbians, Liberation, and the Law," *Willamette Law Journal*, II (1975), pp. 355-76.

Richardson, Diane, "Do Lesbians Make Good Parents?" *Community Care*, (August 2, 1978), pp. 16-7.

Richardson, Diane, "Lesbian Mothers," in *The Theory and Practice of Homosexuality*, D. Richardson and J. Hart (eds.), (London: Routledge & Kegan Paul, 1981).

Ricketts, Wendell and Roberta Achtenberg, "The Adoptive and Foster Gay and Lesbian Parent," in *Gay and Lesbian Parenting*, Frederick W. Bozett (ed.), (New York: Praeger, 1987), pp. 89-111.

Ricketts, Wendell and Roberta Achtenberg, "Adoption and Foster Parenting for Lesbians and Gay Men: Creating New Traditions in Family," in *Homosexuality and Family Relations*, F.W. Bozett and M.B. Sussman (eds.), (New York: Harrington Park, 1990), pp. 83-118.

Rights of Women Lesbian Custody Group, *Lesbian Mothers' Legal Handbook*, (London: Women's Press, 1986).

Riley, Claire, "American Kinship: A Lesbian Account," *Feminist Issues*, (Fall 1988), pp. 75-94.

Riley, Marilyn, "The Avowed Lesbian Mother and Her Right to Child Custody: A Constitutional Challenge That Can No Longer Be Denied," *San Diego Law Review*, 12, 4 (June 1975), pp. 799-864.

Rivera, Rhonda R., "Our Straight-Laced Judges: The Legal Position of Homosexual Persons in the United States," *Hastings Law Journal*, 30 (1979), p. 799.

Rivera, Rhonda R., "Recent Developments in Sexual Preference Law," *Drake Law Review*, 30 (1980).

Rivera, Rhonda R., "Queer Law: Sexual Orientation Law in the Mid-Eighties — Part II," *Dayton Law Review*, 11 (1986).

Rivera, Rhonda R., "Legal Issues in Gay and Lesbian Parenting," in *Gay and Lesbian Parents*, Frederick W. Bozett (ed.), (New York: Praeger, 1987), 199-227.

Robinson, Susan and H.F. Pizer, *Having a Baby Without a Man: The Woman's Guide to Alternative Insemination*, (New York: Simon & Schuster, 1985).

Rofes, Eric, "Loving Your Gay Parent," in *The Kids' Book of Divorce*, (Lewis Publishing, 1981).

Rohrbaugh, Joanna Bunker, "Choosing Children: Psychological Issues in Lesbian Parenting," *Women & Therapy: A Feminist Quarterly*, 8, 1/2 (1988), pp. 51-64.

Saphira, Miriam, *Amazon Mothers*, (Ponsonby, Auckland: Papers Inc., 1984).

Schulenberg, Joy, *Gay Parenting: A Complete Guide for Gay Men and Lesbians with Children*, (New York: Doubleday, 1985).

Shavelson, Eileen, Mary K. Biaggio, Herb H. Cross and Robert E. Lehman, "Lesbian Women's Perceptions of Their Parent-Child Relationships," *Journal of Homosexuality*, 5 (1980), pp. 205-15.

Sheppard, Annamay T., "Lesbian Mothers II: Long Night's Journey Into Day," *Women's Rights Law Reporter*, 8 (1985), pp. 219-46.

Shernoff, M., "Family Therapy for Lesbian and Gay Clients," *Social Work*, 19 (1974), pp. 393-6.

Steinhorn, Audrey I., "Lesbian Mothers," *Women and Therapy*, 1 (Winter 1982), pp. 35-48.

Stevens, Mary L., "Lesbian Mothers in Transition," in *Our Right to Love — A Lesbian Resource Book*, Ginny Vida (ed.), (Englewood, NJ: Prentice-Hall, 1978), pp. 207-11.

Stone, Donald H., "The Moral Dilemma: Child Custody When One Parent Is Homosexual or Lesbian — An Empirical Study," *Suffolk University Law Review*, 23 (1989).

Susoeff, Steve, "Assessing Children's Best Interests When A Parent is Gay or Lesbian: Toward a Rational Custody Standard," *UCLA Law Review*, 32 (1985), pp. 852-903.

Sutton, Stuart, "The Lesbian Family: Rights in Conflict under the Uniform Parentage Act," *Golden Gate Law Review*, 10 (1980), p. 1007.

Turner, P., L. Scadden and M. Harris, "Parenting in Gay and Lesbian Families," *Journal of Gay and Lesbian Psychotherapy*, 1 (1990), pp. 55-67.

Weston, Kath, *Families We Choose: Lesbians, Gays, Kinship*, (New York: Columbia University Press, 1991).

Wickens, Elaine, "Penny's Question: 'I Will Have a Child in My Class With Two Moms — What Do You Know About This?'" *Young Children*, (March 1993), pp. 25-8.

Wolf, Deborah Goleman, "Lesbian Mothers," in *The Lesbian Community*, Deborah Goleman Wolf (ed.), (Berkeley, CA: University of California Press, 1980), pp. 136-65.

Wolfe, Susan J., "Jewish Lesbian Mother," in *Nice Jewish Girls: A Lesbian Anthology*, Evelyn Torton Beck (ed.), (Watertown, MA: Persephone Press, 1982), pp. 164-73.

Wysor, Bettie, "Lesbian Mothers," in *The Lesbian Myth*, Bettie Wysor (ed.), (New York: Random House, 1974), pp. 326-63.

Zuckerman, E., "Second Parent Adoption for Lesbian-Parented Families: Legal Recognition of the Other Mother," *UC Davis Law Review*, 19 (1986), pp. 729 and 731.

Selected Resources for Lesbian Parents

Children of Lesbians and Gays Everywhere
2300 Market Street, P.O. Box 165, San Francisco, CA 94114
In Canada: P.O. Box 187, Station F, Toronto, Ontario M4Y 2L5

Custody Action for Lesbian Mothers
P.O. Box 281, Narbeth, PA 19072

The Family Next Door
P.O. Box 21580, Oakland, CA 94620

Gay and Lesbian Parents Coalition International
P.O. Box 50360, Washington, D.C. 20091
In Canada: P.O. Box 187, Station F, Toronto, Ontario M4Y 2L5

Lambda Legal Defense and Education Fund
666 Broadway, New York, NY 10012

Lavender Families Resource Network
(formerly Lesbian Mothers' National Defense Fund)
P.O. Box 21567, Seattle, WA 98111

Mom's Apple Pie: Lesbian Mothers' National
Defense Fund Newsletter
P.O. Box 21567, Seattle, WA 98111

Momazons
P.O. Box 02069, Columbus, OH 43202

National Center for Lesbian Rights
(formerly the Lesbian Rights Project)
870 Market Street, Suite 570, San Francisco, CA 94102

The MOMS List

BY DORSIE HATHAWAY (LIST OWNER)

The idea for the MOMS list first began to take shape after I had been involved with online women's communities for more than two years. It was hard enough to find many lesbians on the Internet; harder yet to discover those with children, let alone with children of similar ages. The MOMS list was born in 1992; its midwife was my friend Darci Chapman, who pioneered many internet mailing lists supporting LGBO (Lesbian, Gay, Bisexual, Other) persons and interests.

The "moms" mailing list is for lesbian mothers, lesbian co-moms, and lesbian mom-wanna-bes. This list is for women only. All subscription requests will be approved manually by the list owner.

While this list is unmoderated, it is also private, meaning that only subscribers can post to the list and make other queries about the list to majordomo.

All moms requests should be sent to:
majordomo@qiclab.scn.rain.com

To subscribe, in the BODY of your message, send:
subscribe moms yourfirstname yourlastname your e-mail address

> **For example:**
> subscribe moms Darci Chapman @netcom.com
> (Leaving your name out will only delay the subscription process.)

For a complete list of majordomo commands send:
HELP
on a line by itself in a message to:
majordomo@qiclab.scn.rain.com

If all else fails:
If you have tried all the above (especially "help") and your problem still remains unresolved, you may reach the human being responsible for the moms list by sending e-mail to: **moms-approval@qiclab.scn.rain.com.**

Contributors

PERRY ADAMS lives in Kootenay country in the interior of British Columbia with her partner, two grown children and an assortment of animals. She works full-time at a paying job and writes when she can. In 1994, she celebrated twenty-five years as an "out" lesbian.

KAREN ANDREWS has been a long-time activist in the lesbian, gay and feminist communities. She articled with the human rights and labour firm of Cornish Advocates without whose support this article could not have been written. She was called to the Ontario bar in 1995.

TONI ARMSTRONG JR. was publisher/managing editor of *Hot Wire: The Journal of Women's Music and Culture* from 1984-1994. She is a photographer, bass player, and special ed. teacher. Her collection of vampire books exceeds three hundred.

LAURA BARRY is a thirty-three-year-old lesbian mom who co-parents with her partner of two years. Their daughter is five years old and attends school full time. In addition to writing about her parenting experiences, Laura has published many lesbian short stories and mainstream newspaper articles.

JANE BERNSTEIN manages a small family business in Quebec. She and her partner, Laura Stephenson, have one daughter.

ANGELA BOWEN is a black lesbian feminist writer, mother and organizer who speaks out on a variety of issues aimed at radical change. Her work has appeared in *Conditions, Sojourner, The Village Voice, Gay Community News* and *Women of Power.* She has also published a book of short stories, *Aleta in the Forties and Fifties* (Kitchen Table: Women of Color Press).

ELISE CHENIER is currently researching and writing a thesis on twentieth century Canadian lesbian history at Queen's University. Natasha is currently embarassed about the whole sex thing and would rather discuss her tooth fairy money.

JANICE CZYSCON is a senior editor for the Department of Engineering Professional Development at the University of Wisconsin-Madison. She enjoys attending plays and operas with her family, playing tennis and golf, bowling, and playing cards with her partner, Crystal. In her spare time, which is hard to find, she plays guitar and surfs the

Internet. She is also active with the parent liaison committee to the Madison School Board.

VICKY D'AOUST is a mother with disabilities who identifies herself as a lesbian to most people, but continues to pass as straight in some communities. She is a researcher, activist, teacher and writer who works with community based and semi-institutional organizations to empower women with disabilities.

ALIX DOBKIN was born in Manhattan in 1940, and has been a guiding light in the women's music scene since 1973. Her recordings include *Lavendar Jane Loves Women, Living with Lesbians, XXAlix* and *Never Been Better/These Women.* She is the mother of one daughter, Adrian Hood.

DR. SUSAN DUNDAS is a child psychiatrist at the Hinck's Institute. She is currently working on a longterm follow-up study of lesbian mothers and their children. She lives with her children and life partner in Toronto.

ET ALIA is a researcher at a Toronto area university.

GLORIA FILAX is a Ph.D. student in the Department of Educational Policy Studies at the University of Alberta. She lives in Edmonton with her child, three cats and her partner, Debra Shogan.

LOUISE FLEMING considers herself very lucky to be part of a loving, fun lesbian family. She and her lover own *gynergy books* and live with their daughter, Sarah, and Sarah's favorite stuffed animal, Crystal.

SIBYL FREI likes to travel the country and savour different communities by spending some time there — about one decade per region seems to work for her. Her life is filled with her lover Louise, their daughter Sarah, a small but warm lesbian and feminist community, social and political activism and books, books, books.

COLLEEN GLASS' life is "hands on": house- and fence-building, cooking and managing in restaurants, book illustration and production, operating building system technology, learning about horses and tending gardens (as Buckminster Fuller said, "I seem to be a verb."). Two of the most beautiful and rewarding experiences in her life so far have been giving birth to and being raised by her daughter Oona; and coming out as a lesbian with Jan's everpresent love and understanding.

AMY GOTTLEIB is an editor and artist who has only stopped smiling long enough to take four hundred photographs of her son, Sami, since he recently arrived.

TANYA GULLIVER is a twenty-six-year-old lesbian living in Whitby, Ontario. She and her partner, Louise, are raising Louise's youngest sons, Jesse and Jay. From 1991-1994, Tanya was a trustee with the Durham Board of Education. She is currently employed with the Social Development Council of Ajax-Pickering, where she is the anti-racism project coordinator; she is also highly involved in the gay and lesbian community. Her lifelong goal is to become the first dyke Governor-General.

J.A. HAMILTON is the author of a children's book, *Jessica's Elevator* (Beach Holme), two poetry books, *Body Rain* (Brick) and *Steam-Cleaning Love* (Brick), and a volume of short fiction, *July Nights* (Douglas and McIntyre).

DORSIE HATHAWAY: femme, Euro-American, more able-bodied some days than others, mother of three — one child grown, two in their early teens. Her family lives in an expanding rural area with llamas down the road. She started and still maintains many Internet mailing lists for the LGBO community. List wrangling is her labour of love, like her writing, and evidence of her belief in the power of networking. She claims herself to be Creatrix, Lover, Motherbear.

OONA HAYES enjoys balancing her vivid creative and dream lives with blackbody radiation, carbon-oxygen chemistry, the chi-squared distribution and Freud (it's a tough job ...). She hopes to get involved with community health research and planning, and to become a chef in the true sense of the word. She's proud to say that she's straight but not narrow.

ADRIAN HOOD was born in 1970 in Manhattan, and lived there until 1974, when her mother, Alix Dobkin, and her mother's lover, Liza Cowen, moved with Adrian to the Catskill Mountains. Adrian lived both with her father — from ages five to eight — and with her mother. Her article with Alix Dobkin in this collection recounts some of her growing up experiences.

MIRIAM KAUFMAN is the lesbian parent of two children, ages ten and seven. She is a paediatrician at Toronto's Hospital for Sick Children, co-author of *All Shapes and Sizes: Promoting Fitness and Self Esteem in Your Overweight Child* (HarperCollins Canada) and the author of *Easy For You To Say* (Key Porter), a book for teens with a chronic illness or disability.

CATHY KING is a native of Ottawa, where she has worked as a hairdresser for fifteen years and has recently returned to university. She has lived with her partner and best friend Maureen for ten years. Both she and Maureen are very busy raising their three boys.

LEVI is a Toronto-based freelance writer who works from the home she shares with Et Alia, located deep in the mind-numbing suburbs of the big city.

SHIRLEY LIMBERT lives in a little grey house by the sea in Prince Edward Island. She is a writer, art worker and thinker, and shares her time with two cats, Tansy Ragwort and Baby Dyke. She has had many jobs in her fifty-nine years, including riding elephants in a circus, ballet dancer, mother, auto parts truck driver, horse farm operator and grandmother. She now works at a women's shelter and does some private counselling. She loves her sons and her life, and is working on a book of old women poems.

K.S.M. is a P.E.I. resident, a poet and a small business owner. She likes gardening, theatre and cloth sculpture.

HANNAH McLAUGHLIN was born in 1971 in Massachusetts, and grew up in a suburb of Boston. She graduated from Antioch College in Ohio and plans to pursue graduate studies in early childhood education or psychology. She hopes to continue her research into the children of lesbian mothers and homophobia in the schools. Her mother, Eleanor, is a medieval church historian and Episcopal priest who lives with her partner, Betsy, in Massachusetts.

CHRISTINA MILLS is learning to be the mother of a teenager and hoping she figures it out by the time he's twenty. The rest of her immediate family includes her partner and step-cats, No Sé, Sluggo and Alien. She has published short prose, scientific articles and translations, but her preferred genre is poetry. She is looking for a songwriting partner in the Ottawa area.

VANESSA-LYNN NEOPHYTOU is a thirty-year-old single lesbian mother living in South Africa. She is a member of the editorial collective of *Agenda*, the only feminist journal in South Africa, and is involved in LINK (Lesbians in Natal KwaZulu). She also writes poetry on sexual politics, lectures in sociology, works on her Masters thesis on lesbian mothers in South Africa — and raises her four-and-a-half-year-old daughter.

YVETTE PERREAULT works with the AIDS Bereavement Project of Ontario. Her emerging interest in chaos theory has helped her think in new ways about both personal loss and community transformation. She's still wildly in love with Debbie.

JAN RADFORD has worked as a Registered Nurse for the last twenty-one years. Currently, she is employed as a Clinical Nurse Specialist in the area of pediatric rehabilitation. She and her partner and their two daughters live in Vancouver, B.C.

HEIDI RANKIN lives on Prince Edward Island with her partner and three children. She works in community development and women's issues — and tap dances by night.

ANTOINETTE REED is a published poet and has worked as a journalist. She is now a general internist who continues to write as time and energy allow. She lives with her partner and ten-month-old son in Palo Alto, California.

JANE ROUNTHWAITE, a former executive with a major Canadian life insurance company, has just completed a career change and is now the Executive Director of the Women's Legal Education and Action Fund (LEAF). Jane has been "out" to her family and friends for over twenty years, and much more recently in her work and public life.

BRYN SHERIDAN is a human services consultant. She lives with her partner of eleven years, Katherine Stuart.

DEBRA SHOGAN is a professor in women's studies and in physical education and sports studies at the University of Alberta.

MAKEDA SILVERA is Caribbean-born. She lives in Toronto and shares a large part of her life with Stephanie and her two daughters Ayoola and Keisha. She is co-editor of *Pearls of Passion: A Treasury of Lesbian Erotica* (Sister Vision), anthologizer of the groundbreaking Lesbian of Colour anthology *Piece of My Heart* (Sister Vision), editor of *The Other Woman: Women of Colour in Contemporary Canadian Literature* (Sister Vision) and author of two short story collections, *Remembering G* (Sister Vision) and *Her Head a Village* (Press Gang). Her life continues to be hectic and unconventional.

MARY-WOO SIMS has been an activist in the field of human rights and equal opportunity for over ten years. She is currently a Vice-Chair, Equity Tribunals, for the Province of Ontario. In that capacity, she hears and makes decisions on cases related to alleged violations of human rights, pay equity, and employment equity legislation. She has served as Co-Chair of the Minister of Citizenship's Anti-Racism Advisory Working Group, a member of the Cabinet Round Table on Anti-Racism, a member of the Ontario Civilian Commission on Police Services, the Co-Chair of the Gay and Lesbian Issues sub-committee of the Toronto Mayor's Committee on Community and Race Relations, and the Co-Chair for the Campaign for Equal Families.

CHRISTINA STARR is a writer, editor, activist, and mother living in Toronto. Her work has appeared in *Canadian Woman Studies*, *Healthsharing*, and *Herizons*, and her first poetic monologue for the stage was produced at the 1994 Edmonton Fringe Festival. Just as this article was being completed, she had almost found a girlfriend who also has children. Due to conflicting schedules and other demands, it didn't work out.

LAURA STEPHENSON teaches in a university. She and her partner, Jane Bernstein, have one daughter and live in Quebec.

KATHERINE STUART is a career civil servant. She met her partner, Bryn Sheridan, through work. They were friends for almost two years before beginning their relationship eleven years ago.

SUSAN URSEL is a labour and human rights lawyer in Toronto, Ontario. In 1994, she was a member of the Campaign for Equal Families' Steering Committee during the fight for Bill 167.

JESSICA WALKER is a bookseller and aspiring editor who lives in Vancouver with her husband and young son.

KATE WALKER lives in British Columbia and works in the book publishing industry.

KAREN WILLIAMS is a lesbian mother, co-parenting her two children with her partner Pam. Her political activism is primarily focussed on fighting for the rights of lesbian and gay parents and their children. She is a co-founder of Equal Families Action Group (EFAG) of Hamilton, Ontario, and Ontario Regional Co-ordinator of Gay and Lesbian Parents International.

KATHLEEN WYNNE is currently working as a conflict resolution trainer in elementary and secondary schools. As a volunteer, she works as a community mediator, serves on various committees of the Toronto

Board of Education and is involved with a community-based group, Education against Homophobia, which combats homophobia in the education system. Kathleen also helps with cross-country running and volleyball programs at her daughter's junior elementary school. She is completing her M.Ed. at the Ontario Institute for Studies in Education.

SUSAN GENGE

KATHERINE ARNUP is a professor in the School of Canadian Studies at Carleton University. A lesbian mother herself, she has published widely on the subjects of lesbian parenting and reproductive rights for women. She is the award-winning author of *Education for Motherhood* (University of Toronto Press) and she is the co-editor of *Delivering Motherhood* (Routledge).

The Best of gynergy books

The Harriet Hubbley Mystery Series, *Jackie Manthorne.* The Harriet Hubbley Series features gripping mysteries with a lesbian twist and a dash of sly humour. "Manthorne knows how to keep the action moving and she never lets the dialogue sink to polemic." *The Globe and Mail*
Ghost Motel ISBN 0-921881-31-2 $9.95
Deadly Reunion ISBN 0-921881-32-0 $10.95
Last Resort (available September 1995) ISBN 0-921881-34-7 $10.95

By Word of Mouth: Lesbians Write the Erotic, *Lee Fleming (ed.).* "... contains plenty of sexy good writing and furthers the desperately needed honest discussion of what we mean by 'erotic' and by 'lesbian.'" *Sinister Wisdom*
ISBN 0-921881-06-1 $10.95/$12.95 U.S.

Imprinting Our Image: An International Anthology by Women with Disabilities, *Diane Driedger, Susan Gray (eds.).* "In this global tour de force, 30 writers from 17 countries provide dramatic insight into a wide range of issues germane to both the women's and the disability rights movements." *Disabled Peoples' International*
ISBN 0-921881-22-3 $12.95

Patient No More: The Politics of Breast Cancer, *Sharon Batt.* "One of the most comprehensive — and political — books ever written about breast cancer." *Maclean's Magazine* "A spectacular book ... carefully researched and thoroughly engrossing ... As exciting to read as a Grisham thriller, it demonstrates that reality is more compelling than fiction." *Bloomsbury Review*
ISBN 0-921881-30-4 $19.95/$16.95 U.S.

Triad Moon, *Gillean Chase.* Meet Lila, Brook and Helen, three women whose bonds of love take them beyond conventional relationships. *Triad Moon* is an exhilarating read that skilfully explores past and present lives, survival from incest, and healing.
ISBN 0-921881-28-2 $9.95

gynergy books titles are available at quality bookstores. Ask for our titles at your favourite local bookstore. Individual, prepaid orders may be sent to: **gynergy books**, P.O. Box 2023, Charlottetown, Prince Edward Island, Canada, C1A 7N7. Please add postage and handling ($3 for the first book and 75 cents for each additional book) to your order. Canadian residents add 7% GST to the total amount. GST registration number R104383120.